For Dad —
an invitation to explore...

Merry Christmas '94
Love always,
Trish + Ben

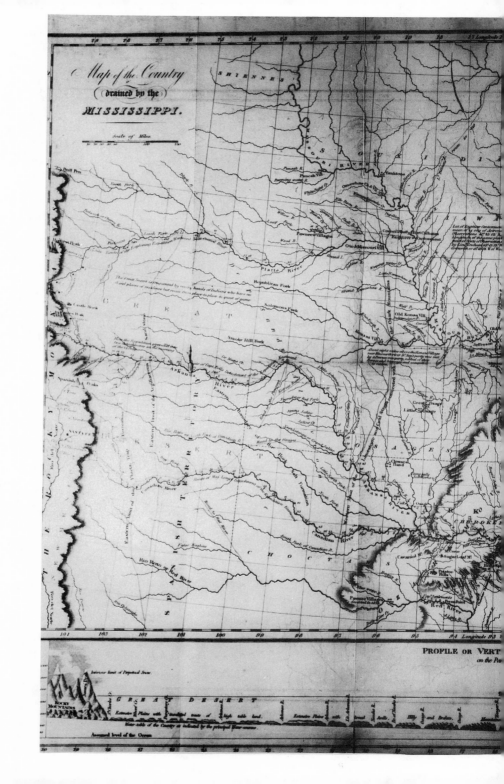

Map of the Country (drained by the) MISSISSIPPI.

FROM PITTSBURGH TO THE ROCKY MOUNTAINS

FROM PITTSBURGH TO THE ROCKY MOUNTAINS

MAJOR STEPHEN LONG'S EXPEDITION
1 8 1 9 - 1 8 2 0

Edited by Maxine Benson

Book Design by Jody Chapel, Cover to Cover Design

Cover Painting
Bison Herd by Pike's Peak by Titian Ramsay Peale,1854, oil painting
Courtesy of the Glenbow Museum, Calgary, Alberta, Canada

Library of Congress Cataloging-in-Publication Data

From Pittsburgh to the Rocky Mountains
Major Stephen Long's Expedition, 1819–1820

      Bibliography: p.
      Includes Index.
      1. West (U.S.)—Description and travel—To 1848.
      2. United States—Exploring expeditions.
      3. Rocky Mountains Region—Description and travel.
      4. Long, Stephen Harriman, 1784–1864—Journeys—West (U.S.)
      I. Benson, Maxine.
F592.F886 1988 917.8'042 88-16369
ISBN 1-55591-022-X

Fulcrum, Inc.
Golden, Colorado

Acknowledgments

We gratefully acknowledge the assistance of the following:

Academy of Natural Sciences of Philadelphia
American Philosophical Society
Columbia University, Rare Book and Manuscript Library
Denver Public Library, Western History Department
Yale University, Beinecke Rare Book and Manuscript Library
Independence National Park Historical Collection
Glenbow Museum

CONTENTS

1 8 2 0

INTRODUCTION

LATE on a July afternoon in 1820, the young botanist Edwin James stood atop the summit of Pikes Peak and surveyed the vast panorama around him. Summer never really comes to the high peaks of the Rockies, and the country to the north and west, he decided, looked much like the mountains of New England in January. It was truly another world, one far removed from the green rolling hills of his native Vermont. Perhaps at this time he reflected on the extraordinary circumstances that had brought him and his companions into these magnificent Rocky Mountains on the scientific expedition led by Maj. Stephen H. Long.[1]

For more than a century and a half, the Long expedition of 1819–1820 has generated controversy among historians who have criticized the explorer and his party for failing to accomplish their objectives, for bringing back insignificant results and, most of all, for characterizing the land between the Mississippi River and the Rockies as the "Great American Desert." Yet their accomplishments in science and art were considerable, and recently some writers have begun to view these achievements in a more positive light. The publication of the 1823 report in this one-volume, abridged edition offers an opportunity for a fresh look at all aspects of the expedition.

When Long and his men embarked on their journey in 1819, the United States was vastly larger than it had been a mere two decades earlier, when Thomas Jefferson assumed the presidency. Termed by historian Donald Jackson "the most towering Westerner of them all," Jefferson had presided over the acquisition of the Louisiana Purchase from France in 1803 and had sent Meriwether Lewis and William Clark out to explore the wilderness from St. Louis north and west to the Pacific (1804–1806). Zebulon Pike then traversed the central plains in 1806–1807, in the process not only failing to ascend the peak that later would bear his name but also running afoul of the Spanish, who imprisoned him for a time in Mexico. "Nothing that Pike ever tried to do was easy," Jackson has remarked, "and most of his luck was bad."[2]

By mid–1807 Pike was back in United States territory, and by 1809 Jefferson had completed his second term and had left office. Meanwhile, the nation continued to grow and expand, and pioneering families pushed ever westward into land that only recently had been covered with pristine forests. Even so, much territory remained uncharted and unexplored, and considerable opportunity awaited Stephen Long and his men as they prepared to leave for the West in 1819.

Like Edwin James, Long was a native New Englander, born in Hopkinton, New Hampshire, in 1784. He was graduated from Dartmouth in 1809 and taught

Stephen Harriman Long

school in Salisbury, New Hampshire, moving on to become a public school principal in Germantown, Pennsylvania. In December 1814 he was commissioned a second lieutenant in the Corps of Engineers, and he spent a year teaching mathematics at West Point before joining the Topographical Engineers in 1816. During 1817 he led expeditions that ranged north to the Falls of St. Anthony on the Mississippi and south into Arkansas that provided him with much valuable field experience.[3]

The scientific expedition placed under his command two years later was part of a much broader plan conceived principally by John C. Calhoun, secretary of war under President James

Monroe. Concerned with British control in the northwest, Calhoun wanted to enlarge American power and influence on the frontier. As he wrote, the Yellowstone expedition (as it was termed originally) was "a part of a system of measures, which has for its objects, the protection of our northwestern frontier, and the greater extension of our fur trade."[4]

The military branch, known as the Missouri expedition, began in 1818 and continued in 1819 under the command of Col. Henry Atkinson. It was to advance to the Mandan villages on the Missouri River, and if practicable to the mouth of the Yellowstone. As *Niles' Weekly Register* commented, it was an expedition "of the most respectable and imposing character," comprising about one thousand men. Beginning in the summer of 1818, the troops advanced to a point near present Leavenworth, Kansas. Proceeding up the Missouri by steamboat, they traveled as far as Council Bluffs, where they spent the winter of 1819–1820. The progress of the expedition had been greatly hampered by the use of steamboats, which, as the *Register* reported, with considerable understatement "do not appear to be fitted for the purpose of ascending the river."[5]

Meanwhile, plans were completed for the scientific expedition, and the men assembled in Pittsburgh, Pennsylvania, in April 1819. Their major objectives were to explore the land between the Mississippi River and the Rocky Mountains, the Missouri and its tributaries, and the Red, Arkansas and Mississippi above the mouth of the Missouri; they were also to make detailed observations on the topography, natural history, botany and geology of the country. In addition to Long, the party included Dr. William Baldwin, botanist; Thomas Say, zoologist; Titian Ramsay Peale, assistant naturalist; Samuel Seymour, painter; Augustus E. Jessup, geologist; as well as Maj. Thomas Biddle, who was to keep the journal, and Lt. James D. Graham and Cadet William Swift, who were to assist the commanding officer.

Baldwin, the physician-botanist, was born in Pennsylvania in 1779 and received a medical degree from the University of Pennsylvania in 1807. He then became increasingly interested in botany and made collecting trips to Georgia (where he was stationed as a naval surgeon at St. Mary's beginning in 1812), Florida and South America. Probably tubercular and in poor health for years, he hoped that additional travel with the Long expedition would prove beneficial.[6]

Zoologist Thomas Say, born in 1787 in Philadelphia, was a charter member of the Academy of Natural Sciences, which had been founded in 1812. Interested particularly in conchology and entomology, Say had published a paper on American shells in 1816 in a British encyclopedia and had issued the prospectus for his *American Entomology* in 1817, destined to become a three-

Thomas Say

volume classic (1824–1828). In 1818, with Titian Peale, he had participated in an expedition along the Georgia and Florida coasts which had been cut short by Indian hostilities. The 1819 trip with Long offered more exciting possibilities for research, and Say was eager to take full advantage of the opportunity. "I have been so continuously occupied in preparing for our Western Expedition that I have hardly time even to write," he told a friend in March.[7]

Say's compatriot, Titian Peale, was just as anxious to go West. Born in 1799 in Philadelphia, the youngest son of artist Charles Willson Peale, he had grown up amidst the exhibits and collections of his father's famed natural history museum. At an early age, in fact, he had painted the two grizzly cubs that Zebulon Pike had presented to Jefferson and that the president in turn had given to Peale. Playful at first, they later terrorized the Peale family and were killed and mounted in the museum. Titian's drawing skills had been recognized by Say, who had engaged him to prepare illustrations for the *American Entomology* prospectus. After returning from the southern trip, Peale had been elected to the Academy of Natural Sciences and as assistant naturalist and artist on the Long expedition he would be able to expand his already considerable accomplishments.[8]

Samuel Seymour also had an unparalleled opportunity to preserve on canvas the first scenes of the area through which the expedition would travel. Almost nothing is known about this pioneer artist, although he was apparently born in England and was associated with other painters in Philadelphia before joining Long's party in 1819.[9]

Augustus Jessup, the geologist, was older than many of the expedition participants, having been born in 1789 in Massachusetts. A Philadelphia merchant, his work in mineralogy and geology was sufficiently well regarded to have brought him an invitation to join the Academy of Natural Sciences in 1818.[10]

James Duncan Graham and William Swift, the topographers and assistants, had both attended West Point. Graham, born in 1799 in Virginia, had graduated in 1817. Swift, a year younger and still a student, left his studies to accompany Long (he was graduated in June 1819 while on the expedition). Thomas Biddle, the journalist, had joined the army in 1812 and had served in the War of 1812, receiving a brevet promotion to major.[11]

From Pittsburgh to Engineer Cantonment

Assembling at Pittsburgh, Long's party left on May 5, 1819, and started down the Ohio River on its steamboat, the *Western Engineer.* This vessel was constructed to draw only a small amount of water, perhaps two or two and a half feet. The wheels were placed in the stern to better avoid trees and snags, and there was a bulletproof house for the helmsmen. Brightly decorated, the boat featured Monroe's name lettered in capitals on the right wheel, Calhoun's on the left, since, as Titian Peale aptly remarked, the president and the secretary of war were "the two propelling powers of the expedition."[12]

By far the most colorful aspect of the *Western Engineer,* and one that created no little stir among the populace, was the large serpent carved on the bow. This creature did serve a useful purpose, as the steam was expelled through its mouth. But it also gave the boat something of the appearance of a sea monster. As an imaginative correspondent wrote in *Niles' Weekly Register,* "The bow of this vessel exhibits the form of a huge serpent, black and scaly, rising out of the water from under the boat, his head as high as the deck, darted forward, his mouth open, vomiting smoke, and apparently carrying the boat on his back." The author of this account was certain that the vessel would so awe the Indians that "it would require a daring savage to approach and accost her."[13]

Traveling down the river in the unique steamer, Long and his men arrived at Cincinnati on May 9, 1819, remaining a few days to make repairs. On their way again, they reached Louisville on May 19 and the mouth of the Ohio on May 30. On June 9 they arrived in St. Louis, where they remained until June 21. "The cause of science is exceedingly interested in the results of this expedition," commented the St. Louis *Inquirer.* The paper was sure that "a region so vast, so different from all others in air and water, must have a vegetable kingdom of its own, and the botanist will doubtless find abundant subjects for the employment of his talent."[14]

By June 22 the group was on the Missouri, joined a few days later by Benjamin O'Fallon, agent for Indian affairs, and interpreter John Dougherty. On July 13 the party reached Franklin, Missouri, where Dr. Baldwin left the group. He had been in ill health from the beginning of the journey, and on July 18 he informed Long that he could no longer continue, stating that he had a pulmonary disease "aggravated by confinement on board of the boat under your command." Long was understandably disappointed at the loss of his botanist. "It is with deep regret that we are compelled to forego the services of this valuable officer," he told Calhoun. Baldwin died about a month later, on August 31, 1819.[15]

Meanwhile, a contingent that included Say, Peale, Seymour, Jessup, Swift and Biddle left on August 6 to visit the Kansa Indians near present Manhattan, Kansas. Warmly welcomed, they were later attacked by a Pawnee war party after their departure. Returning to the Kansa village, they were entertained by dog dancers as Seymour captured the activity, which as Smithsonian ethnologist John Ewers notes is "the first field drawing of a Plains Indian dance group in action, and the earliest picture of the interior of a lodge of a farming tribe on the great plains."[16]

By the latter part of September, the men had all made their way to the vicinity of Council Bluffs on the west bank of the Missouri, named for the meeting of Lewis and Clark and the Indians in 1804. Here, some twenty miles above present Omaha, Long established his winter quarters, which he called Engineer Cantonment. Soon Atkinson and the Missouri expedition troops began arriving to establish Cantonment Missouri nearby. Leaving orders for his men, Long departed for the East on October 11, accompanied by Jessup.[17]

While at Engineer Cantonment the men had an opportunity to make excursions into the surrounding area and to collect much valuable information about the neighboring tribes. Both Seymour and Peale recorded aspects of the scene, Seymour in two watercolors, *Otoe Council* and *Pawnee Council,* and Peale in "the first known white artist's picture of the conical, buffalo hide-covered tipi, typical home of the nomadic Plains tribes," probably in November 1819, according to Ewers. Peale also made numerous drawings of the plant and animal life.[18]

While his men wintered at Engineer Cantonment, Long visited Philadelphia and arrived in Washington early in 1820, where he reported to Calhoun on the progress of the expedition. Recounting the accomplishments of the scientists, he told the secretary that the trip thus far, however, had not been wholly successful. The boat had been found to have "some defects," and the difficulty of navigating the Missouri, he said, had been "far greater than the most exaggerated accounts had authorized me to expect." Added to this was the loss of the botanist, Dr. Baldwin. All of these factors, Long concluded, were "impediments in the way of successful and efficacious operation."[19]

Concurrently, Congress was becoming increasingly dissatisfied with the entire western operation. During the early part of 1820 there was considerable debate in the House and Senate on the results of the enterprises and on the merits of continuing them, particularly in light of the difficult financial conditions after the Panic of 1819. After much discussion the War Department appropriation was cut, and the Missouri expedition was halted halfway to its destination. Calhoun informed Atkinson in April 1820 of the congressional action and told him that his troops were not to proceed beyond Council Bluffs. Among the activities the men then undertook were surveying and road construction.[20]

The congressional decision also made certain alterations necessary in the objectives of Long's scientific party. Instead of proceeding up the Missouri as planned, they were given new orders by the secretary of war to go "by land, to the source of the river Platte, and thence by way of the Arkansas and Red rivers to the Mississippi."

Some changes in personnel also were made for the second year of the expedition. Jessup had left and returned east; Lieutenant Graham was to take charge of the *Western Engineer* and to perform other duties "assigned to him by special order." Major Biddle also had left and had joined Colonel Atkinson's staff. (He and Long had quarreled to such an extent that Biddle had even issued a challenge to a duel; Long turned the other cheek.) Biddle's tasks, primarily keeping the journal, were assumed by Capt. John R. Bell. A West Point graduate, Bell was a veteran of the War of 1812. He was then stationed at Boston Harbor and in 1819 he was appointed an instructor at West Point.[21]

Moreover, another scientist was needed to take the place of the late Dr. Baldwin, and to fill this position Long chose Edwin James. Born in Weybridge, Vermont, in 1797, James had been graduated from nearby Middlebury College in 1816. He then spent most of the next three years in Albany, where he apparently studied medicine under his two physician brothers as well as various scientific subjects, gaining the background that would equip him for the adventures ahead.[22]

After completing preparations for the second part of the expedition, James and Long left Philadelphia on March 22, 1820, for the journey to Council Bluffs. On March 26 they arrived in Pittsburgh, where Captain Bell joined them. Five days later the men started down the Ohio River, having bought passage on the steamboat *Telegraph*, and by April 5 they were in Cincinnati. Proceeding down the river, they entered the Mississippi on April 16. Reaching St. Louis where they obtained needed supplies, the men left May 3 on the last leg of the trip to Engineer Cantonment, arriving there on May 27.[23]

To the Rocky Mountains

With the party together once more, plans were made for departure. Before leaving, however, the group at Engineer Cantonment was visited by a party of Otoe Indians, including several chiefs and a number of braves. A few days after the visit, Long and his men began the difficult journey that would take them many hundreds of miles to the great Rocky Mountains. They must have felt some anxiety at the prospect, and the Indians did little to encourage them. James later wrote that they "affected to laugh at our temerity, in attempting what they said we should never be able to accomplish." And Captain Bell noted that the Otoes said they would either "be destroyed by the Indians of the mountains or perish for provisions & water on the prairies." Perhaps the men remembered these warnings during the hot midsummer trek across the prairie when there was little food and less water available to sustain them. It would take more than a few words to deter them, however, and on June 6, 1820, Long and his party confidently embarked upon the journey to the West. In addition to Long, James and Bell, the group on that date included Swift, Say, Peale and Seymour from the expedition of the previous year, as well as thirteen others who performed various support functions. Long planned later to add two Frenchmen as guides and interpreters.[24]

On June 11 the group arrived at the village of the Grand Pawnees, who informed them of the country through which they were to travel, impressing upon them the dangers of the route. Their motives, however, were perhaps something less than altruistic; as James wrote, they were probably trying to discourage the explorers from going through their hunting grounds.[25]

Next the group visited the Republican Pawnees and also the Pawnee Loups. Continuing on their way, the party came to the Platte River on June 14. Thus they became the first party of record to ascend the river through present Nebraska, traversing the wide waterway that later would be known as the Great Platte River Road, a teeming highway of emigration and commerce. (As the *Account* mentions in *1820* chapter 2, a party led by Robert Stuart returning from Astoria, at the mouth of the Columbia River, first descended the Platte in 1813.) On June 22 the Long expedition reached the confluence of the north and south branches; they forded the north fork and then crossed over to the south side of the South Platte the next day.[26]

The country through which they were traveling was becoming "more arid and sterile," and after some days they were anxious for a change of scenery. In an article written several years later, Edwin James vividly described his feelings:

The traveller journeys, for weeks in succession, over a dreary and monotonous plain, sparingly skirted and striped with narrow undulating lines of timber, which grow only along the margins of considerable streams of water. In these boundless oceans of grass, his sensations are not unlike those of the mariner, who beholds around him only the expanse of the sky and the waste of waters.[27]

Thus after several weeks of travel on the dry and desolate plains, the men were understandably happy to see the outlines of the Rocky Mountains on the horizon. "From this plain the Rocky Mountains are first seen at a distance, in some states of the atmosphere, exceeding one hundred miles," James later recalled. "They first discover themselves, not by emerging from below the sensible horizon, but become distinguishable from the clouds and the sky above it. Their snowy and shining summits, when first seen, were mistaken for clouds by almost every individual of our party." As the men gained their first, faint views of the mountains beginning on June 30, the artist Samuel Seymour recorded his impressions in *Distant View of the Rocky Mountains* and *View of the Rocky Mountains, on the Platte, 50 Miles from their Base.*[28]

Soon the explorers were able to distinguish the peak that would later be named for their commanding officer. Proceeding on the South Platte, the party camped at the present site of Denver on July 5. Turning south, their line of march took them along the foothills, where James and the other scientists were able to make short excursions to observe the plant and animal life. They were also able to see the mountain that Zebulon Pike had sighted during the winter of 1806–1807. Cold, weary, without adequate provisions, Pike and his men were ill equipped to battle the icy November storms. The peak looming starkly above them appeared entirely inaccessible; in fact, Pike wrote that "no human being could have ascended to its pinical." The mountain did not look so forbidding to James in the summer of 1820, and on July 13 he and two other men set out to climb it.[29]

Beginning the ascent late that afternoon, the men found it extremely difficult to proceed across the crumbled granite in their path. After going only a few miles they made camp for the night. The next afternoon they achieved their objective, reaching the summit about four o'clock. The Vermonter was not particularly impressed with the feat he and his companions had accomplished. "The last part of the ascent was less difficult than I had expected to find it, having been informed that many unsuccessful attempts had been made to climb it by the Indians," said the youthful mountaineer.[30]

As a scientist, however, James was quite excited about the new varieties of plant life that he observed at high altitudes. "Soon after the entire disappearance of the timber commences a region of astonishing beauty, and of great interest to a Botanist whose acquaintance with the vegetable kingdom is as limited as mine," he remarked in his diary. The masses of "short but brilliantly flowering plants" he thought especially noteworthy.[31]

The men spent little time on the peak and began their descent almost immediately. The next evening, July 15, they arrived back at the main encampment. In recognition of James's accomplishment Major Long named the mountain James Peak, and it was shown thus on the maps included with the history of the expedition. Today, however, it is known by the name of the explorer who first discovered it, Zebulon Pike.[32]

Two days after his return to camp, on July 17, James, with Bell and two other men, began a short trip into the mountains along the Arkansas River. After some difficulty, they reached a point now known as the Royal Gorge, near present Cañon City, and discovered seven mineral springs, which were named Bell's Springs after Captain Bell.[33]

Traveling Toward Home

Soon afterward the time came for Long's party to leave the mountains and begin the trip home. On July 19 the men started eastward and were soon into country that James characterized as "arid and sterile" and that in his estimation "must remain forever desolate." Bell agreed; to him the land appeared "barren as the deserts of Arabia." The party remained in sight of the mountains for several days; on July 22 James nostalgically observed: "Though we are distant 100 miles by our estimation from the high peak its glorious summit is yet distinctly visible, towering among the broken clouds which rest upon its shoulders."[34]

Two days later, on July 24, the expedition separated into two groups. Captain Bell was placed in command of one party, which was to go down the Arkansas to Belle Point to await the arrival of the other. Major Long led the second detachment, which included James and Peale. They were to go south to the Red River and then east to Belle Point, the site of Fort Smith in present Arkansas.[35]

Thus began one of the most difficult portions of the journey for Long and his party. The hot mid-summer sun beat down on the men as they marched across the prairie, which to James was "a desolate and disgusting tract of country." As they traveled along a stream, which they supposed to be the Red River, they became increasingly anxious to reach their destination. "The weather continues warm and we are growing tired of each other, and of our comfortless and weary pilgrimage," James wrote on August 16.[36]

Finally they noted signs of approaching civilization. Water flowed in the river, timber and game were more abundant, and the soil was more fertile. Before they reached Belle Point, however, the men had an unpleasant surprise. They discovered that they had been on the Canadian River, far north of the Red River, which had been their objective. As James noted ruefully: "We are all of us something [sic] mortified by this mistake which has defeated one principal aspect of our summer's labor." Much disappointed, Long's party arrived at Belle Point on September 13.[37]

The party commanded by Captain Bell, which had reached Belle Point on September 9, also had had an unfortunate experience. Three of the men had deserted, taking with them horses, rifles, clothing and most importantly, several manuscripts containing Swift and Say's notes and observations of the entire trip. Despite this loss, James at least thought they had "accomplished all the objects of their trip" and had achieved "various adventures in many respects superior to ours."[38]

The members of Long's expedition were thus reunited for the first time in nearly two months. They stayed at Fort Smith for a few days making observations about the country, after which they again separated into small parties for the remainder of the journey to Cape Girardeau, where they reconvened in early October. A number of the men became ill with fever, but within a few weeks most had recovered and the explorers separated for the last time. Long had left for Washington, and Bell had departed on October 13. Say, Graham, Peale and Seymour left about the first of November for New Orleans and then Philadelphia, while James and Swift remained until the latter part of the month. On November 23 James set out on horseback, while Swift started down the Mississippi with the *Western Engineer*. He left the boat at Smithland, Kentucky, for the winter, continuing on horseback to Philadelphia to report to his superiors for further topographical duty.[39]

James also made his way to Smithland, where he spent the winter months. About the middle of May, James and the crew started with the *Western Engineer* up the river toward Louisville, where the vessel was to be repaired. After various misadventures he finally arrived back in Philadelphia.[40]

James's duties with the expedition were not completed, however, for late in 1821 he began work compiling the report of the expedition. In addition to his own journal he had the notes of Long, Say and other members on which to rely, but the responsibility for assembling this material and putting it in some kind of order rested squarely on his shoulders. It is known that Say and Long assisted him a good deal and were "constantly attentive to the work, both to the preparation of the manuscript and its revision for the press." [41]

The manuscript was ready for the printer in about six months. After finishing the final draft James left Philadelphia for a short vacation, while Major Long took charge of the work in the final stages of publication. As is sometimes the case in the world of publishing, Long encountered numerous delays and frustrations before the work was finally printed and bound. The publisher promised more than he could deliver, supplies were slow in coming and the printing proceeded at a snail's pace. Finally, on January 3, 1823, the major sent six copies of the long-awaited report to Secretary of War Calhoun. Now he and the American people would be able to read all about the "Expedition from Pittsburgh to the Rocky Mountains." [42]

The volumes that appeared in the bookshops in 1823 contained a wealth of information about the vast country beyond the Mississippi. The main portion of the work was a summary of the expedition, written primarily in day-by-day journal form. The appendices included such material as catalogues of animals seen, Indian language vocabularies, astronomical and meteorological observations and maps.

What was the reaction of the American press to this latest treatise on Western exploration? When the activities of Long and his scientists were made public, both the report and the expedition itself received what might be termed mixed notices. Overall, the reviewers judged the *Account* to be a useful and worthwhile contribution to knowledge. "We deem the work a valuable accession to our stock of travels, which may be safely referred to, as to its principal topics," commented Henry Rowe Schoolcraft, Indian agent at Sault Ste. Marie and himself an explorer of some note. "The public are indebted to Dr. James, for the judicious manner in which he has accomplished the task of compiler, from the manuscript notes of the party." *Niles' Weekly Register* published an extremely favorable notice, along with an extract from the Philadelphia edition. "It is a very valuable work. . . . Those whose opinion is much to be respected, have spoken of it as being very superior in its composition to the usual works of its nature, which, of necessity, must have some dry details of facts, not subject to embellishment."[43]

The scientific accomplishments of the expedition were particularly well received. The public was indebted to James, wrote Schoolcraft, not only for compiling the *Account* but also "for his geological and botanical observations upon the desert plains, and snowy eminences, which fell within his track." And *Niles' Weekly Register* told its readers that the work "abounds with interesting information of the manners and habits of the Indians, and the geography, geology, botany of the regions traversed, with ample notices of its animals, natural curiosities, &c. It will no doubt be extensively read."[44]

Yet the reviews were by no means wholly favorable. Many critics thought that the expedition could have accomplished much more had Congress not reduced the funds for the project. Edward Everett, writing in the *North American Review*, could hardly contain his disgust at the prospect of a country that was "growing in wealth and prosperity beyond any other" and yet was "too poor to pay a few gentlemen and soldiers for exploring its mighty rivers, and taking possession of the empires, which Providence has called it to govern."[45]

Historians in later years also tended to criticize rather than praise the expedition and the report. To many scholars, the party's failure to discover the source of the Platte, along with the mistaken identification of the Red River, were just two examples of the carelessness and scientific ineptitude that characterized the Long expedition. One of the most forceful critics was Hiram M. Chittenden, whose 1902 *American Fur Trade of the Far West* is a classic work in the field of fur trade history. Chittenden felt that the entire expedition had accomplished little, and in comparing "its actual results with what it proposed and what the public expected, the impression left is one of disappointment."[46]

Later works, too, presented a mostly negative view of the expedition. For example, in their textbook *America Moves West*, historians Robert E. Riegel and Robert G. Athearn wrote of Long's "halfhearted effort to find the source of the Red River" and concluded that he "accomplished little" and "added almost nothing to the knowledge of the region he had traversed." Ray Allen Billington was even more outspoken in his *Westward Expansion: A History of the American Frontier*, calling the expedition "Long's fiasco."[47]

The Great American Desert

Of all those who have read the *Account*, however, most have commented not on the financing of the expedition, nor on its scientific achievements, but on the explorers' description of the land east of the Rockies. In their words this was the "Great American Desert," dry, desolate and unfit for cultivation. This concept became fixed in the minds of the American people and to a large extent blocked expansion and settlement in the region until after the Civil War.

Long and James were not the first to report that this was a desert land, destined to be forever barren. Many years earlier Castañeda, the chronicler of Coronado's exploits, had written of the great arid desert through which that expedition had traveled. And only a few years before the Long journey, Zebulon Pike had concluded: "These vast plains of the western hemisphere, may become in time equally celebrated as the sandy desarts [*sic*] of Africa." But it remained for Long and James to bring this concept home to the public and to make it part of the American consciousness.[48]

In several oft-quoted passages, they presented their impressions of the country in no uncertain terms. "In regard to this extensive section of the country," said Long, "I do not hesitate in giving the opinion, that it is almost wholly unfit for cultivation, and of course uninhabitable by a people depending on agriculture for their subsistence." Edwin James agreed. "We have little apprehension of giving too unfavourable an account of this portion of the country," he wrote. The lack of water and timber, he continued, made the land "an unfit residence for any but a nomade population." With the memory of his arduous journey still fresh in his mind, James concluded: "The traveller who shall at any time have traversed its desolate sands, will, we think, join us in the wish that this region may for ever remain the unmolested haunt of the native hunter, the bison, and the jackall."[49]

Their views were almost immediately accepted and the authors of history and geography textbooks hastened to add the legend, "Great American Desert" to their maps. "When I was a schoolboy," Col. Richard Irving Dodge recalled in 1877, "my map of the United States showed between the Missouri River and the Rocky Mountains a long and broad white blotch, upon which was printed in small capitals, 'The Great American Desert—Unexplored.'" Yet a recent study of some five hundred printings of geographies and textbooks from the period 1800–1882 indicates that it is too simplistic to assume that all Americans accepted this image. In "The Great American Desert and the Frontier, 1800–1882," Martyn J. Bowden concludes that "the desert image of the western interior was shared by perhaps a majority of the well-educated in the Northeast during the 1840's and 1850's, a large minority of the same group in the eastern Middle West and the Southeast by the 1850's, and a small minority of the better educated in the old northwest after 1850."[50]

Many twentieth-century historians have roundly criticized Long and James for, as Terry Alford writes, "aiding a 'myth' seemingly so out of place in the generally optimistic national thought of the early nineteenth century." Ray Allen Billington, for example, called the Great American Desert label "a false designation" and accused Long of creating "a psychological barrier that kept others from disproving his falsehoods."[51]

Yet it is difficult to see how Long and James could have come to any other conclusion regarding the usefulness of the area. After tramping across the plains with the brilliant sun beating down on them day after day, they found it impossible to believe that civilization as they knew it could survive and endure in that inhospitable territory. Better leave it to the wild animals and the Indians, they thought; no sensible person would choose to make a life in that country.

During the latter part of the nineteenth century, however, determined farmers by the thousands ignored such negative opinions. They swarmed over the land, bent on making the desert bloom. The railroads lured settlers from the eastern United States and from Europe with promotional pamphlets that pictured the West as a land of milk and honey. All seemed to go well for a time as more and more families joined the great trek westward, confident that they could tame the desert. Many thought that working the land would produce a change in the climate itself. It was widely believed that increased settlement meant increased rainfall, and "Rain follows the plow" became a popular slogan. By the turn of the century, in an article entitled "The Mastery of the Desert," a writer for the *North American Review* assured his readers that "desert conditions are gradually disappearing through the efforts of the man who digs and toils and subdues nature." And in 1975 Everett Dick, in his work *Conquering the Great American Desert*, wrote that "the desert in America has indeed been vanquished."[52]

But was the desert really being vanquished? The farmers who saw their land blowing away in the swirling storms of the Dust Bowl would not have thought so. Even before that great disaster, many plains families had been wiped out by years of drought following an illusory "wet cycle." Slowly and painfully it began to dawn on some that the harsh, unrelenting desert was a severe taskmaster, sometimes beneficent, more often destructive. Perhaps Pike and Long and James had had the right idea after all, however much Westerners disliked admitting such a possibility. As historian Richard Dillon aptly phrased it, "The spectre of the Dust Bowl haunts the West even today for it proved, for all time, that there lurks behind the myth of the Great American Desert of the 1820's a frightening amount of reality."[53]

Although many decades have elapsed since these early explorers first published their findings, the issue of the Great American Desert remains a lively one. Nowhere is this better illustrated than in the response to an article written in 1957 by Walter Prescott Webb. In this essay he suggested that the arid desert was the most important feature of the West, making it a "land of deficiencies" and an "oasis civilization." Westerners immediately rushed to the defense of their region, denying that any part of this assertation was true. The furor that Webb's paper stirred up has not yet subsided, proving once more that any mention of the desert, whether in 1823 or 1957, can provoke a goodly amount of discussion and debate.[54]

Science

The controversy over the Great American Desert has cast a shadow over the work of Long and James and has tended to obscure the very real contributions made by the expedition in the field of natural history. As James DeKay told the New York Lyceum of Natural History in 1826:

> The collections made by this expedition were numerous and important. More than sixty new or rare animals, and several hundred insects were added to the Fauna, and many interesting plants to the Flora of the United States. The minerals and organic remains were extremely interesting, and the zoological notices which are scattered through the work, highly important.[55]

It is instructive to remember that in the early decades of the nineteenth century, American science was in its infancy, struggling toward the twin goals of professionalism and specialization. Botanists and naturalists and geologists were all busily engaged in collecting and classifying plants and in describing the natural features of the country. Men such as Amos Eaton had eagerly awaited reports of explorers who could tell them what the little-known West was really like. "Have you any knowledge of the strata constituting Rocky Mountains?" he inquired of Henry Rowe Schoolcraft in 1820. "I have said, in a note, that, after you and Dr. E. James set foot upon it, we shall no longer be ignorant of it."[56]

In order to answer such questions, several papers describing the findings of the expedition were soon published in leading scientific periodicals, primarily during the 1820s. Long, Say, Jessup, Peale and James contributed articles on the entomology, geology and botany of the vast area through which they had traveled. A number were read before interested groups such as the American Philosophical Society or the Philadelphia Academy of Natural Sciences before appearing in the transactions or journals of such groups.[57]

Among the most notable contributions of the expedition were the papers on botany. Although Edwin James wrote several of them, others were compiled by John Torrey from specimens collected by James and Dr. Baldwin. Included was a paper entitled "Descriptions of some new or rare Plants from the Rocky Mountains," collected in July 1820 by Dr. Edwin James, which was read at a meeting of the New York Lyceum of Natural History on September 22, 1823.

The plants described were some that James had collected on his ascent of Pikes Peak; their habitat, Torrey noted, was "10,000 feet above the level of the ocean, near the region of perpetual snow." James was, in fact, the first botanist in North America to collect specimens above timberline and to gather the brilliant alpine flora. Other papers by Torrey described some new grasses and the plants collected west of the Mississippi. In addition to presenting some of James's discoveries, the three articles marked the first time that an American scientist had written studies classifying plants by the natural rather than the artificial or Linnean system, and thus they constitute a landmark in the development of American botany.[58]

James made important contributions to geology as well. In an assessment in his recent study *New Lands, New Men,* historian William Goetzmann points out that James's account "went far beyond mere descriptions of a desert region. He reconstructed the geological history of the region in a way that was both uncommonly perceptive and very daring for its time. Most significantly, in looking at the vast plains and Rockies region, James assumed it was formed over an exceedingly long span of time." Indeed, it was this vision, Goetzmann continues, that "perhaps accounts for the neglect of his geological report on the part of contemporary reviewers."[59]

Even a brief review of the scientific aspects demonstrates that there was far more to the Long expeditions of 1819 and 1820 than the "Great American Desert" designation or the failure to find the Red River. And even despite this error, the explorers made significant contributions to the art of cartography. In the words of Goetzmann, "Long's expedition did produce, after Lewis and Clark's map of 1814, the most important and comprehensive view of the West. His map of 1821 remains a landmark of American cartography." And in analyzing maps of the "plains and prairies" between 1800 and 1860, John Allen asserts that the Long map "may have been one of the most important of all maps of the plains produced before the Civil War."[60]

Art and Literature

Just as historians are now viewing the scientific and cartographic contributions of the expedition in a more favorable light, so too are they coming more fully to appreciate the drawings and paintings by Peale and Seymour—"the first visualization of the West," as Goetzmann aptly phrases it. In a recent survey of "The Historian and Western Art," Richard Bartlett makes the point that "to fully comprehend Long's expedition, then, it is necessary to be aware of Seymour's sketches, the map accompanying the report . . . and the scientific information."[61]

As has been noted, Seymour's sketches represent several firsts in American exploration—the first drawing of a Plains Indian dance group, the first view of the Rockies. They are, as John Ewers points out, "documents of true historical significance" and "reveal that artist's efforts to picture the Western scene as faithfully as his talents would permit." Yet only a small number of the perhaps 150 images executed by Seymour exist either in engravings or in the original, including one, *View of James Peak in the Rain,* that has just recently been identified after years of misattribution.[62]

Far more of Titian Peale's sketches and drawings survive. From insects to birds to buffalo to squirrels, Peale's images vividly illuminate the day-to-day march of the expedition. Included as well are "the earliest known white artist's portrayal of Plains Indian warriors and buffalo hunters on horseback, as well as the first representations of such typical wildlife of the Great Plains as the antelope, the prairie chicken, and the grasshopper," as Ewers writes. For the most part, Peale's originals are now preserved in the collections of the American Philosophical Society in Philadelphia.[63]

Lastly, it should be pointed out that beyond science and art, the Long expedition had a significant impact on American literature as well. In May 1826, the popular author James Fenimore Cooper was preparing to take up residence in Europe, beginning a seven-year sojourn abroad. When he and his family sailed from New York on June 1 he carried with him the volumes of the *Account,* which served as the basis for *The Prairie,* his novel then in progress. As Orm Overland demonstrates in *The Making and Meaning of an American Classic: James Fenimore Cooper's THE PRAIRIE,* Cooper drew liberally on the *Account* for description and details, at one point apparently even using the illustrations *Otoe Encampment* and *Moveable Skin Lodges of the Kaskaias* to write passages in the novel. In fact, Overland presents abundant evidence to show that "Cooper obviously used the *Account of an Expedition* as a handbook during the whole period of composition of *The Prairie.*"[64]

After the Great Adventure

Thus did the explorers of the Long expedition become part of the literary as well as the historical record. Their scientific findings had been considerable and their artistic representations had portrayed for the first time the natural features and native inhabitants of the West. Yet their depiction of the prairies as the Great American Desert did little to encourage Congress immediately to send out more government-sponsored expeditions in the area, and thus during the 1820s and 1830s the fur traders and trappers took the lead in penetrating the wilderness. Searching for beaver pelts, these mountain men traveled up streams, across mountains and into deep forests, all the while acquiring the knowledge of the terrain that later explorers would find of immense value. This was the age of such storied figures as Kit Carson and Thomas Fitzpatrick, of Jim Beckwourth and Jim Bridger and Jedediah Smith.

While the mountain men were exploiting the riches of the wilderness, other artists were discovering the interior. During the 1830s George Catlin documented the Indian way of life in a series of incomparable portraits and scenes, while Karl Bodmer left a similarly important record as a legacy of his journey up the Missouri in 1833–1834 with Prince Maximilian of Wied-Neuwied.

Therefore, by 1840 much more was known about the continent than at the end of the Long expedition, thanks to the efforts of these independent and adventuresome men. The mood of the country had changed, too, and politicians and journalists now were asserting the need, indeed the right, for the United States to follow its "Manifest Destiny." In the words of William Gilpin, promoter and politician, it was the "*untransacted* destiny of the American people . . . to subdue the continent." The stage was set for the appearance of the controversial and flamboyant John Charles Fremont, who traversed the West five times between 1842 and 1854, surveying, mapping, collecting, analyzing. His reports, which drew in large measure on the writing talents of his wife Jessie, caught the imagination of the nation and provided information for the emigrants who were beginning to cross the continent en route to new lives in the Oregon country or California. During the 1840s, travel along the Platte River, which Long's group had ascended in 1820, increased yearly from a few small parties in 1841 and 1842 to the great throngs of the California gold rush— perhaps 40,000 persons in 1849 and 65,000 in 1850.[65]

Such figures scarcely could have been imagined by the members of the Long expedition in 1820 as they made their difficult and lonely way up the Platte, into the mountains of present Colorado and then on to Fort Smith. Afterward, as mountain men, artists, explorers, missionaries and gold seekers followed in their wake, what happened to those who had participated in this great venture? For Seymour and Say, the year 1823, when the *Account* was published, found them together on another expedition led by Stephen H. Long. This time they were to go north to the 49th parallel, which had been established as the international boundary in an 1818 agreement with Great Britain, and then east to Lake Superior.

Despite Seymour's problems in finishing the artwork from the 1819–1820 expedition (at one point Long had complained that "I cannot get him to complete the Drawings for our Book"), the artist had received the assignment to accompany the major in 1823. During the course of that journey he sketched likenesses of the natives the group encountered as well as various landscape features: Eleven of his images were included in the expedition report. From this point Seymour virtually disappears from the historical record; the circumstances of his death, as well as the disposition of most of his sketches and paintings, are unknown.[66]

Thomas Say served as zoologist for the 1823 expedition, after which he joined the utopian New Harmony, Indiana, colony in 1825, founded in that year by philanthropist Robert Owen. Two years later Say went on a collecting trip to Mexico (1827–1828), returning to New Harmony despite the failure of many of the colony's objectives. There he completed his *American Entomology* and published as well his six-volume *American Conchology* before his death in 1834. (Augustus Jessup, the geologist who had served during the first year of the expedition, collected specimens for this work. He died in 1859.)[67]

Edwin James also might have gone northward with Seymour, Say and Long, for the major had appointed him botanist, geologist and physician to the 1823 expedition. Ordered to join the men along the way, James was never able to intercept their march because of poor communication and he thus lost the opportunity. Long then offered the post of mineralogist and geologist to William Keating, who later prepared the official report. The position of botanist was never filled, although Thomas Say did undertake to collect some specimens.[68]

Subsequently, James served as an assistant army surgeon in the army at various frontier posts, including Forts Crawford, Mackinac and Brady during the period 1823–1833. Interested in the Indians who resided in the Great Lakes region, he produced several grammar and spelling books, a *New Testament* translation, and the 1830 *Narrative of the Captivity and Adventures of John Tanner*. About 1836 he moved to Burlington, Iowa, where he was involved in that state's only recorded fugitive slave case before his death in 1861.[69]

With respect to Long, the 1823 expedition brought an end to his active exploring career, though not to his travels. Continuing as a member of the engineering corps, he was involved in numerous engineering and internal improvements projects ranging from surveying railroads to designing bridges. He also worked to improve river navigation and in 1853 became superintendent of Western rivers. In 1861 he was named chief of the Topographical Engineers, serving until he retired in 1863. A year later he died in Alton, Illinois, where some of his family had settled.[70]

James D. Graham also was active in topographical engineering following his service with the 1819–1820 expedition. During his career he participated in surveys to determine the boundaries between the United States and the Republic of Texas and the United States and Canada, as well as the Maine boundary, the Mexican border and part of the Mason-Dixon line. He also made scientific observations on the Great Lakes in the late 1850s. He died in 1865.[71]

William Henry Swift's later career encompassed similar duties. As a member of the Topographical Engineers, he was associated with the Coast and Geodetic Survey (1833–1843) and worked in the topographical bureau in Washington, D.C., before resigning from the service in 1849 and becoming president of the Philadelphia, Wilmington and Baltimore Railroad. He died in 1879.[72]

As for the two journalists, Maj. Thomas Biddle had left the expedition in 1819 but remained in the army. His hot temper evidently got the better of him and he died in a duel in 1831. Biddle's replacement in 1820, Capt. John R. Bell, served in Georgia and South Carolina during the early 1820s before his death in 1825.[73]

Finally, Titian Peale, the young artist-naturalist, lived a long, full, and adventurous life after returning from the Long expedition. Associated with Peale's museum in Philadelphia, he embarked on trips to Florida (1824–1825) and Colombia (1830–1832) and with the worldwide Wilkes Expedition (1838–1842). From time to time Peale also reworked a number of his sketches from the Long expedition into more finished paintings, one of which is featured on the cover of this volume. In 1849 he became an examiner in the United States Patent Office in Washington, D.C., continuing in that position until 1872. He died in Philadelphia in 1885.[74]

Titian Peale thus had lived through most of the nineteenth century, long enough to see large portions of the Great American Desert turned into farms and ranches and towns. The telegraph and then the railroad had joined the nation from coast to coast, and photographers such as William Henry Jackson now preserved Western images on immense glass plate negatives. Along with

Samuel Seymour, Peale was there in the beginning, recording the great heartland of America on the eve of almost incomprehensible change. While earlier editions of the Long expedition report have included a few illustrations by Peale and Seymour, the advent of computerized technology permits the artwork now to be integrated more directly with the text. Thus it is possible through their sketches and paintings to gain a fresh perspective on the expedition and to appreciate more fully the images as historical documents beyond their illustrative value.

It is hoped also that this one-volume edition will serve as a readable, convenient introduction to the expedition for the general reader and student. Using the text of the Philadelphia edition, the emphasis is on the journey "from Pittsburgh to the Rocky Mountains," and thus some chapters reporting observations of the "Omawhaws" are synopsized in the Interlude, rather than being included in full. Also omitted is a chapter of "Animals, Indian language of signs, and Indian speeches," the two concluding chapters (synopsized in the Epilogue), and Long's 1821 report, as well as the sometimes lengthy notes. A few other deletions in the text are indicated by ellipses; minor typographical errors have been corrected silently. In addition, it should be noted that volume one included two chapters (17 and 18) covering the beginning of the 1820 excursion; these have been placed in the *1820* section and the succeeding chapters from volume two renumbered accordingly (that is, chapter 1 of volume two of the Philadelphia edition is now chapter 3 in the second section of this work). Those who wish to study the expedition in greater depth are directed to the four-volume edition prepared by Reuben Gold Thwaites, which was published in 1905 in the Early Western Travels Series, and to the journals of Captain Bell in the Far West and the Rockies Historical Series.[75]

Return, now, to the spring of 1819 as Long and his men prepare to set out on their epic journey. Travel through the plains (desert or garden?) and visit the Oto, Kiowa and other native peoples. Share the excitement of the first view of the Rocky Mountains and climb Pikes Peak with Edwin James. In these pages are drama, frustration and excitement in full measure—a sweeping yet intimate picture of an era forever gone, yet alive forever.

NOTES

[1] Letter from Edwin James to Amos Eaton, December 8, 1820, Simon Gratz Collection, Historical Society of Pennsylvania, Philadelphia.

[2] Donald Jackson, *Thomas Jefferson & the Stony Mountains: Exploring the West from Monticello* (Urbana: University of Illinois Press, 1981), ix, 263.

[3] Roger L. Nichols and Patrick L. Halley, *Stephen Long and American Frontier Exploration* (Newark: University of Delaware Press, 1980), 23-26; Richard G. Wood, *Stephen Harriman Long, 1784–1864: Army Engineer, Explorer, Inventor* (Glendale: Arthur H. Clark Co., 1966), 26-57.

[4] For more detailed discussions of Calhoun's plan see Cardinal Goodwin, "A Larger View of the Yellowstone Expedition, 1819–1820," *Mississippi Valley Historical Review* 4 (December 1917):299-313 and Edgar B. Wesley, "A Still Larger View of the So-Called Yellowstone Expedition," *North Dakota Historical Quarterly* 5 (July 1931):219-38. The Calhoun quote is from John C. Calhoun to A. Smyth, chairman of the Committee on Military Affairs, December 29, 1819, *American State Papers: Military Affairs*, 2:33.

[5] Calhoun to Smyth, December 29, 1819, *American State Papers: Military Affairs*, 2:33; Roger L. Nichols, *General Henry Atkinson: A Western Military Career* (Norman: University of Oklahoma Press, 1965), 54-68; *Niles' Weekly Register*, April 17, 1819, 143; Nichols, ed., *The Missouri Expedition, 1818-1820: The Journal of Surgeon John Gale, with Related Documents* (Norman: University of Oklahoma Press, 1969), x-xi; *Niles' Weekly Register*, September 18, 1819, 44.

[6] "William Baldwin," *Dictionary of American Biography* (hereinafter *DAB*), 1:547-48.

[7] Biographical information from "Thomas Say," *Dictionary of Scientific Biography* (hereinafter *DSB*), 12:132-34 and "Thomas Say," *DAB*, 16:401-2; the quotation is from Say to John F. Melsheimer, March 13, 1819, printed in Harry B. Weiss and Grace M. Ziegler, *Thomas Say, Early American Naturalist* (Springfield, Ill.: Charles C. Thomas, 1931), 61.

[8] John C. Ewers, *Artists of the Old West* (Garden City, N.Y.: Doubleday and Co., 1965; enlarged ed., 1973), 22-24; Charles Coleman Sellers, *Mr. Peale's Museum: Charles Willson Peale and the First Popular Museum of Natural Science and Art* (New York: W. W. Norton and Co., 1980), 206-7; Jackson, *Thomas Jefferson & the Stony Mountains*, 259-60.

[9] John Francis McDermott, "Samuel Seymour: Pioneer Artist of the Plains and the Rockies," *Annual Report of the Board of Regents of the Smithsonian Institution, 1950* (Washington, D.C.: Government Printing Office, 1951), 497-98.

[10] Wood, *Stephen Harriman Long*, 69; Nichols and Halley, *Stephen Long*, 73.

[11] "James Duncan Graham," *DAB*, 7:476; "William H. Swift" in G. W. Cullum, *Register of the Officers and Graduates of the U.S. Military Academy, at West Point, N.Y., from March 16, 1802, to January 1, 1850* (New York: J. F. Trow, Printer, 1850), 94-95; "Thomas Biddle, Jr.," in Francis B. Heitman, *Historical Register and Dictionary of the United States Army, From its Organization September 29, 1789, to March 2, 1903* (2 vols.; Washington, D.C.: Government Printing Office, 1903), 1:217; Nichols and Halley, *Stephen Long*, 75. Nichols and Halley point out that scholars have often misidentified Thomas Biddle as John Biddle, perpetuating an error made by Reuben Gold Thwaites in his edition of the *Account*. But Titian Peale, in his diary entry of May 3, 1819, uses the name Thomas Biddle. See *Stephen Long*, 239 n. 31.

[12] Quoted in A. O. Weese, ed., "The Journal of Titian Ramsay Peale, Pioneer Naturalist," *Missouri Historical Review* 41 (January 1947):149.

[13] *Niles' Weekly Register*, July 24, 1819, 368.

[14] Quoted in *Niles' Weekly Register,* July 31, 1819, 377.

[15] Reuben Gold Thwaites, ed., "Preface" to Edwin James, *Account of an Expedition from Pittsburgh to the Rocky Mountains. . . .,* vols. 14-17 of *Early Western Travels: 1748–1846* (Cleveland: Arthur H. Clark Co., 1905), 14:11; letter from Dr. William Baldwin to Stephen H. Long, July 18, 1819, and letter from Long to Calhoun, July 19, 1819, Secretary of War, Letters Received, Record Group (RG) 107, Records of the Office of Secretary of War, National Archives, Washington, D.C.

[16] Ewers, *Artists of the Old West,* 25.

[17] Nichols, ed., *Missouri Expedition,* 75-76; Wood, *Stephen Harriman Long,* 83-84. On the location of Council Bluffs, see Merrill J. Mattes, *Platte River Road Narratives: A Descriptive Bibliography of Travel Over the Great Central Overland Route to Oregon, California, Utah, Colorado, Montana, and Other Western States and Territories, 1812–1866* (Urbana: University of Illinois Press, 1988), 6.

[18] Ewers, *Artists of the Old West,* 26.

[19] Letter from Long to Calhoun, January 3, 1820, Secretary of War, Letters Received.

[20] U.S., *Annals of Congress,* 16th Cong., 1st Sess., 1820, 545, 549-50, 555-59, 598-99, 1629, 1633-34, 1783-90; Henry P. Beers, *The Western Military Frontier, 1815-1846* (Philadelphia: n.p., 1935), 44; Nichols and Halley, *Stephen Long,* 100, 108-11.

[21] Nichols and Halley, *Stephen Long,* 75-76, 88-89, 101; Harlin M. Fuller and LeRoy R. Hafen, eds., *The Journal of Captain John R. Bell, Official Journalist for the Stephen H. Long Expedition to the Rocky Mountains, 1820,* vol. 6 of *The Far West and the Rockies Historical Series, 1820-75,* eds. LeRoy R. and Ann Hafen (Glendale: Arthur H. Clark Co., 1957), 19-24. Hereinafter cited as Fuller and Hafen, eds., *Bell Journal.*

[22] Maxine Benson, "Edwin James: Scientist, Linguist, Humanitarian" (Ph.D. diss., University of Colorado, Boulder, 1968), *passim.*

[23] Edwin James, diary entitled "Notes of a part of the Expd. of Discovery Commanded by S. H. Long Maj. U.S. Eng. &c &c.," Rare Book and Manuscript Library, Columbia University, New York, New York, 7-8, 12-13, quoted with permission; Fuller and Hafen, eds., *Bell Journal,* 36-39, 47, 50, 62.

[24] James, *Account,* in *Early Western Travels,* 14:192-93; Fuller and Hafen, eds., *Bell Journal,* 103. (To facilitate further research, references are given when appropriate to the Thwaites edition of the *Account.*)

[25] James, Diary, 57; James, *Account,* in *Early Western Travels,* 15:206-7.

[26] James, Diary, 57; James, *Account,* in *Early Western Travels,* 15:234, 235-39; Fuller and Hafen, eds., *Bell Journal,* 124-32; Mattes, *Platte River Road Narratives,* 17-19.

[27] James, Diary, [75]; James, "Remarks on the Sandstone and Floetz Trap Formations of the Western Part of the Valley of the Mississippi," *Transactions of the American Philosophical Society,* n.s. 2, no. 9 (1825):193.

[28] James, "Remarks on the Sandstone and Floetz Trap Formations," 194; McDermott, "Samuel Seymour," 501.

[29] Pike's journal entry for November 27, 1806, in Donald Jackson, ed., *The Journals of Zebulon Montgomery Pike, With Letters and Related Documents* (2 vols.; Norman: University of Oklahoma Press, 1966):1:351; James, *Account,* in *Early Western Travels,* 16:11.

[30] James, Diary, [102].

[31] Ibid., [104].

[32] Fuller and Hafen, eds., *Bell Journal,* 167, 177-78; Francis P. Farquhar, "Naming America's Mountains: The Colorado Rockies," *American Alpine Journal* 12 (1961):333-36.

[33] James, *Account,* in *Early Western Travels,* 16:32, 34; James, Diary, [107-8]; Fuller and Hafen, eds., *Bell Journal,* 169-73.

[34] James, Diary, [109, 112]; Fuller and Hafen, eds., *Bell Journal*, 178.

[35] Fuller and Hafen, eds., *Bell Journal*, 186-276; James, *Account*, in *Early Western Travels*, 16:58-63.

[36] James, Diary, [144, 184].

[37] Ibid., [215].

[38] Fuller and Hafen, eds., *Bell Journal*, 256-57; James, Diary, [217].

[39] James, *Account*, in *Early Western Travels*, 17:88, 91-93, 103.

[40] James, Diary, [246-49].

[41] Preliminary Notice to the Philadelphia edition, James, *Account*, in *Early Western Travels*, 14:35; Weiss and Ziegler, *Thomas Say*, 79-81.

[42] Letter from Long to Isaac Roberdeau, June 10, 1822, Records of the Office of the Chief of Engineers, Topographical Engineers: Miscellaneous Letters Sent and Received, 1821–24, no. 51, RG 77, National Archives (hereinafter cited as Topographical Engineers: Miscellaneous Letters 1821–24); James, Diary, [279]; Long to Calhoun, January 3, 1823, Secretary of War, Letters Received. The *Account* was published in Philadelphia by Carey and Lea in 1823 in two volumes; in addition, a larger volume containing Long's map, geological charts, and plates of views by Seymour and Peale accompanied the set. A London edition in three volumes, with some text not included in the Philadelphia edition, also appeared in 1823. For full bibliographical information, see Henry R. Wagner and Charles L. Camp, *The Plains & the Rockies: A Critical Bibliography of Exploration, Adventure, and Travel in the American West, 1800–1865*, 4th ed. rev. by Robert H. Becker (San Francisco: John Howell Books, 1982), 94-96.

[43] [Henry Rowe Schoolcraft], review of *La Decouverte des Sources du Mississippi, et de la Riviere Sanglante*, by J. C. Beltrami (1824), *North American Review* 27 (July 1828):94; *Niles' Weekly Register*, February 8, 1823, 353.

[44] [Schoolcraft], review of *La Decouverte des Sources du Mississippi*, 94-95; *Niles' Weekly Register*, February 8, 1823, 353.

[45] [Edward Everett], "Long's Expedition," *North American Review* 16 (April 1823):268.

[46] Hiram M. Chittenden, *The American Fur Trade of the Far West* (2 vols.; New York: Francis P. Harper, 1902):2:580.

[47] Robert E. Riegel and Robert G. Athearn, *America Moves West* (4th ed.; New York: Holt, Rinehart and Winston, 1964), 326; Ray Allen Billington, *Westward Expansion: A History of the American Frontier* (New York: Macmillan, 1949), 452.

[48] W. Eugene Hollon, *The Great American Desert Then and Now* (New York: Oxford University Press, 1966), 40; Walter Prescott Webb, *The Great Plains* (Boston: Ginn and Co., 1931), 153; Jackson, ed., *Journals of Zebulon Montgomery Pike*, 2:27.

[49] Long, "A General Description of the Country Traversed by the Exploring Expedition," in *Early Western Travels*, 17:147; James, *Account*, in ibid., 16:174.

[50] Dodge, *The Hunting Grounds of the Great West* quoted in Webb, *Great Plains*, 152; Martyn J. Bowden, "The Great American Desert and the American Frontier, 1800–1882: Popular Images of the Plains," in *Anonymous Americans: Explorations in Nineteenth-Century Social History*, ed. Tamara K. Hareven (Englewood Cliffs, N.J.: Prentice-Hall, 1971), 57-58.

[51] Terry L. Alford, "The West as a Desert in American Thought Prior to Long's 1819-1820 Expedition," *Journal of the West* 8 (October 1969):516; Billington, *Westward Expansion*, 452-53.

[52] Robert G. Athearn, "The Great Plains in Historical Perspective," *Montana: The Magazine of Western History* 8 (January 1958):21-26; Frank W. Blackmar, "The Mastery of the Desert," *North American Review* 182 (May 1906):686; Everett Dick, *Conquering the Great American Desert* (Lincoln: Nebraska State Historical Society, 1975), xi.

[53] Richard Dillon, "Stephen Long's Great American Desert," *Proceedings of the American Philosophical Society* 111 (April 14, 1967):108.

[54] Walter Prescott Webb, "The American West, Perpetual Mirage," *Harper's* 214 (May 1957):28-29; "The West and the Desert," *Montana: The Magazine of Western History* 8 (January 1958):2-12.

[55] James E. DeKay, *Anniversary Address on the Progress of the Natural Sciences in the United States: Delivered Before the Lyceum of Natural History of New-York, Feb., 1826* (New York: G. & C. Carvill, 1826), 61.

[56] Russel Blaine Nye, *The Cultural Life of the New Nation, 1776–1830* (New York: Harper and Brothers, 1960), ch. 4 *passim*; Jeannette E. Graustein, *Thomas Nuttall, Naturalist: Explorations in America, 1808–1841* (Cambridge, Mass.: Harvard University Press, 1967), 24-31; letter from Amos Eaton to Henry Rowe Schoolcraft, March 18, 1820, as printed in Henry Rowe Schoolcraft, *Personal Memoirs of a Residence of Thirty Years with the Indian Tribes of the American Frontiers: With Brief Notices of Passing Events, Facts, and Opinions, A.D. 1812 to A.D. 1842* (Philadelphia: Lippincott, Grambo and Co., 1851), 48.

[57] See the listing in Max Meisel, *A Bibliography of American Natural History* (Brooklyn: Premier Publishing Co., 1926), 2:386-400. A convenient listing can be found in the appendix to Nichols and Halley, *Stephen Long*, 224-32.

[58] *Annals of the Lyceum of Natural History of New York* 1 (1824):30-36; "Descriptions of some new Grasses collected by Dr. E. James, in the expedition of Major Long to the Rocky Mountains, in 1819-1820," *Annals of the Lyceum of Natural History of New York* 1 (1824):148-56; "Some Account of a Collection of Plants made during a journey to and from the Rocky Mountains in the summer in 1820," *Annals of the Lyceum of Natural History of New York* 2 (1828):161-254; Howard A. Kelly, *Some American Medical Botanists Commemorated in Our Botanical Nomenclature* (New York: D. Appleton and Co., 1929), 138.

[59] William H. Goetzmann, *New Lands, New Men: America and the Second Great Age of Discovery* (New York: Viking, 1986), 122-23.

[60] Ibid., 122; John L. Allen, "Patterns of Promise: Mapping the Plains and Prairies, 1800–1860," in *Mapping the North American Plains: Essays in the History of Cartography*, ed. Frederick C. Luebke, Frances W. Kaye, and Gary E. Moulton (Norman: University of Oklahoma Press, 1987), 46.

[61] Goetzmann, *New Lands, New Men*, 121; Richard A. Bartlett, "The Historian and Western Art: A Review Essay," *Colorado Heritage* (1985:4):26.

[62] McDermott, "Samuel Seymour," 498-99; Ewers, *Artists of the Old West*, 29; Patricia Trenton and Peter H. Hassrick, *The Rocky Mountains: A Vision for Artists in the Nineteenth Century* (Norman: University of Oklahoma Press, 1983), 60, 346 n. 23, 348 n. 61.

[63] Ewers, *Artists of the Old West*, 29; Robert Cushman Murphy, "The Sketches of Titian Ramsay Peale (1799-1885)," *Proceedings of the American Philosophical Society* 101 (December 1957):23-31.

[64] Orm Overland, *The Making and Meaning of an American Classic: James Fenimore Cooper's THE PRAIRIE* (New York: Humanities Press, 1973), 19-20, 83-87, 67.

[65] The Gilpin quote (1846) is in Thomas L. Karnes, *William Gilpin, Western Nationalist* (Austin: University of Texas Press, 1970), 136; the immigration figures are from Mattes, *Platte River Road Narratives*, 1-3.

[66] Lucile M. Kane, June D. Holmquist, and Carolyn Gilman, eds., *The Northern Expeditions of Stephen H. Long: The Journals of 1817 and 1823 and Related Documents* (St. Paul: Minnesota Historical Society Press, 1978), 26-28, 29-30; McDermott, "Samuel Seymour," 503-8.

[67] "Thomas Say," *DSB*, 12:132-34; "Thomas Say," *DAB*, 16:401-2; Wood, *Stephen Harriman Long*, 69; Nichols and Halley, *Stephen Long*, 73.

[68] Kane, Holmquist, and Gilman, eds., *Northern Expeditions*, 23-24; Benson, "Edwin James," 137-40.

[69] Benson, "Edwin James," iv-v.

[70] Wood, *Stephen Harriman Long, passim.* A good modern, concise biography of Long containing details on his later life is Roger L. Nichols, "Stephen H. Long," in Paul Andrew Hutton, ed., *Soldiers West: Biographies from the Military Frontier* (Lincoln: University of Nebraska Press, 1987), 25-41.

[71] "James Duncan Graham," *DAB*, 7:476.

[72] Cullum, *Register of Officers and Graduates*, 94-95; "William Henry Swift," *DAB*, 18:249-50.

[73] Nichols and Halley, *Stephen Long,* 76; Fuller and Hafen, eds., *Bell Journal,* 23-24.

[74] "Titian Ramsay Peale," *DAB*, 14:351-52; "Titian Ramsay Peale," *DSB*, 10:439-40; Jessie Poesch, *Titian Ramsay Peale, 1799–1885, and His Journals of the Wilkes Expedition* (Philadelphia: American Philosophical Society, 1961), 42-108.

[75] Also of note is a one-volume abridgment with an introduction by Howard Lamar, published by the Imprint Society, Barre, Massachusetts, in a 1972 limited edition (fewer than two thousand copies). For full information on all previous editions, see Wagner and Camp, *The Plains & the Rockies,* 94-97.

ACCOUNT

OF

AN EXPEDITION

FROM

PITTSBURGH TO THE ROCKY MOUNTAINS,

PERFORMED IN THE YEARS 1819 AND '20,

BY ORDER OF

THE HON. J.C. CALHOUN, SEC'Y OF WAR

UNDER THE COMMAND OF

MAJOR STEPHEN H. LONG.

FROM THE NOTES OF MAJOR LONG, MR. T. SAY,
AND OTHER GENTLEMEN OF THE EXPLORING PARTY.

COMPILED

BY EDWIN JAMES,

BOTANIST AND GEOLOGIST FOR THE EXPEDITION.

TO THE

HONOURABLE J. C. CALHOUN,

SECRETARY OF WAR,

WHOSE LIBERAL VIEWS, ENLIGHTENED POLICY, AND

JUDICIOUS MEASURES,

WHILE THEY HAVE BEEN PROSECUTED WITH THE

UTMOST CIRCUMSPECTION AND ECONOMY,

HAVE AT THE SAME TIME CONTRIBUTED

IN AN EMINENT DEGREE

TO THE ADVANCEMENT OF THE

NATIONAL CHARACTER OF THE UNITED STATES

BOTH IN SCIENCE AND POLITICS;

THESE VOLUMES ARE MOST RESPECTFULLY DEDICATED

BY THE AUTHORS,

AS AN HUMBLE TESTIMONIAL

OF THEIR

HIGH SENSE OF HIS TALENTS AND PATRIOTISM,

AND AS A GRATEFUL ACKNOWLEDGMENT

OF HIS

INDULGENCE AND PATRONAGE.

PRELIMINARY NOTICE.

In selecting from a large mass of notes and journals the materials of the following volumes, our design has been to present a compendious account of the labors of the Exploring Party, and of such of their discoveries as were thought likely to gratify a liberal curiosity. It was not deemed necessary to preserve uniformity of style, at the expense of substituting the language of a compiler for that of an original observer. Important contributions of entire passages from Major Long and Mr. Say, will be recognized in various parts of the work, though we have not always been careful to indicate the place of their introduction. Those gentlemen having indeed been constantly attentive to the work, both to the preparation of the manuscript and its revision for the press.

In the following pages we hope to have contributed something towards a more thorough acquaintance with the Aborigines of our country. In other parts of our narrative where this interesting topic could not be introduced; we have turned our attention towards the phenomena of nature, to the varied and beautiful productions of animal and vegetable life, and to the more magnificent if less attractive features of the inorganic creation.

If in this attempt we have failed to produce any thing to amuse or instruct, the deficiency is in ourselves. The few minute descriptions of animals and plants that were thought admissible, have been placed as marginal notes, and we hope they will not be the less acceptable to the scientific reader, for being given in the order in which they occurred to our notice.

Descriptions of the greater number of the animals and plants collected on the Expedition, remain to be given. These may be expected to appear from time to time, either in periodical journals or in some other form.

Not aspiring to be considered historians of the regions we traversed, we only aimed at giving a sketch true at the moment of our visit, and which, as far as it embraces the permanent features of nature, will we trust, be corroborated by those who shall follow our steps. Much remains to be done not only on the ground we have occupied, but in those vast regions in the interior of our continent, to which the foot of civilized man has never penetrated. We cannot but hope, that the enlightened spirit which has already evinced itself in directing a part of the energies of the nation, towards the development of the physical resources of our country, will be allowed still farther to operate; that the time will arrive, when we shall no longer be indebted to the men of foreign countries, for a knowledge of any of the products of our own soil, or for our opinions in science.

We feel it a duty incumbent upon us, to acknowledge our obligations to many distinguished individuals both military and scientific, and particularly to several members of the Philosophical Society of Philadelphia, for their prompt offers of any aid in their power to contribute towards advancing the objects of the expedition at its commencement. We are indebted more especially to Professors James, Walsh, and Patterson, to Dr. Dewees and Mr. Duponceau; each of whom furnished a number of queries, and a list of objects, by which to direct our observations. These we found eminently useful, and we regret to state that, with many of our manuscripts they were inadvertently mislaid, otherwise, they should have been published in this place, for the information of future travellers.

An interesting communication from Messrs. Gordon and Wells, of Smithland, Kentucky, was received after the first volume had gone to press, consequently too late for insertion.

As a farther introduction to our narrative, we subjoin an extract from the orders of the Honourable Secretary of War to Major Long, exhibiting an outline of the plan and objects of the Expedition.

"You will assume the command of the Expedition to explore the country between the Mississippi and the Rocky Mountains."

"You will first explore the Missouri and its principal branches, and then, in succession, Red river, Arkansa and Mississippi, above the mouth of the Missouri."

"The object of the Expedition, is to acquire as the rough and accurate knowledge as may be practicable, of a portion of our country, which is daily becoming more interesting, but which is as yet imperfectly known. With this view, you will permit nothing worthy of notice, to escape your attention. You will ascertain the latitude and longitude of remarkable points with all possible precision. You will if practicable, ascertain some point in the 49th parallel of latitude, which separates our possessions from those of Great Britain. A knowledge of the extent of our limits will tend to prevent collision between our traders and theirs."

"You will enter in your journal, every thing interesting in relation to soil, face of the country, water courses and productions, whether animal, vegetable, or mineral."

"You will conciliate the Indians by kindness and presents, and will ascertain, as far as practicable, the number and character of the various tribes, with the extent of country claimed by each."

"Great confidence is reposed in the acquirements and zeal of the citizens who will accompany the Expedition for scientific purposes, and a confident hope is entertained, that their duties will be performed in such a manner, as to add both to their own reputation and that of our country."

"The Instructions of Mr. Jefferson to Capt. Lewis, which are printed in his travels; will afford you many valuable suggestions, of which as far as applicable, you will avail yourself."

It will be perceived that the travels and research of the Expedition, have been far less extensive than those contemplated in the foregoing orders:—the state of the national finances, during the year 1821 having called for retrenchments in all expenditures of a public nature,—the means necessary for the farther prosecution of the objects of the Expedition, were accordingly withheld.

1 8 1 9

CHAPTER I

Departure from Pittsburgh—
North-Western slope of the Alleghany mountains—Rapids of the Ohio.

EARLY in April, 1819, the several persons constituting the exploring party had assembled at Pittsburgh. It had been our intention to commence the descent of the Ohio, before the middle of that month; but some unavoidable delays in the completion of the steam boat, and in the preparations necessary for a long voyage, prevented our departure until the first of May. On the 31st March the following instructions were issued by the commanding officer, giving an outline of the services to be performed by the party, and assigning to each individual the appropriate duties.

"Pursuant to orders from the Hon. Secretary of War, Major Long assumes the command of the expedition about to engage in exploring the Mississippi, Missouri, and their navigable tributaries, on board the United States steam boat Western Engineer.

"The commanding officer will direct the movements and operations of the expedition, both in relation to military and scientific pursuits. A strict observance of all orders, whether written or verbal, emanating from him will be required of all connected with the expedition. The prime object of the expedition being a topographical description of the country to be explored, the commanding officer will avail himself of any assistance he may require of any persons on board to aid in taking the necessary observations. In this branch of duty Lieutenant Graham and Cadet Swift will officiate as his immediate assistants.

"The journal of the expedition will be kept by Major Biddle, whose duty it will be to record all transactions of the party that concern the objects of the expedition, to describe the manners and customs, &c. of the inhabitants of the country through which we may pass; to trace in a compendious manner the history of the towns, villages, and tribes of Indians we may visit; to review the writings of other travellers, and compare their statements with our own observations; and in general to record whatever may be of interest to the community in a civil point of view, not interfering with the records to be kept by the naturalists attached to the expedition.

"Dr. Baldwin will act as Botanist for the expedition. A description of all the products of vegetation, common or peculiar to the countries we may traverse, will be required of him, also the diseases prevailing among the inhabitants, whether civilized or savages, and their probable causes, will be subjects for his investigation; any variety in the anatomy of the human frame, or any other phenomena observable in our species, will be particularly noted by him. Dr. Baldwin will also officiate as physician and surgeon for the expedition.

"Mr. Say will examine and describe any objects in Zoology and its several branches, that may come under our observation. A classification of all land and water animals, insects, &c. and a particular description of the animal remains found in a concrete state will be required of him.

"Geology, so far as it relates to earths, minerals and fossils, distinguishing the primitive, transition, secondary, and alluvial formations and deposits, will afford subjects of investigation for Mr. Jessup. In this science, as also in Botany and Zoology, facts will be required without regard to the theories or hypotheses that have been advanced on numerous occasions by men of science.

"Mr. Peale will officiate as assistant naturalist. In the several departments above enumerated his services will be required in collecting specimens suitable to be preserved, in drafting and delineating them, in preserving the skins, &c. of animals, and in sketching the stratifications of rocks, earths, &c. as presented on the declivities of precipices.

"Mr. Seymour, as painter for the expedition, will furnish sketches of landscapes, whenever we meet with any distinguished for their beauty and grandeur. He will also paint miniature likenesses, or portraits if required, of distinguished Indians, and exhibit groups of savages engaged in celebrating their festivals, or sitting in council, or in general illustrate any subject, that may be deemed appropriate in his art.

"Lieutenant Graham and Cadet Swift, in addition to the duties they may perform in the capacity of assistant Topographers, will attend to drilling the boat's crew, in the exercise of the musket, the field piece, and the sabre.

"Their duties will be assigned them, from time to time, by the commanding officer.

"All records kept on board the steam boat, all subjects of Natural History, Geology, and Botany, all drawings, as also journals of every kind relating to the expedition will at all times be subject to the inspection of the commanding officer, and at the conclusion of each trip or voyage, will be placed at his disposal, as agent for the United States' government.

"Orders will be given, from time to time, whenever the commanding officer may deem them expedient.

S. H. Long, *Major U. S. Engineers,*
Commanding Expedition."

On the third of May we left the arsenal, where the boat had been built, and after exchanging a salute of twenty-two guns, began to descend the Alleghany, towards Pittsburgh. Great numbers of spectators lined the banks of the river, and their acclamations were occasionally noticed by the discharge by ordnance on board the boat. The important duties assigned the expedition rendered its departure a subject of interest, and some peculiarities in the structure of the boat attracted attention.

We were furnished with an adequate supply of arms and ammunition, and a collection of books and instruments.

On Wednesday the 5th of May, having completed some alterations, which it appeared necessary to make in our engine, and received on board all our stores, we left Pittsburgh and proceeded on our voyage. All the gentlemen of the party except Dr. Baldwin were in good health, and entered upon this enterprise in good spirits and with high expectations. Fourteen miles below Pittsburgh we passed a steam boat lying aground; we received and returned their salute, as is customary with the merchants' boats on the Ohio and Mississippi.

At evening we heard the cry of the whip-poor-will; and among other birds saw the pelicanus carbo, several turkey vultures, and the tell tale sandpiper. The spring was now rapidly advancing, the dense forests of the Ohio bottoms were unfolding their luxuriant foliage, and the scattered plantations assuming the cheering aspect of Summer.

A few weeks residence at and near Pittsburgh, and several journies across the Alleghany mountains, in different parts, have afforded us the opportunity of collecting a few observations relative to that important section of the country, which contains the sources of the Ohio.

In the Alleghany river we found several of those little animals, which have been described as a species of Proteus, but which to us appear more properly to belong to the genus Triton.

The northwestern slope of that range of mountains, known collectively as the Alleghanies, has a moderate inclination towards the bed of the Ohio, and the St. Lawrence, which run nearly in opposite directions along its base. This mountain chain extends uninterrupted along the Atlantic coast, from the Gulf of St. Lawrence southwest to the great alluvial formation of the Mississippi. It crosses the St. Lawrence at the rapids above Quebec, and has been supposed to be connected as a spur to a group of primitive mountains occupying a large portion of the interior of the continent, north of the great Lakes. An inspection of any of the late maps of North America, will show that this range holds the second place among the mountain chains of this continent. All our rivers of the first magnitude have their sources, either in the Rocky Mountains, or in elevated spurs, projecting from the sides of that range. The largest of the rivers, flowing from the Alleghanies, is the Ohio; and even this, running almost parallel to the range; and receiving as many, and, with a few exceptions, as large rivers from the north as from the south, seems in a great measure independent of it. From the most elevated part of the continent, at the sources of the Platte, and Yellow Stone branches of the Missouri, the descent towards the Atlantic, is at least twice obstructed by ranges of hills nearly parallel, in direction, to each other. Erroneous impressions have heretofore prevailed, respecting the character of that part of the country called the Mississippi Valley. If we consider attentively that extensive portion of our continent, drained by the Mississippi, we shall find it naturally divided into two nearly equal sections. This division is made by a range of hilly country, to be hereafter particularly described, running from near the northwestern angle of the Gulf of Mexico north-eastwardly to Lake Superior. Eastward, from this range, to the summit of the Alleghanies, extends a country of forests, having usually a deep and fertile soil, reposing upon extensive strata of argillaceous sandstone, compact limestone, and other secondary rocks. Though these rocks extend almost to the highest summits of the Alleghanies, and retain even there the horizontal position which they have in the plains, the region they underlay, is not to be considered as forming a district of table lands. On the contrary, its surface is varied by deep vallies, and lofty hills; and there are extensive tracts elevated probably not less than eight hundred feet above the Atlantic ocean. The north-western slope of the Alleghany mountains, though more gradual than the south-eastern, is, like it, divided by deep vallies, parallel to the general direction of the range. In these vallies, many of the rivers, which derive their sources from the interior and most elevated hills of the group, pursue their courses for many miles, descending either towards the south-west, or the north-east, until they at length acquire sufficient force to break through the opposing ridges, whence they afterward pursue a more direct course. As instances, we may mention the Alleghany river, which runs nearly parallel, but in an opposite direction, to the Ohio—the great Kenhawa, whose course above the falls forms an acute angle with the part below—also the Cumberland, and Tennessee, which run a long distance parallel to each other, and to the Ohio. This fact seems to justify the inference, that some other agent than the rivers has been active in the production of the vallies between the subordinate ridges of the Alleghany. There appears some reason to believe that the rocky hills, along the immediate course of the Ohio, and the larger western rivers, have received, at least their present form, from the operation of streams of water. They do not, like the accessary ridges of the Alleghany, form high and continuous chains, apparently influencing the direction of rivers, but present groups of conic eminences separated by water-worn vallies, and having a sort of symmetric arrangement. The structure of these hills, does not so much differ from that of the Alleghany mountains, as their form and position. The long chains of hills, which form the ascent of the Alleghany, on the western side, are based either on metalliferous limestone, or some of the inclined rocks belonging to the transition formation of Werner, and have their summits capped with the more recent secondary aggregates in strata without inclination, and greatly resembling those found in the plains west of the Ohio. It is not easy to conceive how these horizontal strata, unless originally continuous, should appear so similar at equal elevations in different hills, and hills separated by vallies of several miles in width. If that convulsion which produced the inclination of the strata, of the metalliferous limestone, the clay slate, and the graywacke, happened before the deposition of the compact limestone, and the argillaceous sandstones, why are not these later aggregates found principally in the vallies where their integrant particles would be supposed most readily to have accumulated? On the other hand, if the secondary rocks had been deposited previous to that supposed change, how have their stratifications retained the original horizontal position, while that of the transition strata has been changed?

Most of the rivers which descend from the western side of the Alleghany mountains, are of inconsiderable magnitude, and by no means remarkable on account of the straightness of their course, or the rapidity of their currents. The maps accompanying this work, will, in the most satisfactory manner, illustrate the great contrast in this respect, between the district now under consideration and the eastern slope of the Rocky mountains. The Tennessee, the Cumberland, the Kentucky, the Kenhawa and Alleghany rivers, though traversed in their courses by rocky dikes, sometimes compressing their beds into a narrow compass, occasioning rapids, and in other instances causing perpendicular falls, yet compared to the Platte, and the western tributaries of the Missouri generally, can be considered neither shoal nor rapid. Their immediate banks are permanent, often rocky, and the sloping beach covered with trees or shrubs, and the water, except in time of high floods, nearly transparent. The waters of the Ohio, and its tributaries, and perhaps of most other rivers, when they do not suspend such quantities of earthy matter as to destroy their transparency, reflect, from beneath their surface, a greenish colour. This colour has been thought to be, in some instances, occasioned by minute confervas, or other floating plants, or to result from the decomposition of decaying vegetable matter. That it depends on neither of these causes, however, is sufficiently manifest, for when seen by transmitted light, the green waters are usually transparent and colourless. Some rivers of Switzerland, and some of South America which descend from lofty primitive mountains, consisting of rocks of the most flinty and indestructible composition, covered with perpetual snows, and almost destitute of organic beings, or exuviæ either animal or vegetable, and whose waters have a temperature, even in summer, raised but a few degrees above the freezing point, which circumstances, together with the rapidity of their currents, render them unfit for the abode of vegetable life, and is incompatible with the existence of putrefaction, notwithstanding the transparency of their waters, and the reddish, or yellowish colour of the rocks which pave their beds, have a tinge of green, like the Ohio and Cumberland, at times of low water. It is well known that the water of the ocean, though more transparent than any other, is usually green near the shores; and on soundings, while at main ocean, its colour is blue. Perhaps the power which transparent waters have of decomposing the solar light, and reflecting principally the green rays, may have some dependence upon the depth of the stratum. If this were the case, we might expect all rivers, equally transparent and of equal depth, to reflect similar colours, which is not always the case.

In the southern part of Pennsylvania, the range called particularly the Alleghany ridge, is near the centre, and is most elevated of the group. Its summit divides the waters of the Susquehannah, on the east, from those of the Ohio on the west.

This mountain consists principally of argillite and the several varieties of gray wacke, gray wacke slate, and the other aggregates, which in transition formations usually intervene between the metalliferous limestone and the inclined sandstone. The strata have less inclination than in the Cove, Sideling, and South mountains, and other ridges east of the Alleghany. The summit is broad, and covered with heavy forests. Something of the fertility of the Mississippi valley seems to extend, in this direction, to the utmost limits of the secondary formation. The western descent of the Alleghany ridge is more gradual than the eastern, and the inclination of the strata, in some measure, reversed. It is proper to remark, that, throughout this group of mountains, much irregularity prevails in the direction as well as of the dip and inclination of strata. If any remark is generally applicable, it is, perhaps, that the inclination of the rocks is towards the most elevated summits of the vicinity.

Laurel ridge, the next in succession, is separated from the Alleghany by a wide valley. Its geological features are, in general, similar to those of the eastern ranges; but about its summit the sandstones of the coal formation, begin to appear alternating with narrow beds of bituminous clay slate. Near the summit of this ridge, coal-beds have been explored, and, at the time of our visit, coals were sold at the pits, for ten cents per bushel. In actual elevation, the coal strata, at the summit of Laurel-hill, fall but little below the summits of the Alleghany. Thus in transversing from east to west, the state of Pennsylvania, there is a constant but gradual ascent from the gneiss at Philadelphia, the several rocky strata occurring one above another, in the inverse order of their respective ages, the points most elevated being occupied by rocks of recent origin, abounding in the remains of animal and vegetable life.

Near the summit of this ridge some change is observed in the aspect of the forest. The deep umbrageous hue of the hemlock spure, the Weymouth pine, and other trees of the family of the coniferæ is exchanged for the livelier verdure of the broad leaved laurel, the rhododendron, and the magnolia acuminata.

Chestnut ridge, the last of those accessary to the Alleghany on the west, deserving the name of a mountain, is somewhat more abrupt and precipitous, than those before mentioned. This ridge is divided transversely by the bed of the Loyalhanna, a rapid but beautiful stream, along which the turnpike is built. Few spots in the wild and mountainous regions of the Alleghanies, have a more grand

and majestic scenery, than this chasm. The sides and summits of the two overhanging mountains, were at the time of our journey brown, and to appearance almost naked; the few trees which inhabit them, being deciduous, while the laurels and rose bays, gave the deep and narrow vallies the luxuriant verdure of spring.

The Monongahela rises in Virginia, in the Laurel ridge, and running northward receives in Pennsylvania the Yohogany, whose sources are in the Alleghany mountain, opposite those of the Potomac. This river, like most of those descending westward from the Alleghany, has falls and rapids at the points, where it intersects Laurel-hill, and some of the smaller ranges. Along the fertile bottoms of the Alleghany river, we begin to discover traces of those ancient works so common in the lower parts of the Mississippi valley, the only remaining vestiges of a people once numerous and powerful, of whom time has destroyed every other record. These colossal monuments, whatever may have been the design of their erection, have long since out-lived the memory of those who raised them, and will remain for ages, affecting witnesses of the instability of national, as well as individual greatness; and of the futility of those efforts, by which man endeavors to attach his name and his memorial to the most permanent and indestructible forms of inorganic matter.

In the deep vallies west of the Alleghany, and even west of the Laurel-ridge, the metalliferous limestone, which appears to be the substratum of this whole group of mountains, is again laid bare. In this part of the range, we have not observed those frequent alternations of clay-slate with this limestone, which have been noticed by Mr. Eaton and others in New England. In its inclination, and in most particulars of external character, it is remarkably similar to the mountain limestone of Vermont, and the western counties of Massachusetts. Many portions of the interior of the state of Pennsylvania, have a basis of this limestone. When not overlaid by clay-slate, and particularly when not in connexion with sandstone, the soils resting on the transition limestone, are found peculiarly fertile and valuable, having usually a favorable disposition of surface for agricultural purposes, and abounding with excellent water.

The transition limestone is not, however, of frequent occurrence westward of the Alleghany ridge. It appears only in the vallies, and is succeeded by clay-slate and the old sandstone lying almost horizontally. The coal, with the accompanying strata of argillaceous sandstone and shale, are, as far as we have seen, entirely horizontal.

The country westward from the base of the Chestnutridge, has an undulating surface. The hills are broad and terminated with a rounded out-line, and the landscape presenting a grateful variety of fields and forests is often beautiful, particularly when, from some elevation, the view overlooks a great extent of country, and the blue summits of the distant mountains, are added to the perspective.

Pittsburgh has been so often described, the advantages and disadvantages of its situation, and the gloomy repulsiveness of its appearance, have been so often and so justly portrayed, that we should not think ourselves well employed in recounting our own observations. The Alleghany and the Monogahela at Pittsburgh, where they unite to form the Ohio, are nearly equal in magnitude; the former, however, on account of the rapidity of its current, and the transparency of its waters, is a far more beautiful river than the latter. Its sources are distributed along the margin of Lake Erie, and a portage, of only fifteen miles, connects its navigation with that of the St. Lawrence.

About the sources of the Alleghany are extensive forests of pine, whence are drawn great supplies of lumber, for the country below as far as New Orleans. On French Creek and other tributary streams, are large bodies of low and rather fertile lands, closely covered with forests, where the great Weymouth pine, and the hemlock spruce are intermixed with beech, birch, and the super maple. The great white or Wemouth pine, is one of the most beautiful of the North American species. Its trunk often attains the diameter of five or six feet, rising smooth and straight from sixty to eighty feet, and terminated by a dense conifer top. This tree, though not exclusively confined to the northern parts of our continent, attains there its great magnitude and perfection. It forms a striking feature in the forest scenery of Vermont, New Hampshire, and some parts of Canada, and New York; rising by nearly half its elevation above the summits of the other trees, and resembling, like the palms of the tropics, so beautifully described by M. De Sainte Pierre, and M. De Humboldt, "a forest planted upon another forest." The sighing of the wind in the tops of these trees, resembles the scarce audible murmurings of a distant water-fall, and adds greatly to the impression of solemnity produced by the gloom and silence of the pine forest. In the southern parts of the Alleghany mountains, pines are less frequent, and in the central portions of the valley of the Mississippi, they are extremely rare.

The Coal formation containing the beds, which have long been wrought near Pittsburgh, appears to be of great extent; but we are unable particularly, to point out its limits towards the north and east. One hundred miles above Pittsburgh, near the Alleghany river, is a spring, on the surface of whose waters, are found such quantities of a bituminous oil, that a person may gather several gallons in a day. This spring is most probably connected with coal strata, as are numerous similar ones in Ohio, Kentucky, &c. Indeed it appears reasonable to believe that the coal strata are continued along the western slope of the Alleghanies with little interruption, at least as far northward as the Brine springs of Onondago. Of all the saline springs belonging to this formation, and whose waters are used for the manufacture of salt, the most important are those of the Kenhawa, a river of Virginia. Others occur in that country of ancient monuments, about Paint-creek, between the Sciota and the Muskinghum, near the Silver-Creek hills in Illinois; and indeed in almost all the country contiguous to the Ohio river. Wherever we have had the opportunity of observing these brine springs, we have usually found them in connexion with an argillaceous sandstone, bearing impressions of phytolytes, culmaria, and those tessellated zoophytes, so common about many coal beds. It appears to us worthy of remark, that in many places, where explorations have been made for salt water, and where perpendicular shafts have been carried to the depth of from two to four hundred feet, the water, when found, rises with sufficient force to elevate itself several feet above the surface of the earth. This effect appears to be produced by the pressure of an aerial fluid, existing in connexion with the water, in those cavities beneath the strata of sandstone, where the latter is confined, or escaping from combination with it, as soon as the requisite enlargement is given, by perforating the superincumbent strata. We have had no opportunity of examining attentively, the gaseous substances which escape from the brine pits, but from their sensible properties, we are induced to suppose that carbonic acid, and carburetted hydrogen, are among those of most frequent occurence.

The little village of Olean, on the Alleghany river, has been for many years of point of embarkation, where great numbers of families, migrating from the northern and eastern states, have exchanged their various methods, of slow and laborious progression by land, for the more convenient one of the navigation of the Ohio. From Olean downward, the Alleghany and Ohio bear along with their currents fleets of rude arks laden with cattle, horses, household furniture, agricultural implements, and numerous families having all their possessions embarked on the same bottom, and floating onward toward that imaginary region of happiness and contentment, which like the "town of the brave and generous spirits," the expected heaven of the aboriginal American, lies always "beyond the places where the sun goes down."

This method of transportation, though sometimes speedy and convenient, is attended with uncertainty and danger. A moderate wind blowing up the river, produces such swells in some parts of the Ohio, as to endanger the safety of the ark; and these heavy unmanageable vessels are with difficulty so guided in their descent, as to avoid the *planters,* sunken logs, and other concealed obstructions to the navigation of the Ohio. We have known many instances of boats of this kind so suddenly sunk, as only to afford time for the escape of the persons on board.

On the 6th we arrived at Wheeling, a small town of Virginia, situated on a narrow margin along the bank of the Ohio, at the base of a high cliff of sandstone. Here the great national road from Cumberland, comes in conjunction with that of Zanesville, Columbus, and Cincinnati. The town of Cumberland, from which this great national work has received the appellation of the Cumberland road, lies on the north side of the Potomac, one hundred and forty miles E. by S. from Wheeling. The road between these two points, was constructed by the government of the United States, at a cost of one million eight hundred thousand dollars. The bridges and other works of masonry, on the western portion of this road, are built of a compact argillaceous sandstone, of a light gray or yellowish white colour, less durable than the stone used in the middle and eastern sections, which is the blue metalliferous limestone, one of the most beautiful and imperishable among the materials for building which our country affords. A few miles from Wheeling, a small but beautiful bridge, forming a part of this road, is ornamented with a statue of that distinguished statesman Mr. Clay—erected, as we were informed, by a gentleman, who resides in that neighbourhood.

In an excursion on shore, near the little village of Charleston in Virginia, we met with many plants common to the eastern side of the Alleghanies; beside the delicate sison bulbosum, whose fruit was now nearly ripened. In shady situations we found the rocks, and even the trunks of trees to some little distance from the ground, closely covered with the sedum ternatum, with white flowers fully unfolded. The cercis canasendis, and the cornus florida, were now expanding their flowers, and in some places occurred so frequently, as to impart their lively colouring to the landscape. In their walks on shore, the gentlemen of the party, collected great numbers of the early flowering herbaceous plants, common to various parts of the United States. . . .

The scenery of the banks of the Ohio, for two or three hundred miles below Pittsburgh is eminently beautiful, but is deficient in grandeur and variety. The hills usually approach on both sides, nearly to the brink of the river; they have a rounded and graceful form, and are so grouped as to produce a pleasing effect. Broad and gentle swells of two or three hundred feet, covered with the verdure of the almost unbroken forest, embosom a calm and majestic river, from whose unruffled surface, the broad out line of the hills is reflected with a distinctness, equal to that with which it is imprinted upon the azure vault of the sky. In a few instances near the summits of the hills, the forest trees become so scattered, as to disclose here and there a rude mass, or a perpendicular precipice of gray sandstone, or compact limestone, the prevailing rocks of all this region. The hills are however usually covered with soil on all sides, except that looking towards the river, and in most instances are susceptible to cultivation to their summits. These hilly lands are found capable of yielding, by ordinary methods of culture, about fifty bushels of maize per acre. They were originally covered with dense and uninterrupted forests, in which the beech trees were those of most frequent occurrence. These forests are now disappearing before the industry of man; and the rapid increase of population and wealth, which a few years has produced, speak loudly in favor of the healthfulness of the climate, and of the internal resources of the country. The difficulty of establishing an indisputable title to lands, has been a cause operating hitherto to retard the progress of settlement, in some of the most fertile parts of the country of the Ohio; and the inconveniences resulting from this source, still continue to be felt.

On the 7th, we passed the mouth of the Kenhawa, and the little village of Point Pleasant. The spot now occupied by this village, is rendered memorable, on account of the recollections connected with one of the most affecting incidents, in the history of the aboriginal population. It was here that a battle was fought, in the "autumn of 1774, between the collected forces of the Shawanees, Mingoes, and Delawares on one side, and a detachment of the Virginia militia, on the other. In this battle, Logan, *the friend of the whites*, avenged himself in a signal manner, for the injuries of one man, by whom all his women and children had been murdered. Notwithstanding his intrepid conduct, the Indians were defeated, and sued for peace; but Logan disdained to be among the suppliants. He would not turn on his heel to save his life. "For my country," said he, "I rejoice in the beams of peace, but, do not harbor a thought that mine is the joy of fear. Logan never felt fear. Who is there to mourn for Logan! Not one." This story is eloquently related by Mr. Jefferson, in his "Notes on Virginia," and is familiar to the recollection of all who have read that valuable work.

In the afternoon of the 8th, we encountered a tremendous thunder storm, in which our boat, in spite of all the exertions we were able to make, was driven on shore; but we fortunately escaped with little injury, losing only our flagstaff with the lantern attached to it, and some other articles of little importance. On the following day we passed Maysville, a small town of Kentucky. On our return to Philadelphia, in 1821, we were delayed some time at this place; and taking advantage of the opportunity thus afforded, we made an excursion into that beautiful agricultural district, southeast of Maysville, about the large village of Washington. The uplands here are extremely fertile, and in an advanced state of cultivation. The disposition of the surface, resembles that in the most moderately hilly parts of Pennsylvania, and to the same graceful undulation of the landscape, the same pleasing alternation of cultivated fields, with dense and umbrageous forests, is added an aspect of luxuriant fertility, surpassing any thing we have seen eastward of the Alleghanies. Having prolonged our walk many miles, we entered after sunset a tall grove of elms and hickories; towards which we were attracted by some unusual sounds. Directed by these, we at length reached an open quadrangular area of several acres, where the forest had been in part cleared away, and much grass had sprung up. Here we found several hundreds of people, part sitting in tents and booths, regularly arranged around the area, and lighted with lamps, candles, and fires; part assembled about an elevated station, listening to religious exhortations. The night had now become dark, and the heavy gloom of the forests, rendered more conspicuous by the feeble light of the encampment, together with the apparent solemnity of the great numbers of people, assembled for religious worship, made considerable impression on our feelings.

As long as we remained among them, we observed nothing incompatible with the most rigid requirements of decorum, nothing in ill accordance with the solemn grandeur of the scene, they had chosen for their place of worship.

On the 9th May, we arrived at Cincinnati. Since our departure from Pittsburgh, Dr. Baldwin's illness had increased, and he had now become so unwell, that some delay appeared necessary on his account; as we wished also for an opportunity for making some repairs, and alterations in the machinery of the boat, it was resolved, to remain at Cincinnati some days. Dr. Baldwin was accordingly moved on shore, to the house of Mr. Glen, and Dr. Drake was requested to attend him. Cincinnati is the largest town on the Ohio. It is on the north bank of the river, and the ground on which it stands is elevated, rising gradually from the water's edge.

Compact limestone appears here, in the bed of the Ohio, and extends some distance in all directions. This limestone has been used in paving the streets, for which purpose its tabular fragments are placed on edge, as bricks are sometimes used in flagging. The formation of limestone, to which this rock belongs, is one of great extent, occupying a large part of the country from the shores of Lake Erie, to the southern boundary of the state of Tennessee. It appears, however, to be occasionally interrupted, or over-laid by fields of sandstone. It abounds in casts, and impressions of marine animals. An orthocer-

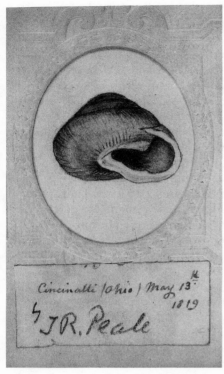

Shell, T.R. Peale, May 13, 1819, watercolor.

Within the image: *Cincinnatti (Ohio) May 13 1819* / *JR. Peale*

ite in the museum of the college at Cincinnati, measures near three feet in length. Very large specimens of what has been considered lignite, have also been discovered, and parts of them deposited in that collection. We saw here no remains of ammonites. Numerous other species, appear to be similar to those found in the limestone of the Catskill, and Hellebergh mountains.

The soil, which overlays the limestone of Cincinnati, is a deep argillaceous loam, intermixed with much animal and vegetable matter. Vegetation is here luxuriant, and many plants unknown eastward of the Alleghany mountains, were constantly presenting themselves to our notice. Two species of Æsculus are common. One of these has a nut as large as that of the Æ. Hippocastanum, of the Mediterranean, the common horse-chestnut of the gardens.

These nuts are round, and after a little exposure, become black, except in that part which originally formed the point of attachment to the receptacle, which is an oblong spot three fourths of an inch in diameter, the whole bearing some resemblance to the eye ball of a deer, or other animal. Hence the name *buck-eye*, which is applied to the tree. The several species of æsculus are confined principally to the western states and territories. In allusion to this circumstance, the indigenous backwoodsman is sometimes called buck-eye, in distinction from the numerous immigrants who are introducing themselves from the eastern states. The opprobrious name of Yankee is applied to these last, who do not always stand high in the estimation of the natives of the south and west. Few of these sectional prejudices, are, however, to be discovered in Ohio, the greater part of the population here having been derived from New England. Cincinnati, which in 1810 contained 2,500 inhabitants, is now said to number about 12,000. Its plan is irregular, and most of the buildings are of brick. The dwellings are neat and capacious, and sometimes elegant.

The site of the town was heretofore an aboriginal station, as appears from the numerous remains of ancient works still visible. We forbear to give any account of these interesting monuments, as they have already been repeatedly described.

On Tuesday, the 18th, the weather becoming clear and pleasant, Dr. Baldwin thought himself sufficiently recovered to proceed on the voyage; accordingly having assisted him on the boat, we left Cincinnati at 10 o'clock.

During our stay at that place, we had been gratified by the hospitable attentions of the inhabitants of the town. Mr. Glen was unremitting in his exertions to promote the recovery of Dr. Baldwin's health; to him, as well as to Dr. Drake, and several other gentlemen of Cincinnati, all the members of our party are indebted for many friendly attentions.

Below Cincinnati the scenery of the Ohio becomes more monotonous than above. The hills recede from the river, and are less elevated. Heavy forests cover the banks on either side, and intercept the view of all distant objects. This is, however, somewhat compensated by the magnificence of the forests themselves. Here the majestic platanus attains its greatest dimensions, and the snowy whiteness of its branches is advantageously contracted with the deep verdure of the cotton-wood, and other trees which occur in the low grounds.

The occidental plane tree is, perhaps, the grandest of the American forest trees, and little inferior in any respect to the boasted plane tree of the Levant. The platanus orientalis attains, in its native forests, a diameter of from ten to sixteen feet. An American plane tree, which we measured, on the bank of the Ohio, between Cincinnati and the rapids at Louisville, was fourteen feet in diameter. One which stood, some years since, near the village of Marietta, was found, by M. Michaux, to measure 15. 7-10 ft. in diameter, at twenty feet from the ground. They often rise to an elevation of one hundred and fifty feet. The branches are very large and numerous, forming a spreading top, densely covered with foliage. Many of those trees, which attain the greatest size, are decayed in the interior of the trunk, long after the annual increase continues to be added at the exterior circumference. The growth of the American plane tree does not appear to be very rapid. It was remarked by Humboldt, that in the hot and damp lands of North America, between the Mississippi and the Alleghany mountains, the growth of trees is about one fifth more rapid than in Europe, taking for examples the platanus occidentalis, the liriodendron tulipifera, and the cupressus disticha, all of which reach from nine to fifteen feet in diameter. It is his opinion that the growth of these trees does not exceed a foot in diameter in ten years. As far as our observation has enabled us to judge, this estimate rather exceeds than falls short of the truth. This growth is greatly exceeded in rapidity by the baobab, and other trees in the tropical parts of America; also by the gigantic adansonia of the eastern continent, and equalled, perhaps, by several trees in our own climate, whose duration is less extended than that of those above mentioned.

The sycamore, or occidental plane tree has been cultivated for more than one hundred and eighty years in England, yet it does not appear to have become entirely naturalized there, as we are informed by president Smith that great numbers were killed by the severe frost of the winters of 1810-11. In America this tree is very widely distributed, and extends northward beyond the forty-fifth degree of north latitude. In the fertile alluvial lands of Otter Creek, and other rivers which discharge into Lake Champlain, this tree attains more than one half the magnitude which it is seen to reach in the most prolific portions of the Mississippi valley; it appears, therefore, that some other cause than the frigidity of the climate, must have occasioned the destruction of the plane trees of England, since it is well known that the winters of Vermont and Lower Canada, far surpass in severity those of the island of Great Britain.

The fruit of the sycamore is the favourite food of the paroquet, and large flocks of these gaily plumed birds constantly enliven the gloomy forests of the Ohio.

During the night of the 18th, the weather being clear, we continued on our voyage, as is customary with most of the steam boats navigating the Ohio.

It was long since remarked by Mr. Schultz, and considered by him as an inexplicable circumstance, that the reflection, by night, of the images of the banks of the Ohio, does not furnish an infallible guide to the middle of the bed of the river. Nothing is more manifest than that the banks at different places, having different degrees of elevation, and being sometimes naked, and sometimes covered with very tall trees, must, of necessity, cast shadows of different lengths, upon the surface of the water, consequently that the luminous stripe along the middle of the river, from the surface of which the sky and the stars are reflected, must be greatly subject to irregularities in position and direction. This cumstance often proves very annoying to inexperienced pilots, who attempt to navigate the Ohio, or any other river of similar character, by night, as we have had occasion in many instances to experience.

On the morning of the 19th we arrived at Louisville, having passed, in the night, the boats containing the sixth regiment of infantry, then on their way to the Missouri. At Louisville we stopped to procure a pilot to conduct our boat over the rapids. Two or three pilots appointed pursuant to an act of the legislature of Kentucky reside at Louisville, always holding themselves in readiness to go on board such boats as are about to descend the rapids, and leaving them again at Shippingsport, for which service they are entitled to receive two dollars for each ark or raft.

At these rapids, called usually the rapids of the Ohio, the river descends about twenty-two feet, in a distance of less than two miles. At times of high water an acceleration of current, not usual in other parts of the river, is all that is perceived in passing down this descent: at other times the water is dashed and broken upon the rocky and uneven bed of the channel, called the *Indian chute,* through which a great part of the water passes. The magnificence of a cataract is however at no time displayed here, and it is only in peculiar conditions of the atmosphere, that the noise of the fall can be heard at the distance of one fourth of a mile from the bank of the river.

Large boats ascend the rapids at the time of the Spring floods, by the aid of a cable made fast to a tree, or some other object above, and taken in by the capstan. In 1821, the Maysville, a steam boat of about two hundred tons, was taken up, and had nearly reached the head of the rapid, when the cable broke, and the boat swinging round, was thrown against the rocks, in the bed of the river, and placed in such a situation as to render hopeless all attempts to get her off before the next annual rise of the water. Arks and small barges descend, by the aid of skilful pilots, for great part of the year. It is expected that the navigation of this dangerous rapid will soon be rendered more convenient, by canaling, which can be accomplished at a very inconsiderable expense. The direction of the Ohio, above and below the rapids, is nearly from north-east to south-west, but where the stream passes the rocky obstruction occasioning the fall, it is a little deflected from its course, making a bend towards the west. Thus a point is formed on the south-eastern side projecting from the elevated bank, which, from its present position, would seem to indicate that the bed of the river had changed its place, having formerly traversed the point from north-east to south-west, in a direct line. In times of high floods the water is, in part, discharged through this old channel, and large boats are said to have ascended by that route within a few years past.

On this point stands the small town of Shippingsport, at the foot of the rapids. The proposed canal will traverse the point in the rear of this village. The obstacles to be encountered in opening a canal at this place are but trifling. The soil is firm and gravelly, being based on horizontal strata of compact limestone, and fine argillaceous sandstone.

The sandstone, which is the rock of most common occurrence about the rapids, very closely resembles that of Pittsburgh. It is commonly of a compact texture, having an argillaceous cement, with a laminated structure. At Shippingsport, and at Clarksville, in Indiana, it is succeeded by bituminous clay slate. While we were waiting at the rapids, several of the party made an excursion to visit the boiling spring, at the foot of the Silver Creek hills, in Indiana, at a little distance from New Albany. This spring is small, discharging no water above the surface of the ground. It is an artificial excavation in the clayey bank of a small stream, called Fountain Creek. It is filled to the level of the water in the creek, the spring itself evidently discharging very little, if any water. That which fills the basin is turbid, being kept in constant agitation by the bubbles of inflammable air which rise through it. The smell of sulphuretted hydrogen is perceptible at considerable distance about the spring, and a piece of silver, held near the surface of the water, was quickly tarnished. The Silver Creek hills are of argillaceous sandstone, and secondary clay slate; and this spring seems to be placed near the meeting of the two strata.

In the bed of the Ohio opposite Shippingsport, is a tabular mass of rocks visible above water for great part of the year, and called Corn Island. On the highest parts of this, are remaining some small portions, of the limestone stratum, which appears in many places to have been worn through, and removed by the river. Five or six acres of the surface of this island are of the smooth compact argillaceous sand rock, before mentioned, lying horizontally, and divided into squares and paralellograms by the natural fissures. These fissures contain some soil which supports, in the summer, a dense growth of herbaceous plants. Among these we noticed the Hypericum sphærocarpum of Michaux (apparently not the plant mentioned by Nuttall, under that name, which has been noticed near Philadelphia, by Collins, and others, but without doubt that originally described by Michaux). Two species of Andropogon, the Panicum virgatum, Solanum nigrum, Polygala verticillata, Leplanthus gramineus, Chenopodium botrys, &c. The lower part of the island is covered with loose sand; being some small cotton–wood and willow trees.

The unenclosed grounds, about Louisville and Shippingsport are extensive and afford pasturage to great numbers of domestic animals. They are, however, much overrun with luxuriant weeds. The Datura strammonium, which is common in every part of Ohio, is sometimes eaten by sheep, and the spiny capsules of the seed, when about half ripened, we have seen eaten with apparent avidity by cows. In addition to this loathsome plant, the common may-weed (anthemis cotula) has become abundant in all the waste grounds, to the exclusion of the native plants. A few of these, which keep their places with the greatest obstinacy by the road sides, are the Sida abutibon and S. spinsoa, and the verbena hastata, while the thistles, Chrysanthemums, and Johnsworths so common about old fields, in New England, are not to be met with. The Eleusine mucronata of *Pursh,* is one of the most frequent grasses along the streets.

The Silver Creek hills, are elevated about one hundred and fifty, or two hundred feet above the level of the country in the rear of Jeffersonville. They form a continuous range, crossing the country from north to south. On the Kentucky side they constitute the commencement of a rugged and barren district, called the *Knobs,* and extending far to the south. At some remote period this range may have formed a barrier, extending across what is now the immediate valley of the Ohio, and retarding the retreat of the waters from the tract above the falls. Coal occurs frequently in this range of hills, on the north side of the Ohio; quarries have been opened near the Blue river, in Indiana, about the two Pidgeons, opposite the mouth of Green river, and in various other places.

The larger steam boats which run on the Mississippi, and the Ohio, ascend usually no farther than Shippingsport, and several of them remain at this place, during several months of the summer, while the water is too low to admit their passing up and down the rivers. This time it is often necessary to spend in repairs of various kinds. The high steam engines require frequent repairs, and in the difficult navigation of the Mississippi the hulks of vessels are often injured. It frequently happens that the boats, built at Pittsburgh, and other places near the sources of the Ohio, are within three or four years after they are launched, in a condition to require the planking of the hull to be replaced with new timber. These boats are usually planked with the upland white-oak: we have been informed that those boats which are built lower down on the river, and of such timber as is found in the low grounds, are more durable.

CHAPTER II

The Ohio below the Rapids at Louisville—
ascent of the Mississippi from the mouth of the Ohio to St. Louis.

OUR small boat descended over the rapids without injury, and having taken on board some wood near New Albany, we proceeded on our voyage, with a pressure of steam equalling one hundred pounds to the square inch, upon all parts of the engine, exposed to its immediate operation. This enabled us to descend, at the rate of ten miles per hour. A small island in the Ohio, about twenty-three miles below the rapids, is called Flint Island, from the great numbers of fragments of flints, broken arrow points, and various instruments of stone, heretofore used by the Indians, which are found there on turning up the soil. This island has probably been the favourite residence of some tribe, particularly expert in the manufacture of those rude implements, with which the wants of the aboriginal Americans were supplied. Some stone employed in these manufactures appears to have been in most instances, that compact flint, which occurs in nodular masses, in the secondary limestones. In one instance we met with a triangular prism, of a very hard and compact aggregate of feldspar, and hornblende, unlike any rock we have seen in the valley of the Mississippi. This prism was about five inches long, with faces of about an inch in width, and was

27

perforated, from end to end, forming a complete tube, with an orifice, about half an inch in diameter, and smoothly polished, both within and without. We were never able to discover, to what use this implement could have been applied; nor do we recollect to have met with accounts of any thing analogous to it, except, perhaps, those "tubes of a very hard stone," mentioned by the Jesuit Venegas, as used by the natives of California, in their treatment of the sick. That it may have passed, by means of the intercourse of various tribes of Indians, from the primitive mountains of California, to the rapids of the Ohio, is not perhaps, improbable. Indirect methods of communication may have conveyed the productions of one part of the continent to another, very remote from it. The savages of the Missouri, receive an intoxicating bean, from their neighbours on the south and west; these again, must probably procure it from other tribes inhabiting, or occasionally visiting, the tropical regions.

Western Engineer, T.R. Peale, 1819, ink and wash.

In the Philadelphia museum, are many Indian pipes, of that red indurated clay, found only, (as far as hitherto known,) on the Pipe Stone branch of the little Sioux river of the Missouri; one of these, however, was found on the banks of the Rio de la Plata, in South America; several were found in the territory now called New England, and in the north-eastern part of the continent.

On the 26th we passed the mouth of the Wabash, and arrived at Shawaneetown, ten miles below. Near the mouth of the Wabash, an accident happened to the engine, which rendered it necessary for us to drift down, until we should arrive at some place, where repairs might be made. Some of the gentlemen of the party, determined to go on shore, and walk to Shawaneetown. In swimming across a creek, three miles above that place, Lieutenant Graham dropped his rifle in the water, and, having spent some time, in attempts to recover it, did not arrive at Shawaneetown, until after the boat had reached that place.

On the 27th, several of the party went out to hunt in the forest, and swamps, north-west of the Shawaneetown. At about four miles distance from the Ohio, they arrived at the banks of a small pond, three miles long, and only three or four hundred yards wide. Here they killed a turkey, and some small birds. On the bank of the pond, was found a specimen of the Lake Erie tortoise, depositing its eggs in the sand, at about twenty yards distance from the water. It had made, with its feet, a hole in the sand, two inches in diameter and four inches in depth, enlarging towards the bottom to three inches. This species occurs frequently in the pools and stagnant waters along the Ohio. We first met with it near the rapids at Louisville. Among other birds, we noticed about Shawaneetown, the pileated woodpecker, the minute tern, numerous flocks of the psittacus caroliniensis, two broods of young wood duck, some gulls, and semipalmated sandpipers. The terns appear to be attracted hither by great numbers of a species of phryganea, with which we found the stomachs of some of them filled. The semipalmated sandpipers were in large flocks, and did not appear stationary.

Tern, T.R. Peale, May 28, 1819, watercolor.

We left Shawaneetown at twelve o'clock on the 28th, and stopped three miles below, to take in wood; then proceeding forward, at four P.M. we ran aground on a sand bar, seven miles above the "Cave Inn," or "House of Nature." After much exertion, by means of anchors and poles, with the aid of the engine, and all the men, who were under the necessity of jumping into the river, we at length succeeded in getting her off, and we ran down to the Cave, where we laid by for the night.

Early the next morning, we went to visit the cave, of the entrance to which two views were sketched by Mr. Seymour. It is a perpendicular fissure, extending about one hundred and sixty feet, into the horizontal limestone cliffs, which here, form the north bank of the river. At times of high water, the Ohio flows in, and fills the cave nearly to its roof. In this cave, it is said, great numbers of large bones were some time ago found, but we saw no remains of any thing of this kind. Impressions and casts of the shells of submarine animals were seen in the rocks, forming the sides of the cave, as in all the stata of compact limestone, in this region. The organic remains here, do not appear to be so numerous as those of the rocks at the falls, and at Cincinnati; and are much less distinct, and visible in the fracture; indeed the fracture generally exhibits to the eye no vestige of organic remains. It is upon the surface only, and more especially in parts of it as are in a certain stage of decomposition, that they are at all to be distinguished.

As far as we could discover, they consist, chiefly of the caryophyllæ, similar to the radiated species so common at the falls of Ohio; of the encrinus, but of this our specimens were not so perfect, as to enable us to determine the analogy. Numerous other remains were exhibited, but not sufficiently characterized, to be referred to their proper places in the system. The top of the cliff, into which this fissure opens, is said to be the favourite haunt of great numbers of birds of prey. This is not improbable, as many hawks and birds of prey always choose high and inaccessible cliffs to build their nests in. We saw about the tops of these rocks, only one pair of hawks, which we took to be of the red shouldered species, (Falco lineatus,) but a heavy rain, which commenced soon after we had ascended, prevented us from procuring a specimen. About the cave, we found some fragments of pottery, arrow points, and other articles of Indian manufacture.

Near Shawaneetown are extensive salt manufactories, at a place heretofore called the United States' Saline, affording employment and a source of trade to a part of the inhabitants of that village. Common salt, with the nitrates of lime, potash, &c. occur in great plenty, in connexion with the horizontal limestones and sandstones on the Ohio. . . .

On the 29th of May we passed the mouths of the Cumberland and Tennessee, the two largest rivers, tributary to the Ohio. At the mouth of the Cumberland, is a little village called Smithland, where, for a considerable part of the year, such goods are deposited as are designed for Nashville and other places in the Cumberland.

The Cumberland and Tennessee rivers are, for many miles, nearly parallel in direction, and at no great distance apart. Between them are some low sandstone hills; but, we believe, no lofty range of mountains, as has been sometimes represented. About these hills, also, in the low ridges north of the Ohio, we found the sandstone, which appears to be the basis rock, often overlaid with extensive beds of puddingstone, wherein pebbles of white yellow and various coloured quartz are united in a cement highly tinged by oxide of iron; extensive fields of compact limestone also occur in the same connexion.

About half way between the mouth of the Cumberland and Tennessee, near the old deserted settlement, originally called Smithland, are several large catalpa trees. They do not, however, appear to be native, nor have we here, or elsewhere, been able to discover any confirmation of the opinion, that this tree is indigenous to any part of the United States.

It is here called *petalfra*, which as well as catalpa, the received appellation, may be a corruption from Catawba, the name of the tribe by whom, according to the suggestion of Mr. Nuttall, the tree may have been introduced. Following the directions of the Pittsburgh navigator, we kept near the left shore, below the

Cave inn, by which means we again run our boat aground, on a sandbar, where we spent considerable part of the night in the most laborious exertions. These were at length crowned with success, and having the boat once more afloat, we proceeded with greater caution.

On the 30th, we arrived at a point a little above the mouth of Cash river, where a town had been laid out, called America. It is on the north bank of the Ohio, about eleven miles from the Mississippi, and occupies the first heights on the former, secure from the inundation of both these rivers, (if we except a small area three and a half miles below, where there are three Indian mounds, situated on a tract containing about half an acre above high water mark.) The land on both sides of the Ohio, below this place, is subject to be overflowed to various depths, from six to fourteen feet in time of floods; and on the south side, the flat lands extend four or five miles above, separated from the high country by lakes and marshes. The aspect of the country, in and about the town, is rolling or moderately hilly, being the commencement of the high lands, between the two rivers above mentioned; below it, however, the land is flat, having the character of the low bottoms of the Ohio. The growth is principally cottonwood, sycamore, walnut, hickory, maple, oak, &c. The soil is first rate, and well suited to the cultivation of all products, common to the climate of 37 Deg. N. Lat. From the extensive flat, or bottom, in its neighbourhood, and the heavy growth of timber, which here generally prevails, it is probable that the place will be unhealthy, till extensive clearings are made in its vicinity.

This position may be considered as the head of constant navigation for the Mississippi. The Mississippi from New Orleans to the Ohio, is navigable for boats of the largest size, and America may be considered as the head of constant as well as heavy navigation. Ice is seldom to be found in the Mississippi, as low down as the mouth of the Ohio and never in so large quantities as to oppose any serious obstruction to the navigation.

The navigation of the Ohio has a serious impediment about four and a half miles above the town, occasioned by a limestone bar, extending across the river, called the Grand Chain. This bar is impassable in the lowest stage of the water, and will not admit boats of any considerable burden, except in the higher stages.

The Mississippi has, in like manner, two bars, called the Big and Little Chain, which appear to be a continuation of the same range of rocks as that in the Ohio, extending across the point of land situated between the two rivers. These bars are situated a little above the Tyawapatia Bottom, about thirty miles above the mouth of the Ohio, and in low water have but a moderate depth of water across them, which, added to the rapidity of the current, occasions a serious obstacle to the navigation.

Boats suited to the navigation of both rivers above the bars here specified, should be of inferior size; those for the Mississippi, not exceeding one hundred tons burden, and those for the Ohio, from fifty to seventy-five tons.

Any position on the Mississippi in the neighbourhood of the Ohio, would be objectionable for the following reasons: First, The rapidity of the current, which renders it difficult to find a safe and commodious landing, there being no rocky-bound shore within thirty miles above and a far greater distance below the point.—The Iron Banks, seventeen miles below the mouth of the Ohio, have been thought by some, an eligible position for the extensive business, which, it is admitted by all, must center in this neighbourhood.—But at this place there is no safe landing; and besides the banks are composed of layers of sand and clay alternating with each other, of an acclivity nearly perpendicular, and annually wearing away, by the current of the river, which sets strongly against them. These banks are elevated about one hundred and thirty feet above the common level of the river, and are insurmountable, except by a circuitous rout, leading from the river a considerable distance above and below them.

Second, There are no positions on the Mississippi, except the Iron and Chalk Banks, for a great distance below the Ohio, secure from inundation. The bottom directly opposite the mouth of the Ohio, on the west side of the Mississippi is elevated a little above high water, but as it is an alluvial shore, having no permanent foundation, and the banks often falling in, it affords no conveniences or security as a place of business.

Third, No places of anchorage for boats or heavy burden are to be found, except in the main channel of the river, where they would be exposed to drift wood, great quantities of which are brought down in times of freshet,—and when borne along with the rapid current of the river occasion serious danger to the boats lying in its way.

The town of America is almost entirely exempt from any of these objections;—although it has not a rocky foundation, (which may be said of most of the towns of the Ohio,) the current of the river is so gentle, that no such guard against the undermining and wasting away of the banks, is required. In case of an excessive flood, or an unusual quantity of floating ice, (which may possibly be apprehended in remarkably cold seasons) the mouth of Cash river, five miles below the town, is a harbour, in which boats may lie in perfect security.

We would not encourage the idea, that the site is now fixed upon as a town is exclusively the point where business is to be done; but that the town will eventually extend along on that side of the river about four miles, to the Big Chain above described.

In view of the extent of inland navigation centering at this place, and the incalculable amount of products, to be realized at no distiant period, from the cultivation of the rich vallies and fertile plains of the west; a great proportion of which must find a market here; no doubt can be entertained that it will eventually become a place of as great wealth and importance, as almost any in the United States.

In the afternoon of the 30th we arrived at the mouth of the Ohio.

This beautiful river has a course of one thousand and thirty-three miles, through a country surpassed in fertility of soil by none in the United States. Except in high floods, its water is transparent, its current gentle and nearly uniform. For more than half of its course its banks are high, and its bed gravelly. With the exception of about two miles at the rapids, at Louisville, it has sufficient depth of water, for a part of the year, to float vessels of 300 tons burthen to Cincinnati. The country which it washes, may, with propriety, be considered under two divisions. The first, extending from its head at Pittsburgh, to the little town of Rockport, about 150 miles below the falls or rapids at Louisville, is hilly. This district forms a portion of one of the sides of the great formation of secondary rocks, which occupies the basin of the Mississippi and its tributaries. This formation, like others in the same period, is rough, with small elevations, which are most considerable on its borders, and diminish in proprtion, as we approach nearer its central parts.

Compact limestone, and sandstone of several varieties, are the rocks which invariably occur along that portion of the Ohio we are now considering. Sandstone of a light gray or ashen colour, of a compact texture, an argillaceous cement, and a slaty or lamellated structure, is the most abundant, and occupies the lowest points which we have hitherto been able to examine. This rock frequently contains alternating beds of coal, bituminous shale, and its accompanying minerals. The beds of compact limestone, which occur in this region, usually rest upon the sandstone just mentioned. Considered as a stratum, its distribution is the reverse of that of the sandstone. It occupies the central and least elevated portions of the formation, and on the borders where the sandstone is most abundant, the limestone is of less extent and of more uncommon occurrence. These remarks are applicable to the hilly district of the upper portion of the Ohio river. From Pittsburgh to Cincinnati, the prospect from the river is that of hills of moderate elevation, sometimes rocky and abrupt, but often sufficiently gradual in their ascent, to admit of cultivation to their summits.

Their character, as to extent, direction, &c. seems to be determined by the number, direction and magnitude of the streams which traverse them. They are the remains of what was formerly a continuous and nearly horizontal stratum, with a large deposit of superincumbent soil, which the flowing of water, during the lapse of ages, has channelled and excavated to its present form. These hills diminish in altitude as you approach the falls from above; there they again rise to a height nearly equal to what they attain at the head of the river, and from thence gradually diminish, until they disappear, a little above the confluence of the Ohio and Green rivers. Here commences the low country, which extends west to the Mississippi. It is characterized by the great extent of the river alluvion, the increased width and diminished velocity of the stream. The river banks are low, but thickly wooded with sycamore, cotton wood, river maple, the planera aquatica, cypress, &c. The river hills, which terminate the alluvial district, are distant and low, and often happens that the surface descends on both sides, from the immediate banks of the river to these hills. Hence when the waters of the river are sufficiently swollen to flow over its banks, they inundate extensive tracts, from which they cannot return to the channel of the river, and are left stagnant during the summer months, poisoning the atmosphere with noxious exhalations. Many of these inundated tracts have a soil of uncommon fertility, which it is probable will hereafter be recovered from the domination of the river, by dykes or levees.

The beach or sloping part of the immediate bank of the Ohio, throughout its whole extent, is of rather gradual ascent, and covered with timber a considerable distance below high-water mark. The average rapidity of the current of the Ohio is about two and an half miles per hour, and the descent of its surface nine inches per mile, as estimated by Dr. Drake of Cincinnati. The annual innundations happen in the spring. The range between extreme high and low water, in the upper part of the river, is more than 60 feet; but below, where it is not confined by high banks, it is much less.

About the falls of Ohio, the cane, (myegia macrosperma of Persoon,) begins to be seen, and increases in quantity thence westward to the Mississippi. The "Cave inn Rock," or "House of Nature," which we have before mentioned, is an immense cavern, penetrating horizontally into a stratum of compact limestone, which forms the river bank for some distance above Golconda in Illinois. Its entrance is a large and regular arch, placed immediately on the brink of the river, and a similar form is preserved in some degree through its whole extent. The Battery rock is a high mural precipice of the same stratum, running in a straight line, and forming the northern bank of the river, which washes its base. The face of this precipice is smooth and naked, and it is surmounted by a heavy growth of timber. This limestone is compact, entirely horizontal in its position and filled with organic remains. It is traversed by veins containing sulphuret of lead, and at several places near Golconda, this is accompanied by fluat of lime, in beautiful yellow and violet coloured crystals. Fluat of lime is also found disseminated in small and irregular masses throughout the rock. At Golconda, six miles below the cave, a coarse, gray, flinty sandstone is found, extending some distance to the west. This rock forms broad hills on the Kentucky side, between the Cumberland and Tennessee rivers; where it abounds in iron ore of several kinds. Perhaps these hills ought to be considered as a spur from the Cumberland hills. At the mouth of the Tennessee river, is a locality of the columnar argillaceous oxide of iron, which rises from the surface in pyramidal and columnar masses, somewhat resembling the cypress knees.

An extensive tract of land between the Tennessee and Mississippi rivers, included in the recent purchase from the Cherokees, is rocky and broken, abounding in ores of iron and lead, and probably some other minerals. We have seen a specimen of sulphuret of Antimony, in possession of an inhabitant, who being a sort of alchemist, greatly delighting in mystery, thought it imprudent to reveal the secret of its particular locality. It is to be hoped, future and more minute examinations than we had the opportunity of making, may hereafter detect the valuable mineral depositions in this tract.

The confluence of the Ohio and Mississippi, is in latittude 37° 22' 9" north according to the observations of Mr. Ellicott, and in longitude 88° 50' 42" west from Greenwich. The lands about the junction of these two great rivers are low, consisting of recent alluvion and covered with dense forests. At the time of our journey, the spring floods having subsided in the Ohio, this quiet and gentle river seemed to be at once swallowed up, and lost in the rapid and turbulent current of the Mississippi. Floods of the Mississippi, happening when the Ohio is low, occasion a reflux of the waters of the latter, perceptible at fort Massac, more than thirty miles above. It is also asserted that the floods of the Ohio occasion a retardation in the current of the Mississippi, as far up as the little chain, ten miles below Cape Girardeau. The navigation of the Mississippi above the mouth of the Ohio, also that of the Ohio, is usually obstructed for a part of the winter by large masses of floating ice. The boatmen observe that soon after the ice from the Ohio enters the Mississippi, it becomes so much heavier by arresting the sands, always mixed with the waters of that river, that it soon sinks to the bottom. After ascending the Mississippi about two miles, we came to an anchor, and went on more on the eastern side. The forests here are deep and gloomy, swarming with innumerable mosquitoes, and the ground overgrown with enormous nettles. There is no point near the confluence of the Ohio and Mississippi, from which a distant prospect can be had. Standing in view of the junction of these magnificent rivers, meeting almost from opposite extremities of the continent, and each impressed with the peculiar character of the regions from which it descends, we seem to imagine ourselves capable of comprehending at one view all that vast region, between the summits of the Alleghanies and the Rocky Mountains, and feel a degree of impatience at finding all our prospects limited, by an inconsiderable extent of low muddy bottom lands, and the unrelieved, unvaried, gloom of the forest.

Finding it necessary to review the packing of the piston in the steam engine, which operation would require some time, most of the gentlemen of the party were dispersed on shore in pursuit of their respective objects, or engaged in hunting. Deer, turkies, and beaver, are still found in plenty in the low grounds, along both sides of the Mississippi, but the annoyance of the mosquitoes and nettles preventing the necessary caution and silence approaching the haunts of these animals, our hunting was without success.

We are gratified to observe many interesting plants, and among them several of the beautiful family of the Orchidæ, particularly the orchis spectabile, so common in the mountainous parts of New England.

The progress of our boat against the heavy current of the Mississippi, was of necessity somewhat slow. Steam boats in ascending, are kept as near the shore as the depth of water will admit; and ours often approached so closely as to give such of the party as wished, an opportunity to jump on shore. On the first of June, several gentlemen of the party went on shore six miles below the settlement of Tyawapatia bottom, and walked up to that place through the woods. They passed several Indian encampments, which appeared to have been recently tenanted. Under one of the wigwams they saw pieces of honey comb, and several sharpened sticks, that had been used to roast meat upon, on a small tree near by was suspended the lower jaw-bone of a bear. Soon after leaving these they came to another similar camp, where they found a Shawanee Indian and his squaw with four children, the youngest lashed to a piece of board and leaned against a tree.

The Indian had recently killed a deer, which they purchased of him, for one dollar and fifty cents—one-third more than is usually paid to white hunters. They afterwards met with another encampment, where were several families. These Indians have very little acquaintance with the English language, and appeared reluctant to use the few words they knew. The squaws wore great numbers of trinkets, such as silver arm bands and large ear rings. Some of the boys had pieces of lead tied in various parts of the hair. They were encamped near the Mississippi, for the purpose of hunting on the islands. Their village is on Apple creek, ten miles from Cape Girardeau.

June 2nd. As it was only ten miles to Cape Girardeau, and the progress of the boat extremely tedious, several of the party, taking a small supply of provisions, went on shore, intending to walk to that place.

Above the settlement of Tyawapatia, and near cape a la Bruche, is a ledge of rocks, stretching across the Mississippi, in a direct line, and in low water forming a serious obstacle to the navigation. These rocks are of limestone, and are placed at the commencement of the hilly country on the Mississippi. Here the landscape begins to have something of the charm of distant perspective. We seem released from the imprisonment of the deep monotonous forest, and can, occasionally, overlook the broad hills of Apple Creek, and the Au Vaise, or Muddy river of Illinois, diversified with a few scattered plantations, and some small natural meadows.

About five miles above Cape Girardeau we found the steam boat Jefferson, destined for the Missouri. She had been detained some time waiting for castings which were on board the Western Engineer. Several other steam boats, with stores for the troops about to ascend the Missouri, had entered that river, and were waiting to be overtaken by the Jefferson, and the Calhoun, which last we had left at the rapids of the Ohio. On the 3d of June we passed that insular rock in the middle of the Mississippi, called the Grand Tower. It is about one hundred and fifty feet high, and two hundred and fifty in diameter. Between it and the right shore is a channel of about one hundred and fifty yards in width, with a deep and rapid current.

In the summer of 1673, Father Marquette and M. Joliet descended the Mississippi, probably as far as the mouth of the Arkansas. Their narrative contains sufficient evidence that they passed the mouth of the Missouri, the Grand Tower, the mouth of the Ohio, &c. . . .

Turkey, T.R. Peale, June 3, 1819, watercolor.

The strata of sandstone containing the extensive beds of coal which have been explored, about the Muddy river of Illinois, are here divided transversely by the bed of the Mississippi. The Grand Tower, the precipice opposite the mouth of the Obrazo, containing the singular cavity called the Devil's Oven, the Cornice Rock, and other remarkable cliffs, are monuments indicating the great extent to which the Mississippi has channelled its bed in these strata of horizontal sandstone.

The Grand Tower, from its form and situation, strongly suggests the idea of a work of art. It is not impossible that a bridge may be constructed here, for which this rock shall serve as a pier. The shores, on both sides, are of substantial and permanent rocks, which undoubtedly extend across, forming the bed of the river. It is probable, however, that the ledge of rocks called the two chains, extending down to cape a la Bruche, presents greater facilities for the construction of a bridge than this point, as the highlands there approach nearer the river, and are less broken than in the neighbourhood of the Grand Tower. The Ohio would also admit of a bridge at the chains, which appear to be a continuation of the range of rocks here mentioned, crossing that river fifteen miles above its confluence with the Mississippi. We look forward to the time when these great works will be completed.

Compact and sparry limestones are frequent in this region; but all the rocks seem to be acted upon with great rapidity by currents of water. The country on the east side of the Mississippi, back of fort Chartres, and about the river St. Mary, is much broken by sink holes, having the form of a funnel, and occasioned, probably, by the action of subterraneous streams of water finding their way through the friable sandstones, which underlay the deep and fertile soils in those places. We passed in succession the mouths of the river St. Mary, opposite to which is the fine settlement of the Bois Broule bottoms, the Ocoa, or Kaskaskia river, the St. Lora, a handsome stream, from the west, and the Gabaree Creek, on which stands the old French town of St. Genevieve. The navigation of the Mississippi, above the mouth of the Ohio, is at times difficult. The current is considerably accelerated by the descent of the river over the rocky traverses which cross its bed. At times of low water, innumerable sand-bars occur in various parts of the channel, rendering the navigation extremely precarious.

A little below the mouth of the Kaskaskia, is a creek called the Saline, entering on the west side. A grant of a tract of land, one league square, was here made by the Spanish government, in favour of a Frenchman named Pegreau, the founder of the deserted town called New Bourbon. The tract included a valuable brine spring, near the mouth of the creek. The proprietor built a house near the bank of the Mississippi, where he resided for some time, and carried on a manufacture of salt; but having occasion to go to France, he rented his works to a man, who for want of funds, or for some other reason, failed to keep them in operation. After the transfer of Louisiana to the United States' Government, this grant, among others, became an object of speculation; and advantage being taken of Pegreau's absence, the worthless tenant was instigated to prosecute his landlord for breach of contract, and by a legal process recovered damages to the amount of nine thousand dollars, for the disbursement of which the property was sold and fell into the hands of the present proprietors.

At the mouth of the Kaskaskia river, on the east bank of the Mississippi, a town has been recently commenced called Portland. The highlands approach here to the brink of the river, affording an elevated and advantageous site, the landing is said to be good, and there is reason to expect that Portland will soon rival the old town of Kaskaskia, the present seat of great portion of the mercantile business in this part of Illinois.

On the 5th the wind blew from the south-east, and with the aid of sails we were enabled to ascend the river with considerable rapidity. As we were proceeding briskly forward, our boat struck upon one of those concealed trunks of trees so frequent in the Mississippi, and soon afterwards we discovered that a leak had occurred, which made it necessary for us to lay by. By the constant use of the pumps during the remainder of the day, and the following night, we were able to prevent the water from gaining further upon us, and the next day having discovered the leak, we raised the stern of the boat, by means of a pair of shears, and succeeded in repairing the injury.

On the beach opposite the place where we lay by for these repairs, was a large flock of pelicans, which remained in sight for several hours. We had met with some wild geese; and a swan, which we saw was unable to fly, having at that time cast its feathers. The yellow breasted chat, chuck-wills-widow, the falco haliatus, the king fisher, bank swallow, and numerous other birds occurred.

At the mouth of the Kaskaskia river, on the east side of the Mississippi, commences the celebrated valley called the American bottom, extending along the eastern bank of the river last mentioned to the Piasa hills, four miles above the mouth of the Missouri. It is several miles in width, and has a soil of astonishing fertility, consisting of comparatively recent depositions from the river. It has all the disadvantages usually attending tracts of recent river alluvion, the most valuable parts of it being liable to be swept away by the current of the Mississippi, and its surface descending from the brink of the water to the stagnant pools and lagoons, at the outskirts of the valley. But the inexhaustible fertility of its soil makes amends for the insalubrity of the air, and the inconveniences of a flat marshy situation, and this valley is undoubtedly destined to become one of the most populous parts of America. We were formerly shown here a field that had been cultivated, without manure, one hundred years in succession, and which, when we saw it, (in August 1819) was covered with a very luxuriant growth of corn.

The town of Kaskaskia, the villages of Prairie de Roches, Kahokia, Prarie Dupont, Harrisonville, and Fort Chartres, are situate in this tract. Some of them are in a flourishing condition. Fort Chartres, which was built by the French government, at the expense of one million and an half of dollars, stood near the bank of the river, about twenty miles from Kaskaskia. Not long after they were erected, a part of the works were undermined by the washing of the river, since which time the whole has been suffered to remain in ruins, which are now one fourth of a mile distant from the river.

The country west of the Mississippi, opposite the American bottom, is of a very different character. The highlands approach the river, presenting abrupt declivities, prominent points, and in many places perpendicular precipices from one to two hundred feet high, frowning over the brink of the river. One of the most remarkable of these is known by the name of the Cornice rock. It bounds a narrow arm of the river, which has generally sufficient water to admit the passage of boats. The rock extends nearly in a straight line, having a front of about four hundred yards, the brow of the precipice at some points impending over the channel through which boats pass. The rock rises above, to the height of fifty or sixty feet, smoothly rounded by the attrition of the water, which never rising to the upper part of the precipice, leaves that to project in the form of a cornice. Though the lands on the west side of the Mississippi are less fertile than those of the American bottom, they are of great value, and have long been objects of scandalous speculation.

Among a variety of stratagems, practiced in this part of the country, to obtain titles to lands, was one which will be best explained, by the following anecdote, related to us by a respectable citizen of St. Genevieve. Preparatory to taking possession of Louisiana, in 1805, the legislature passed a law, authorising a claim to one section of land, in favor of any person, who should have actually made *improvements*, in any part of the same, previous to the year 1804. Commissioners were appointed, to settle all claims of this description; more commonly known, by the name of improvement rights. A person, some where in the county of Cape Girardeau, being desirous of establishing a claim of this kind to a tract of land, adopted the following method. The time having expired for the establishment of a right, agreeably to the spirit of the law, he took with him two witnesses, to the favourite spot, on which he wished to establish his claim, and in their presence, marked two trees, standing on opposite sides of the spring; one with the figures 1803, the other 1804, and placed a stalk of growing corn, in the spring. He then brought the witnesses before the commissioners, who upon their declaration, that they had seen corn growing at the place specified, in the spring between 1803 and 1804, admitted the claim of the applicant, and gave him a title to the land. In the old district of Cape Girardeau, as in other parts of Louisiana, the difficulty of establishing the indisputable titles to the lands, arising out of the great number of Spanish grants, preemption, and improvement claims, has greatly retarded the settlement of the country. Establishments were made here more than one hundred and fifty years since; yet the features of the country are little changed, retaining the rudeness and gloominess of the original forest.

At five o'clock, on the afternoon of the sixth, we passed the Platteen rock, a perpendicular precipice, not unlike the Cornice rock, near the mouth of a creek of the same name. Along the base of this cliff, we found water three and sometimes four fathoms deep. In the evenings we arrived at Herculaneum, a small village on the west side of the Mississippi, depending principally upon the lead mines, for its business.

Here are three shot manufactories, all of them built at the summit of perpendicular precipices; by which means, the expense of erecting high towers has been avoided. Thirty or forty miles to the south-west of Herculaneum, commences the region of the lead mines, which, though not yet satisfactorily explored, is known to extend for many miles through the hilly country, at the sources of the Merameg, the St. Francis, and the other small rivers, rising in the angle between the Mississippi and Missouri, below the mouth of the latter river.

Soon after the cession of Louisiana, to the United States, particular care was taken to have all claims to land investigated and registered. Some few, may have been omitted, which may be hereafter revived, but these cannot be numerous. In all the recent sales of public lands in the western states and territories, liberal reservations have been made for the encouragement of learning. . . . It is probable, similar grants will be made to the Eastern States.

On the 7th, after taking in wood at Herculaneum, we moved up the river; but had scarcely passed the mouth of the Merameg, when we found ourselves unable to stem the heavy current of the Mississippi, on account of the great quantities of mud, that had accumulated in the boilers, and prevented our raising the requisite pressure of steam. While we were lying at anchor, to afford the steam engineer an opportunity to clean the boilers, some gentlemen of the party, returned along shore, to the Merameg, a beautiful river, whose limpid and transparent waters present a striking contrast to the yellow and turbid Mississippi. They were fortunate in meeting with many interesting objects and, among others, an undescribed mud, which has received, from Mr. Ord, the name of floridanus. Upon the specimen, which was a male, was a dilated, glabrous, ventral line, 2 1-4 inches long. This species is well known in some districts, under the name of large hairy tailed rat, and is by no means rare in Florida. It is as large as the ordinary stature of the Norway rat, and is equally troublesome. The contents of its stomach were entirely vegetable; consisting of the green bark of trees, and the young shoots of plants. Their nests are large, and are composed of a great quantity of brush. Dr. Baldwin had rarely been able to join in the excursions on shore. Plants were, however, collected and brought to him on board the boat, where he spent much of his time in the examination of such as were interesting or new.

A few rods above our anchoring ground, were two graves, supposed to be those of Indians. One of them was quite recent, and both were covered with heaps of loose stones, probably designed as monuments, and to protect the graves from the ravages of wolves or other animals. The eighth of June, brought us to the small village of Vide Poche, and the following day to St. Louis, where our arrival was noticed by a salute, from a six pounder on the bank of the river, and the discharge of ordnance on board several of the steam boats lying in front of the town.

CHAPTER III

Tumuli and Indian graves about St. Louis, and on the Merameg—
Mouth of the Missouri—Charboniere—
Journey by land from St. Charles, to Loutre Island.

SAINT Louis, formerly called Pain Court, was founded by Pierre La Clade and his associates in 1764, eighty-four years after the establishment of Fort Crevecœur, on the Illinois river. Until a recent period, it was occupied almost exclusively by people of French extraction, who maintained a lucrative traffic with the Indians. The history, and present condition of this important town, are too well known to be dwelt upon in this place. Its population has been rapidly augmented within a few years, by the immigration of numerous families, and its wealth and business extended by the accession of enterprising merchants and mechanics from the Eastern States. As the town advances in importance and magnitude, the manners and customs of the people of the United States, are taking the place of those of the French and Spaniards, whose numbers are proportionately diminishing. As this place seems destined to be the depot for such articles of merchandize, as are to be sent from New Orleans to the upper rivers, it is unfortunate, that no good harbour offers for the protection of boats against the impetuosity of the current, and from the danger occasioned by floating ice. In this respect, the site of a projected town, a few miles below, has a decided advantage over Saint Louis, as it possesses a good harbour. It was selected many years since, by some Canadian Frenchman who formed a settlement there.

The horizontal strata of limestone which underlay the town of Saint Louis and the surrounding country, have strongly attracted the attention of the curious, on account of having been found in one or two instances, to contain distinct impressions of the human foot. There is now in the possession of Mr. Rapp, of the Society of the Harmonites, a stone, which has upon its surface, marks that appear to have been formed by the naked feet of some human being, who was standing upon it while in a plastic state; also an irregular line, apparently traced by a stick or wand, held in the hand of the same person. This stone was taken from the slope of the immediate bank of the Mississippi below the range of the periodical floods. To us there seems nothing inexplicable or difficult to understand in its appearance.

Nothing is more probable, that the impressions of human feet made upon that thin stratum of mud, which was deposited on the shelving of the rocks, and left naked by the retiring of the waters, may, by the induration of the mud, have been preserved, and at length have acquired the appearance of an impression made immediately upon the limestone. This supposition will be somewhat confirmed, if we examine the mud and slime deposited by the water of the Mississippi, which will be found to consist of such an intimate mixture of clay and lime, as under favourable circumstances, would very readily become indurated. We are not confident that the impressions above mentioned have originated in the manner here supposed, but we cannot by any means adopt the opinion of some, who have considered them as contemporaneous to those casts of submarine animals, which occupy so great a part of the body of the limestone. We have no hesitation in saying, that whatever those impressions may be, if they are produced, as they appear to have been by the agency of human feet, they belong to a period far more recent, than that of the deposition of the limestone on whose surface they are found.

The country about St. Louis, like that in the rear of Fort Chartres, and indeed like the horizontal limestone country generally, abounds in sink holes sometimes of great depth. These are very numerous, from five to seven miles back of the town. They are in the form of vast funnels, having at the surface, a diameter of from twenty to fifty yards. Mr. Say descended into one of these, for the purpose of ascertaining the medium temperature below the surface of the earth. This sink opens at the bottom of a deep ravine. It has two apertures near each other, through which water is admitted, and each large enough to afford passage to the body of a man. Within are two chambers from six to twelve feet in breadth, and thirty-five feet long. At the bottom of the second chamber, is a pool of water rather difficult of access. In this apartment the Mercury stood at 60° Fah.: in a shady part of the ravine about twenty-five feet below the general surface at 75°. The grassy plains to the west of St. Louis, are ornamented with many beautifully flowering herbaceous plants. Among those collected there, Dr. Baldwin observed the aristolochia Sipho, cypripedium spectabile, lilium catesbeiana, bartsia coocinnea, triosteum perfoliatum, cistus canadensis, clematis viorna, and the tradescantia virginica. The borders of this plain begin to be overrun with a humble growth of black jack and the witch hazle, it abounds in rivulets, and some excellent springs of water, near one of which was found a new and beautiful species of viburnum. On the western borders of this prairie, are some fine farms. It is here that Mr. John Bradbury, so long and so advantageously known as a botanist, and by his travels into the interior of America, is preparing to erect his habitation. This amiable gentleman lost no opportunity during our stay at St. Louis, to make our residence there agreeable to us. Near the site selected for his house is a mineral spring, whose waters are strongly impregnated with sulphuretted hydrogen gas. Cattle and horses which range here throughout the season, prefer the waters of this spring to those of the creek in whose bed it rises, and may be seen daily coming in great numbers, from distant parts of the prairie, to drink of it.

Tumuli, and other remains of the labours of nations in Indians that inhabited this region many ages since, are remarkably numerous about St. Louis. Those tumuli immediately northward of the town, and within a short distance of it, are twenty-seven in number, of various forms and magnitudes, arranged nearly in a line from north to south. The common form is an oblong square, and they all stand on the second bank of the river. . . .

It seems probable these piles of earth were raised as cemeteries, or they may have supported altars for religious ceremonies. We cannot conceive of any useful purpose to which they can have been applicable in war, unless as elevated stations from which to observe the motions of an approaching enemy; but for this purpose a single mound would have been sufficient, and the place chosen, would probably have been different.

Nothing like a ditch, or an embankment, is to be seen about any part of these works.

Indian graves are extremely numerous about St. Louis, though none are found in the immediate vicinity of the town: they are most frequent on the hills about the Merameg and the north side of the Missouri. On the 12th June, Mr. Say and Mr. Peale, accompanied by one man, descended the Mississippi, in a small boat to the mouth of the Merameg, and ascended the latter river about fifteen miles, to a place where great numbers of graves have been explored, and have been represented to contain the bones of a diminutive race of men. Most of these graves are found near the bank of the Merameg. They do not rise above the general surface, but their presence is ascertained by the vertical stones which enclose them, and project a little at either end of the grave. When the included earth, and the numerous horizontal flat stones, are removed, we find the sides neatly constructed of long flat stones, vertically implanted and adapted to each other, edge to edge, so as to form a continuous wall. The graves are usually three or four feet, though sometimes six feet in length. The bones they contained appeared to have been deposited after having been separated from the flesh, and from each other, according to the custom of some tribes of Indians at the present day.

In the first grave opened by Mr. Say, were found the fragments of an earthen pot, and the bones of an infantile skull; the second contained what appeared to be the remains of a middle aged man of the ordinary stature, laid at full length; the bones much confused and broken. An inhabitant residing here informed them, that many similar graves had been found along the summits of most of the neighbouring hills. In one of these he had found two pieces of earthen ware, one having nearly the form of a porter bottle; the other with a wide mouth; but this grave contained no bones. After spending a night at this place, they crossed the river to the town of Lilliput, (one of the projected towns here has received this name) the place so often mentioned as the locality of the graves of a pigmy race. Appearances here are in general similar to those already described. One head, that had been dug up, was that of an old person, in whom the teeth had been loose, and the alveolæ obliterated, leaving the sharp edge of the jaw bone. From this the neighbouring settlers had inferred the existence of a race of men without teeth, having their jaws like those of the turtle. Having satisfied themselves that all the bones found here were those of men of the common size, Mr. Say and Mr. Peale "sold their skiff, shouldered their guns, bones, spade, &c. and bent their weary steps towards St. Louis, (distance 16 miles) where they arrived at eleven o'clock P.M., having had ample time by the way to indulge sundry reflections on that quality of the mind, either imbided in the nursery or generated by evil communications, which incites to the love of the marvellous, and by hyperbole, casts the veil of falsehood over the charming features of simple nature."

These graves evidently contain the relics of a more modern people than those who erected the mounds.

On the summit of one of the large hillocks, near St. Louis, . . . are several of these graves; we opened five of them, but in one only, were we fortunate in finding any thing interesting, and all that this contained, was a solitary tooth, of a species of rat, together with the vertebrae and ribs of a serpent of moderate size, and in good preservation; but whether the animal had been buried by the natives, or had perished there, after having found admittance through some hole, we could not determine. If they were buried by the Indians, they are probably the bones of a species of Crotalus, as it is known that many Indians of the present day have a sort of veneration for animals of that genus. The circumstance of the discovery of these bonds renders it somewhat probable, that rattlesnakes were formerly worshipped by the natives of America, and their remains, like those of the Ibis of Egypt, religiously entombed after death.

Whilst we were at Cincinnati, Dr. Drake exhibited to us, in his cabinet of Natural History, two large marine shells, that had been dug out of ancient Indian tumuli in that vicinity. These shells were each cut longitudinally, and the larger half of each only remained. From this circumstance it seems probable that they had been used by the aborigines as drinking cups; or, consecrated to supersti-tuion, they may have been regarded as sacred utensils, and either used in connection with the rites of sacrifice, or in making libations to their deities; they may, however, like the Cymbium of the Archipelago, have served a more useful and salutary purpose in bathing.

One of these specimens seems to be a *Cassis cornutus*, of authors, or great conch shell, though it is proper to observe, that of the three revolving bands of tubercles, characteristic of that species, the inferior one in this specimen is dou-ble. In length it is about nine inches and a quarter, and in breadth seven inches.

The other specimen is a heterostrophe shell of the genus *Fulgur* of Montfort; and, as far as we can judge, in every respect the same with those which are, at the present day, found on the coast of Georgia and East Florida, known to naturalists, under the name of *F. perversus*, though it is certainly much larger than any of the recent specimens we have seen; its length being nine inches and breadth six and a half.

Several different countries have been mentioned by the authors as the habitation of the *cornutus*; according to Rumphius it inhabits Amboyna, the straits of Malacca, and the shores of the island of Boeton; Humphreys says it is brought from the East Indies and China; Linnæus believed it to inhabit the coasts of America; but Bruguiere, a more recent author, informs us that Linnæus was probably mistaken, in the habitation of this shell, and states it to be a native of the Asiatic ocean.

The *cornutus* becomes of some importance in the question relative to the Asiatic origin of the American Indians. All the authorities to which we have been able to refer, correspond in assigning the shores of Asia, or those of the islands which lie near that continent, as the native territory of this great species of conch, with the sole exception of Linnæus; but as no other author has discovered it on the coasts of this continent, we must believe with Bruguiere, that it is only to be found in the Asiatic ocean.

The circumstance then of this shell being discovered in one of the ancient Indian tumuli affords, at least, an evidence that an intercourse formerly existed between the Indians of North America and those of Asia; and leads us to believe that even a limited commerce was carried on between them, as it undoubtedly was with the Atlantic coast, from which the Fulgur was obtained.

But although this isolated fact does not yield a positive proof of the long asserted migration of the ancestors of the present race of American Indians from Asia to this country, yet, when taken in combination with other evidence, which has been collected by various authors, with so much industry it will be regarded as highly corroborative of that popular belief.

In the prairies of Illinois, opposite St. Louis, are numbers of large mounds. We counted seventy-five in the course of a walk of about five miles, which brought us to the hill a few years since occupied by the monks of La Trappe. This enormous mound lies nearly from north to south, but it is so overgrown with bushes and weeds, interlaced with briers and vines, that we were unable to obtain an accurate account of its dimensions.

The survey of these productions of human industry, these monuments without inscription, commemorating the existence of a people once numerous and powerful, but no longer known or remembered, never fails, though often repeated to produce an impression of sadness. As we stand upon these mouldering piles, many of them now nearly obliterated, we cannot but compare their aspect of decay, with the freshness of the wide field of nature, which we see reviving around us: their insignificance, with the majestic and imperishable features of the landscape. We feel the insignificance and the want of permanence in every thing human; we are reminded of what has been so often said of the pyramids of Egypt, and may with equal propriety be applied to all the works of men, "these monuments must perish, but the grass that grows between their disjointed fragments, shall be renewed from year to year."

June 21st. After completing our arrangements at St. Louis, we left that place at noon, and at 10 o'clock on the following day, entered the mouth of the Missouri. From St. Louis upward to the Missouri, the water of the Mississippi, for a part of the year, is observed to be clear and of a greenish colour on the Illinois side, while it is turbid and yellow along the western bank. But at the time of our ascent every part of the Mississippi appeared equally turbid, its waters soon becoming blended with the heavy flood of the Missouri.

The Missouri being now swollen by the spring floods, which had subsided in the Mississippi, entered that river with such impetuosity, as apparently to displace almost the whole body of the waters in its channel. We had occasion to observe that the water of the Missouri, passes under that of the Mississippi, rising and becoming mingled with it on the opposite shore, so that a portion of the clear, green waters of the latter river, run for some distance in the middle of the channel, and along the surface of the Missouri waters, rendered perhaps specifically heavier, by the great quantities of earthy matter mingled with them. The waters of the Missouri are so charged with mud and sand, as to be absolutely opake, and of a clay colour; while those of the Mississippi being comparatively clear, and having a somewhat olivaceous tint, afford an opportunity of tracing their respective courses, after their junction in the same channel. At some stages of water they run side by side, and in a great measure unmingled, as far as Herculaneum, forty-eight miles below their confluence.

We had the pleasure to find, notwithstanding the furnace was supplied with wood of an indifferent quality, that the force of our steam engine was sufficient to propel the boat against the current of the Missouri, without recourse to the aid of the *cordelle*, which we had expected to find necessary.

We were somewhat surprised to see here, a flock of blackheaded terns. It is remarkable that these birds, whose ordinary range is in the immediate vicinity of the sea coast, should ascend this river to so great a distance. They are not seen on the Delaware as high as Philadelphia, unless driven up by storms.

In ascending from the mouth of the Missouri to Bellefontain, a distance of four miles, our boat grounded twice on the point of the same sand bar, and considerable time was consumed in efforts to get her afloat. A military post was established at Bellefontain, under the direction of the government of the United States, by general Wilkinson, in 1803; but the soil on which his works were erected has disappeared, the place being now occupied by the bed of the river. A few fruit trees only, which stood in the end of his garden, are yet standing, but are now on the brink of the river. The first bank is here ten or twelve feet high, rising perpendicularly from the water. Near its base are the trunks of several trees with one end imbedded, and the other projecting horizontally over the surface of the water, affording an evidence of the recent deposition of the soil of the low plains, and an admonition of the uncertainty of tenure, on the first bank of the river. One of these projecting trunks is still in good preservation. It is about three feet in diameter, and from its direction must pass immediately under the roots of two large trees, now occupying the surface of the soil. Similar appearances are frequent along the Mississippi and Missouri, and furnish abundant evidence that these rivers are constantly changing their bed, and, from the great rapidity of the stream, as well as from the appearances presented, we must suppose these changes are not very slowly produced; but their range is confined to the valley, within the second banks, which are here raised about seventy feet. On this second bank, in the rear of the site of the former works, the buildings belonging to the present military establishment have been erected. They were commenced in 1810. The houses are of one story, constructed of logs, based upon masonry, and united in the form of a hollow square. At the foot of the second bank rises a fine spring of water, which has given name to the place. Cold Water creek, a very small stream not navigable, discharges itself a few hundred yards above; in times of high water its mouth might afford harbour to small boats. Before the recent change in the bed of the Missouri, this creek entered higher up than at present, and then afforded a good harbour for boats of all sizes. The fifth regiment were encamped here at the time of our arrival, waiting for the contractor's steam boats, three of which we had passed at the mouth of the river.

Here we found it necessary to adjust a tube to the boilers of our steam engine, in order to form a passage, through which the mud might be blown out: the method heretofore adopted, of taking off one end, for the purpose of admitting a man to clean them, proving too tedious, when it was found necessary to repeat the operation daily. The expedient of the tube succeeded to our entire satisfaction.

Dr. Baldwin found here a plant, which he considered as forming a new genus, approaching astragalus; also the new species of rose, pointed out by Mr. Bradbury, and by him called Rosa mutabilis. This last is a very beautiful species, rising sometimes to the height of eight or ten feet. The linden tree attains great magnitude in the low grounds of the Missouri; its flowers were now fully expanded.

In ascending from Bellefontain to Charboniere, where we came to an

Sparrow, T.R. Peale, June 23, 1819, watercolor and pencil.

anchor, on the evening of the 24th, we were opposed by a very strong current, and much impeded by sand-bars. On the upper ends of these sand-bars, are many large rafts of drift wood; these are also frequent along the right hand shore. In several places we observed portions of the bank, in the act of falling or sliding into the river. By this operation, numerous trees, commonly cotton-woods and willows are overturned into the water.

The forests, on the low grounds immediately in the vicinity of the Missouri, are remarkably dense; but in many instances, the young willows and poplars, (which are the first and almost the only trees, that spring up on the lands left naked by the river) have not attained half their ordinary dimensions, before, by another change in the direction of the current, they are undermined and precipitated down, to be borne away by the river. The growth of the cotton tree is very rapid, that of the salix angustata, the most common of the willows found here, is more tardy, as it never attains to great size. The seeds of both these trees are produced in the greatest profusion, and ripened early in the summer, and being furnished by nature, with an apparatus to ensure their wide dissemination they have extended themselves, and taken root in the fertile lands along all the ramifications of the Mississippi, prevailing almost to the exclusion of other trees.

Charboniere is on the right bank of the Missouri. This name was given it

Landscape, T.R. Peale, June 23, 1819, watercolor.

by the boatmen, and the earliest settlers, on account of several narrow beds of coal, which appear a few feet from the water's edge, at the base of a high cliff of soft sandstone. The smell of sulfur is very perceptible along the bank of the river, occasioned doubtless, by the decomposition of pyrites, in the exposed parts of the coal beds. Some small masses of sulphate of lime also occur, and have probably derived their origin from the same source.

At St. Charles we were joined by Maj. O'Fallon, agent for Indian affairs in Missouri, and his interpreter, Mr. John Dougherty, who had travelled by land from St. Louis. When Lewis and Clark ascended the Missouri, the town of St. Charles was said to contain one hundred houses, the inhabitants deriving their support principally from the Indian trade. This source having a great measure failed, on account of the disappearance of the aborigines, before the rapid advances of the white population, the town remained in a somewhat declining condition for several years; but as the surrounding country was soon occupied by an agricultural population, a more permanent, though less lucrative exchange is taking the place of the Indian trade. Accordingly within two or three years, many substantial brick buildings had been added, and several were now in progress: we could enumerate, however, only about one hundred houses. There are only two brick kilns, a tanyard, and several stores.

A mile or two below St. Charles, are many trunks of trees projecting from the bank, like those mentioned at Bellefontain. In the face of the banks, are usually great numbers of the holes made by the bank-swallow for its nest, and the birds themselves are fequently seen.

At St. Charles, arrangements were made for the purpose of transporting baggage for such of the gentlemen of the party as should choose to ascend the

Catfish, T.R. Peale, June 23, 1819, watercolor.

Missouri by land, that they might have the better opportunities for investigating the natural history of the country. Messrs. Say, Jessup, Peale, and Seymour, having provided themselves with a horse and packsaddle, on which they fastened their blankets, a tent, and some provisions, accompanied by one man, left St. Charles at 7 o'clock on the morning the 26th, intending to keep nearly an equal pace with the steam boat, in order to rejoin it as occasion might require. Dr. Baldwin, still confined by debility and lameness, was compelled to forego the pleasure of accompanying them.

The Western Engineer proceeded on her voyage, soon after the departure of Mr. Say and his detachment. Having grounded several times in the course of the day, and contending all the way against a heavy current, she proceeded but a few miles. We passed some rocky cliffs; but in general, the immediate banks of the river presented the same appearance as below, consisting of a recent alluvium. After we had anchored at evening, Dr. Baldwin was able to walk a short distance on shore, but returned much fatigued by his exertions.

On the morning of the 27th, after having taken in a small supply of indifferent fuel, we crossed over to the right hand side of the river, and took on board one of the party, who had left the boat at an early hour, to visit a friend residing a short distance from the river. At evening we came to anchor half a mile below point Labidee, a high bluff, where observations for latitude were taken. Here we were detained a day making some necessary repairs.

A fine field of wheat, which appeared to be ripe, extended down to the brink of the river opposite the spot where we lay. This belonged to the plantation of a farmer, recently from Virginia. From him we obtained a plentiful supply of milk, and some bacon hams. A portion of the bank had lately fallen into the river, and with it, a part of the wheat field, and the dwelling house and other buildings seemed destined soon to follow.

The shore here was lined with the common elder, (Sambucus canadensis) in full bloom, and the cleared fields were yellow with the flowers of the common mullien. This plant, supposed to have been originally introduced from Europe, follows closely the footsteps of the whites. The liatris pycnostachia here called "pine of the Prairies," which was now in full bloom, has a roundish tuberous root, of a warm somewhat balsamic taste, and is used by the Indians and others, for the cure of Gonnorhæa.

The Indian interpreter Mr. Dougherty also showed us some branches of a shrub, which he said was much used among the natives, in the cure of Lues venerea. They make a decoction of the root, which they continue to drink for some time. It is called "blue wood" by the French, and is the Symphoria racemosa of Pursh, common to the maritime states, the bank of the St. Lawrence, and the Missouri. It is here rather taller, and the branches less flexuous than in the eastern states.

Without meeting any remarkable occurrences, we moved on, from day to day, encountering numerous obstacles in the navigation of the river, and being occasionally delayed, by the failure of some part of the steam engine, till on the 2d of July, we arrived at Loutre Island, where we found Mr. Say and his companions.

After leaving the steam boat at St. Charles, on the 25th of June, this party had travelled over a somewhat hilly country, covered with open oak woods, for about ten miles, to a small creek, called the Darden, entering the Mississippi a few miles above the Illinois. This stream they crossed three miles from the Missouri, having in their walk suffered greatly from thirst. At evening they tied their pack-horse to a bush, and as they returned after being absent a few minutes for water, the animal took fright, and breaking loose, disencumbered himself of his pack, and set off on a gallop to return to St. Charles, and it was not without great exertion that he was overtaken, and brought back. They then pitched their tent, and were so fortunate as to find a house at the distance of half a mile. This belonged to a family from Carolina, and exhibited great appearance of neatness and comfort, but the owner was found particularly deficient in hospitality. He refused to sell, or to give any refreshments for the use of the party, and even granted them some water with apparent reluctance, marching haughtily about his piazza, while some person was annoying his family by playing wretchedly on the flute. Mr. Say and the gentlemen of his party had on the fatigue dress of common soldiers, to which they probably owed the coldness of their reception. We are however glad to be able, from much experience, to say that there are few houses in the lately settled parts of the United States, where common soldiers would have met such a reception, as was accorded by this Mr. N. to the gentlemen of the party. Want of hospitality is rarely the fault of the inhabitants of the remote settlements. Being refused refreshments, they returned to their camp, and with the addition of a hawk which they had killed, made a supper from the contents of their pack.

On the 27th they crossed the Perogue, about nineteen miles from St. Charles, and after a fatiguing march of several miles, were entertained at the house of a very worthy man, who supplied them with whatever his place afforded. From too long fasting, and from the effect of exposure, and fatigue, Mr. Say and others became somewhat unwell, and on their account, the party remained at the house of their friendly host till evening, when they walked four miles to a place called Fort Kennedy. They purchased a ham, and a loaf of corn bread of Mr. Kennedy, paying ten cents per pound for the ham, and twenty-five cents for all the bread, milk, and corn consumed during their stay.

The next morning having travelled about seven miles, they halted for breakfast, and having fettered their horse, dismissed him to feed, but when sought for the purpose of continuing their journey, he could not be found. Two travellers at length arrived, and informed them that the horse had been seen at about six miles distance, on the way towards St. Charles: a horse was therefore hired, and a person returned in pursuit, but he was not to be found, having proceeded on his journey, previously to the arrival of the messenger.

The prairie flies (a species of Tabanus), are exceedingly troublesome to horses and cattle, in so much that people who cross these grassy plains, usually travel very early in the morning, and again at evening, resting greater part of the day; some indeed journey only by night. If they travel at all in the day, they have the precaution to defend the horse, by a covering thrown loosely over him. The Tabani appear about the 10th of June, and are seen in immense numbers, until about the 10th of August, when they disappear. Near the farm houses we observed, that cattle when attacked by them, ran violently among the bushes, to rid themselves of their persecutors.—Mosquitoes were not numerous.

As they were fearful of being unable to overtake the steam boat on the Missouri, if they made a longer delay to prosecute the search for their horse, it was determined to abandon him altogether, rather than return to St. Charles, whither he had doubtless gone; accordingly on the 29th of June, they made a division of their baggage, and each one shouldering his respective portion, proceeded towards the margin of Loutre Prairie. When they arrived here, they determined to take the most direct route towards the Missouri, as it seemed folly for them to attempt, in the drought and heat, which then prevailed, to cross the extensive plains of Loutre, and the grand Prairie with their heavy burthens. They therefore, followed a path leading nearly south, along a naked ridge, where they travelled twelve miles, without finding water, and arrived at Loutre Island in the evening. They were all day tormented with excessive thirst, and being unaccustomed to travelling on foot, they were much fatigued, and several became lame. The soil of the extensive Prairies which they passed, was not very good, but mixed at the surface, with so much vegetable matter, accumulated by the successive growth, and decomposition of the yearly products, as to give it the aspect of fertility.

On the south side of Loutre Prairie, a well has been sunk, sixty-five feet without obtaining water; on the north, water is readily found, by digging to a moderate depth. Loutre Prairie is twenty-three, and Grand Prairie is twenty-five miles in length: on the borders of each are some scattering settlements.

Near Loutre island are several forts, as they are called by the inhabitants, built by the settlers during the late war, and designed to afford protection, against the attacks of the Aborigines, chiefly the Kickapoos, and Saukees, who were most feared in this quarter. They are simple, strong log houses, with a projecting upper story, and with loop holes for musketry.

It was within a few miles of this place, that a company of mounted rangers, commanded by captain Calloway, were attacked by the Indians. The assault commenced as the rangers were entering a narrow defile, near the confluence of the Prairie-Forks of Loutre Creek. Several men were killed at the first fire, and captain Calloway received in his body a ball, that had passed through his watch. So furious was the onset, that there was no time for reloading their pieces, after they had discharged them. Captain Calloway threw his gun into the creek, that it might not add to the booty of the Indians, and though mortally wounded, drew his knife, and killed two of the assailants, but seeing no prospect of success he ordered a retreat, hoping thereby to save the lives of some of his men. He was the last to leave the ground, when springing into the creek he received a shot in his head, and expired immediately.

Loutre island, is something more than nine miles long, and about one mile wide, and is the residence of several families. Between it, and the main land, is an isthmus which is left naked at times to low water. Loutre creek enters at the lower end of the island. It is not navigable. Mr. Talbot formerly from Kentucky, has been resident here for nine years. His farm is in a high state of cultivation, and furnishes abundant supplies of poultry, eggs, potatoes, and the numerous products of the kitchen garden, of which he sent a handsome present on board our boat. He informed us that peach trees succeed well in the most fertile parts of the island.

The first dwellings constructed by the white settlers, are nearly similar in every part of the United States. Superior wealth and industry are indicated by the number, and magnitude of corn-cribs, smoke houses, and similar appurtenances; but on the Missouri, we rarely meet with any thing occupying the place of the barn in the northern States. The dwellings of people who have emigrated from Virginia, or any of the more southern states, have usually the form of double cabins, or two distinct houses, each containing a single room, and connected to each other by a roof, the intermediate space, which is often equal in area to one of the cabins, being left open at the sides, and having the naked earth as a floor, affords a cool, and airy retreat, where the family will usually be found in the heat of the day. The roof is composed of from three to five logs, laid longitudinally, and extending from end to end of the building; on these are laid the shingles, four or five feet in length; over these are three or four heavy logs, called weight poles, secured at their ends by withes, and by their weight supplying the place of nails.

They have corn mills, consisting of a large horizontal wooden wheel, moved by a horse, and having a band passed round its periphery, to communicate motion to the stone. These are called band mills, and are the most simple, and economical of those in which the power of the horses is employed. The solitary planter, who has chosen his place remote from the habitation of any other family, has some times a mill of a more primitive character, called a handmill, probably differing, little from those used among the ancient Egyptians. It consists of two stones, and while one person causes the uppermost to revolve horizontally upon the disk of the other, a second, who is usually a child or a woman, introduces the corn a few grains at a time, through a perforation in the upper stone. Some are content with the still ruder apparatus, consisting of an excavation in the top of a stump, into which the corn is thrown, and brayed with a pestle. This is the method in use among many of the agricultural Indians.

A large species of Lampyris is common on the lower part of the Missouri. It is readily distinguished from the smaller species, the common fire fly, by its mode of coruscating. It emits from three to seven or eight flashes, in rapid succession, then ceases; but shortly after renews its brilliancy. This species appears early in May; we saw many of them in returning by night, from the Merameg to St. Louis; but before our arrival at Loutre island they had disappeared, and were succeeded by great numbers of the Lampyris pyralis, whose coruscations are inferior in quantity of light, and appear singly.

The black walnut attains, in the Missouri bottoms, its greatest magnitude. Of one, which grew near Loutre island, there had been made two hundred fence-rails, eleven feet in length, and from four to six inches in thickness. A cotton tree in the same neighbourhood produced thirty thousand shingles, as we were informed by a credible witness.

CHAPTER IV

*Settlement of Cote Sans Dessein—Mouths of the Osage—
Manito rocks—Village of Franklin.*

THE left bank of the Missouri at the confluence of Loutre creek is precipitous, terminating a group of hills which can be distinguished, running far to
the north-east. Towards the river, these fall off in perpendicular precipices,
whose bases are concealed in a dense growth of trees and underwood. From
their summits huge masses of rock have fallen, and some of these are of such
magnitude, that their summits rise above the surrounding forest. One standing
opposite the head of the Island next above Loutre, is marked with numerous
rude drawings, executed by the Indians, some representing men with the heads
of bisons, spears, arrows, bows &c. Half a mile above this rock, the Gasconade
enters the Missouri from the south. The sources of this river are in the hilly country, near those of some of the larger tributaries of the Yungar fork of the Osage;
its waters are transparent, and its current rapid. Traversing a rocky and broken
country, it has not the uniformity of current common to many of the branches
of the Missouri, but is varied by numerous cataracts and rapids, affording convenient stations for water-mills. Some saw-mills have already been erected, and

from them, a supply of pine timber is brought to the settlements of the Missouri, that tree being rarely met with here, except in the hilly country. The Gasconade is navigable for a few miles. As might be expected a projected town is placed at the confluence of this river, and the Missouri, and is to be called Gasconade.

Above the Gasconade, the aspect of the shores of the Missouri, is the same as below, except that the hills are discontinued on the left side, and make their appearance on the right, extending along eight or nine miles; above this both shores are low bottom grounds.

Having received on board Mr. Say and his companions, we left Loutre island on the 3d of July, and passing in succession the mouths of the Gasconade, Bear Creek, the Au Vase and other tributaries, we anchored on the evening of the 5th, above the little village of Cote Sans Dessein. This place contains about thirty families mostly French, occupying as many small log cabins, scattered remotely along the left bank of the river. Nearly opposite the village is the lower mouth of the Osage. Just above the town is the elevated insular hill, which has given name to the place; it extends about eight hundred yards, parallel to the bank of the river, and terminates at a small stream called Revoe's creek. Back of the hill is a marsh, discharging a small stream of water into the creek. The site of the settlement of Cote Sans Dessein is remarkable on account of the fertility of the soil, the black mould extending to the depth of about four feet. The soil is very rich for twenty or thirty miles, in the rear of the village, but the uncertainty of the titles, arising from the conflicting claims, founded on the basis of pre-emption, New Madrid grants, and the concession of a large tract opposite the mouth of the Osage, made by the Spanish authorities in favor of Mr. Choteau, still operates to retard the increase of population.

At the time of the late war, the inhabitants of this settlement relying on mutual protection, did not retire, but erected two stockades, and block houses for their defence; the Sauks, assisted by some Foxes and Ioways, having by a feigned attack and retreat, induced the greater part of the men to pursue them, gained their rear by means of an ambuscade, and entering the village, raised their war cry at the doors of the cabins. The women and children fled in consternation to the block-houses. At this juncture, a young man was seen, who would not abandon his decrepid mother, even though she entreated him to fly and save his own life, leaving her, who could at best expect to live but a few days, to the mercy of the savages. The youth, instead of listening to her request, raised her upon his shoulders, and ran towards the stockade, closely pursued by the Indians. They fired several times upon him, and he must have been cut off had not a sally been made in his favor.

After killing the villagers who had fallen into their hands, the Indians proceeded to attack the lower stockade. The block-house at this work was defended by two men, and several women. On hearing the war cry, this little but determined garrison responded to it in such a manner as to communicate to the Indians the idea that the block-house contained a considerable number of men. They, therefore, proceeded to the attack with caution. In the first onset, one of the two men received a mortal wound, which made him incapable of further exertion—the other continued to discharge the guns at the besiegers, they being loaded and put into his hands by the women. One mode of attack, adopted by the Indians, had nearly proved successful. They threw burning torches upon the roof, which was several times on fire, but the women, with admirable presence of mind, and undaunted intrepidity, ascended to the top of the building and extinguished the flames. This scene continued during the entire day, and at evening, when the assailants withdrew, a small portion only of the roof remained, so often had the attempt to fire the building been repeated. The loss sustained by the enemy was never correctly ascertained; it has since been stated by an Indian, that fourteen were killed and several wounded, but many are of opinion that two or three only were killed.

We saw the hero of this affair at the block-house itself, now converted into a dwelling, but he did not appear to be greatly esteemed, having perhaps few qualities except personal intrepidity to recommend him. Cote Sans Dessein contains a tavern, a store, a blacksmith's shop, and a billiard table.

The Cane is no where met with on the Missouri; but its place is in part supplied by the equisetum hiemale, which, remaining green through the winter, affords an indifferent pasturage for horned cattle and horses; to the latter, it often proves deleterious. The inhabitants of St. Genevieve placed their horses upon an island covered with rushes, where great numbers of them shortly after died; but it was observed that such as received regularly a small quantity of salt remained uninjured. Of a large number of horses, placed on an island near the mouth of the Nishnebottona, to feed upon this plant, no less than twenty were found dead at the end of five days. May not the deleterious properties of the equisetum hiemale depend, in some measure, on the frozen water included in the cavity of the stalk?

We were told the cows on this part of the Missouri, at certain seasons of the year, give milk so deleterious, as to prove fatal, when taken into the stomach; and this effect is commonly attributed to a poisonous plant, said to be frequent in the low grounds, where it is eaten by the cattle. They have a disease called the *milk sickness;* it commences with nausea and dizziness, succeeded by headache, pain in the stomach and bowels, and finally, by a prostration of strength, which renders the patient unable to stand; a general torpor soon ensues, succeeded by death. It is a common belief that the flesh of animals, that have eaten of this poisonous weed, is noxious, and that horses are destroyed by it.

We have heard it remarked by the inhabitants of the Ohio below the rapids, that the milk of cows running at large in August is poisonous; and this they do not fail to attribute to the effect of noxious plants, and in some places they point out to you one, and in another place, another vegetable, to which they assign these properties. The inhabitants generally seem to have no suspicion that milk, unless it is poisoned, can be an unwholesome article of diet, and we have been often surprised to see it given to those labouring under fever. Throughout the western states, and particularly in the more remote settlements, much use is made of butter milk, and soured milk in various forms; all of which they sell to travellers. Below Cote Sans Dessein we paid, for new milk, twenty-five cents per gallon, and for soured milk, eighteen and three-fourth cents. At that place twenty-five cents per quart were demanded by the French settlers. It is commonly remarked that the French, as well as the Indians, who have been long in the immediate vicinity of the whites, charge a much higher price for any article than the Anglo-Americans, under the same circumstances. Emigrants from the Southern states prefer sour milk, and the traveller's taste in this particular, we have often observed, forms a test to discover whether he is entitled to the opprobrious name of *Yankee*, as the people of the northern and eastern states rarely choose sour milk. We have found that in some of the sickliest parts of the valley of the Mississippi, where bilious and typhoid fevers prevail, through the summer and autumn, the most unrestrained use is made of butter, milk, eggs, and similar articles of diet. Dr. Baldwin was of opinion that the *milk sickness* of the Missouri, did not originate from any deleterious vegetable substance eaten by the cows, but was a species of typhus, produced by putrid exhalations, and perhaps aggravated by an incautious use of a milk diet.

During the few days we remained at Cote Sans Dessein, Dr. Baldwin, though suffering much from weakness, and yielding perceptibly to the progress of a fatal disease, was able to make several excursions on shore. His devotion to a fascinating pursuit, stimulated him to exertions for which the strength of his wasted frame seemed wholly inadequate; and it is now, perhaps, improbable that his efforts may have somewhat hastened the termination of his life.

Between Loutre island and Cote Sans Dessein, compact limestone occurs, in horizontal strata, along the sides of the Missouri valley. It is of a bluish white colour, compact structure, and a somewhat concoidal fracture, containing few organic remains. It alternates with sandstones, having a silicious cement. These horizontal strata, are deeply covered with soil; usually a calcareous loam, intermixed with decayed vegetable matter.

July 6th. Soon after leaving the settlement of Cote Sans Dessein we passed the upper and larger mouth of the Osage River. Here, to use the language of the country, a town has been *located,* and the lots lately disposed of at St. Louis at various prices, from fifty to one hundred and eighty dollars each. Within the limits of this town is a considerable hill, rising at the point of the junction of the two rivers, and running parallel to the Missouri. From its summit is an extensive view of the village of Cote Sans Dessein, and the surrounding country.

The river of the Osages, so called from the well known tribe of Indians inhabiting its banks, enters the Missouri one hundred and thirty-three miles above the confluence of the latter river with the Mississippi. Its sources are in the Ozark mountains opposite those of the White River of the Mississippi, and of the Neosho, a tributary of the Arkansas. Flowing along the base of the north-western slope of a mountainous range, it receives from the east several rapid and beautiful rivers, of which the largest is the Yungar, (so named, in some Indian language, from the great number of springs tributary to it,) entering the Osage one hundred and forty miles from the Missouri.

In point of magnitude the Osage ranks nearly with the Cumberland and Tennessee. It has been represented as navigable for six hundred miles, but as its current is known to be rapid, flowing over great numbers of shoals and sandbars, it must be considered an exaggeration. In the lower part of its course it traverses broad and fertile bottom lands, bearing heavy forests of sycamore and cotton trees. We may expect the country along the banks of this river will soon become the seat of a numerous population, as it possesses in a fertile soil and a mild climate, advantages more than sufficient to compensate for the difficulty of access, and other inconveniences of situation.

The northern bank of the Missouri, for some distance above the confluence of the Osage, is hilly. Moreau's Creek enters three miles above, and at its mouth is Cedar Island, where we anchored for the night. This island is three miles long, and has furnished much cedar timber for the settlements below; but its supply is now nearly exhausted.

In the afternoon of the following day we were entangled among great numbers of *snags* and *planters,* and had a cat head carried away by one of them. In shutting off the steam for this occasion, one of the valves was displaced, and as we were no longer able to confine the steam, the engine became useless, the boat being thus exposed to imminent danger. At length we succeeded in extricating ourselves, and came to an anchor near the entrance of a small stream, called Mast Creek by Lewis and Clark.

At evening dense cumulostratus and cirrostratus clouds skirted the horizon: above these we observed a comet bearing north-west by north. Above the mouth of the Osage, the immediate valley of the Missouri gradually expands, embracing some wide bottoms, in which are many settlements increasing rapidly in the number of inhabitants. The Manito rocks, and some other precipitous cliffs, are the terminations of low ranges of hills running in, quite to the river. These hills sometimes occasion rapids in the river, and in the instances of the Manito rocks, opposite which commences a group of small islands stretching obliquely across the Missouri, and separated by narrow channels, in which the current is stronger than below. Some of these channels we found obstructed by collections of floating trees, which usually accumulate about the heads of islands, and are here called rafts. After increasing to a certain extent, portions of these rafts, become loosened, float down the river, sometimes covering nearly its whole surface, and greatly endangering the safety, and impeding the progress of such boats as are ascending. The group above mentioned is called the Thousand Islands.

Nashville, Smithton, Rectorsville, and numerous other towns of similar character and name, containing from one to half a dozen houses each, are to be met with in a few miles above the Little Manito rocks. Almost every settler, who has established himself on the Missouri, is confidently expecting that his farm is, in a few years, to become the seat of wealth and businesss, and the mart for an extensive district.

The banks of the Missouri, in this part, present an alternation of low alluvial bottoms and rocky cliffs. Roche a Pierce creek is a small stream entering nearly opposite another, called Splice creek, a few miles above the Manito rocks. Here is a range of rocky cliffs, penetrated by numerous cavities and fissures, hence called by the French boatmen, Roche a Pierce, and giving name to the creek. These rocks we found filled with organic remains, chiefly encrinites. About eight or ten miles above this point the Missouri again washes the base of the rocky hills, which bound its immediate valley. The rocks advance boldly to the brink of the river, exhibiting a perpendicular front, variegated with several colours arranged in broad stripes. Here is a fine spring of water gushing out at the base of the precipice; over it are several rude paintings executed by the Indians. These cliffs are called the Big Manito rocks, and appear to have been objects of peculiar veneration with the aborigines, and have accordingly received the name of their Great Spirit.

It is not to be understood that the general surface of the country, of which we are now speaking, is traversed by continuous ridges, which, in their course across the valley of the Missouri, occasion the alternation of hill and plain, which, to a person ascending the river, forms the most conspicuous feature of the country. The immediate valley of the Missouri preserves great uniformity in breadth, and is bounded on both sides by chains of rocky *bluffs* rising from one to two hundred feet above the surface of the included valley, and separating it from those vast woodless plains which overspread so great a part of the country. Meandering from right to left along this valley the river alternately washes the base of the bluffs on either side, while, from a person passing up or down the stream, the heavy forests intercept the view of the bluffs, except at the points where they are thus disclosed. Opposite the Big Manito rocks, and the island of the same name, is the Litttle Saline river, on the left side; and three or four miles above, on the opposite side, a stream called the Big Manito creek. Here we passed the night of the 12th of July. About midnight so violent a storm arose that we were compelled to leave our encampment on shore, the tent being blown down, and to seek shelter on board the boat. Though the storm did not continue long, the water fell to the depth of one inch and a half.

After taking in a supply of wood, we departed on the morning of the 13th, and the same day arrived at Franklin. This town, at present increasing more rapidly than any other on the Missouri, had been commenced but two years and an half before the time of our journey. It then contained about one hundred and twenty log houses of one story, several framed dwellings of two stories, and two of brick, thirteen shops for the sale of merchandise, four taverns, two smiths' shops, two large team mills, two billiard rooms, a court house, a log prison of two stories, a post office, and a printing press issuing a weekly paper. At this time bricks were sold at ten dollars per thousand, corn at twenty-five cents per bushel, wheat one dollar, bacon at twelve and an half cents per pound; uncleared lands from two to ten or fifteen dollars per acre. The price of labour was seventy-five cents per day.

In 1816 thirty families only of whites, were settled on the left side of the Missouri, above Cote Sans Dessein. In three years, their numbers had increased to more than eight hundred families.

The Missouri bottoms about Franklin are wide, and have the same prolific, and inexhaustible soil as those below. The labor of one slave is here reckoned sufficient, for the culture of twenty acres of Indian corn, and produces ordinarily about sixty bushels per acre, at a single crop. In the most fertile parts of Kentucky, fifteen acres of corn are thought to require the labour of one slave, and the crop being less abundant, we may reckon the products of agriculture there, at about one third part less than in the best lands on the Missouri. Franklin is the seat of justice for Howard county. It stands on a low and recent alluvial plain, and has behind it, a small stagnant creek. The bed of the river near the shore, has been heretofore obstructed by sand bars, which prevented large boats from approaching the town; whether this evil will increase or diminish, it is not possible to determine, such is the want of stability, in every thing belonging to the channel of the Missouri. It is even doubtful, whether the present site of Franklin, will not in some future day be occupied by the river, which appears to be at this time encroaching on its banks. Similar changes have happened in the short period, since the establishment of the first settlements on the Missouri. The site of St. Anthony, a town which existed about thirteen years since, near Bonhomme, is now occupied by the channel of the river. Opposite Franklin is Boonsville, containing at the time of our visit eight houses, but having in some respects a more advantageous situation, and probably destined to rival, if not surpass its neighbour.

Numerous brine springs are found in the country about Franklin. Boon's Lick, four miles distant, was the earliest settlement in this vicinity, and for some time gave name to the surrounding country. Some furnaces have been erected, and salt is manufactured, in sufficient quantities to supply the neighbouring settlements. Compact limestone appears to be the prevailing rock, but it is well known that coal-beds, and strata of sandstone, occur at a little distance from the river. We visited one establishment, for the manufacture of salt. The brine is taken from a spring at the surface of the earth, and is not remarkably concentrated, yielding only one bushel of salt to each four hundred and fifty gallons. Eighty bushels are manufactured daily, and require three cords of wood for the evaporation of the water. The furnace consists of a chimney-like funnel, rising obliquely along the side of a hill, instead of the vertical and horizontal flues, commonly used in these manufactories. The fire being kindled in the lower orifice of this, the ascent of the air drives the flame against forty or fifty iron pots, inserted in a double series; to these the water is conveyed by small pipes. The banks of the ravine, in which this spring rises, still retain the traces of those numerous herds of bisons, elk, and other herbivorous animals, which formerly resorted here, for their favourite condiment.

While at Franklin, the gentlemen of the exploring party, received many gratifying attentions, particularly from Gen. T. A. Smith, at whose house they were often hospitably received, and where they all dined by invitation on the 17th of July. Here we met several intelligent inhabitants of the village, and of the surrounding country, from whose conversation we were able to collect much information of the character of the country, and the present condition of the settlements.

Mr. Munroe, a resident of Franklin, related to us that being on a hunting excursion in the year 1816, he remained sometime on a branch of the Le Mine river, where he found the relics of the encampment of a large party of men, but whether of white troops, or Indian warriors, he could not determine. Not far from this encampment, he observed a recent mound of earth, about eight feet in height, which he was induced to believe must be a cache, or place of deposit, for the spoils which the party, occupying the encampment, had taken from an enemy, and which they could not remove with them on their departure. He accordingly opened the mound, and was surprised to find in it the body of a white officer, apparently a man of rank, and which had been interred with extraordinary care.

The body was placed in a sitting posture, upon an Indian rush mat, with its back resting against some logs, placed around it in the manner of a log house, enclosing a space of about three by five feet, and about four feet high, covered at top with a mat similar to that beneath. The clothing was still in sufficient preservation to enable him to distinguish a red coat trimmed with gold lace, golden epaulettes, a spotted buff waistcoat, finished also with gold lace, and pantaloons of white nankeen. On the head was a round beaver hat, and a bamboo walking stick with the initials J. M. C., engraved upon a golden head, reclined against the arm, but was somewhat decayed, where it came in contact with the muscular part of the leg. On raising the hat, it was found the deceased had been hastily scalped.

To what nation this officer belonged, Mr. Munroe could not determine. He observed, however, that the button taken from the shoulder, had the word Philadelphia moulded upon. The cane still remains in the possession of the narrator, but the button was taken by another of his party.

In relation to this story, Gen. Smith observed, that when he commanded the United States troops in this department, he was informed of an action, that had taken place near the Le Mine, in the Autumn of 1815, between some Spanish dragoons, aided by a few Pawnee Indians, and a war party of Sauks and Foxes. In the course of this action, a Spanish officer had pursued an Indian boy, who was endeavouring to escape, with a musket on his shoulder, but who finding himself nearly overtaken, had discharged the musket behind him at random, and had killed the officer on the spot. The skirmish continuing, the body was captured, and recaptured several times, but at last remained with the Spanish party. This may possibly have been the body discovered by Mr. Munroe, but by whom it was buried in a manner so singular, is unknown.

About the middle of July, the summer freshets in the Missouri began to subside at Franklin. On the 17th the water fell twelve inches, though in the preceding week more than two inches of rain had fallen. We were informed that the floods had continued longer this year, and had risen higher than usual, owing to the unusual quantities of rain that had fallen.

CHAPTER V

Death of Dr. Baldwin—Charaton River, and Settlement.—
Pedestrian Journey from Franklin to Fort Osage.

DR. BALDWIN'S health had so much declined that, on our arrival at Franklin, he was induced to relinquish the intention of ascending farther with the party. He was removed on shore to the house of Dr. Lowry, intending to remain there until he should recover so much strength as might enable him to return to his family. But the hopes of his friends, even for his partial recovery, were not to be realized. He lingered a few weeks after our departure, and expired on the thirty-first of August. His diary, in which the latest date is the eight of August, only a few days previous to his death, shows with what earnestness, even in the last stages of weakness and disease, his mind was devoted to the pursuit, in which he had so nobly spent the most important part of his life. He has left behind him a name which will long be honoured;—his early death will be regretted not only by those who knew his value as a friend, but by all the lovers of that fascinating science, to which his life was dedicated, and which his labours have so much contributed to advance and embellish. We regret that it is not in our power to add to this inadequate testimony of respect, such notices of the life and writings of Dr. Baldwin, as might be satisfactory to our readers. His manuscripts were numerous but his works were left unfinished. The remarks on the Rotbollia, published in Silliman's Journal, are his only productions, as far as we are informed, hitherto before the public. His Herbarium, it is well known, has contributed to enrich the works of Pursh and Nuttall. He was the friend and correspondent of the venerable Muhlenbergh, and contributed materials for the copious catalogue of North American plants published by that excellent botanist. In South America he met with Bonpland, the illustrious companion of Humboldt, and a friendly correspondence was established between them, which continued until his death. He had travelled extensively, not only in South America, but in Georgia, Florida, and other parts of North America. His notes and collections are extensive and valuable. During the short period of his connection with the exploring party, the infirmities, resulting from a long established and incurable pulmonary disease, then rapidly approaching its fatal termination, could not overcome the activity of his mind, or divert his attention entirely from his favourite pursuit. Though unable to walk on shore, he caused plants to be collected and brought on board the boat; and not disheartened by the many vexations attending this method of examination, he persevered, and in the course of the voyage from Pittsburgh to Franklin, detected and described many new plants, and added many valuable observations relating to such as were before known. . . .

Messrs. Say, Jessup, Seymour, and Dougherty, accompanied by major Biddle, left Franklin on the 19th July, intending to traverse the country by land, to Fort Osage, where they proposed to await the arrival of the steam boat. A pack horse was purchased for the transportation of their baggage, and a tent, blankets, and provisions, furnished for their accommodation.

The party now remaining on board the steam boat, consisted of major Long, major O'Fallon, Mr. Peale, and lieutenants Graham and Swift. Having completed some repairs of machinery, and other necessary operations, which had occasioned a delay of six days at Franklin, we left that place on the same day, at four o'clock in the afternoon. The inhabitants of the village were assembled on the bank of the river to witness our departure, and signified their good wishes by repeated cheers and acclamations. The fuel we had taken on board, being of an indifferent quality, we were able to make small progress against the rapid current of the Missouri. We anchored, for the night, three miles above Franklin. Finding the valves, and other parts of the steam engine, so much worn by the fine sand, suspended in the water of the river, as to become leaky, we were compelled to lay by, and were occupied for a day in making repairs. In the meantime the boat's crew were employed in taking on board a supply of dry mulberry wood,

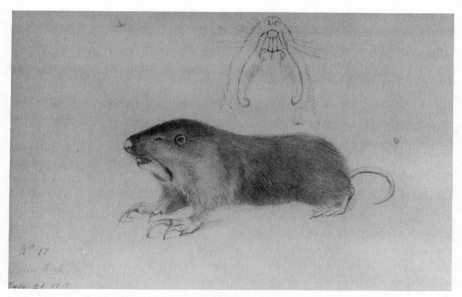

Pocket gopher, T.R. Peale, July 21, 1819, watercolor and pencil.

which is the best that the forests along the Missouri afford. The water in the river was now subsiding, and the rapidity of the current consequently diminishing; we did not, therefore, so much regret the necessary delays, as we might otherwise have done. Some of the party went out on the south-west side of the river, to search for game. Most of the deer, and larger animals, as well as the turkies, had fled from this part of the country, though it is but a few years since they were extremely abundant; they met however, with a raccoon, the Maryland arctomys, some small birds, and some interesting little animals. After leaving the river bottom, they passed some groves of small and scattered oak trees, and bushes, and arrived at the margin of a wide grassy plain, which spread before them as unvaried, and apparently as boundless as the ocean, and which is said to extend uninterrupted, near three hundred miles to the Arkansa.

At evening a soldier came on board the boat, who had been sent express from colonel Chambers' command. He brought intelligence that the detachment had arrived within fifteen miles of Fort Osage, and that their provisions were nearly exhausted.

Charaton, where we arrived on the 22d, is a small village, its settlement having been commenced in the year 1817. It is, however, in a flourishing condition, and from the advantages of its situation, promises to become one of the most important towns on the Missouri. It does not stand immediately on the bank of the Missouri, but of the Charaton river, about seven hundred yards above its mouth. Charaton will be the depot of merchandise, for a large extent of fertile country, which lies towards the north and east. At this time, the settlement contained about fifty houses, and near five hundred inhabitants, on a spot where two years previous, no permanent inhabitation had been established. Such is the rapidity, with which the forests of the Missouri are becoming filled with an enterprising and industrious population.

Charaton river is seventy-five yards wide at its mouth, and navigable, at high water, one hundred and fifty miles. Half a mile from its confluence with the Missouri, it receives the Little Charaton, also a considerable stream, and navigable for many miles. The Charaton originates near the De Moyen river of the Mississippi, and traverses a country which is of great importance, both on account of the fertility of its soil, and its inexhaustible mines of coal. The Western Engineer, being the first steam boat that had ever ascended the Missouri, above Charaton, great numbers of settlers were attracted to the banks of the river, on both sides to witness our progress. So numerous were the obstacles to be encountered, that many were of opinion our progress would soon be arrested. It sometimes happened, that mistaking the channel, we ran our boat aground in shoal places, and in some instances it was necessary to fall back, in order to extricate ourselves from these difficulties. In this way much time was consumed.

The expansions of the Missouri bottom above Franklin have, since their settlement, received distinctive names. We pass on the south of the Chney au Barre, Tabeau, Titesaw, and Miami bottoms; on the north, those of Charaton, Sugar tree, and Grand river. These are wide and fertile plains, usually covered with heavy forests of cottonwood, sycamore, ash, and sugar maple, and partly encircled by the bluffs, rising abruptly, about to the elevation of the highest trees, thence sloping gradually to the prairies, the region of the Gramina, and the Cyperacæa. Eighteen miles above Charaton is the entrance of Grand river, an important tributary of the Missouri, from the north. This river is one hundred and fifty yards wide at its mouth, and is navigable, for boats of small burthen, about two hundred miles. Its waters are transparent, except in times of high floods, and its current less rapid than that of the Missouri. There are no settlements on its banks, except at the mouth, where is a trading house, and the residence of a single family. The lands are, however, of a good quality, and the adequate supply of timber, and numerous springs of water, will ensure their speedy settlement. The Sauks, Foxes, and Ioways, hunt in the plains towards the sources of Grand river, where elk, and deer are still numerous, and the latter dispose of their peltries to the traders on the Missouri.

The navigation of the Missouri, for a few miles above and below the mouth of the Grand river, is supposed to be more difficult than at almost any other place, owing to the rapidity of the current, and the numerous sand bars and snags. Two miles above the confluence, is the channel called Grand river Cut-Off, so thickly set with snags as to be almost impassable. The distance by the Cut-Off, to the head of the island, is three fourths of a mile; by the course of the river, to the same point, it is six miles. We followed the old channel, which is much obstructed by trunks of trees and sand bars, and after a few hours succeeded in ascending this dangerous pass. Compact limestone, and argillaceous sandstone, occur frequently along the Missouri, above the mouth of Grand river, and indications of coal are often met with. In a country affording but an insufficient supply of timber for the consumption of a dense population, these extensive beds of fossil coal will be considered of great value, and the necessities of the inhabitants will lead to their early exploration. Whenever the dominion of man is sufficiently established in these vast plains, to prevent the annual ravages of fires, trees will spring up; but we may expect that before forests, originating in this manner can arrive at maturity, the population along the

Sunset on the Missouri, T.R. Peale, July 28, 1819, watercolor.

banks of the Missouri will become so dense, as to require the greater part of the soil for the purposes of culture.

The beds of coal, in this district, lie horizontally, varying much in thickness, and occuring often at an elevation of a few feet above the surface of the water, in the Missouri.

On the first of August we arrived at Fort Osage, one hundred and five miles above the mouth of Grand river. Here Mr. Say and his party had been some days encamped, having arrived on the 24th July, from their pedestrian journey, across the country from Franklin. After leaving that place on the 19th, we passed through a fine bottom on the left side of the river, closely covered with forests of oaks, elms, hackberry, walnut, the mulberry, the gleditschia, the guilandina and the other trees common on the Missouri, for twelve miles, when they arrived at Arrow Rock, where is a ferry by which they crossed the Missouri. In this walk they passed a field of corn, containing seven hundred acres. The ferry boat used at Arrow Rock is one peculiarly adapted to the navigation of a rapid stream. It consists of two canoes, on which rests a platform, with a slight railing to prevent cattle from falling off.

Arrow Rock is so called from its having been formerly resorted to, by the neighbouring Indians, for the stone used to point their arrows. It is a beautiful situation, and rises to considerable elevation above the water. From its summit is a pleasing view of the river, and near the base is a remarkable eddy, which, as they were crossing, whirled their ferry boat entirely round. On the second day they left their encampment at an early hour, and travelled forward through plains, where very few trees were to be seen. They turned off from the Osage trace, in which they had been travelling, and went eight miles to visit the salt works, and some remarkable diggings, on the saline fork of the Le Mine. Here, at one establishment, one hundred bushels of salt are manufactured per week; eight men are employed, and one hundred and eighty gallons of water are evaporated to produce a bushel of salt.

Two miles from the confluence of the Camp Fork with the Saline, are the salt works, and the residence of Mr. Lockhart, who received the detachment with much hospitality.

His works were not then in operation, but were sufficiently extensive for the manufacture of five hundred bushels of salt per week. Near his house, are the *diggings* so often mentioned in this region as objects of curiosity. These are irregular, but very numerous excavations of little depth, but evidently the result of the united labours of many persons, who were possessed of instruments of iron and steel, as no others could have penetrated, and removed the compact rocky soil, of which the points and brows of the hills are composed. These excavations occur frequently in an extent of two or three miles; and from the amount of labour, which appears to have been expended on them, it has been thought by some, that several hundred men, must have been occupied two or three years in digging them; but this is, doubtless, much overrated. Whoever were the labourers, it is probable their search was for the precious metals, though at present no indications of any metallic ores, except of a little iron, are perceptible about the diggings. Mr. Lockhart had sunk a shaft to the depth of twenty-two feet, but the appearances continued the same as at the surface.

After travelling forty miles from Arrow Rock, for great part of the way through open plains, where the high grass and weeds rendered their progress difficult and laborious, they pitched their tent, on the evening of July 21st, on a branch of the Le Mine. Here they saw four Mississippi kites. The forks of the tail of this bird are so much elongated, as to resemble some fortuitous append-age, for which at first sight, they are often mistaken. Sandhill cranes, and flocks of prairie hens were also seen, but were so shy as not to be taken without much difficulty.

The country about the Le Mine is beautiful and fertile. The unaccus-tomed eye, in roving over those extensive undulating prairies, is beguiled by the alteration of forests and meadows, arranged with an appearance of order, as if by the labour of men, and seeks in vain to repose upon some cottage or mansion embosomed in the little copses of trees, or in the edge of the forest, which margins the small streams and ravines in the distance.

Their provisions being nearly exhausted, the detatchment delayed a short time at their encampment on the Le Mine, to replenish their stock by hunting. This camp was near a place called the Grand Pass, a narrow neck of prairie between the timber of the Saline, and that of a small creek discharging directly into the Missouri. Here the Osage trace passes, and a little beyond falls into a waggon road leading to the Tabeau Settlement.

On the 22nd Maj. Biddle experienced a severe attack of cramp in the stomach, but soon found some relief from swallowing a quantity of ginger, the only medicine with which they were provided. On the following day they entered the forests of the Missouri bottom, and soon after crossed the Tabeau, where a town of the same name, at that time containing two houses, had been estab-lished. Tabeau is the name of a Canadian hunter, who formerly frequented this region. The creek is navigable to the site of the projected town, about one mile from the Missouri, having for its distance about six feet of water. Four miles from this place they crossed the Little Tabeau, and at evening pitched their tent on a stream called the Little Chneij au Barre, about a mile and a half from the Missouri. Here is a good mill seat. The Great and Little Chneij au Barre are two creeks entering the Missouri about a mile and a half from each other. Before the mouths of these two creeks is a large island, the slough, or *Chneij* dividing this island from the shore, received the additional name of Au Barre from a hunter known by that appellation, who was lost here for some time, successively ascending the two creeks, which he mistook for the Missouri; hence the name of Chneij au Barre island, Great and Little Chneij au Barre creek, &c.

In the afternoon they halted to rest at the cabin of a hunter on Fire Prairie creek, so called from the circumstance of three or four Indians having been burned to death by the sudden conflagration of the dry grass in the meadows at its source. Here Mr. Say had an opportunity to examine a young black wolf, which was confined by a chain at the door of the hut. These animals are common in this part of the country. This individual was one of five that had been taken from the same den. It had become familiar with the hunter and his family, but was shy towards strangers. When fed on meat the ferocity of his disposition manifested itself in attempts to bite the children. It was ordinarily fed on bread and milk.

This man had been settled here two years, but had not "made a crop," having subsisted himself and his family by hunting, wherein he had been very successful. In the preceding autumn he had killed seventy deer, and fifty bears. He took great pleasure in relating his hunting adventures, particularly his engagements with bears. One bear, which he had killed, he said, weighed seven hundred pounds; but in this instance he was probably mistaken. He had seen, in the winter of 1818, a large herd of bisons near the Grand Pass; but they had been driven down by the severity of the weather, and were not ordinarily to be found within the limits of his hunting excursions. During the severe winter weather, he affirmed that bears make for themselves a shelter of brushwood, into which they creep to secure themselves from the cold.

From May until July the female of the common deer conceals her young whilst she goes to feed. It is at this time that the hunters take advantage of the maternal feelings of the animal to secure her prey. They conceal themselves and imitate the cry of the fawn. The solicitude of the parent animal for her young overcomes her usual care for her own safety; and believing she hears the cries of her offspring in distress, she hurries toward the spot where the hunter lies concealed, and falls an easy prey.

Mr. Say and his companions were very politely received by Col. Chambers, then at Fort Osage. The rifle regiment was encamped here, waiting the arrival of the contractor's boats.

Fort Osage was established in 1808, by Gov. Lewis. It stands on an elevated bluff, commanding a beautiful view of the river, both above and below. The works are a stockade, of an irregular pentagonal form, with strong log pickets perforated with loop holes; two block houses are placed at opposite angles; one of them, however, flanks one of its curtains too obliquely to be of much service in defending it. There is also a small bastion at a third angle. Within are two series of buildings for quarters, store houses, &c. The position of the fort is not a secure one, on account of numerous ravines and declivities that would cover an enemy within a short distance; but is such that boats ascending or descending the river must be exposed to its fire. The stream in the middle of the river, and on the opposite side, is so remarkably rapid that it is in vain to contend against it with the oar or paddle; it is, therefore, usually necessary for ascending boats to enter the eddy, which brings them within musket shot of the fort.

At the time of our journey Fort Osage, which, according to our estimate, is one hundred and forty-two miles, by the course of the river, above Charaton, was the extreme frontier of the settlements. For a great distance below, the establishments of the white settlers were confined to the immediate banks of the Missouri. The inhabitants of this frontier are mostly emigrants from Tennessee, and are hospitable to strangers. Many of them possessed a considerable wealth. In the inhabitants of the new States and Territories there is a manifest propensity, particularly in the males, to move westward, for which it is not easy to account. The women, having their attention directed almost exclusively to domestic pursuits, form local attachments, and establish habits, which are not interrupted without occasioning some disquietude. They are at first discontented in their new abode; in a few weeks they become reconciled, but less attached than to their former home; and, at length, by the habit of frequent migration, they acquire the same fondness for an adventurous, unsettled life, as characterises the men.

Daniel Boon, whose history is connected with that of all the new settlements from Kentucky westward, answered to an inquiry concerning the cause of his frequent change of residence, "I think it time to remove when I can no longer fall a tree for fuel, so that its top will lie within a few yards of the door of my cabin." The charms of that mode of life, wherein the artificial wants, and the uneasy restraints inseparable from a crowded population are now known, wherein we feel ourselves dependent immediately and solely on the bounty of nature, and the strength of our own arm, will not be appreciated by those to whom they are known only from description, though they never fail to make an impression upon such as have acquired a knowledge of them from experience. A settler on the Missouri observed to us, that the land he at present occupied was not better than that he had left in Tennessee; but he did not wish to spend all his life in one place, and he had learned, from experience, that a man might live in greater ease and freedom where his neighbours were not very numerous.

A person upwards of sixty years old, who had recently arrived at one of the highest settlements of the Missouri, inquired of us very particularly of the river Platte, and of the quality of the lands about its source. We discovered that he had the most serious intention of removing with his family to that river. On the last day of July and the first of August about two inches of rain fell: the prevailing winds were from the north-east; but the superior strata of the atmosphere carried clouds of different descriptions in different, and sometimes opposite directions. The moon, soon after rising, passed behind a long dense body of cirrus clouds, that floated over the eastern horizon. Long and distinct radii were soon after seen converging to a point fifteen or twenty of the moon's diameters to the eastward of its disk. Such is the refracting power of the aqueous vapors sometimes suspended in the atmosphere.

Horizontal strata of sandstone, and compact limestone, are disclosed in the cliffs on both sides of the valley of the Missouri. These rocks contain numerous remains of Caryophilla, Productus, and Terebratulæ.

Some days passed, after our arrival at Fort Osage, before the weather admitted our making the astronomical observations necessary to ascertain its position. The mean of the results of several observations of the meridian altitude of the sun's lower limb gave 39° 9' 33 1-2" north, for the latitude of the place.

CHAPTER VI

Mouth of the Konzas—Arrival at Wolf River—
Journey by land from Isle au Vache to the village of the Konzas.

WISHING to extend our examinations between Fort Osage and the Konzas river, also between that river and the Platte, a party was detached from the steam boat, with instructions to cross the Konzas, at the Konza village, thence to traverse the country by the nearest route to the Platte, and to descend that river to the Missouri. The party consisted of Mr. Say, to whom the command was entrusted, Messrs. Jessup, Peale and Seymour, Cadet Swift, Mr. J. Dougherty, and five soldiers. They were furnished with three packhorses, and a supply of provisions for ten days. Thus organized and equipped, they commenced their march on the afternoon of August 6th, accompanied by Maj. Biddle and his servant.

After their departure, the steam boat was delayed a few days at Fort Osage. On the ninth a part of the troops destined for the Missouri service arrived in keelboats. Col. Chambers, with the principal part of his regiment, were still at Fort Osage, awaiting the arrival of supplies of provisions, now daily expected.

On the following day we resumed our journey, and were accompanied about ten miles by Mr. Sibley, agent of Indian affairs, and his lady, to whom the gentlemen of the party were indebted for numerous hospitable attentions during their stay at Fort Osage; also by captain Bissel, and lieutenant Pentland, of the rifle regiment, who returned in a skiff. Our progress was much impeded by shoals and rapids in the river, but we succeeded in passing these without warping, and anchored at sun-set, having ascended eighteen miles.

Between Fort Osage and the mouth of the Konzas river, a distance of about fifty-two miles, are many rapid places in the Missouri. We were able to ascend all these, except one, without towing. It was with some difficulty we supplied our furnace with wood of a suitable quality. The forests of the Missouri, though limited in extent, are deep and shady, and, though the atmosphere is perceptibly less humid than in the forests of the Mississippi, fallen trees, whose wood is soft and porous like that of the linden and cotton tree, absorb much moisture from the ground. It was only when we were so fortunate as to find a dry mulberry, ash, or cotton-wood still standing, that we could procure fuel well adapted to our purpose. Much time was of necessity expended in cutting and bringing on board our supplies of this article, and the additional delay occasioned by the numerous obstacles to the easy navigation of the river, made our ascent somewhat tedious.

The mouth of the Konzas river was so filled with mud, deposited by the late flood in the Missouri, as scarcely to admit the passage of our boat, though with some difficulty we ascended the river about a mile, and then returning dropped anchor opposite its mouth. The spring freshets subside in the Konzas, the Osage, and all those tributaries that do not derive their sources from the Rocky Mountains, before the Missouri reaches its greatest fulness; consequently the waters of the latter river, charged with mud, flow into the mouths of its tributaries, and there becoming nearly stagnant deposit an extensive accumulation of mud and slime. The Konzas river has a considerable resemblance to the Missouri; but its current is more moderate and the water less turbid, except at times of high floods. Its valley, like that of the Missouri, has a deep and fertile soil, bearing similar forests of cotton-wood, sycamore, &c. interspersed with meadows, but in ascending, trees become more and more scattered, and at length disappear almost entirely, the country, at its sources, being one immense prairie.

We sailed from the mouth of the Konzas on the 13th of August. Numerous sandbars occur in the Missouri above that point, and these occasioned us some delay. The water having fallen several feet, we had less velocity of current to contend against, but found it more necessary to keep in the channel, and could not so often take advantage of the eddy currents, below the points and along the shore.

A party of white hunters were encamped on the Missouri, not far above the Konzas. In the rudeness of their deportment and dress, they appeared to us to surpass the Savages themselves. They are usually the most abandoned and worthless among the whites, who adopt the life of wandering hunters: frequently they are men whose crimes have excluded them from society.

Eighteen miles above the Konzas river, and five above the Little Platte, is a large island, which from its rhombic form, has received the name of Diamond island. The principal channel is on the north side. It is difficult to pass, being much obstructed by sandbars. Four miles above this is a small group, called the Three Islands; and two miles further another cluster, known as the Four Islands, and by the French as the Isles des Parcs, or Field Islands. At each of these places, as in the neighbourhood of islands generally, the navigation is difficult.

The site of an old village of the Konzas, and the remains of a fortification erected by the French, were pointed out a few miles below Isle au Vache. This island, which lies about one hundred miles above Fort Osage, was the wintering post of Capt. Martin's detachment, destined to proceed in advance of the troops ordered to the Missouri. Captain Martin, with three companies of the rifle regiment, left Bellefontain in September 1818, and arrived at Isle au Vache in October, with the expectation of resuming his march, as early in the following spring as the weather would permit. But not having received the necessary supplies of provisions as anticipated, they had been compelled to remain till the time of our arrival, subsisting themselves principally by hunting. Fortunately, this part of the country afforded so much game, that a competent supply was easily obtained. Between two and three thousand deer, beside great numbers of bears, turkies, &c. had been taken. The arrival of the boats, laden with provisions, now furnished them the means of continuing their ascent, and they had the prospect of departing within a few days.

Previous to our departure from Fort Osage, major O'Fallon, the Indian agent who accompanied us, had sent a messenger across the country by land to the Konzas nation of Indians, residing on the Konzas river, summoning their chiefs to a council, to be held at Isle au Vache, on the arrival of the Western Engineer. Agreeably to the message sent by an interpreter, the Indians had been expected on the 18th, but did not arrive until the 23d of August, having been absent, when the messenger reached their village, on a hunting excursion. As soon as they received the invitation they repaired, with all convenient speed, to the appointed place, having sent runners before, to apprise us of their approach.

The interpreter, who returned with them, brought intelligence of the safe arrival of Mr. Say and his party, and of their kind reception at the Konza village. We were sorry to learn that Mr. Say had been in ill health, and had not entirely recovered.

On the 24th, the chiefs and principal men of the Konzas, to the number of one hundred and fifty, assembled under an arbour prepared for their reception. The Indian agent addressed them in a speech adapted to the occasion, setting forth the causes of complaint, which they had given by their repeated insults and depredations upon the whites, giving them notice of the approach of a military force, of sufficient strength to chastise their insolence, and advising them to seize the present opportunity of averting the vengeance they deserved, by proper concessions, and by their future good behaviour, to concilate those, whose friendship they would have so much occasion to desire.

The replies of the chiefs were simple and short, expressive of their conviction of the justice of the complaints made against them, and of their acquiescence in the terms of reconciliation proposed by the agent. There were present at this council, one hundred and sixty-one Konzas, including chiefs and warriors, and thirteen Osages. The most distinguished men were Na-he-da-ba, or *Long Neck*, one of the principal chiefs. Ka-he-ga-wa-ta-ning-ga, *Little Chief*, second in rank. Shon-ga-ne-ga, who had been one of the principal chiefs, but had resigned his authority in favor of Ka-he-ga-wa-ta-ning-ga. Wa-ha-che-ra, *Big Knife*, a partizan or leader of war parties. Wom-pa-wa-ra, *He who scares all men*, more commonly known to the whites as Plume Blanche, or White Plume, a man rising rapidly in importance, and apparently destined to become the leader of the nation. In addition to the Indians the officers of the garrison, and a few gentlemen were present at the council. There ceremonies were commenced by a discharge of ordnance from the steam boat; the flags were hoisted in their appropriate places, a council flag being placed near the chair occupied by the agent. The Indians appeared gratified at the displays made on the occasion, but their attention was more particularly aroused by the exhibition of a few rockets and shells, fired for their entertainment. At our departure, which, on account of the Indians, was delayed until the 25th of August, many of them were present, and manifested some surprise at witnessing the operations of the steam boat.

It was thought adviseable to make some addition to our force at Isle au Vache, as we should soon be in advance of the troops on the Missouri, and might be exposed to insults and depredations, from some of the numerous tribes of Indians. Accordingly, on application to colonel Morgan, a boat and fifteen men, under the command of lieutenant Fields, were detailed for this duty, and directed to regulate their movements agreeably to the orders of the commanding officer of the exploring expedition. These men were furnished with provisions for sixty days, and having embarked on board a keel boat, called the Gen. Smith, they sailed in company with the Western Engineer. A favourable wind springing up, we proceeded in the course of the day about twenty-three miles, and encamped at night near the entrance of a small stream called Independence Creek. A little above, and on the south side of the river, is the site of an old Konza town, called formerly the village of the Twenty Four. Above Cow Island the Missouri is more serpentine in direction than below, and the difficulties of the navigation we found by no means diminished as we ascended. The bed of the river, in many places, is broad, and the water distributed into small channels separated by sandbars. About fifty miles above Cow Island we passed a spot that had lately been occupied as a hunting camp by captain Martin, who had been here to procure the requisite provisions for the subsistence of his party.

At the Yellow Banks we found the bluffs elevated about one hundred and fifty feet above the surface of the valley. Barometric observations, several times repeated, gave nearly the same result at some points below. One hundred and fifty feet may, therefore, be assumed as the medium depth of the immediate valley of the Missouri; its aggregate width, for the first five hundred miles above the Mississippi, may be estimated at about three miles. The corresponding appearances in the strata of the opposite sides of this valley, as well as its entire form and character, indicate it to have been formed by the river. But far more than that vast body of soil and rocky strata which formerly filled the space now occupied by the immediate valley of the river, has been removed by the Missouri. From the summit of the bluffs there is a sloping ascent towards the interior of the country, and it is probable the aggregate elevation of the great plains, is not less than three hundred feet above the surface of the river. If we admit that this great valley, with its numerous ramifications, has resulted from the operation of currents, wearing down, and transporting to the ocean the solid materials of the earth's surface, it would appear necessary still farther to acknowledge that this channel was once much deeper than at present, for we usually meet with thick alluvial depositions covering the rocks that line the bottom of the Missouri valley. The manifest tendency of the operation of the Mississippi, at this time, upon its valley, is to fill up rather than to excavate; but it may be doubted whether this is equally, or even to any degree, the case with the Missouri. The aggregate mass of alluvion within the valley of the Missouri is, undoubtedly, moving downwards, with considerable rapidity, for the quantity of earthy matter carried into the Mississippi is, at all times, very great. In their descent the alluvial substances are alternately deposited and swept away, as by the variations in the direction of the current any particular point is, from time to time, either exposed to, or sheltered from, the action of the stream.

About eighty-seven miles above Cow Island is the mouth of the Nodowa, a river of some importance, being about seventy yards wide, and navigable to some distance. It is not usually seen in passing, being concealed by the island called the Great Nodowa, which is about five miles long, and covered with heavy forests. The lands on the Nodowa are of an excellent quality.

On the 1st of September, we were under the necessity of remaining encamped near the mouth of the Wolf river, that some repairs might be made to the steam engine. Here we sent out some persons to hunt, who after a short time returned, having taken a deer, a turkey, and three swarms of bees, which afforded us about half a barrel of honey. On the trees which margin the river, we frequently observed a fine species of squirrel, which possesses all the graceful activity of the common grey squirrel, as it leaps from bough to bough. After our machinery was adjusted, we resumed our ascent, and had proceeded a short distance, when we were hailed from shore by Mr. Dougherty, who had accompanied Mr. Say's party across the country. We were not surprised at this unexpected meeting, and were apprehensive some disaster had befallen the detachment.

Mr. Dougherty being received on board, informed us that Mr. Peale, Mr. Swift, Mr. Seymour, Chaboneau the Indian interpreter, and one of the soldiers were at a little distance in the rear, having accompanied him across the country, from Cow Island, where they had arrived five days after our departure. Mr. Say and Mr. Jessup had been left sick at Cow Island. We encamped immediately, to give those, who were near, an opportunity of joining us. It will now be necessary to return to the time of Mr. Say's departure from Fort Osage, and briefly to trace the progress of his detachment to the place where a rencontre with a war party of Pawnees, frustrated their design, and made it necessary for them to rejoin the steam boat.

Mr. Say's detachment consisting of twelve men and a boy, furnished with three pack horses for the transportation of baggage, departed from Fort Osage on the evening of August 6th. Their route lay westward across the woodless plains, about the sources of the Hay Cabin, Blue Water, and Warreruza Creek. The cliffs along the Blue Water are naked perpendicular rocks. In the vallies numerous Indian encampments occurred, which appeared not long since to have been occupied. These were most frequently seen at the points, where the streams making almost a complete circuit, and nearly enclosing a small tract of ground, afforded an important protection against the approach of an enemy.

The prairies about the head waters of the Warreruza abound in game. Here ravens were first seen by the party, and numbers of large banded rattle-snakes were killed. The blowing flies swarmed in inconceivable numbers, attacking not only the provision of the party, but depositing their eggs upon the blankets, clothing, and even on the furniture of the horses. On the 11th of August they arrived at some elevated ridges, from which they overlooked an extensive country, and could trace the whole course of the Wahrengeho, or Full Creek, diverging slightly from the Konzas, and could readily perceive timber upon several of its head branches. The lands between the head waters of Full Creek and the Konzas are not so good as those about the sources of the Warreruza, and produce less timber. The settlement of this region, will be much retarded on account of the want of trees, these being confined to the margins of the water courses, while tracts of valuable soil, of many miles in extent, have not a single tree or bush upon them. The soil is, however, well adapted to the culture of some of our most valuable forest trees. The sugar maple, and several of the most important species of carya, the oaks, the tulip tree, and the linden, would unquestionably succeed.

In consequence of the excessive heat of the weather, the great fatigues of the party, and their constant exposure in the open plains, the health of several of them began to be impaired. The high and coarse grasses which now covered the plains greatly impeded their progress, and very rapidly destroyed their clothing and mockasins. Their journey was, therefore, slow and laborious. On the night of the 13th they encamped on the bank of the Konzas, having travelled some distance parallel to the course of that river. The next day several of the party, already much debilitated, began to be afflicted with dysentery; some accidents also occured to retard their progress, and on that and the following day they advanced only two miles. On the 16th they marched about fifteen miles, and encamped on the bank of the Konzas. Being now in doubt, as to the situation of the Konza village, and the illness of some of the party continuing, they determined to remain encamped, while some persons should be sent out to reconnoitre the country, and discover, if possible, whether that part of the river, at which they had arrived, was above or below the village they designed to visit. The Konzas river in this part bears the closest resemblance to the Missouri, both in the turbulence and rapidity of its current, and the aspect of the country along its banks; it is, however, so shoal as at almost any point to admit of being forded without difficulty.

Willow islands, moving sandbars, and *falling-in* banks, are as frequent as in the Missouri. The line of forest which skirts the banks, including the bed of the river, is about half a mile wide, but not entirely uninterrupted. The course of the river is remarkably serpentine, forming woodland points alternately on both sides.

After crossing, and recrossing the river, and extending their search in every direction, they had the satisfaction at last to fall in with a beaten path, leading up to the river, and which their guide and interpreter was confident would conduct them to the Konzas village.

On the morning of the 19th, they passed across a wide and fertile prairie to the Vermillion, a stream which enters the Konzas from the north-west. It is four feet deep, and about twenty yards wide. Here they halted in the middle of the day, and dined on the flesh of a black wolf, the only game they were able to procure.

About Vermillion Creek are some open forests of oak, not extending far on either side. The trees are from fifteen to twenty-five feet high, and from one foot to eighteen inches in diameter, standing at a considerable distance from each other.

On the day following, the Konza village was descried at a distance. The detachment immediately halted to arrange their dress, and inspect their fire arms. This was thought the more necessary, as no party of whites had visited the village since a number of the Konzas had received a whipping at Isle au Vache, and it was a matter of doubt, whether the party would meet with a friendly reception.

As they approached the village, they perceived the tops of the lodges red with the crowds of natives; the chiefs and warriors came rushing out on horseback, painted and decorated, and followed by great numbers on foot. Mr. Say and his party were received with the utmost cordiality, and conducted into the village by the chiefs, who went before on each side, to protect them from the encroachments of the crowd. On entering the village the crowd readily gave way before the party, but followed them into the lodge assigned to them, and completely and most densely filled the spacious apartment, with the exception only of a small space opposite to the entrance, where the party seated themselves on the beds, still protected from the pressure of the crowd by the chiefs, who took their seats on the ground immediately before them. After the ceremony of smoking with the latter, the object which the party had in view in passing through their territories was explained to them, and seemed to be perfectly satisfactory. At the lodge of the principal chief, they were regaled with jerked bison meat, and boiled corn, and were afterwards invited to six feasts in immediate succession. Chaboneau and the old Frenchman, who had been despatched from Fort Osage, to summon the Konzas to meet the agent at Isle au Vache, had arrived some days previous; but the nation being at that time absent on a hunting excursion, the interpreters, after reaching the village, had proceeded immediately into the plains in pursuit of them. At the time of the arrival of our detachment, the village was in confusion, the hunters having lately returned, and being then engaged in preparations for the journey to Isle au Vache. Two runners were despatched to give notice to major O'Fallon, that his summons had been received; and at the same time the chiefs and principal warriors departed for the place appointed. Before his departure, the principal chief was careful to appoint a fit person to attend Mr. Say's party, and arrangements were made to promote their comfort and convenience, while they should remain at the village.

Many reports had been circulated among the Konzas, respecting the invitation to council their chiefs had received. They were conscious of having recently offended, by firing on major O'Fallon, and by insulting and plundering several soldiers of captain Martin's command. For these offences they had been in some measure punished at the time, major O'Fallon having returned their fire from his boat, and not entirely without effect, as was supposed; several also had been flogged by the orders of captain Martin, yet they did not consider themselves secure from the vengeance of the whites. Many believed that at the time of the anticipated council, barrels of gunpowder were to be placed in the earth to destroy them at once. The two runners, who had been despatched, quarrelled before they had gone far; one saying all the things that had been told them by the interpreters were lies, for which assertion he was struck to the ground by his companion. In this situation they were found by the advancing chiefs. Finally a dispute happened between the chiefs themselves, respecting rank, in consequence of which ten or twelve of them returned to the village.

Mr. Say, who spent some time among the Konzas, gives in his notes, the following account of that nation.

"The approach to the village is over a fine level prairie of considerable extent; passing which, you ascend an abrupt bank of the height of ten feet, to a second level, on which the village is situate in the distance, within about 1-4 of a mile of the river. It consists of about 120 lodges, placed as closely together as convenient, and destitute of any regularity of arrangement. The ground area of each lodge is circular and is excavated to the depth of from one to three feet, and the general form of the exterior may be denominated hemispheric.

"The lodge, in which we reside, is larger than any other in the town, and being that of the grand chief, it serves as a council house for the nation. The roof is supported by two series of pillars, or rough vertical posts, forked at top for the reception of the transverse connecting pieces of each series; twelve of these pillars form the outer series, placed in a circle; and eight longer ones, the inner series, also describing a circle; the outer wall, of rude frame work, placed at a proper distance from the exterior series of pillars, is five or six feet high. Poles, as thick as the leg at base, rest with their butts upon the wall, extending on the cross pieces, which are upheld by the pillars of the two series, and are of sufficient length to reach nearly to the summit. These poles are very numerous, and, agreeably to the position which we have indicated, they are placed all around in a radiating manner, and support the roof like rafters. Across these are laid long and slender sticks or twigs, attached parallel to each other by means of bark cord; these are covered by mats made of long grass or reeds, or with the bark of trees; the whole is then covered completely over with earth, which, near the ground, is banked up to the eaves. A hole is permitted to remain in the middle of the roof to give exit to the smoke. Around the walls of the interior, a continuous series of mats are suspended; these are of neat workmanship, composed of a soft reed, united by bark cord, in straight or undulated lines, between which, lines of black paint sometimes occur. The bedsteads are elevated to the height of a common seat from the ground, and are about six feet wide; they extend in an unin- terrrupted line around three-fourths of the circumference of the apartment, and are formed of the simplest manner of numerous sticks, or slender pieces of wood resting on their ends on cross pieces, which are supported by short notched or forked posts, driven into the ground; bison skins supply them with a comfortable bedding. Several medicine or mystic bags are carefully attached to the mats of the wall, these are cylindrical, and neatly bound up; several reeds are usually placed upon them, and a human scalp serves for their fringe and tassels. Of their contents we know nothing.

"The fireplace is a simple shallow cavity, in the centre of the apartment, with an upright and a projecting arm for the support of the culinary apparatus. The latter is very simple in kind, and limited in quantity, consisting of a brass kettle, an iron pot, and wooden bowls and spoons; each person, male as well as female, carries a large knife in the girdle of the breech cloth behind, which is used at their meals, and sometimes for self-defence. During our stay with these Indians they ate four or five times each day, invariably supplying us with the best pieces, or choice parts, before they attempted to taste the food themselves.

"They commonly placed before us a sort of soup, composed of maize of the present season, of that description which having undergone a certain prepa- ration, is appropriately named sweet corn, boiled in water, and enriched with a few slices of bison meat, grease, and some beans, and to suit it to our palates, it was generally seasoned with rock salt, which is procured near the Arkansa river.

"This mixture constituted an agreeable food; it was served up to us in large wooden bowls, which were placed on bison robes or mats, on the ground; as many of us as could conveniently eat from one bowl sat round it, each in as easy a position as he could contrive, and in common we partook of its contents by means of large spoons made of bison horn. We were sometimes supplied with uncooked dried meat of the bison, also a very agreeable food, and to our taste and reminiscence, far preferable to the flesh of the domestic ox. Another very acceptable dish was called *leyed corn;* this is maize of the preceding season *shelled* from the cob, and first boiled for a short time in a ley of wood ashes until the hard skin, which invests the grains, is separated from them; the whole is then poured into a basket, which is repeatedly dipped into clean water until the ley and skins are removed; the remainder is then boiled in water until so soft as to be edible. They also make much use of maize roasted on the cob, of boiled pumpkins, of muskmelons, and watermelons, but the latter are generally pulled from the vine before they are completely ripe.

"Ca-ega-wa-tan-ninga, or the Fool Chief, is the hereditary principal chief, but he possesses nothing like monarchical authority, maintaining his distinction only by his bravery and good conduct. There are ten or twelve inferior chieftains, or persons who aspire to such dignity, but these do not appear to command any great respect from the people. Civil as well as military distinction arises from bravery or generosity. Controversies are decided amongst themselves; they do not appeal to their chief, excepting for counsel. They will not marry any of their kindred, however remote. The females, before marriage, labour in the fields, and serve their parents, carry wood and water, and attend to the culinary duties; when the eldest daughter marries, she commands the lodge, the mother and all the sisters; the latter are to be also the wives of the same individual. When a young man wishes to marry a particular female, his father gives a feast to a few persons, generally old men, and acquaints them with his design; they repair to the girl, who generally feigns an unwillingness to marry, and urges such reasons as her poverty, youth, &c.—the old men are often obliged to return six or seven times before they can effect their object—when her consent is obtained, the parents of the young man take two or three blankets and some meat to the parents of the female that they may feast, and immediately return to their lodge. The parents put on the meat to cook, and place the same quantity of meat and merchandize on two horses, and dress their daughter in the best garments they can afford; she mounts one of the horses, and leads the other, and is preceded by a crier announcing, with a loud voice, the marriage of the young couple, naming them, to the people; in this way she goes to the habitation of her husband, whose parents take from her every thing she brings, strip her entirely naked, dress her again in clothes as good as she brought, furnish her with two other horses, with meat and merchandize, and she returns with her crier to her parents. These two horses she retains as her own, together with all the articles she brings back with her. Her parents then make a feast, to which they invite the husband, his parents and friends; the young couple are seated together, and all then partake of the good cheer, after which the father of the girl makes a harangue, in which he informs the young man that he must now assume the command of the lodge, and of every thing belonging to him and his daughter. All the merchandize which the bride returned with, is distributed in presents from herself to the kindred of her husband in their first visit. The husband then invites the relatives of his wife to a feast. Whatever peltries the father possesses are at the disposal of the son to trade with on his own account; and in every respect the parents, in many instances, become subservient to the young man.

"After the death of the husband the widow scarifies herself, rubs her person with clay, and becomes negligent of her dress until the expiration of a year, when the eldest brother of the deceased takes her to wife without any ceremony, considers her children as his own, and takes her and them to his house; if the deceased left no brother, she marries whom she pleases. They have, in some instances, four or five wives, but those are mostly sisters; if they marry into two families the wives do not harmonize well together, and give the husband much inquietude; there is, however, no restriction in this respect, except in the prudence of the husband. The grandfather and grandmother are very fond of their grandchildren, but these have very little respect for them. The female children respect and obey their parents; but the males are very disobedient, and the more obstinate they are and the less readily they comply with the commands of their parents, the more the latter seem to be pleased, saying, 'he will be a brave man, a great warrior, he will not be controlled.'

"The attachment of fraternity is as strong, if not stronger, than with us. The niece has great deference for the uncle. The female calls her mother's sister *mother*, and her mother's brother *uncle*. The male calls his father's brother *father*, his father's sister *aunt*, his mother's sister *mother*, and his mother's brother *uncle*. Thirteen children have occurred in one family. A woman had three children at a birth, all lived.

"The young men are generally coupled out as friends; the tie is very permanent, and continues often throughout life.

"They bear sickness and pain with great fortitude, seldom uttering a complaint; bystanders sympathize with them, and try every means to relieve them. Insanity is unknown; the blind are taken care of by their friends and the nation generally, and are well dressed and fed. Drunkenness is rare, and is much ridiculed; a drunken man is said to be bereft of his reason, and is avoided. As to the origin of the nation, their belief is, that the Master of life formed a man, and placed him on the earth; he was solitary and cried to the Master of life for a companion, who sent him down a woman; from the union of these two proceeded a son and daughter, who were married, and built themselves a lodge distinct from that of their parents; all the nations proceeded from them, excepting the whites, whose origin they pretend not to know. When a man is killed in battle the thunder is supposed to take him up, they do not know where. In going to battle each man traces an imaginary figure of the thunder on the soil; and he who represents it incorrectly is killed by the thunder. A person saw this thunder one day on the ground, with a beautiful mockasin on each side of it; having much need of a pair, he took them and went his way; but on his return by the same spot the thunder took him off, and he has not been since heard of. They seem to have vague notions of the future state. They think that a brave warrior, or good hunter, will walk in a good path; but a bad man or coward will find a bad path. Thinking the deceased has far to travel they bury with his body, mockasins, some articles of food, &c. to support him on the journey. Many persons, they believe, have become reanimated, who have been, during their apparent death, in strange villages; but as the inhabitants used them ill they returned. They say they have never seen the Master of life, and therefore cannot pretend to personify him; but they have often heard him speak in the thunder; they wear often a shell which is in honour, or in representation of him, but they do not pretend that it resembles him, or has any thing in common with his form, organization, or dimensions.

"This nation having been at profound peace with the Osages since the year 1806, have intermarried freely with them, so that in stature, features and customs they are more and more closely approaching that people. They are large and symmetrically well formed, with the usual high cheek bones, the nose more or less aquiline, colour reddish coppery, the hair black and straight. Their women are small and homely, with broad faces. We saw but a single squaw in the village who had any pretensions to beauty; she was recently married to an enterprizing warrior, who invited us to a feast, apparently in order to exhibit his prize to us. The ordinary dress of the men is a breech cloth of blue or red cloth, secured in its place by a girdle; a pair of *leggins*, made of dressed deer skin, concealing the leg, excepting a small portion of the upper part of the thigh; a pair of mockasins made of dressed deer, elk, or bison skin, not ornamented; and a blanket to cover the upper part of the body, often thrown over one arm in hot weather, leaving that part naked; or it is even entirely thrown aside. The outer cartilage of the ear is cut through in three places, and upon the rims, thus separated, various ornaments are suspended, such as wampum, string beads, silver or tin trinkets, &c. The hair of most of their chiefs and warriors is scrupulously removed from the head, being careful however to leave enough, as in honour they are bound to do, to supply their enemy with a scalp, in case they should be vanquished. This residuum consists of a portion of the back of the head of about the breadth of the hand, rounded at its upper termination near the top of the head, the sides rectilinear, and nearly parallel, though slightly approaching each other towards the origin of the neck, where it abruptly terminates; on the exterior margin, the hair is somewhat longer and erect; this strip of hair is variously decorated; it is sometimes coloured on the margin with vermillion, sometimes a tail feather of the *war eagle* is attached transversely with respect to the head; this feather is white at base, and black at tip; but the principal ornament, which appears to be worn by some of their chief warriors, and which is at the same time by far the most handsome, is the tail of the common deer; this is attached by the base near the top of the patch of hair, the back of it resting on the hair, and the tip secured near the termination of the patch; the bristly hair of the tail is dyed red by a beautiful permanent colour, and parted longitudinally in the middle by a broad silver plate, which is attached at top, and suffered to hang loose. Many of them are tatooed on different parts of the body. The young boys are entirely naked, with the exception of a girdle generally of cloth, round their protruding abdomen. This part of the body in the children of this nation is remarkably prominent; it is more particularly so when they are very young, but gradually subsides as they advance in age. In hot weather the men, whilst in the village, generally use fans, with which they cool themselves, when in the shade, and protect their heads from the sun whilst walking out; they are made of the wing or tail of the turkey. The women rarely use them. The dress of the female is composed of a pair of mockasins, leggins of blue or red cloth, with a broad projecting border on the outside, and covering the leg to the knee or a little above; many, however, and perhaps almost a majority of them, do not in common wear this part of the dress. Around the waist, secured by a belt or cestus, is wrapped a piece of blue cloth, the sides of which meet, or come nearly in contact on the outside of the right thigh, and the whole extends downward as far as the knee, or to the mid-leg; around the left shoulder is a similar piece of cloth, which is attached, by two of the corners, at the axilla of the right arm and extends downward as far as the waist. This garment is often laid aside, when the body, from the waist upward, is entirely exposed. Their hair is suffered to grow long; it is parted longitudinally on the top of the head; and flows over the shoulders, the line of separation being coloured with vermillion. The females, like those of other aborigines, cultivate the maize, beans, pumpkins, and watermelons, gather and prepare the two former, when ripe, and pack them away in skins, or in mats, for keeping; prepare the flesh of the bison, by drying, for preservation; attend to all the cooking; bring wood and water; and in other respects manage the domestic concerns, and appear to have over them absolute sway. These duties, as far as we could observe, they not only willingly performed as a mere matter of duty, but they exhibited in their deportment a degree of pride and ambition to acquit themselves well; in this respect resembling a good housewife amongst the civilized fair. Many of them are tattooed.

"Both sexes, of all ages, bathe frequently, and enter the water indiscriminately. The infant is washed in cold water soon after its birth, and the ablution is frequently repeated; the mother also bathes with the same fluid soon after delivery. The infant is tied down to a board, after the manner of many of the Indian tribes.

"The chastity of the young females is guarded by the mother with the most scrupulous watchfulness, and a violation of it is a rare occurrence, as it renders the individual unfit for the wife of a chief, a brave warrior, or good hunter. To wed her daughter to one of these, each mother is solicitous; as these qualifications offer the same attractions to the Indian mother as family and fortune exhibit to the civilized parent. In the nation, however, are several courtezans; and during our evening walks we were sure to meet with respectable Indians who thought pimping no disgrace. Sodomy is a crime not uncommonly committed; many of the subjects of it are publicly known, and do not appear to be despised, or to excite disgust; one of them was pointed out to us: he had submitted himself to it, in consequence of a vow he had made to his mystic medicine, which obliged him to change his dress for that of a squaw, to do their work, and to permit his hair to grow. The men carefully pluck their chins, axilla of the arms, eye brows, and pubis, every hair of beard that presents itself: this is done with a spiral wire, which, when used, is placed with the side upon the part, and the ends are pressed towards each other so as to close the spires upon the hairs, which can then be readily drawn out; this instrument we observed to be an article of dress of the chiefs, who departed to attend the council at the Isle au Vache."

CHAPTER VII

Further account of the Konza nation—
Robbery of Mr. Say's detachment by a war party of Pawnees—Arrival at the Platte.

THE Konza warriors, like those of some others of the Missouri tribes, on their departure on a war excursion, sometimes make vows, binding themselves never to return until they have performed some feat which they mention, such as killing an enemy, striking an enemy's dead body, or stealing a horse. An instance lately occurred, of a warrior who had been long absent under a vow of this sort, and finding it impossible to meet an enemy, and being in a starving condition, he returned to his own village by night, with the determination of accomplishing his vow, by killing and scalping the first person he should meet. This person happened to be the warrior's own mother, but the darkness of the night prevented the discovery until he had accomplished his bloody purpose.

On the 23d of August, Mr. Say's party began to prepare for leaving the Konza village, where they had been treated with much hospitality. They purchased a number of articles for their use on the journey they proposed to take, such as jerked bison meat, pounded maize, bison fat put up like sausages, mockasins, leggings, spoons made of the horn of the bison, two large wooden

95

dishes, &c. They received also an addition to their cavalcade of two horses, one belonging to Maj. O'Fallon, and another which they procured from a Frenchman residing in the village.

A Pawnee prisoner, an interesting young man, was brought to them, who said he was desirous to accompany them to his nation, but at the same time, was afraid his people would not recognize him, and would kill him for a Konza. He was promised protection, but at the same time it was remarked to him, that if he should attempt to steal the horses of the party on the way, they would certainly pursue him and take his scalp.

On the 24th, says Mr. Say, having been detained until afternoon in searching for our horses, we departed, accompanied by several Indians, who intended to pass the night with us, and to return to the village the following morning.

Our path led along the margin of Blue Earth creek, a stream of the width of twenty-five yards, and greatest depth of three feet, which discharges into the river a mile or two above the Konza village. The soil supports but a thin growth of grass, and the timber is far from abundant, consisting principally of different sorts of oak, confined to the margin of the creek, its ravines and tributaries. One of our Indian followers, who, although a chief of the extinct Missouri nation, has yet much influence with the Konzas, wished to exchange a horse he had with him, for one of ours, which was evidently a less valuable animal. The reason he assigned, in explanation of his desire, of such an apparently disadvantageous exchange was, that his horse had been presented to him by a person, who, he feared, intended to reclaim him, but that if he should exchange him for another horse, he would be secure in the possession of the individual so obtained, as an Indian will not reclaim a present which is not identically the same he had given. At the distance of seven miles from the village, our party encamped by the side of the creek, in a narrow but beautiful, and level prairie bottom, which was bounded by an abrupt, though verdant, range of bluffs.

Mr. Dougherty and one of the Indians went in quest of game, and having supplied the two remaining Indians with a pipe and tobacco, we were partaking of some refreshment, when one of the party suddenly drew our attention to an extensive cloud of dust, which arose from the plain, and which we soon perceived but partially concealed a body of Indians, who had already approached within a quarter of a mile, and were now running with great swiftness. Our Indian followers now displayed all their activity; the chief seized his gun, and ran towards the advancing multitude to obtain his horse, which he mounted and rode off at full speed, whilst his companion disappeared in the bushes in an instant. This was a sufficient intimation that a hostile party was before us, and a timely admonition of the approach of danger. Our men were therefore drawn up in a line, and all prepared themselves for defence in case of extremity.

The advancing party were armed, decorated and painted for battle, but they manifested, as they rushed up to us, the most pacific deportment, shaking us by the hand, putting their arms about our necks, and raising their hands with the palm towards us, in token of peace. We were not, however, disposed to rely upon these assurances of friendship, being fully aware of the difficulties which their partizans would have to surmount, in checking the inconsiderate prowess of the younger warriors. We now observed some of them seizing our horses, which were staked at some distance: they mounted them and rode swiftly in the direction that the chief had taken, but they soon returned. It soon became necessary to protect our baggage by arranging ourselves around it; still, however, in despite of our vigilance many of our small articles were stolen. They begged for whiskey and tobacco, and a small portion of the latter was given them. Amidst the confusion arising from the incessant and rapid movements of the Indians, we observed an individual bearing off a small package of very fine pounded meat; I immediately pointed out the circumstance to the partizan, and directed him to recover it and punish the thief; he complied by wresting the meat from the grasp of the latter, and from that of several others who had been contending for portions of it, placed it beneath his feet, and defended it with his lance; but Chabonneau, to whom the meat belonged, declaring that he had given it to them, they were permitted to retain it. A tent which had been pitched for me in consideration of my illness, and in which my blanket, pistols, together with some small articles had been deposited, was plundered of its contents; it was finally cut down and would have been taken away, had we not made an effort to preserve it. During the whole transaction those warriors, who stood at a short distance, intently watched our movements, as if they were led to believe, from the attitude we assumed, that we would attempt to repel them, even with our inadequate force. No sudden action or notion of any one of the party escaped them, and individuals were frequently observed to draw their arrows, to test the elasticity of the bows. At a critical juncture, a tall and graceful Indian cocked his gun fiercely, and put his war whistle to his mouth, but the signal was not blown. Amongst numerous incidents that occurred during the half hour that we were surrounded by them, an individual attempted to seize a knapsack belonging to one of the soldiers, and immediately under his observation; the latter placed his foot upon the knapsack to detain it, and at the same time prepared his gun as if to shoot the offender, who leaped backward with great agility, and with an ejaculation of pleasure, drew his arrow to the head. The whole party precipitately retreated just as Mr. Dougherty returned from hunting; being briefly informed of the nature of their visit, he called aloud to the fugitives in their own language, but they passed on without heeding him, taking our horses with them. I had by a rough estimate fixed their number at one hundred and forty; they were chiefly armed with the bow and arrow and lance, with the usual accompainments of tomahawks, war-clubs and knives, together with a few guns. Fortunately no personal indignity was offered us, yet we could not repress a sensation of much mortification, at the prospect of a frustration of our enterprise, which now seemed inevitable, and of extreme vexation at the irreparable loss of our horses, which no exertions of ours could have saved: an appeal to arms, except in the last extremity, would have been the height of imprudence, conquest being hopeless and escape almost impossible.

Soon after their departure Mr. Jessup and Chabonneau, set out for the village to procure assistance, for the purpose of removing our camp to that place from which we recommenced our journey at a moment so unpropitious, whilst we busied ourselves in removing the baggage to a situation amongst the neighbouring bushes, which appeared favourable for concealment, and for defence, in case of a night attack, which was confidently anticipated. Several alarms occured during the night, and on the return of day we observed thirty mounted Indians riding swiftly towards us. The chief, who left us so precipitately the preceding evening, on his arrival at the village, hastily assembled a little band of warriors for the purpose of returning immediately to our assistance, and it was he and his party, that we had now the pleasure to greet. They expressed great satisfaction, when they learned that we were all uninjured. After saluting us cordially, they pursued the trail of the Pawnees for some distance, and from the footsteps in the grass, and other appearances, to be duly appreciated only by the eye of an Indian, they estimated the number of the Pawnees at 130. On their return they restored to us some bacon and other articles, which had been carried off by the fugitives, and rejected as not at all to their taste. We were now supplied with a conveyance for ourselves and our baggage, and were conducted back to the village.

The Indians who committed this robbery, were a war party of the Republican Pawnees, and were about one hundred and forty in number. Their nation was at war with the Konzas.

Mr. Say's party were kindly received at the village they had left on the preceding day. In the evening they had retired to rest in the lodge set apart for their accommodation, when they were alarmed by a party of savages, rushing in armed with bows, arrows and lances, shouting and yelling in the most frightful manner. The gentlemen of the party had immediate recourse to their arms, but observing that some squaws, who were in the lodge, appeared unmoved, they began to suspect that no molestation of them was intended. The Indians collected around the fire in the centre of the lodge, yelling incessantly; at length their howling assumed something of a measured tone, and they began to accompany their voices with a sort of drum and rattles. After singing for some time, one who appeared to be their leader, struck the post over the fire with his lance, and they all began to dance, keeping very exact time with the music. Each warrior had, besides his arms, and rattles made of strings of deer's hoofs, some part of the intestines of an animal inflated, and inclosing a few small stones, which produced a sound like pebbles in a gourd shell. After dancing round the fire for some time, without appearing to notice the strangers, they departed, raising the same wolfish howl, with which they had entered; but their music and yelling continued to be heard about the village during the night.

This ceremony, called the *dog dance*, was performed by the Konzas for the entertainment of their guests. Mr. Seymour took an opportunity to sketch the attitudes and dresses of the principal figures. . . .

Finding it impracticable to obtain horses by purchase, out of their almost exhausted stock of merchandize, to enable them to prosecute their march to Council Bluff, after due deliberation, they saw no alternative, but to endeavour to hire horses on credit, and to make the best of their way for Cow Island, in hopes of meeting the steam boat there. A Frenchman, Mr. Gunville, resident with this nation, agreed to furnish two pack horses, and a saddle horse for Mr. Say, whose state of health would not admit of his continuing the journey on foot. Thus furnished they prepared to depart, and in the meantime two runners were dispatched to inform Major Long of their situation by letter.

On the 25th of August, Mr. Say and his party again left the Konza village, accompanied by the French trader, who had furnished them two horses, and by a Missouri Indian; but this last had followed them only a few miles, when he repented of his undertaking and returned.

In pursuing the most direct route from the Konza village to the Missouri, they crossed at the distance of seventeen miles, the Vermillion, a small stream bordered with handsome forests. Nineteen miles beyond this they arrived at the sources of Grasshopper creek, where they encamped on the evening of the 27th. Here the soil changes somewhat abruptly. The high Prairies about the Vermillion and Blue Earth creeks are barren, almost naked, and inhabited by some orbicular lizards. About Grasshopper creek the soil is fertile, the grass dense and luxuriant.

On the 29th they arrived at Isle au Vache, and were hospitably received by Col. Morgan and the officers of his command, but had the mortification to learn that major Long, after waiting a sufficient time to enable the Indian agent to complete his negotiations with the Konzas, had departed with the steam boat before the arrival of the messengers, that had been sent to notify him of their disaster. These runners had been despatched immediately after their arrival, with instructions to overtake the steam boat, and to deliver Mr. Say's letter, but after some days they returned, without having been able to effect any thing.

It was now determined that Mr. Say and Mr. Jessup, who on account of ill health, were unable to travel farther on foot, should for the present remain at Isle au Vache, while the other gentlemen of the detachment, should continue their journey. Mr. Dougherty, from his intimate acquaintance with the country, was of opinion that by crossing in the nearest direction from Isle au Vache to the mouth of Wolf river, they might yet overtake the steam boat. They accordingly placed themselves under his guidance, and by great exertion, fortunately arrived at the mouth of the Wolf river, on the evening of the 1st of September, as the steam boat was passing.

The country southwest of the Missouri, between the Konzas and the Platte, is drained principally by Wolf river and the Great Nemahaw. These rivers, like the Nodowa and Nishnebottona, which enter the Missouri nearly opposite them, from the northeast, rise in the prairies at an elevation probably of forty or fifty feet above the level of the Missouri. As they descend, their vallies becoming gradually wider, embosom a few trees, and at length, near their entrance into the Missouri valley, are forests of considerable extent. The surface of these prairies presents a constant succession of small rounded hills, becoming larger and more abrupt, as you approach the beds of the rivers. The soil is deep, reposing usually on horizontal beds of argillaceous sandstone, and secondary limestone. In all the limestones along the Missouri, we observe a tendency to crystalline structure, and they have often a reddish or yellowish white colour. There is however always something in the arrangement and the aspect of the crystals, to distinguish these sparry varieties from the primitive granular limestone, to which they have something of general resemblance. The horizontal disposition of the strata of this limestone, the great numbers of organic relics contained in it, and its intimate connexion with coal strata, indicate with sufficient clearness its relation to the secondary rocks. No person who shall examine this stratum with the least attention either about the Nemahaw and the Konzas, or in the mining district at the sources of the Gasconade, the Merameg, and the St. Francis, will for a moment mistake it for any of those varieties of transition of primitive limestone, which it in some respects so closely resembles. The crystalline varieties, no less than the compact blue limestones, embrace numerous masses of chert or hornstone. This occurs of various colours, and these are arranged in spots or stripes. Some specimens have several distinct colours arranged in zigzag lines, somewhat resembling the fortification agate. The hunters use fragments of this stone for gun flints; the savages also formerly employed it in the manufacture of arrow points and other implements.

The soil superimposed upon these strata of limestone, is a calcareous loam. Near the rivers it is intermixed with sand; this is also the case with the soil of the high prairies around the Konzas village. In ascending the Konzas river, one hundred, or one hundred and twenty miles from the Missouri, you discover numerous indications, both in the soil, and its animal and vegetable productions of an approach to the borders of that great Sandy Desert, which stretches eastward from the base of the Rocky Mountains. You meet there with the orbicular lizard or "horned frog," an inhabitant of the arid plains of New Mexico. You distinguish also some cacti, as well as many of those plants allied to chenopodium, and salsola, which delight in a thirsty muriatiferous soil. The catalogue of the forest trees belonging to the vallies of this region is not very copious. The cotton wood, and the plane tree, every where form conspicuous features of the forests. With these are intermixed the tall and graceful acacia, the honey locust, the bonduc or coffee tree, and several species of juglans, carya and fraxinus, with pinnated or many-parted leaves. Trees of the family of the coniferæ are not of frequent occurrence on the Missouri. About the summits of rocky cliffs are here and there a few cedars or junipers, the only trees that retain their verdure during the winter.

The prairies, for many miles on each side of the Missouri, produce abundance of good pasturage; but as far as our observation has extended, the best soil is a margin from ten to twelve miles in breadth, along the western bank of the river. In the summer very little water is to be found in the prairies, all the smaller streams failing, even though the season be not unusually dry. On account of the want of wood and of water, the settlements will be, for a long time, confined to the immediate vallies of the Missouri, the Konzas, and the larger rivers; but it is probable, forests will hereafter be cultivated in those vast woodless regions, which now form so great a proportion of this country; and wells may be made to supply the deficiency of running water.

We have seen at Bellefontain, as well as at several other points on this river, a pretty species of sparrow, which is altogether new to us; and several specimens of a serpent have occurred, which has considerable affinity with the pine snake of the Southern States or bull snake of Bartram.

Having received on board the detachment that had arrived from the Konza village, except Messrs. Say and Jessup, who, on account of ill health, remained at Isle au Vache, we left the mouth of Wolf River on the 2nd of September. A party of hunters, furnished with a horse for the transportation of game, were despatched at the same time with instructions to hunt on the south side of the river, and to join us again in the evening. We had little difficulty in procuring a constant supply of venison. Deer are very numerous on this part of the Missouri, and we had several opportunities to kill them from on board, as they were swimming across the river.

Twenty-one miles above the mouth of the Wolf River, and on the same side, is the entrance of the Grand Nemahaw, a considerable river, which rises in the plains between the Platte and the Republican Fork of the Konzas river, and running eastwardly about one hundred and fifty miles, discharges into the Missouri a little north of latitude forty degrees. In the straightness of its course,

Squirrel, T.R. Peale, September 5, 1819, ink and pencil.

the rapidity and turbulence of its stream, it has a general resemblance to the other western tributaries of the Missouri. A few miles above the Nemahaw, and on the opposite side is the mouth of the Tarkio a small stream.

On the 4th of September we were joined by the hunters, who brought two deer, and informed us they had killed several others. Lieutenant Field's boat was allowed to remain at the encampment of the preceding night, after the departure of the steam boat, for the purpose of taking on board a large quantity of honey. Swarms of bees were found here in great numbers, and the honey they afforded made a valuable addition to our provisions, consisting now in a great measure of hunters' fare.

Finding one of the valves of the steam engine much worn and leaky, we were now under the necessity of stopping for a day to have a new one, which we had brought, adapted to its place. Several of the men amused themselves by hunting and fishing. We had now a plentiful supply of game, and many large catfish were taken, some of them weighing more than fifty pounds.

We passed in succession the mouths of the Nishnebottona, and the Little Nemahaw, and arrived on the 7th at the Grand Pass. Here the Nishnebottona, a beautiful river about sixty yards wide, approaches within one hundred and fifty yards of the Missouri, being separated from it by a sandy prairie, rising scarcely twenty feet above the surface of the water. After pursuing for a short distance a parallel course, the two rivers diverse, and the Nishnebottona meanders along the side of the Missouri valley, about sixty miles, to its confluence with the latter river. From this point is a pleasing view of the hills called the Bald Pated Prairie, stretching along the north-eastern side of the Nishnebottona, and diminished to the size of ant-hills in the distant perspective. Here the navigation is much obstructed by sandbars, and the ordinary current of the Missouri, according to the statement of Lewis and Clark, corroborated by our observation, is something more than one fanthom per second. In many places the Missouri hurries across concealed sandbars and other obstructions, with the velocity of seven, eight or even twelve feet in a second. Between these obstructions, the channel becomes deeper, and the current more moderate; consequently the aggregate velocity at times of low water may be reckoned something less than six feet to the second. As the volume of water is increased by the heavy rains, and the melting of snows within the Rocky Mountains, the current is proportionably accelerated, and becomes more equable, running for many miles in succession, not less than seven hundred and twenty feet per minute. At the time of our ascent the summer floods had not entirely subsided, and in contending against the current, we found occasion in a few instances to make use of the towing rope.

About thirteen miles above the Grand Pass, is a point where Lewis and Clark witnessed the falling of a portion, about three-fourths of a mile in length, of a high cliff of sandstone and clay. Appearances have considerably changed since the time of their journey. There is still an indentation along the bluff, showing the upper part of the portion which had slid down, but the whole is now covered with grass. The river has retired from the base of the cliff it was then undermining. The grassy plain, to some extent, occupies the spot where the bed of the river must have been; but this prairie is, in its turn, experiencing the vicissitude incident to every thing along the bank of the Missouri, and is evidently very soon to disappear entirely. A mile or two above this point are cliffs of sandstone and indurated clay, in a state of rapid disintegration. Here we observed extensive beds of aluminous earth, of a dark gray colour, alternating with red and yellowish white sandstone. Here are also numerous vegetable remains, which Mr. Say thought to consist of the limbs of trees included in the rock, carbonized and often intermixed with pyrites; smaller limbs in short fragments lay intermixed, and crossing each other in every direction.

Among other things, we observed here what appeared to be the cast of the seed vessel of the nelumbium, of uncommon magnitude. Fragments of mineral coal were observed scattered about the surface.

The mouth of the Platte, where we arrived on the 15th of September, is, according to our observations, in latitude 41° 3' 13" north. We shall hereafter have occasion to speak more particularly of this river. Its mouth now exhibited a great extent of naked sandbars, the water, which was transparent and of a greenish colour, flowing almost unseen through a number of small channels. Masses of sand accumulate at the mouth of the Platte, rendering the navigation of the Missouri at this point extremely difficult. The Platte, during its floods, pours into the Missouri a volume of water, considerably exceeding in magnitude that of the latter river, occasioning a reflux of the waters for many miles. From the Platte upward, the annual range from high to low water in the Missouri, may be rated at about eighteen feet.

Above the Platte, the scenery of the Missouri becomes much more interesting. The bluffs on each side are more elevated and abrupt, and being absolutely naked, rising into conic points, split by innumerable ravines, they have an imposing resemblance to groups of high granitic mountains, seen at a distance. The forests within the valley, are of small extent, interspersed with wide meadows covered with Carices and Cyperaceæ, with some species of Limnetis, Polypogon, and Arundo, sometimes sinking into marshes occupied by Saggittarias, Alismas, and others of the Hydrocharidæ. The woodlands here, as on the whole of the Missouri below, are filled with great numbers of pea vines, which afford an excellent pasturage for horses and cattle. The roots of the Apios tuberosa were much sought after, and eaten by the soldiers, who accompanied us in our ascent. They are little tubers about half an inch in diameter, and when boiled are very agreeable to the taste. Two and an half miles above the mouth of the Platte, and on the same side, is that of the Papilion, a stream of considerable length, but discharging little water. Here we found two boats belonging to the Indian traders at St. Louis. They had passed us some days before, and were to remain for the winter at the mouth of the Papilion, to trade with the Otoes, Missouries, and other Indians.

The banks of the Missouri above the Platte, have long been frequented by the Indians, either as places of permanent or occasional residence. Deserted encampments are often seen. On the northeast side, near the mouth of Mosquito river, are the remains of an old Ioway village. Four miles above, and on the opposite side, was formerly a village of the Otoes. On the 17th September, we arrived at the trading establishment of the Missouri fur company, known as Fort Lisa, and occupied by Mr. Manuel Lisa, one of the most active persons engaged in the Missouri fur trade. We were received by a salute from this establishment, and encamped a little above, on the same side of the river.

CHAPTER VIII

Winter Cantonment near Council Bluff—
Councils with the Otoes, Missouries, Ioways, Pawnees, &c.

THE position selected for the establishment of winter quarters for the exploring party, was on the west bank of the Missouri, about half a mile above Fort Lisa, five miles below Council Bluff, and three miles above the mouth of Boyer's river. At this place we anchored on the 19th September, and in a few days, had made great progress in cutting timber, quarrying stone, and other preparations for the construction of quarters.

Cliffs of sparry limestone rise in the rear of the site we had selected, to an elevation of near three hundred feet. At times of low water, strata of horizontal sandstone, are disclosed in the bed of the Missouri. These pass under and support the limestone. Both these strata probably extend in connexion, some distance to the west; but as they are deeply covered with soil, we could not accurately ascertain their boundary in that direction. . . .

Both these strata, embrace numerous relicks of marine animals, many of which we collected.

Immediately after our arrival, an interpreter had been sent across the country, to intercept the traders, then on their way to the Pawnees, with considerable quantities of merchandize. It was thought proper to suspend all intercourse with those Indians, until an adjustment of the recent difficulties should take place. In addition to the outrage committed on Mr. Say's party, they had made prisoners of two white hunters from the Arkansa, a father and son, who had been found hunting in the Indian territories. These men had been liberated through the interference of some of the members of the Missouri Fur Company, and had recently arrived at Fort Lisa. During their captivity, they had been treated with such severity by the Pawnees, that they had often entreated an end might be put to their lives.

The interpreter returned on the 20th, having accomplished the object of his mission. Soon afterwards, Mr. Dougherty arrived from the Oto village, whither he had been sent with a deputation of Konzas, to aid in effecting a reconciliation between those nations. This proposition, which originated with the Konzas, was favorably received by the Otoes. Mr. D. was soon afterwards dispatched to the Pawnees, with instructions to demand of them, the property plundered from Mr. Say's party, also to require that the persons who had committed that outrage, should be given up. He was accompanied by two Frenchmen acquainted with the Pawnees and their language.

A party of Otoes arrived at Fort Lisa on the 26th September, with pack horses, laden with peltries, and bringing with them a soldier, who, having been accidentally separated from a small detachment, that were driving some beeves from Martin's Cantonment, towards Council Bluff, had wandered about in the prairie for five days, without tasting food, when he at last, had the good fortune to fall in with the Otoes, who hospitably fed and conducted him to their trading house.

The Council Bluff, so called by Lewis and Clark, from a council with the Otoes and Missouries held there, on the 3d of August 1804, is a remarkable bank, rising abruptly from the brink of the river, to an elevation of about one hundred and fifty feet. This is a most beautiful position, having two important military features, security, and a complete command of the river. Its defects are a want of wood within a convenient distance, there being little within a mile above, and much farther below, also a want of stone and of water, except that of the river. From the summits of the hills, about one mile in the rear of the Bluff, is presented the view of a most extensive and beautiful landscape. The bluffs on the east side of the river, exhibit a chain of peaks stretching as far as the eye can reach. The river is here and there seen meandering in serpentine folds, along its broad valley, chequered with woodlands and prairies, while at a nearer view you look down on an extensive plain interspersed with a few scattered copses or bushes, and terminated at a distance by the Council Bluff.

This position is about five miles above that selected for the wintering post of the exploring party. At the last mentioned place, a very narrow plain or beach, closely covered with trees, intervenes between the immediate bank of the river, and the bluffs, which rise near two hundred feet, but are so gradually sloped as to be ascended without great difficulty, and are also covered with trees. This spot presented numerous advantages for the cantonment of a small party like ours. Here were abundant supplies of wood and stone, immediately on the spot where we wished to erect our cabins, and the situation was sheltered by the high bluffs from the northwest winds. The place was called Engineer Cantonment. On the 26th of September, Mr. Say and Mr. Jessup, arrived in the flotilla from Cow Island, in company with Col. Morgan, Dr. Gale, and captain Magee. They had both nearly recovered their health, and entertained the liveliest sense of the eminent politeness and hospitality, which had been conferred on them by the above named gentlemen, as well as the other officers of the military expedition.

About one hundred Ottoes, together with a deputation of the Ioway nation, who had been summoned to a council by Major O'Fallon, presented themselves at our camp on the 3d of October. The principal chiefs advanced before their people, and upon invitation seated themselves. After a short interval of silence *Shonga-tonga*, the *Big-horse*, a large, portly Indian of a commanding presence, arose, and said, "My father, your children have come to dance before your tent agreeably to our custom of honouring brave or distinguished persons."

After a suitable reply, by Major O'Fallon, the amusement of dancing was commenced by the striking up of their rude instrumental and vocal music; the former consisting of a gong made of a large keg, over one of the ends of which a skin was stretched, which was struck by a small stick; and another instrument consisting of a stick of firm wood, notched like a saw, over the teeth of which a smaller stick was rubbed forcibly backward and forward; with these, rude as they were, very good time was preserved with the vocal performers, who sat around them, and by all the natives as they sat in the inflection of their bodies, or the movements of their limbs; after the lapse of a little time three individuals leaped up and danced around for a few minutes, then, at a concerted signal from the master of ceremonies, the music ceased, and they retired to their seats uttering a loud noise, which by patting the mouth rapidly with the hand, was broken into a succession of similar sounds, somewhat like the hurried barking of a dog.

Several sets of dancers succeeded, each terminating as the first. In the intervals of the dances, a warrior would step forward and strike a flag staff they had erected, with a stick, whip, or other weapon, and recount his martial deeds. This ceremony is called *striking the post*, and whatever is then said may be relied upon as rigid truth, being delivered in the presence of many a jealous warrior and witness, who could easily detect and would immediately disgrace the *striker* for exaggeration or falsehood. This is called the beggars' dance, during which some presents are always expected by the performers, as tobacco, whiskey, or trinkets. But on this occasion, as none of those articles were immediately offered, the amusement was not, at first, distinguished by much activity. The master of the ceremonies continually called aloud to them to exert themselves; but still they were somewhat dull and backward. *Ietan* now stepped forward and lashed a post with his whip, declaring that he would thus punish those who did not dance; this threat from one whom they had vested with authority for this occasion had a manifest effect upon his auditors, who were presently highly wrought up by the sight of two or three little mounds of tobacco twist which were now laid before them, and appeared to infuse new life.

After lashing the post and making his threat, Ietan went on to narrate his martial exploits. He had stolen horses seven or eight times from the Konzas; he had first struck the bodies of three of that nation slain in battle. He had stolen horses from the Ietan nation, and had struck one of their dead. He had stolen horses from the Pawnees, and struck the body of one Pawnee Loup. He had stolen horses several times from the Omawhaws, and once from the Puncas. He had struck the bodies of two Sioux. On a war party, in company with the Pawnees, he had attacked the Spaniards, and penetrated into one of their camps; the Spaniards, excepting a man and boy, fled, himself being at a distance before his party, he was shot at and missed by the man, whom he immediately shot down and struck. "This, my father, said he, is the only martial act of my life that I am ashamed of." After several rounds of dancing, and of striking at the post by the warriors, Mi-a-ke-ta, or the *Little Soldier*, a war-worn veteran, took his turn to strike the post. He leaped actively about, and strained his voice to its utmost pitch while he portrayed some of the scenes of blood in which he had acted. He had struck dead bodies of individuals of all the red nations around, Osages, Konzas, Pawnee Loups, Pawnee Republicans, Grand Pawnees, Puncas, Omawhaws, and Sioux, Padoucas, La Plais or Bald Heads, Ietans, Sauks, Foxes and Ioways; he had struck eight of one nation, seven of another, &c. He was proceeding with his account when Ietan ran up to him, put his hand upon his mouth and respectfully led him to his seat. This act was no trifling compliment paid to the well known brave. It indicated that he had still so many glorious acts to speak of, that he would occupy so much time as to prevent others from speaking, and put to shame the other warriors by the contrast of his actions with theirs.

Their physical action in dancing is principally confined to leaping a small distance from the ground with both feet, the body being slightly inclined, and upon alighting, an additional slight but sudden inclination of the body is made, so as to appear like a succession of jerks; or the feet are raised alternately, the motions of the body being the same. Such are the movements, in which the whole party correspond; but in the figures, as they are termed in our assembly rooms, each individual performs a separate part, and each part is a significant pantomimic narrative. In all their variety of action they are careful to observe the musical cadenses. In this dance *Ietan* presented one, who was in the act of stealing horses. He carried a whip in his hand, as did a considerable number of the Indians, and around his neck were thrown several leathern thongs, for bridles and halters, the ends of which trailed upon the ground behind him; after many preparatory manoeuvres, he stooped down and with his knife represented the act of cutting the *hopples* of horses; he then rode his tomahawk, as children ride their broomsticks, making such use of his whip as to indicate the necessity of rapid movement lest his foes should overtake him. *Wa-sa-ba-jing-ga* or *Little black Bear*, after a variety of gestures, threw several arrows, in succession, over his head, thereby indicating his familiarity with the flight of such missiles; he at the same time covered his eyes with his hand to indicate that he was blind to danger. Others represented their manoeuvres in battle, seeking their enemy, discharging at him their guns or arrows, &c. &c. Most of the dancers were the principal warriors of the nation, men who had not condescended to amuse themselves or others, in this manner, for years before; but they now appeared in honour of the occasion, and to conciliate, in their best manner, the good will of the representative of the government of the *Big Knives*. Amongst these veteran warriors *Ietan* or *Sha-mon-e-kus-se*, *Ha-she-a* the broken arm, commonly called Cut-nose, and *Wa-sa-ba-jing-ga*, or little Black Bear, three youthful leaders, in particular attracted our attention. In consequence of having been appointed soldiers on this occasion to preserve order, they were painted entirely black. The countenance of the former indicated much wit, and had, in its expression, something of the character of that of Voltaire; he frequently excited the mirth of those about him by his remarks and gestures. *Ha-she-a*, called Cut-nose, in consequence of having lost the tip of his nose in a quarrel with Ietan, wore a handsome robe of white wolf skin, with an appendage behind him called a *crow*. This singular decoration is a large cushion, made of the skin of a crow, stuffed with any light material, and variously ornamented; it has two decorated sticks projecting from it upward, and a pendant one beneath; this apparatus is secured upon the buttocks by a girdle passing round the body. The other actors in the scene were decorated with paints of several colours fantastically disposed upon their persons. Several were painted with white clay, which had the appearance of being grooved in many places. This grooved appearance is given by drawing the finger nails over the part, so as to remove the pigment from thence in parallel lines. These lines are either rectilinear, undulated, or zigzag; sometimes passing over the forehead transversely or vertically; sometimes in the same directions, or obliquely over the whole visage, or upon the breast, arms, &c. Many were painted with red clay, in which the same lines appeared. A number of them had the representation of a black hand with outspread fingers, on different parts of the body, strongly contrasting with the principal colour with which the body was overspread; the hand was depicted in different positions upon the face, breast and back. The face of others was coloured, one half black, and one half white, or red and white, &c.; many coloured their hair with red clay; but the eye-lids, and base of the ears, were generally tinged with vermillion. At the conclusion of the ceremony, whiskey, which they always expect on similar occasions, was produced, and a small portion was given to each. The principal chiefs of the different nations,

Oto Council, Samuel Seymour, engraving.

who had remained passive spectators of the scene, now directed their people to return to their camp. The word of the chiefs was obeyed, excepting by a few of the Ioways, who appeared to be determined to keep their places notwithstanding the reiterated command of the chiefs. Ietan now sprang towards them, with an expression of much ferocity in his counternance, and it is probable a tragic scene would have been displayed had not the chiefs requested him to use gentle means, and thus he succeeded, after which the chiefs withdrew.

October 4th. At ten o'clock, the hour appointed for the council, the Indians, headed by their chiefs, arrived; and after shaking us all by the hand took their seats. There were about one hundred Ottoes, seventy Missouries, and fifty or sixty Ioways. They arranged themselves, agreeably to their tribes, on puncheon benches, which had been prepared for them, and which described a semicircle, on the chord of which sat the whites, with Major O'Fallon and his interpreters in the centre. Sentinels walked to and fro behind the benches; and a handsome standard waved before the assembly. The council was opened by a few rounds from the howitzers. A profound silence reigned for a few mintues, when Major O'Fallon arose, and in a very animated and energetic manner addressed his Indian auditors. Suitable replies were given by Shonga-tonga, the Crenier and others, with all the extravagant gesticulation which is one of the prominent features of Indian oratory.

At the termination of the council, presents were made of blankets, kettles, strouding, tobacco, guns, powder and ball, &c. The Big Horse and the Crenier only were acknowledged as chiefs, and to the latter, who did not possess a large medal, one was given in exchange for a smaller one which he possessed. No chief was acknowledged amongst the Missouries, as it is the wish of Major O'Fallon to extinguish as much as possible national prejudices between these two nations or tribes.

Cut-nose now presented to the agent his crow and bison robe ornamented with hieroglyphicks. The Little Black Bear presented his robe of white wolf and bison skin, and a pair of handsome leggins. The Black Bird presented a robe and the serrated instrument of music before mentioned, observing, significantly, that the latter was then the only weapon he possessed with which he could defend his father.

October 5th. Last evening *Loutre*, an old Missouri Indian, died; he had spoken in the council a few hours before, and remarked then that he had not long to live. He was buried without ceremony near the trading house.

October 9th. Messengers, who had been sent yesterday for the Pawnees, returned, having met with them on the Elk Horn creek, twenty-five miles distant, on their way hither. They arrived about noon, seventy in number, consisting of individuals of each of the three tribes called *Grand Pawnees, Pawnee Republicans* and *Pawnee Loups,* or *Pawnemahas,* and halted at some distance from our camp. As we approached them we observed the majority of them standing in a forest of young willow trees, holding their mules by the bridles, and looking dubiously around. The chief of the principal band, *Long Hair,* was haranguing them in a loud voice, "Take off your saddles; why do you stand peeping and trembling in the bushes; you ought to have trembled when the whites were seen near the Konza village, &c." We saluted the principal men in the usual manner, of shaking by the hand, though not with much cordiality. Major O'Fallon then said, "Pawnees encamp here and smoke your pipes in security; you have conducted yourselves badly, but the whites will not harm the red-skins when they have them thus in their power; we fight in the plains, and scorn to injure men seated peaceably by their fires. Think well of what you will have to say to me in council to-morrow." These assurances appeared to annul their present apprehensions, and they proceeded to encamp.

Three boats came from camp Missouri to take on board a quantity of provisions which are stored here for the troops; we exchanged salutes with them. The noise of the artillery excited the apprehensions of the Indians, who, being sensible of having grossly offended the whites, now anticipated some exemplary punishment, and were not at ease until reassured of their safety, and the cause of the firing of such great guns so near them, was explained.

In the evening, accompanied by several gentlemen of the party, we visited the camp of the Pawnees, whom we found sitting round their fires smoking their pipes in silence. Some were employed in making bows, having found plenty of *hickory,* and *hop horn beam* wood here, which are not to be procured in the vicinity of their villages. Their mules were tied to trees, feeding on the bark of the cotton wood. The three tribes were seated around different fires. We sat down in the group of Grand Pawnees and smoked with their chief *Tar-ra-re-ca-wa-o* or *Long-hair.* This is an hereditary chief, of a lofty and rather haughty mein; his mouth is, perhaps through habit, drawn down a little at the corners. He has the appearance and character of an intrepid man, although not distinguished as a warrior, having, during his life, killed but a single man, who was a Spaniard. He is, however, artful and politic, and has performed some laudable actions. The following anecdote may serve in part to illustrate the more amiable traits of his character. Dorion, a Mestizo, on a trading expedition had accumulated a considerable quantity of peltry at the Pawnee republican village, when it was situate on the Republican fork of the Konza river. As he had no horses to transport his merchandize, he requested the chief of that village to assist him in conveying it to the Grand Pawnees on the Platte, as he intended to descend that river to trade with the Otoes, on his way to St. Louis; the chief directly ordered horses to be brought, the furs were packed upon them and they departed on the journey; but owing to some alleged misconduct on the part of Dorion, the chief, when halfway, ordered the goods to be taken from the horses and to be left on the plain. He then, with his followers, returned to his village. The trader, after bewailing his unfortunate condition, at length resolved to go to the Grand Pawnee village, and solicit the aid of Long-hair. Having arrived at the residence of the chief he related to him in what manner he had been used by the Republican chief, and concluded by requesting assistance to bring in his goods. Long-hair, without reply, ascended to the top of his lodge and called out to his people to bring him one hundred horses. Taking the best of these, and a sufficient number of attendants, he accompanied Dorion, and assisted him to transport all his peltries, and did not cease with his good offices, until he had aided him in building a skin canoe, and had packed all the merchandize aboard, although previously told by Dorion that he had nothing to reward him with, having as he said, traded every thing away, though at the same moment he had a number of Indian goods concealed in his packs of buffaloe robes. After all was completed, "now," said the chief, "Dorion, I know that you are a bad man; I have no doubt but you have a quantity of such goods as we want, concealed in those packs, and could reward me if you were liberal enough; but I ask nothing. You have a forked tongue. You have abused me to the whites, by calling me a rascal, saying I robbed the traders, &c.; but go, I will not harm you; tell the red head (governor Clarke) that I am a rascal, robber, &c. I am content."

At another fire, surrounded by his particular band, sat the *Knife Chief, La-che-le-cha-ru*, principal chief of the Pawneemahas. He is a large, portly man, with a very prepossessing countenance; the hair on the sides of his head is gray; he has a deep scar on the right side, from a wound which was inflicted by a female prisoner, of the Padouca nation, whom he had adopted and taken into his family. This squaw, becoming infuriated at the prospect of the state of slavery to which she supposed herself now reduced, stabbed her child to the heart, mortally wounded the brother of this chief, and, before she could be des-patched, had inflicted this wound, through which the bowels protruded. The individuals of this band live in great harmony amongst themselves, owing probably to their having but two chiefs, who are unrivalled. The second chief is Mestizo. Against this band we have no accusation, they have always demeaned themselves well towards the American whites.

In a third group were collected the representatives of the Pawnee Republicans; this nation or clan stands accused of whipping, robbing, and otherwise abusing a white American and his son, whom they found trapping beaver on the Arkansa river, this season; of killing two American citizens, two years since, who were also trapping beaver on the same river; and of robbing our party of sundry articles and horses near the Konza village, whilst under the protection of the flag of our country, of the nature of which they had been instructed and perfectly well understood. These outrages, and many others, they had committed on lands, to which they do not pretend to have any claim, situated far from their own territories, and in the immediate vicinity of nations with whom they then were, and still are, at war.

On the following day the Pawnees were summoned to council, and in a short time they appeared marching leisurely in a narrow pathway, in *Indian file*, led by the grand chief; near this pathway the musical band was stationed, and when Long-hair arrived opposite, they struck up, suddenly and loudly, a martial air. We wished to observe the effect which instruments, that he had never seen or heard before, would produce on this distinguished man, and therefore eyed him closely, and were not disappointed to observe that he did not deign to look upon them, or to manifest, by any emotion whatever, that he was sensible of their presence. The Indians arranged themselves on the benches prepared for them, and the cessation of the music was succeeded by stillness, which was suddenly interrupted by loud explosions from our howitzers, that startled many of us, but did not appear to attract the notice of the Pawnees.

Major O'Fallon rose and addressed them in a very austere tone and manner, stating the offences they had committed against the white people, and admonishing them to a reformation in their conduct, and to restore the articles they had stolen from us; this was chiefly directed against the Pawnee Republicans; the Loups were applauded for their uniformly good deportment.

The council terminated after much of the property taken from us near the Konza village was restored, and a promise given that the offenders should be punished by whipping. . . .

The leisure we enjoyed after our arrival at Engineer cantonment, afforded the opportunity of making numerous excursions to collect animals, and to explore the neighbouring country. . . .

Early in October the cabins for winter quarters were completed. Having made arrangements for the subsistence of the party, and being about to return to Washington, Maj. Long issued orders to the officers and gentlemen of the expedition, for their government during his absence. The following extract will show to what objects they were instructed to direct their attention.

"Mr. Say will have every facility afforded him that circumstances will admit, to examine the country, visit the neighbouring Indians, procure animals, &c. for the attainment of which, he will call on Lt. Graham, who is authorized to make any expenditures in behalf of the expedition, that may be deemed reasonable and necessary, and afford any aid in his power, consistent with the performance of other duties. Mr. Seymour, or Mr. Peale will accompany him, whenever their services are deemed requisite.

"Maj. O'Fallon has given permission to Mr. Dougherty to aid the gentlemen of the party, in acquiring information concerning the Indians, &c.; this gentleman will, therefore, be consulted in relation to visits, and all kinds of intercourse with the Indians, that may be necessary in the prosecution of the duties of the expedition.

"In regard to these duties, the gentlemen of the expedition will consult my orders of March last. The documents transmitted from the Philosophical Society of Philadelphia, by the Secretary of War; and the instructions of Mr. Jefferson to Capt. Lewis, to be found in vol. 1st of Lewis and Clark's expedition, and regulate their observations and inquiries accordingly.

"Lt. Graham will embrace every opportunity for celestial and barometric observations, and calculate the latitude, longitude, magnetic dip and variation, with the utmost attainable precision; also the heights of the neighbouring hills, and the adjacent high table lands. He will also continue the meteorologic observations as usual, noticing the changes of weather, and all celestial and atmospheric phenomena. To aid him in these duties, he will call on Lieut. Swift, or any other gentleman of the expedition, who may not be particularly engaged at the time in other important duties.

"It is believed that the field for observation and inquiry is here so extensive, that all the gentlemen of the expedition will find ample range for the exercise of their talents, in their respective pursuits, and it is hoped that through their unremitted exertions and perserverance, a rich harvest of useful intelligence will be acquired."

On the 11th of October, Major Long and Mr. Jessup took leave of their friends at Engineer Cantonment, and accompanied by several other persons, began to descend the Missouri by a canoe, on their way towards Washington and Philadelphia.

CHAPTER IX

Animals—Sioux and Omawhaw Indians—
Winter residence at Engineer Cantonment.

THE subsequent account of the transactions at and near Council Bluff, one of the observations made there, we copy from the journal of Mr. Say. . . .

The prairie wolves roam over the plains in considerable numbers, and during the night, the principal season of their hunts, they venture very near to the encampment of the traveler. They are by far the most numerous of our wolves, and often unite in packs for the purpose of chasing deer, which they very frequently succeed in running down, and killing. This, however, is an achievement attended with much difficulty to them, and in which the exertion of their utmost swiftness and cunning, are so often unavailing, that they are sometimes reduced to the necessity of eating wild plums, and other fruits, to them almost indigestible, in order to distend the stomach, and appease in a degree the cravings of hunger.

Their bark is much more distinctly like that of the domestic dog, than of any other animal; in fact the first two or three notes could not be distinguished from the bark of a small terrier, but these notes are succeeded by a lengthened scream.

The wonderful intelligence of this animal, is well worthy of note, and a few anecdotes respecting it may not be amiss. Mr. Peale constructed and tried various kinds of traps to take them, one of which was of the description called "a live trap," a shallow box reversed, and supported at one end, by the well known kind of trap sticks, usually called the "figure four," which elevated the front of the trap upwards of three feet above its slab flooring; the trap was about six feet long, and nearly the same in breadth and was plentifully baited with offal. Notwithstanding this arrangement, a wolf actually burrowed under the flooring, and pulled down the bait through the crevices of the floor; tracks of different sizes were observed about the trap. This procedure would seem to be the result of a faculty beyond mere instinct.

This trap proving useless, another was constructed in a different part of the country, formed like a large cage, but with a small entrance on the top, through which the animals might enter, but not return; this was equally unsuccessful; the wolves attempted in vain to get at the bait, as they would not enter by the rout prepared for them.

A large double "steel trap" was next tried; this was profusely baited, and the whole, with the exception of the bait, was carefully concealed beneath the fallen leaves. This was also unsuccessful. Tracks of the anticipated victims, were next day observed to be impressed in numbers on the earth near the spot, but still the trap, with its seductive charge, remained untouched. The bait was then removed from the trap, and suspended over it from the branch of a tree; several pieces of meat were also suspended in a similar manner, from trees in the vicinity; the following morning the bait over the trap, alone remained. Supposing that their exquisite sense of smell, warned them of the position of the trap, it was removed and again covered with leaves, and the baits being disposed as before, the leaves to a considerable distance around were burned, and the trap remained perfectly concealed by ashes; still the bait over the trap was avoided. Once only this trap was sprung, and had fastened for a short time upon the foot of a species, which was shot the following day at no great distance; it proved to be a species distinct from the prairie wolf, and we have described it under the name of *C. nubilus.*

In no respect disheartened by these futile attempts, many times repeated, and varied in every obvious manner, another scheme was executed, which eventuated in complete success. This was the log trap, in which one log is elevated above another at one end, by means of an upright stick, which rests upon a rounded horizontal trigger stick, on the inferior log.

The *latrans* does not diffuse the offensive odour, so remarkable in the two species of jackalls, *(C. aureus* and *C. anthus,)* though in many respects it resembles those animals. Like the *Mexicanus,* the hair on the vertebral line is elongated; and we should be disposed to regard it as the same animal, but it differs from the description of that species, both in colour and physiognomy. The ears are proportionally longer than those of *C. cancrivorous,* and, as well as the tail, shorter than the corresponding parts of *C. mesomelas.*

This animal, which does not seem to be known to naturalists, unless it should prove to be the *mexicanus,* is most probably the original of the domestic dog, so common in the villages of the Indians of this region, some of the varieties of which, still retain much of the habit, and manners of this species.

On the 14th of October, four hundred Omawhaw Indians assembled at Camp Missouri. Major O'Fallon addressed them in an appropriate speech, stating the reasons for their being called to council, upon which *Ong-pa-ton-ga* the *Big Elk* arose, and after shaking by the hand each of the whites present, placed his robe of Otter skins, and his mockasins under the feet of the agent, whom he addressed to the following effect, as his language was interpreted by Mr. Dougherty.

"He had heard that his father wished to see him, and he had wished to see and hear the words of his father, ever since he learned that he was ascending the river. He was informed last fall of his being at the river Platte, and as he could not then go to see him, he had now come to visit him—And here I am, my father. All these young people you see around here are yours, although they are poor and trifling, yet they are your children. I have always loved the whites since I first remember to have seen them, and this affection increases with my age. All my nation love the whites, and always have loved them. Amongst all the good things of this world I place the whites first. But it appears, that there are many nations that live nearer to you than I, that do not love you, though you have done more for them, than you have done for me. When they meet with you, they flatter you, in order to get presents from you, notwithstanding which, they would not hesitate to kill some of your people on their way home. Some of them shake hands with you in a friendly manner, whilst their hands are yet stained with your blood; and if you examine your own hands, my father, I think you would find some of it adhering to them yet. For my part, my father, I am proud to boast, that my hands are clean. Never has one of my nation stained his hands with the blood of a white man. I do not understand, my father, your mode of treating those well, who treat you ill. It is true I know that you have more sense than I have, but I cannot understand it. I have heard that the Pawnees have been to see you, a nation that has killed, robbed, and insulted your people. I was also informed that you feasted them, and at their departure you put weapons in their hands. I should not be surprised to hear, that those very weapons were stained with white man's blood, before they reached the Pawnee village. This is what I cannot understand. This circumstance led me to believe, that if you treated those, that have injured you, so well, you surely would treat your poor children the Omawhaws, who have never done harm to your people, with much kindness also. But I am afraid the transaction will have a bad effect on my young men. When they heard of American troops ascending this river, they feared and respected them. But I am fearful that this transaction will throw them off their guard, make them lose their respect for you, and cause them to do something, that they would not otherwise have done, and thus create trouble and difference between us. You said, my father, that those troops do not come to harm us. I believe it is true. I consider them all my brothers and friends. So far from thinking they come to injure me, I regard them as my shield, to guard me against bad nations around me. You say, that if ever there is a difference between us, that it will be our fault; but I hope not, my father. I cannot think that the Omawhaws will offer any indignity to your people, now that they have seen all those troops, when they have not harmed individuals who have resided years in their village unprotected, although we were then less enlightened than we now are. Some think, my father, that you have brought all these warriors here to take our land from us, but I do not believe it. For although I am but a poor, simple Indian, yet I know that this land will not suit your farmers; if I even thought your hearts bad enough to take the land, I would not fear it, as I know there is not wood enough on it for the use of whites. You might settle along this river, where timber is to be found; but we can always get wood enough in our country to make our little fires. There is one thing I fear, my father, my nation is coming down here to hunt this winter, and if you send out your soldiers to hunt also, they will drive off all the game, and our women and children will starve. We have heard of the ascent of the troops up this river ever since last fall, and we have been told by other nations, that if they chance to meet with any squaws unprotected, they ravish them. But, my father, we shall soon know if this is true or not, because, having but little to eat, our squaws will be obliged to go out into the prairies to dig roots; I shall trust to you, and not hesitate to let them go." He also observed that he could not see the necessity of stationing so many troops here, as there was no one to oppose; he thought it desirable that they should go higher up the river, to chastise those refractory Indians, who will not listen to our words. "There is one thing, my father," he observed, "which I wish you to inform me of. We have heard of your tying up and whipping individuals of several nations, as you ascended this river. What is the offence which will subject us to this punishment. I wish to know, that I may inform my people, that they may be on their guard." He then observed that all his children were poor, and that they had come with the expectation of receiving something from their father.

This speech, contrary to the usual mode of Indian orators, was commenced in a low tone, the voice gradually rising as the speaker proceeded, until it attained its full intonation.

Several speakers subsequently went forward and delivered their sentiments, generally alluding to the circumstance of our treating those who injure us, kindly, and neglecting our friends.

Ta-sone, the *White Cow*, spoke with that allusion, and added, "Look at me, my father, look at my hands, examine me well, I am a wild man, born in the prairie;" and subsequently, "I told you, my father, to look at me, that you might see if there is any of the blood of your people upon me. Some, whose hands have been stained with blood, endeavour to wash it off, but some of it will still remain."

It is proper to mention, as explanatory of some of the allusions in the above speeches, that the Pawnees, at the conclusion of their council, had been invited to dine at Camp Missouri, and that many of their chiefs were there presented with sabres, as I before stated. It was to this circumstance that the above mentioned speakers had reference, as being inexplicable to them, as it seemed as if we wished to conciliate the good will of those evil-doers through fear, and yet they could hardly accuse us of fear, surrounded as we were by so formidable an array of troops.

It was evident, however, that the speakers had mentally no reference to Major O'Fallon, as they knew he had not committed or sanctioned the acts, of which they complained in their truly delicate and peculiar manner. But they looked upon him as responsible for the actions of his people, knowing him to be the representative of the government, and that in case of wrong, they could not obtain redress from any other person. How much soever Major O'Fallon may have disapproved of the treatment which the Pawnees had received from the military, he was perfectly conscious of having conducted himself towards them, according to their deserts, so far as power had been placed in his hands. But being thus verbally accused, pointedly and repeatedly, of injustice, for acts not his own, he arose and said, "Omawhaws, you say I called the Pawnees here to feast them, and make them presents, after they have killed and insulted us, but it is not true. I did not smoke the pipe of peace with them, neither will I, until our differences are settled. I told the Pawnees that, even if I stood unsupported before them, I would, nevertheless, either compel them to make reparation for their offences, or leave my bones among them for my nation to come and bury."

The Big Elk, and Big Eyes, were the only chiefs acknowledged by Major O'Fallon, who then made liberal presents to them for their people.

Some of these presents were distributed by the Indians after a peculiar manner, but which I learn is very common amongst the Indians of this country. A certain portion of them is placed upon the ground, and whoever can *strike the post* the most frequently, gains them. Another portion is then staked for any other competitors who may choose to advance. A valuable stake was then offered, and an aged veteran stepped forth, and looking round upon his nation with a majestic mien, in which there was not a little expression of triumph, he seemed to challenge the bravest of the brave, to come forward and compete with him for the possesion of it; but agreeably to his expectations no one advanced, and he bore off the prize by common consent, without going through the ceremony of *striking*.

From the 24th of October to the 10th of November, the atmosphere was generally filled with a dense smoke like a fog or stratus, which proceeded from the conflagrated prairies. It sometimes affected our vision painfully, sometimes it so far intercepted the rays of the sun, that the disk of that luminary appeared of a blood red, and the eye could repose upon it uninjured. On the morning of the 8th instant it occured in greater quantity than at any other time, when it was so extremely dense as to intercept a view of the opposite shore of the Missouri from Engineer Cantonment.

On the 9th November some rain fell attended with thunder and lightning. The rain continued on the day following with the wind from the southeast; at evening the smoke was almost entirely dissipated, and the clouds, which were cirrocumuli passing to the north-north-west, became visible.

A party of Sioux visited us on the 15th of November, to view the steam boat. As Major Long had left orders to put the steam machinery in action occasionally, in order to preserve it from rust, Lieutenant Graham concluded to exhibit the boat with the engine in action. The Indians hesitated to enter the boat, fearing, as they said, that it was, or that it contained, some *great medicine* of the Big-knives that might injure them. But when on board and at their ease, one of them observed doubtingly, "he hardly thought the Big-knives had any medicine to hurt them." They appeared much delighted with the boat; its size seemed to surprise them; several measured the width of the deck by straddling, instead of pacing as we do. We exhibited to them the air-gun, magnet, &c. which considerably excited their attention. Two of the howitzers were discharged, loaded with case-shot; the effect produced, of the shot falling into the water, at unequal distances and times, was new and unexpected, and they covered their mouths with the hand, to express their astonishment. Of these warriors, three are *Tetons*, one a *Yancton* and a *Sa-ho-ne*, three different tribes of the great Dacota, or Sioux nation. They are fine looking men, with very prominent cheek bones. They are more attentive to their dress, and are much neater than the other Indians we have seen, though it is proper to observe that, as visitors, they are clothed in their best attire. They decorate their hair with a profusion of feathers of the war eagle, and of a species of owl, which we have not seen. They also suspend in the head dress an entire skin of the paroquet. The hair is in great profusion, and is thrown upon the back in very long rolls, but upon close inspection the greater portion of it is perceived to be false hair artificially attached to their own, the points of junction being indicated by small masses of clay, with which the attachment is effected. Two of these Tetons are inseparable friends, were raised together from their infancy, and although not allied by blood, there is a strong personal resemblance between them, which is not a little enhanced by a studied similarity in dress and ornaments. These two individuals are firm friends to the whites. One of them was a few years since at the Sa-ho-ne village in company with a trader, and being invited to a feast, they had proceeded but a short distance, when a Sa-ho-ne rushed from his concealment and knocked the trader down with his war club. The Teton immediately attacked the assailant, felled him in his turn to the earth, gashed his body with the spear of his war-club and left him for dead. This is a strong evidence of the determination of the savages, as they are called, to protect those whom they consider under their guardianship. The Teton retaliated the blow given to the trader, not only at the immediate risk of his life in the combat, but of having to expiate the deed to many a kindred exasperated warrior, and also at the hazard of originating a war between the two bands.

In the course of the winter we received frequent supplies of provisions from camp Missouri, and by means of some exertion and diligence in hunting, we were able to procure plenty of fresh venison and other game. For coffee we substituted the fruit of the Gymnocladus *canadensis*, which afforded a palatable and wholesome beverage. The flesh of the *skunk* we had sometimes dressed for dinner, and found it a remarkably rich and delicate food.

On the 5th of December, the gentlemen of the party dined by invitation with Mr. M. Lisa.

The principal Ioway chief was once at our camp; he is a very intelligent

Indian, with a solemn dignity of deportment, and would not deign to enter our houses or even to approach them until invited. He is said to have a more intimate knowledge of the manners of the whites, than any other Indian of the Missouri, and to be acquainted with many of the words of our language, but will not willingly make use of them, fearing to express himself improperly, or not trusting to his pronunciation. He remained near Council Bluff in the autumn in order to be present at the councils with the different nations, and to observe the conduct of the whites towards them respectively, a considerable time after his nation had departed down the river to their beaver trapping. After this he went with his family to the head waters of the Boyer, and during his stay there trapped sixty beaver; when with us, he was about to go in search of his people. He had three wives with him, one of whom appeared to be about nine or ten years of age, and whom we mistook for his daughter, until he undeceived us. We showed him our books of engravings, with which he was highly pleased. The Indians almost all of them, delight to look over engravings, particularly those which represent animals; they are not soon fatigued when employed in this way.

This Indian is known by several names, as Grand Batture, Hard-heart, Sandbar, and in his own language, Wang-e-wa-ha. During our late contest with Great Britain, he turned his back upon his nation, in consequence of their raising the tomahawk upon our citizens, and crossing the Missouri, united his destiny with the Otoes, who received and treated him with distinguished respect. Last autumn his nation joined him, and submitted to his guidance; so that the Otoes, Missouries, and Ioways were then united.

Some time since in a transaction with a captain, formerly of the United States army, he thought himself grossly insulted, and demanded on the spot personal satisfaction, agreeably to the custom of the whites, challenging his opponent to single combat, with pistols or such other weapons as he might choose.

He is esteemed the bravest and most intelligent of the Ioways, and amongst the Otoes he was associated with many equally brave with himself. But as there are national prejudices among the Indians as well as amongst the whites, he has not escaped from many a keen allusion to his nation. In a quarrel, which arose from some expressions of this nature, Ietan knocked him down with a war-club.

He has been in fifty battles, and has commanded in seven.

He says the white people often request the Indians to abstain from war, and yet the white people continue to fight each other, as if they wished to monopolize the occupation of war, and thereby deprive the Indian of his principal avenue to honour and dignity.

Several Omawhaws, who have been trapping in the country opposite to Blackbird hill, remained with us last night. The principal one, *A-ha-ga-nash-he*, or the *Upright horn*, has a rather handsome Sioux squaw, to whom he appears to be much attached, paying her great attention in conversation, giving her a portion of his whiskey, and handing her the pipe to smoke. She is, however, not exempted from the ordinary employments of the Indian women, and we had an opportunity today of seeing her depart from Mr. Lisa's with a heavy load, consisting of the goods which her husband had received in exchange for his beaver, on her back, whilst he carried only a keg of whiskey slung over his shoulders, and his gun and hunting apparatus. Previously to the departure of the Omawhaws from our establishment this morning, the brother of one of them, who, report said, had been killed by the Sioux, arrived; he has been with about ten lodges (about twenty men) of his tribe trapping on the Elk-horn, and they have taken about two hundred beavers. He has taken sixty himself, of which he presented his elder brother twenty, and is on his way to Mr. Lisa, to have a trader with merchandize sent to his party to deal for the skins. It is a singular circumstance, that this is the second instance of these two brothers meeting in this vicinity, after the one had been supposed to have been killed by the Sioux.

A-ha-ga-nash-he, whom we invited to take up his lodgings for the night in our room, became alarmed at my repute as a medicine man, fearing that I would cast some spell upon him, or otherwise injure him by the operation of some potent mystic medicine: he removed his quarters to the adjoining room, where he seemed to think he was safe from my incantations.

Our hunter, whose name is *No-zun-da-je*, or *He that does not dodge*, is esteemed a good hunter by his nation; but he is not a distinguished warrior, although he has been in numerous battles. He says he has killed several red skins in action, but never yet had the honour to *strike* a body. He showed us the scars of many wounds, most of which he had inflicted on himself, when in mourning for the death of his relatives and friends, by thrusting arrows through the skin and a portion of the flesh of his arm. His brother, at the same time, showed many scars which he had caused by cutting out pieces from his body with a knife, on the same occasions.

Several Omawhaws visited us on the 8th, and a party of three of them, who were in possession of a keg of whiskey, invited our hunter to accompany them, for the night, to "make his heart glad" with a portion of its contents. The Omawhaws, Otes, Missouries, and Ioways are excessively attached to this destructive liquor.

On the 9th December, Lieutenant Swift, in company with Mr. Pilcher of the Missouri Fur Company, set out on a visit to the Omawhaws. His course was first directed towards the Elk Horn river, tributary to the Platte, and afterwards along the valley of the former, to the Omawhaw encampment, which he reached at the distance of about one hundred and twenty miles. The country over which he travelled was almost entirely destitute of woodland; the surface generally cut by numerous ravines; the soil for the most part sandy, but in some instances enriched by a black loam. He returned to camp on the 23d, his companion having purchased of the Indians one hundred and thirty beaver skins, besides raccoon and deer skins.

10th. By a recent occurrence, the late treaty of peace between the Otoes and Konzas was, on the eve of being infracted. The Otoes, who were encamped for hunting near the mouth of the Platte, had four horses stolen from them about two weeks since, and subsequently ten more. These robberies were immediately attributed to the Konzas, and a war party prepared themselves to march and retaliate upon that nation. Hashea however prevented them from going, saying that their father (Major O'Fallon) had been instrumental in reconciling them to a peace with the Konzas, and it would be highly improper for them to strike a blow, without asking his opinion upon the subject. It seems more probable that the horses have been taken either by the Sauks or Ioways. The latter appears to be a faithless people; they obtained a considerable quantity of goods on credit, last fall, from the Missouri Fur Company, and now, we are informed, instead of returning to discharge their debts, they are on their way down the river to barter their beaver at Fort Osage. It is said they will inhabit their old village, on the river Des Moines, the ensuing season.

12th. Many Indians visited us yesterday and to-day, some of whom brought jerked deer meat, mockasins, &c. to exchange for their favourite drink, and for trinkets. But as we have none of the latter, and as the former is interdicted from them by our laws, we are not authorized to make any purchases. That they do contrive to get whiskey elsewhere, perhaps of the traders, we have abundant proof. Yesterday a squaw got drunk, and made much noise; but her companions, after much ado, carried her off to their encampment.

As we were cutting up a log for fuel, one of the Omawhaws seeing a knot or protuberance of the wood, suitable to form into a bowl, requested us to cut it off for him; but not choosing to gratify him in this manner, we offered the axe we were using, that he might cut it in his own way; he, however, would not accept of it, but pointed to the palm of his hand, giving us to understand that such labour would make his hand sore and hard; he then called one of his squaws, who immediately went to work, and handled the axe very dexterously. Observing several young Indians passing, I indicated to her the propriety of requesting one of them to assist her, but she laughed significantly, as if she would say—you are ironical.

The Indians are very fickle in bargaining. An Indian, some time since, exchanged his rifle for Mr. Dougherty's shot gun; yesterday he reversed the bargain, giving a pair of mockasins in return; and this morning he requested to exchange again, in which he was gratified.

A squaw offered to exchange mockasins for a couple of our military stocks. We could not conceive of what use she would apply them, but, upon inquiry, we learned she wished to ornament the crupper of her horse with them.

The stone quarry, which supplied limestone for building chimnies at camp Missouri, was situate at the distance of an hundred yards below our cantonment. The labourers that were employed in this quarry opened upon many large fissures, in which were found a number of serpents that had entered there for the purpose of hybernating. Of these, three species appear to be new.

This morning three Omawhaws were fired upon by a war party of five Ioway Indians, and two were wounded; this occured on the east side of the river, nearly opposite to our cantonment. When they fired, each one called out his name agreeably to the Indian custom. A party of Omawhaws then assembled, and pursued them about 15 miles, but without success.

Two Oto warriors, and a boy, nephew of Ishta-gre-ja, *Gray Eyes* the elder, visited us this afternoon. They have been hunting on Blue-Water creek, in the neighbourhood of the Konzas hunting camps, and not distant from the village of the latter; they have been so fortunate as to take one hundred and forty beavers, the skins of which they left at their village, under the care of the son of Gray Eyes and their squaws; their business in this quarter is to look out for the best market for their peltries. They say it was certainly not the Konzas who stole the horses from their brethren, who are encamped near the confluence of the Platte. They attribute the theft to the Ioways, who, they say, are still fools, as they always have proved themselves to be.

30th. In the morning a nimbus from the north. An imperfect parhelion appeared at sunrise, consisting of three luminous spots, at about 22° distant from each other, in the horizon; one of them was the real place of the sun, and the others were to the north and south of it. As the sun ascended towards the zenith, the mock suns continued to ascend equally and parallel with it, but became gradually fainter, until they disappeared near the zenith.

Evening. A complete paraselene appeared about the moon, of the diameter of 45 degrees.

The mercury was below Zero the greater part of the day, in Fahrenheit's thermometer.

31st. Several Canadians, in the employ of the Missouri Fur Company, came this evening to dance and sing before us, agreeably to the custom of their countrymen, in celebration of the termination of the year. They were adorned with paint after the Indian manner, clothed with bison robes, and had bells attached to different parts of their dress. So completely were they disguised, that three of their employers, who happened to be present, had much difficulty in recognizing them. This dance is called *La Gineolet*, and may have had its origin in the same cause that produced our *Belshnickles*, who make their appearance on Christmas eve. We gave them what was expected, whiskey, flour, and meat.

January 6th 1820. Mr. Graham and I measured the width of the river in two places, a short distance below our cantonment, and a short distance above; the latter gave two hundred and seventy-seven and one third yards, and the former one hundred yards.

We hear the barking of the prairie wolves every night about us; they venture close to our huts; last night they ran down and killed a doe, within a short distance of our huts; this morning the remains of the carcase were found, consisting only of bones and skin.

Mr. Fontenelle, in the employ of the Missouri Fur Company, who has been absent for some time trading with one of the bands of the Omawhaws, called to-day on his return; this band had been much necessitated for food, subsisting for some time upon the fruit of the *red haws*, which the squaws sought for beneath the proper trees, under the snow. He met with some of the nation of Sioux, called Gens de Feuille by the French. They have been much thinned in numbers by a disorder, which, from the description given of it, may be the quinsy. This same band is said to have suffered much from the small pox last autumn. They were also now nearly starved for want of food; but they said if they could hold out until they arrived at Min-da-wa-cong, or Medicine lake, (on the maps Spirit lake) they would do very well, as they had there a considerable quantity of wild oats buried or *caché* as the French say.

13th. Ietan, an Oto, of whom we have before spoken, visited us today, for the purpose of getting two gunlocks mended. He left his people at the Republican fork of the Konza river, and intends as soon as he returns, to lead a party in pursuit of bisons, which he says are in plenty on the Loup fork of the Platte, about sixty miles distant from us.

14th. Ietan called this morning, and as some of our party were going to visit at Camp Missouri, he accompanied them, in order to obtain Major

O'Fallon's permission for his nation to go to war with the Konzas. He informed the agent that individuals of that nation had sometime since stolen horses from them. That one of the losers, *Big Soldier*, had gone to the Konza village to demand the horses; but seeing a number of horses belonging to that nation, when he arrived near the village, he could not resist the temptation of immediately retaliating by seizing several, and appropriating them to his own use. But, Ietan said, he thought the honour of his nation still called for war, and he solicited the acquiescence of the agent in that measure. The Major replied, that his opinion ought to have been asked previously to the retaliatory measure, which had already been prematurely taken, as they were not certain that the Konzas were the offenders, and that this ought to have been ascertained before any depredation on the Konzas had been committed. But the course which he would now advise them to pursue was, to send a deputation to the Konzas, for the purpose of ascertaining the fact, to return the Konzas' horses, and to demand their own. This course seemed satisfactory to the warrior, who, however, stated that if the Konzas attempted to steal horses from them in future, he would certainly lead a war party himself against them.

15th. Mr. Woods, of the Missouri Fur Company, has returned from a trading excursion. He reports that he saw several of the Pawnee *caches*, which had been broken open and robbed of their corn by the Omawhaws. This is by no means a rare occurrence with the Indians, but it does not appear that it has ever led to hostilities between nations; they say that when a person is in want of food, he has a right to take any he can find.

Corporal Norman, who went out this morning to kill rabbits, returned, about noon, with twenty-seven, which he had killed with single balls.

February 9th. Several Oto Indians have visited us within this day or two, and one of them, Ca-he-ga-in-ya, remained with us last night; he was finely dressed, had on a chief's coat laced with silver, and a profusion of wampum about his neck, and suspended to his ears; he departed this morning, on his way to the Omawhaws, to trade for horses.

The ice on the Missouri is sixteen inches in thickness, that on the Boyer creek fifteen and three fourths.

12th. Messrs. Dougherty, Peale, and myself, with an assistant, encamped at a pond near the Boyer to obtain fish; we cut several holes in the ice of the pond, and obtained one Otter and a number of small fishes, amongst which three species appeared to be new; several specimens were of the genus Gasterosteus.

15th. Mr. Zenoni, of the Fur Company, who departed the twenty-seventh ultimo on a trading expedition, returned, and remained with us last night. He and two men had ascended the Elk Horn about twenty-five miles higher than Mr. Swift had been, but were not successful in finding any Indians. And although they saw a few bisons and antelopes and Elks, they were not so fortunate as to kill any game for subsistence, excepting three turkeys; so that they returned in a state of considerable exhaustion, having been, for some time, on an allowance of a little maize per day. He found that the upper part of the Elk Horn had not frozen during the severe weather, but still remained open. This circumstance seems to indicate the flow of a great quantity of spring water, or water of a medium temperature, in that part of the stream, requiring time to cool in its passage, before it can congeal.

19th. The sand is blown by the violence of the wind from the sand bars of the river, so as to resemble a dense fog. We have been hitherto very well supplied with fresh meat, from game killed principally by Mr. Peale, who, on one occasion, killed two deer at a single shot and with one ball, but we are now reduced again to salt pork of a very inferior quality. The party, with the exception of myself, continue to enjoy good health.

22nd. Messrs. Dougherty and Peale returned from a hunt, having killed twelve bisons, out of a herd of several hundreds they met with near Sioux river, and brought us a seasonable supply of meat. They saw several herds of elk, and yesterday they saw swans, geese, and ducks flying up the river. A dinner and ball were given at Camp Missouri, in honour of the day, to which our party were invited.

24th. Mr. Graham and I endeavoured to ascertain the rapidity of the current of this part of the Missouri, at the present low water. We availed ourselves of a long vacancy in the ice to float a porter bottle, to which the proper specific gravity was given, by partially filling it with water, it was attached to a cord of one hundred and twenty-two feet in length; it floated this distance in six successive experiments in the following several times 1'07"—1'04"—1'07 1-2"—1'05"— 1'07"—1 07" [sic], the mean of which is 1'06 1-2" nearly, giving a velocity of 1 mile 441 yards 1 1-2 feet per hour.

By these experiments, however, the superficial current or stratum only was indicated, and as we had reason to suppose that this stratum was more impeded by friction against the inferior surface of the ice than it would be by the atmosphere it became an object to ascertain the average velocity of the different depths. With this view a staff *ten feet* long was made to float vertically, by means of a weight attached to its inferior extremity; a line of one hundred and seventy-eight feet in length was run out, by this arrangement, during the following intervals of time, in four experiments, viz. 1'21"—1'21"—1'19"—1' 21", of which the mean is 1' 20 1-2", which would seem to indicate a current of the velocity of 1 mile 893 yards 1 foot per hour. Thus the average velocity of ten feet in depth of the current of the Missouri, is greater by almost 452 yards, in a single hour, than that of a superficial stratum of about *six* inches depth, during the ice-bound state of the river. During these experiments the atmosphere was nearly calm.

25th. Cooked for dinner the entire hump of a bison, after the manner of the Indians; this favourite part of the animal was dissected from the vertebræ, after which the spinous processes were taken out, and the denuded part was covered with skin, which was firmly sewed to that of the back and sides of the hump; the hair was burned and pulled off, and the whole mass exhibiting something of a fusiform shape, was last evening placed in a hole dug in the earth for its reception, which had been previously heated by means of a strong fire in and upon it. It was now covered with cinders and earth, to the depth of about one foot, and a strong fire was made over it. In this situation it remained until it was taken up for the table to-day, when it was found to be excellent food. Mr. Lisa and family dined with us by invitation. That we have sometimes food in great sufficiency, the provision upon our table this day will sufficiently attest. It consisted of the entire bison hump, above mentioned; the rump of a bison roasted; boiled bison meat; two boiled bison tongues; the spinous processes roasted in the manner of spare ribs; sausages made of minced tender loin and fat, &c. It is true that we have no vegetables whatever; but having been so long estranged from them we scarcely regret their absence. Their place is supplied by excellent wheat flour, of which our cook prepares us bread fully equal, in point of excellence, to any that we have ever eaten. The above repast was prepared for eleven persons, of whom two were ladies. The collation was succeeded by coffee as a dessert.

February 28th. I ascertained the temperature of spring water, which, however, was somewhat exposed to the atmosphere, but in a shaded situation, and in a ravine, to be 47°; that of the atmosphere being at the same time 56°, and that of the river 32°, of Fahrenheit's scale.

Wednesday, March 8th. The Big Elk, Big Eyes, and Wash-co-mo-ne-a visted us today on their way, with their attendants, to the traders with jerked bison meat. They presented us with five large pieces. The Big Elk, principal Omawhaw chief, is much pitted with the small pox, and is of commanding presence. He speaks with great emphasis, and remarkably distinct. He observed that we must think them strange people to be thus constantly wandering about, during the cold of winter, instead of remaining comfortably housed in their village; "but," said he, "our poverty and necessities compel us to do so, in pursuit of game; yet we sometimes venture forth for our pleasure, as in the present instance, to visit the white people whom we are always delighted to see." Big Eyes is a large and remarkably muscular man. His nose is that of the European, the opposite to the Roman curve; he is second chief of the Omawhaws.

The Omawhaw chiefs remained with us the greater part of the following day, and presented us with eight more pieces of jerked meat. We presented them in return with some tobacco, &c. The Big Elk made us a considerable harangue, with all the remarkable vivacity, fluency, and nerve of Indian eloquence, in which he said that he would address me by the title of father; "and you," said he to Mr. Dougherty, "whom I know so well, I will call brother." "The Indians around," said he, "who tell the white people that they love them, speak falsely, as is proved by their killing the white people; but my nation truly love you, they have never stained their hands with the blood of a white man, and this much cannot be said by any nation of this land." He added a strong expression, that such was his attachment to us, that he believed that he should, at a future day, be a white man himself.

When they took their leave, we advised them not to visit camp Missouri, telling them, what in fact they had already been informed of, that many of the soldiers were sick; (we did not wish them to observe the extent of the malady, with which that camp was afflicted,) but Big Elk remarked, that it had been his intention to go there, and it was not fear that could prevent him; his life was at the disposal of the great Wahconda only, and he could not die before his time; "but," said he, "agreeably to your request I certainly will not go."

Of all the objects which we exhibited to the view of the chiefs, quicksilver (mercury) seemed to excite the most surprise; they weighed the vessel, in which it was contained, in their hands, dipped their fingers into it, and were surprised at the resistance which it offered to the immersion, and what appeared most singular was, that they should be withdrawn without any appearance of moisture upon them; that they might not be deceived they repeated the experiment again and again. A couple of iron nails were then thrown upon the mercury, and as these did not sink to the bottom, they pressed them down with their fingers; but finding that the nails constantly arose again to the surface, the Big Elk returned the vessel to me, saying, with a smile of pleasure strongly impressed on his strongly marked countenance, that the fluid was the Omawhaw's Wahconda.

The last load of stone, which was taken from the quarry early in December last, was prevented from reaching camp Missouri by the floating ice; the boat was driven ashore and abandoned. It was now observed floating down the river, with a large quantity of drift ice, and, when opposite our cantonment, was readily secured by Major Ketchum, without having received any injury whatever.

Major Ketchum, with a detachment of men, has been engaged for two or three days past in cutting out of the ice, three of the boats from our harbour. These, together with one, which is at Camp Missouri, are intended to convey the sick from that camp down the river to Fort Osage. Camp Missouri has been sickly, from the commencement of winter; but its situation is at this time truly deplorable. More than three hundred soldiers are, or have been sick, and nearly one hundred have died. This fatality is occasioned by the Scurvy (Scorbutus). Individuals who are seized rarely recover, as they cannot be furnished with the proper aliments; they have no vegetables, fresh meat, nor antiscorbutics, so that the patients grow daily worse, and entering the hospital is considered by them as a certain passport to the grave. Yet it is some consolation to reflect that all the science, care, and attention of the healing art have been exerted for the relief of the sufferers by Doctors Gale and Moore, as far as their present insulated situation will admit. The causes, which have been productive of all this disease, are not distinctly known, although there are many supposed ones to which it has been imputed. But it was generally remarked that the hunters, who were much employed in their avocation, and almost constantly absent from Camp Missouri, escaped the malady.

On the 19th Mr. Immel, of the Missouri Fur Company, returned from an expedition to the Sioux. During his stay in the vicinity of the pseudo volcanoes, which occur on the banks of the Missouri, a tremendous subterranean explosion occurred, which much alarmed the Indians, as well as the whites; the concussion was succeeded by a large volume of dense smoke from the aperture of the volcano, by the sinking in of a portion of the hill in the rear, and by the cracking of the ice in the river. Messrs. Peale, Swift, and Dougherty departed in a periogue yesterday, on their way to the Bowyer creek to hunt.

An igneous meteor, or Jack o' lantern was seen on the evening of the 20th, near our cantonment; it was described to me as the size of a double fist, with a caudate appendage or tail of the length of about two feet; it emitted a light of the colour of the flame of burning sulphur; it passed along the river shore nearly over the observer's head, at but a very small elevation, nearly in a right line, with an equable motion, about as rapid as the flight of a bird, and with an audible sound like the blowing of a moderate stream of air through a thicket; it was visible about one half a minute, when it crossed the river, became paler, and disappeared.

The waters of the Missouri have been as clear during the winter as ordinary rivers; the earthy matter, which they hold in suspension during the temperate and warm weather, and which every person, who views the river, remarks as characteristic of its waters, subsides as soon as the winter temperature occurs, but is again renewed in the Spring. They have been gradually more and more turbid, these two or three days past. The ice in the river broke up on the 29th ult., and entirely disappeared on the 19th instant.

Great flights of geese, swans, ducks, brant, and cranes have been passing up the river, at their usual migrating altitude above the surface of the earth; but this migration of these aquatic birds has nearly ceased.

April 5th. A war party of Omawhaws arrived at the trading house of the Missouri Fur Company. They are one of three parties, which have been for ten days past in pursuit of a war party of thirteen Sauks, who carried off a number of horses from near the Omawhaw village. They pursued the trail of the Sauks until they lost it nearly opposite to this place; they nevertheless continued the pursuit in the direction which they supposed the enemy had taken, but are now returning unsuccessful; they say they are in hopes that one of the other parties may overtake them. It seems probable that it was this same party of Sauks who fired upon a soldier on the 30th ult.

6th. The war party mentioned yesterday visited us this morning, on their way home. They danced for us, and after receiving bread, buffaloe meat, and tobacco, departed well pleased. In the afternoon another war party of eleven Omawhaws, who had also been in pursuit of the same Sauks, arrived. We were notified of their proximity by hearing their war song, and going out, we observed them at a short distance arranged in a line, from the centre of which were elevated two handsome streamers, which, upon their approach, we found to be two long lances, to which feathers of different colours, fancifully arranged, were attached. The partizan advanced, and made us a speech, as usual, in which he began an account of their adventures, and concluded by praising the kindness of the whites, their hospitality, and their greatness in arts and arms. This address being well understood to aim at food and lodging, though neither of these were mentioned, we supplied them with bison meat, bread, and maize, and invited them to remain with us during the night to rest themselves in comfort and safety. They immediately sat down, and, the food being portioned out by one of the warriors, they proceeded to eat with the appearance of such appetites as convinced us that their fast had been of long duration. In conversation during the evening the partizan said that they had followed a considerable trail, supposing that the Sauks had taken that direction; that they observed stakes stuck in the ground at certain distances, and the trees *blazed* as far as they went upon that trail. He inquired if we knew the reason of such marks; he was then informed that it was to indicate the course of a road which was to be made in that direction, and that if he had travelled far enough upon the trail he would have met with towns of white people, who would have treated him well. After musing sometime, he observed, that they had travelled a good distance on that rout, and having occasion to deviate a short distance from it, they found when they returned that a white man and three horses had passed along during their absence; (this was Lieutenant Fields, the express,) they immediately dispatched two of their young men back to follow him, and to learn if he had met the fugitive Sauks; but they could not overtake him. "We continued on," said *Naugh-ken-ne* (or the *Left hand,*) "with all speed; but at length, being almost famished, we were necessitated to halt and hunt; of course we gave over the pursuit. Not wishing to return to our nation without obtaining some trophy, we resolved to go to Nishnebottona in order to strike upon the Ioways, who, we had been informed, were at that place; but when we arrived there, we had the mortification to learn that they were gone; we must therefore, return without these poor young men having any opportunity to distinguish themselves." "Did you not," we asked, "make peace with the Ioways last season?" "Yes, it is true we made a kind of peace with them, but you know they are bad men; we do not like them; the whites do not like them; perhaps it was a party of that nation, and not Sauks, that stole our horses, and you know it was very hard to be obliged, after all our difficulties and starvations, to return to our people without either scalps or horses. We wished to obtain some trophy that should repay us for our toils." In the evening they sang for our amusement a number of tunes, whilst two or three danced as well as they could in our small chamber. A negro belonging to the Fur Company coming in on an errand, they spoke of him as the *black whiteman,* and one of them jokingly said, he was a Wasabajinga, or little black bear.

The Indians departed early on the 7th, with many thanks for the attention they had received. Before they went, they presented to us a wild cat, which they had shot, but we advised them to keep it to eat on the way home, upon which they thanked us for it, as if they had never owned it.

11th. We learn that a third war party of Omawhaws, who departed in pursuit of the Sauks before either of the others, were met by a strong party of that nation, who were on their way to the Omawhaw village; they however escaped from them with the loss of one man killed and several wounded; the loss of the Sauks is not known. The party speak highly of one of their number, a boy of twelve years, who, at a critical juncture of the engagement, ran up to several of the enemy and flashed his gun three times at them; he escaped unhurt.

Western Engineer at Council Bluffs, T.R. Peale, February, 1820, pencil.

INTERLUDE

FOLLOWING chapter 9, chapters 10-15 present information on the "Omawhaws,"
much of it gathered from John Dougherty, who related "such points in their manners,
habits, opinions and history, as we had no opportunity of observing ourselves." Some idea
of the topics discussed can be gained from the chapter titles: 10, "Account of the
Omawhaws—Their Manners and Customs and religious rites—Historical notices of
Blackbird, late principal chief."; 11, "Further account of the Omawhaws—Of their
marriages—of infancy, and the relationship of parents and children—Their old age."; 12,
"Diseases—Medical and Surgical knowledge—Drunkenness, and other vices—Ideas of
God, and of a future state—Superstition, and practice of the Magi—Expiatory tortures.";
13, "Death—Mourning for the Deceased—Physical Character—Senses—Manufactures
and Arts—Domestic and Warlike Implements—War."; 14, "War—Negociation for
peace—Revenge—Self-esteem—Hospitality—Mimickry."; and 15, "Tribes and Bands—
Fabulous Legends—Wit—Ninnegahe or mixed tobacco—Dances—Otoes—Migrations—
Language."

Chapter 16 contains one of the most dramatic episodes in the entire Account,
centering around the heroic actions of the handsome Pawnee Loup chief Petalesharoo, who
later served as the model for Hard-Heart in The Prairie. *On April 20, 1820, a sizeable*
party led by Major O'Fallon set out from Engineer Cantonment to visit the villages of the

Grand Pawnees and the Pawnee Loups. On April 27, having visited the Grand Pawnees, the group traveled to within two miles of the Loups, when they were requested to halt so that the chiefs would have time to receive them properly. The story continues in the Account:

After waiting a short time, we observed, at the distance of a mile before us, a great number of mounted Indians emerging suddenly, apparently from the plain itself, for we could not then see a ravine that had previously concealed them from our view. They immediately began to ride in various directions, and to perform numerous evolutions until the whole were arranged in a widely extended line. These rapid movements, which attracted our attention from other objects, having ceased, we perceived a small body of men in front, whose movements were independent of the others, and who were advancing at a moderate pace. When all were formed, they set forwards, slowly at first, but gradually increasing their speed as they approached, until they surrounded us at a full charge. It is impossible by description to do justice to the scene of savage magnificence that was now displayed. Between three and four hundred mounted Indians, dressed in their richest habiliments of war, were rushing around us in every direction, with streaming feathers, war weapons, and with loud shouts and

Indians, T.R. Peale, February, 1820, pencil.

Pawnee Council, Samuel Seymour, watercolor.

"Ottoes," T.R. Peale, May 1820, watercolor.

Pronghorn antelope, T.R. Peale, June 19, 1820,
watercolor.

Indian on horseback, T.R. Peale, February, 1820, watercolor and pencil.

Bison hunt, T.R. Peale, February, 1820, watercolor and ink.

"Cows," T.R. Peale, February, 1820, watercolor.

Badgers, T.R. Peale, 1819, watercolor.

Fox, T.R. Peale, October, 1819, watercolor.

Jaw structure for Pocket Gopher, T.R. Peale,
July 21, 1819, pencil.

Mole and vole, T.R. Peale, 1819, watercolor and ink.

Sandhill Crane, T.R. Peale, 1820, watercolor.

Watercolors of birds executed by T.R. Peale at Engineer Cantonment, 1820.

Distant view of the Rocky Mountains, Samuel Seymour, engraving.

yells. The few whom we had observed in advance of the main body, and whom, as we came near, we recognized to be the chief men, presented a perfect contrast to the others in their slow movements, and simplicity of dress. Courtesy obliged us to shake hands with each individual, as they came to us in succession for that purpose, nor was a single soldier of our train forgotten on this occasion by any one of them. They expressed great satisfaction on account of our visit, rubbing their breasts in token of the sincerity of this pleasure. Many remarked that the nation had been mourning for their grievous losses in a recent battle with an enemy, but that now grief should give place to rejoicing. Major O'Fallon addressed the Indians as usual, after which we again moved on towards the village. Latelesha, the grand chief, perceiving that the division of his warriors that were on our left, raised some dust on the march, ordered them all to leeward, that we might not be incommoded. Almost from the beginning of this interesting fete, our attention had been attracted to a young man who seemed to be the leader or partizan of the warriors. He was about twenty-three years of age, of the finest form, tall, muscular, exceedingly graceful, and of a most prepossessing countenance. His head dress of war eagles' feathers, descended in a double series upon his back like wings, to his saddle croup; his shield was highly decorated, and his long lance was ornamented by a plaited casing of red and blue cloth. On inquiring of the interpreter, our admiration was augmented by learning that he was no other than Petalesharoo, with whose name and character we were already familiar. He is the most intrepid warrior of the nation, eldest son of Latelesha, destined as well by mental and physical qualifications, as by his distinguished birth, to be the future leader of this people. Seeing that his father had taken a place in our cavalcade on the left of Major O'Fallon, he rode up on his right to the exclusion of a brave officer who had previously occupied that situation, and who now regarded him with an apparently stern aspect, but in which there was perhaps more of admiration than of irritation at this unexpected intrusion. The young chief caught the look, and retorted with an eye that seemed never to have been averted through fear. The name of Petalesharoo is connected with the abolition of a custom formerly prevalent in this nation, at which humanity shudders.

The Pawnee Loups heretofore exhibited the singular anomaly, amongst the American natives, of a people addicted to the inhuman, superstitious rite, of making propitiatory offerings of human victims to Venus, the *Great Star*. The origin of this sanguinary sacrifice is unknown; probably it existed previously to their intercourse with the white traders. This solemn ceremony was performed annually, and immediately preceded their horticultural operations, for the success of which it appears to have been instituted. A breach of this duty, the performance of which they believed to be required by the Great Star, it was supposed would be succeeded by the total failure of their crops of maize, beans, and pumpkins, and the consequent total privation of their vegetable food.

To obviate a national calamity so formidable, any person was at liberty to offer up a prisoner of either sex, that by his prowess in war he had become possessed of.

The devoted individual was clothed in the gayest and most costly attire; profusely supplied with the choicest food, and constantly attended by the magi, who anticipated all his wants, cautiously concealed from him the real object of their sedulous attentions, and endeavoured to preserve his mind in a state of cheerfulness, with the view of promoting obesity, and thereby rendering the sacrifice more acceptable to their Ceres.

When the victim was thus sufficiently fattened for their purpose, a suitable day was appointed for the performance of the rite, that the whole nation might attend.

The victim was bound to a cross, in presence of the assembled multitude, when a solemn dance was performed, and after some other ceremonies, the warrior, whose prisoner he had been, cleaved his head with the tomahawk, and his speedy death was insured by numerous archers, who penetrated his body with their arrows.

A trader informed us that the squaws cut pieces of flesh from the deceased, with which they greased their hoes; but this was denied by another who had been present at one of these sacrifices. However this may be, the ceremony was believed to have called down a blessing upon their labours of the field, and they proceeded to planting without delay.

The present mild and humane chief of the nation, Latelesha, or Knife-chief, had long regarded this sacrifice as an unnecessary and cruel exhibition of power, exercised upon unfortunate and defenceless individuals, whom they were bound to protect, and he vainly endeavoured to abolish it by philanthropic admonitions.

An Ietan woman who was brought captive into the village, was doomed to the Great Star by the warrior, whose property she had become by the fate of war. She underwent the usual preparations, and, on the appointed day, was led to the cross, amidst a great concourse of people, as eager, perhaps, as their civilized fellow men, to witness the horrors of an execution. The victim was bound to the cross with thongs of skin, and the usual ceremonies being performed, her dread of a more terrible death was about to be terminated by the tomahawk and the arrow. At this critical juncture, Petalesharoo (son of the Knife-chief) stepped forward into the area, and in a hurried but firm manner declared that it was his father's wish to abolish this sacrifice; that for himself, he had presented himself before them, for the purpose of laying down his life upon the spot, or of releasing the victim. He then cut the cords which bound her to the cross, carried her swiftly through the crowd to a horse, which he presented to her, and having mounted another himself, he conveyed her beyond the reach of immediate pursuit; when, after having supplied her with food, and admonishing her to make the best of her way to her own nation, which was at the distance of at least four hundred miles, he was constrained to return to his village. The emancipated Ietan had, however, the good fortune, on her journey of the subsequent day, to meet with a war party of her own people, by whom she was conveyed to her family in safety.

This daring deed would, almost to a certainty, have terminated in an unsuccessful attempt, under the arm of any other warrior, and Petalesharoo was, no doubt, indebted for this successful and noble achievement to the distinguished renown, which his feats of chivalry had already gained for him, and which commanded the high respect of all his rival warriors.

Following chapter 16, with its description of Petalesharoo's feat, the Account *continues with an appendix containing a list of the animals "observed at Engineer Cantonment, or at other indicated places, on our journey to that post"; a list of "Indian Language of Signs"; and a section on speeches of the Pawnees, Pawnee Loups, and Pawnee Republicans at Engineer Cantonment in October 1819. Chapter 1 of 1820 (chapter 17 in volume 1 of the Philadelphia edition) then begins with a description of the May journey of Long, James, and Bell from St. Louis to Engineer Cantonment and continues with an account of the preparations for the departure of the party in June.*

Deer, T.R. Peale, February, 1820, pencil.

1 8 2 0

CHAPTER I

Journey by land from St. Louis to Council Bluff—Grand River—
Plains at the sources of the Little Platte, the Nishnebottona, &c.—
Departure of the Expedition from Engineer Cantonment.

... IN the early part of June, 1820, arrangements were completed for the departure of the Exploring Expedition from their winter cantonment near Council Bluff. By an order of the Honourable Secretary of War, dated 28th February, Major Long had been instructed to explore the country from the Missouri westward to the Rocky Mountains, and thence proceeding southward along the base of these mountains to the Arkansa, to despatch a division of his party down that river. The following orders were issued by Major Long, briefly sketching the proposed route, and assigning appropriate duties to each individual of the party.

Engineer Cantonment, Council Bluff
June 1st, 1820

147

Orders.

Agreeably to the instructions of the Honourable Secretary of War, the further progress of the Exploring Expedition up the Missouri is arrested during the present season. By the same authority an excursion, by land, to the source of the river Platte, and thence by way of the Arkansa and Red rivers to the Mississippi, is ordered. The Expedition will accordingly proceed on this duty as soon as practicable, and be governed by the order of the 31st March, 1819, issued at the United States' Arsenal, near Pittsburgh, so far as it may be applicable. The duties therein assigned to Major Biddle will be performed by Captain J. R. Bell attached to the expedition by order of the War Department, with the exception of those parts which relate to the manners, customs, and traditions of the various savage tribes which we may pass. The duties thus excepted will be performed by Mr. Say. The duties assigned to Dr. Baldwin and Mr. Jessup, by the order alluded to, will be performed by Dr. E. James, employed for these purposes by the sanction of the Secretary of War. In these duties are excepted those parts which relate to Comparative Anatomy, and the diseases, remedies, &c. known amongst the Indians; which will also be performed by Mr. Say.

Lieutenant Graham will take charge of the United States' steam boat Western Engineer, and proceed down the Missouri to the Mississippi with the remaining part of the crew originally attached to the boat, on the performance of duties assigned him by special order.

The detachment from the rifle regiment, attached to the Expedition by order from the commanding officer of the 9th military department, will accompany the expedition in their route from this place to Belle Point on the Arkansa, under the immediate command of Lieutenant Swift, who will inspect daily their arms and accoutrements, and report their condition to the commanding officer. He will receive such instructions from the commanding officer as occasion may require in relation to the discharge of his duties.

Guides, interpreters, hunters, and others attached to the expedition, will perform such duties as may be assigned, from time to time, by the commanding officer.

The duties of the expedition being arduous, and the objects in view difficult of attainment, the hardships and exposures to be encountered, requiring zealous and obstinate perseverance, it is confidently expected, that all embarked in the enterprize will contribute every aid in their power, tending to a successful and speedy termination of the contemplated tour.

The party, as now arranged, consisted of the following persons:

S. H. Long, Maj. U. S. Topographical Engineers, commanding the expedition.

J. R. Bell, Captain Lt. Artillery, to act as Journalist.

Lt. W. H. Swift, assistant Topographer, commanding guard.

Thos. Say, Zoologist, &c.

E. James, Botanist, Geologist, and Surgeon.

T. R. Peale, assistant Naturalist.

Saml. Seymour, Landscape Painter.

Stephen Julien, Interpreter, French and Indian.

H. Dougherty, Hunter.

D. Adams, Spanish Interpreter.

Z. Wilson, Baggage Master.

Oakley and Duncan, Engagees.

Corporal Parish, and six privates of the U. S. Army.

To these we expected an addition, on our arrival at the Pawnee villages, of two Frenchmen, to serve as guides and interpreters, one of them having already been engaged.

Twenty-eight horses and mules had been provided, one for each individual of the party, and eight for carrying packs. Of these, six were the property of the United States, being furnished by the commanding officer at Camp Missouri; the remaining sixteen were supplied by Maj. Long, and others of the party. Our saddles, and other articles of equipage, were of the rudest kind, being, with few exceptions, such as we had purchased from the Indians, or constructed ourselves.

Our outfit comprised the following articles, of provisions, Indian goods, &c.; viz. 150lb. of pork, 500lb. of biscuit, 3 bushels of parched corn meal, 5 gallons of whiskey, 25lb. coffee, 30lb. sugar, and a small quantity of salt, 5lb. vermillion, 2lb. beads, 2 gross of knives, 1 gross of combs, 3 doz. fire steels, 300 flints, 1 doz. gun worms, 2 gross of hawk's bells, 2 doz. mockasin awls, 1 doz. scissors, 6 doz. looking glasses, 30lb. tobacco, and a few trinkets, 2 axes, several hatchets, forage bags, canteens, bullet-pouches, powder horns, tin canisters, skin canoes, packing skins, pack cords, and some small packing boxes for insects, &c.

The gentlemen of the party were supplied with such instruments as were deemed indispensably requisite in their several pursuits. The instruments for topographical purposes were, three travelling, and several pocket compasses; one sextant, with radius of five inches; one snuff box sextant; one portable horizon with glass frame and mercurial trough; one and an half pounds mercury, in case of boxwood; two small thermometers; several blank books, port folios, &c.

The hunters, interpreters, and attendants were furnished with rifles or muskets; the soldiers were armed exclusively with rifles, and suitably equipped. Our stock of ammunition amounted in all to about 30 pounds of powder, 20 of balls, and 40 of lead, with a plentiful supply of flints, and some small shot.

Several of the Indians about Council Bluff, to whom our proposed route had been explained, and who had witnessed our preparations, affected to laugh at our temerity, in attempting what they said we should never be able to accomplish. They represented some part of the country, through which we intended to travel, as so entirely destitute of water and grass, that neither ourselves nor our horses could be subsisted while passing it. Barony Vasquez, who accompanied Captain Pike in his expedition to the sources of the Arkansa, assured us there was no probability we could avoid the attacks of hostile Indians, who infested every part of the country. The assault which had been recently made by a party of the Sauks and Foxes, upon a trading boat belonging to Messrs. Pratte and Vasquez, on the Missouri above Council Bluff, in which one man was killed, and several wounded, had at this time spread considerable terror among those in any degree exposed to the hostilities of the Indians.

With these prospects, and with the very inadequate outfit above described, which was the utmost our united means enabled us to furnish, we departed from Engineer Cantonment, at 11 o'clock, on the 6th of June.

The path leading to the Pawnee villages runs in a direction a little south of west from the cantonment, and lies across a tract of high and barren prairie for the first ten miles. At this distance it crosses the Papillon, or Butterfly creek, a small stream discharging into the Missouri, three miles above the confluence of the Platte. Lieutenant Graham and Mr. J. Dougherty accompanied us about five miles on our way; we were also met by Lieutenant Talcott from Camp Missouri, who crossed the bluffs on foot to take leave of us. Much delay was occasioned, as we passed along, by the derangement of the packs, the obstinacy of the mules, and the want of dexterity and experience in our engagees; we however arrived early in the afternoon at the Papillon, where we encamped.

The Papillon, although it traverses a considerable extent of country, was at this time but a trifling stream. Its channel is narrow, the banks steep, and like many other streams, which have their whole course in these arid plains, it is nearly destitute of water, except in rainy seasons.

During the night some rain fell, but as we were furnished with three tents, sufficiently large to shelter all our party, we experienced little inconvenience from the storm. Our baggage was also effectually protected, being laid in heaps, and covered with bear-skins; which were also spread over it when placed upon the pack-horses, during our march by day.

We had each two small blankets, which were carried upon our horses, one being placed under the saddle, and the other upon it. These, with the addition, in some instances, of a great coat, or a blanket-capot, and a valise or a pair of holsters, to supply the place of a pillow, were our only articles of bedding.

On the morning of the 7th a new disposition was made, in relation to the pack-horses, a man being appointed to attend particularly to each. We break-fasted, and recommenced our journey at an early hour, and moving forward at an easy pace, arrived about ten o'clock at the Elk-horn, a considerable river, tributary to the Platte. On the preceding evening, we had been joined at our camp by a party of three or four Frenchmen, on their way to a hunting camp of the Omawhaws to trade. We purchased of them two small brass kettles, to com-plete our supply of camp furniture. One of these men had been of Pratte and Vasquez's party, at the time of the late attack, and had received, in that affair, a wound in the back from a rifle ball, which was yet unhealed. In the morning they accompanied us to the Elk-horn, where the wounded Frenchman was one of the first to strip and plunge into the river. Surprising accounts are given of the hardihood, and patience under suffering, manifested by the Indians; but we have rarely seen one of them exhibit a more striking instance of insensibility to pain, than this Frenchman.

The Elk-horn, called *Wa-ta-tung-ya* by the Otoes, is, where we crossed it, about thirty yards wide, and during a great part of the year, too deep and rapid to admit of being forded. At this time our horses were barely able to keep their feet, in crossing the deepest part of the channel. Our heavy baggage was ferried across in a portable canoe, consisting of a single bison hide, which we carried constantly with us. Its construction is extremely simple; the margin of the hide being pierced with several small holes, admits a cord, by which it is drawn into the form of a shallow basin. This is placed upon the water, and is kept sufficiently distended by the baggage which it receives; it is then towed or pushed across. A canoe of this kind will carry from four to five hundred pounds. The squaws, who are exceedingly expert in this sort of nagivation, transport not only their baggage, but their children, and sometimes adults, across large rivers, in these canoes and with the most perfect safety. They place their children on the baggage, and convey the whole across the stream, by swimming themselves, and urging their charge before them to the opposite shore. It is rare that any unpleasant accident occurs in this primitive mode of ferrying. The Elk-horn enters the Platte about fifty miles above the confluence of that river and the Missouri. Its whole course is through a country nearly destitute of timber. The low plains which extend along its banks have a fertile soil; but the want of timber opposes a serious obstacle to their settlement.

The soil and climate here are so entirely similar to those of the country about Grand river and the Little Platte, already described, that no change in the vegetable productions could be expected. A species of onion, with a root about as large as an ounce ball, and bearing a conspicuous umbel of purple flowers, is very abundant about the streams, and furnished a valuable addition to our bill of fare.

Soon after crossing the Elk-horn we entered the valley of the Platte, which presented the view of an unvaried plain, from three to eight miles in width, and extending more than one hundred miles along that river, being a vast expanse of prairie, or natural meadow, without a hill or other inequality of surface, and with scarce a tree or a shrub to be seen upon it. The woodlands, occupying the islands in the Platte, bound it on one side; the river-hills, low and gently sloped, terminate it on the other.

At about 3 o'clock P.M. a party of ten Indians were seen crossing the plain, towards the Platte, at a great distance before us. Soon after we arrived at a small creek, where was some scattered timber: here we determined to halt for the night, being informed by our guide that we would meet with no wood for twenty miles beyond.

As Indians had been seen in the afternoon, and we were aware of their being still in our neighbourhood, it was thought proper to stake the horses as near as possible to the camp, and to station two sentinels, who were to be relieved during the night.

In our encampment we observed the following order. The three tents were pitched in a right line, all fronting in the same direction. In advance of these, at the distance of four feet, our baggage was arranged in six heaps one at the right, and one at the left of the entrance of each tent, and protected from the weather by bear-skins, thrown over them. This disposition was made, not only for the convenience of the party, but that our baggage, in case of an attack of the Indians, might serve as a kind of breastwork, behind which we might be, in some measure, sheltered from danger. At any rate, having our baggage thus arranged, we should know where to find it, and where to rally, in any emergency by day or night.

On the ensuing morning, (8th,) we continued our journey along the north side of the valley of the Platte, at the distance of four or five miles from the river, the direction of our course South, 85° West, which we followed near twenty miles.

In all our marches we observed the following order. Capt. Bell, mounted on a horse whose gate was regular and uniform, and well calculated for the estimation of distances, preceded the party, attended by our guide.—The soldiers and attendants, formed into two squads, for the better management of the pack horses, followed in single file.—The scientific gentlemen occupied any part of the line that best suited their convenience.—Major Long followed in the rear, for the purpose of superintending the re-adjustment of deranged packs, and urging any disposed to linger, to the observance of a close order of march; a duty attended with no inconsiderable trouble and perplexity.

Though our route lay at the distance of several miles from the Platte, we could distinctly see the narrow and interrupted line of timber which grows along its course, and, occasionally, we had a transient view of the river itself, spreading like an expansive lake, and embosoming innumerable islands. About eighteen miles from our encampment, our course led us into the valley of a small river, called La petite Coquille or Muscleshell creek, which we ascended six miles, not deviating from the course we had taken. In the middle of the day we encountered a violent thunder-storm without dismounting from our horses. The plain about us, for a great distance, was destitute of timber, and so level that our party formed the most prominent object in an extent of several miles. It is not surprising that, in this situation, we were a little startled at seeing the lightning strike upon the ground, at the distance of two hundred yards from us. We could not have been deceived, in relation to this appearance, as we distinctly saw the water and mud thrown several feet into the air by the shock. The storm was so violent that, notwithstanding all our care, we could not prevent our baggage from being wet. We crossed the Coquille six miles above the place where it enters the valley of the Platte. This we effected with some difficulty, the banks being steep and muddy, and immediately afterwards encamped to dry our baggage.

The Coquille is about eight yards across; its bed muddy, and the current moderate. Its course is circuitous, traversing some inconsiderable tracts of fertile and well wooded bottom land: in one of these our camp was placed. The night was warm and the mosquitoes swarming in inconceivable multitudes.

Our baggage had been wet on the preceding day, and again by a heavy shower in the night: as the morning was cloudy, we remained in camp for some time, and attempted to dry out clothes and blankets by a large fire. After breakfasting we again got upon our horses, and, travelling nearly southwest, arrived in the afternoon at the valley of the Wolf river, or Loup fork of the Platte.

This river is called by the Indians the Little Missouri, on account of its resemblance, in the velocity of its current, the turbidness of its waters, and other respects, to that river.

Its sources are in the country of the Poncaras, opposite those of the Quicurre. Like the Platte, its immediate valley is a broad and woodless plain, almost without any perceptible unevenness of surface, and bounded on each side by parallel ranges of low and barren hills.

During our ride, as we were approaching the Loup fork, we met two Pawnee Indians, handsomely mounted, and, as they informed us, on their way to dance the calumet dance with the Omawhaws. We gave them a small quantity of tobacco, and they departed, appearing highly pleased. In the fertile grounds, along the valley of the Loup fork, we observed several plants which we had not before seen: among these was one belonging to the family of the *Malvaceæ*, with a large tuberous root which is soft and edible, being by no means ungrateful to the taste. We observed also the downy spike of the rabbit's-foot plaintain (Plantago *Lagopus,* Ph.) intermixed with the short grasses of the prairie. The long flowered Puccoon, (Batschia *longiflora,* N.) a larger and more beautiful plant than the B. *canescens* is here frequent. As we proceed westward, some changes are observed in the character of the soil and the aspect of vegetation. The Larkspurs and Lichnedias, (species of Phlox and Delphinium,) so common and beautiful in all the country between St. Louis and Council Bluff, are succeeded by several species of Milk vetch, some Vicias, and the superb Sweet pea (Lathyrus *polymorphus*). Every step of our progress to the west brought us upon a less fertile soil. We had as yet seen no game except a few antelopes, too wild and watchful to be taken without much trouble. In the low prairies we saw several curlews and marbled godwits, with their young; Bartram's sand-piper was also very frequent.

A little before sun-set we crossed Grape creek, a small and rapid stream of clear water, and soon after arrived at the Loup fork, where we encamped. The banks of this river are of a fine white sand, and are elevated no more than about eight feet above the surface of the stream, at a time of low water. It does not however appear that the low plains, contiguous to the Loup fork, are at any season inundated, the channel being sufficiently wide, and the current rapid enough to discharge all the water, which may at any time be brought down from above.

In the evening, and on the following morning, observations were taken to ascertain the magnetic variation, which was found to be 13 1/2° east.

On the morning of the 10th, we crossed Beaver creek, six miles southwest of our encampment. Here we were compelled to carry our baggage by hand, the creek being too deep and muddy to admit risking it on the pack-horses.

In fording this difficult stream, we had the misfortune to lose an important part of the lock of an air-gun, and as there were no means of replacing the lost article, it was determined to send back the gun, from the Pawnee villages by one of the traders, who was soon to return to the Missouri.

Whilst we were encamped at this spot, being detained by a heavy shower, three Frenchmen, and two Indians, arrived at the ford, on their way to the Pawnee villages. They told us they had eaten nothing since they left the Missouri. One of the Frenchmen brought a letter from lieutenant Graham, and a box containing a quantity of vaccine virus, transmitted to the exploring party, for the purpose of introducing vaccination among the Indians. The box alluded to, had been sent to the war department, by Mr. Sylvanus Fancher, a gentleman in Connecticut, and forwarded to the commanding officer of the expedition. It contained a considerable quantity of virus, carefully enclosed in a variety of packing apparatus, together with instructions relative to the disposition and application of it. But as it was not transmitted till after the departure of the expedition, from Pittsburgh, it had been forwarded by mail to St. Louis, whence it was conveyed up the Missouri, by a gentleman of the military expedition, under Colonel Atkinson. Unfortunately, the keel-boat, on board of which it had been deposited, was wrecked in ascending the river, and the box and its contents, although saved from the wreck, was thoroughly drenched, and the virus completely ruined. It was received three or four weeks after the catastrophe just mentioned, and was still drenched with water.

The Frenchmen, had, on their way, caught a horse, belonging to Mr. J. Dougherty, and intended for the use of his brother, who was of our party. He had escaped several weeks previous, from Engineer Cantonment, and since that time had been wandering in the prairies. This formed a valuable addition to our stock of horses, as a number of them were already unfit for service, on account of sore backs.

The Frenchmen and Indians were supplied with provisions from our packs, and proceeded immediately on their way, intending to reach the Pawnee villages the same evening.

At a late hour in the afternoon we resumed our journey, and at the distance of four miles from Beaver creek, crossed the creek of Souls, a small and muddy stream, in which two of the pack-horses fell, again wetting our baggage.

At sunset we arrived at a small creek, eleven miles distant from the village of the Grand Pawnees, where we encamped.

On the following morning, having arranged the party according to rank, and given the necessary instructions for the preservation of order, we proceeded forward and in a short time came in sight of the first of the Pawnee villages. The trace on which we had travelled since we left the Missouri, had the apppearance of being more and more frequented as we approached the Pawnee towns; and here, instead of a single footway, it consisted of more than twenty parallel paths, of similar size and appearance. At a few miles distance from the village, we met a party of eight or ten squaws with hoes and other instruments of agriculture, on their way to the corn plantations. They were accompanied by one young Indian, but in what capacity, whether as assistant, protector, or task master, we were not informed. After a ride of about three hours, we arrived before the village, and despatched a messenger to inform the chief of our approach.

Answer was returned that he was engaged with his chiefs and warriors at a medicine feast, and could not, therefore, come out to meet us. We were soon surrounded by a crowd of women and children, who gazed at us with some expressions of astonishment, but as no one appeared to welcome us to the village, arrangements were made for sending on the horses and baggage to a suitable place for encampment, while Major Long, with several gentlemen, who wished to accompany him, entered the village.

The party which accompanied Major Long, after groping about some time, and traversing a considerable part of the village, arrived at the lodge of the principal chief. Here we were again informed that *Tarrarecawaho*, with all the principal men of the village, were engaged at a medicine feast.

Notwithstanding his absence, some mats were spread for us upon the ground, in the back part of the lodge. Upon these we sat down, and after waiting some time, were presented with a large wooden dish of hominy, or boiled maize. In this was a single spoon of the horn of a bison, large enough to hold half a pint, which, being used alternately by each of the party, soon emptied the dish of its contents.

The interior of this capacious dwelling was dimly lighted from a hole at the top, through which the sun's rays, in a defined column, fell aslant upon the earthen floor. Immediately under this hole, which is both window and chimney, is a small depression in the centre of the floor, where the fire is made; but the upper parts of the lodge are constantly filled with smoke; adding much to the air of gloominess and obscurity, which prevail within. The furniture of the Long-hair's lodge consisted of mats, ingeniously woven of grass or rushes, bison robes, wooden dishes, and one or two small brass kettles. In the part of the lodge immediately opposite the entrance, we observed a rude niche in the wall, which was occupied by a bison skull. It appeared to have been exposed to the weather, until the flesh and periosteum had decayed, and the bones had become white.

In this lodge we saw a number of squaws of different ages, but all as we supposed the wives of Long-hair. This chief, who is somehat of a Turk in his domestic establishment, has eleven wives, nine of whom are quiet occupants of the same lodge. He has but ten children.

Our visit to this village seemed to excite no great degree of attention. Among the crowd, who surrounded us before we entered the village, we observed several young squaws rather gaily dressed, being wrapped in clean and new blankets, and having their heads ornamented with wreaths of gnaphalium and the silvery leaves of the prosalea canescens. On the tops of the lodges we also saw some display of finery, which we supposed to have been made on account of our visit. Flags were hoisted, shields, and bows, and quivers, were suspended in conspicuous places, scalps were hung out; in short, the people appeared to have exposed whatever they possessed, in the exhibition of which, they could find any gratification of their vanity. Aside from these, we received no distinguished marks of attention from the Grand Pawnees.

After spending an hour or two at their village, we retired to our camp about a mile distant. Here we were shortly afterwards visited by Long-hair, the Malicious chief, and several others. They had with them a young Spaniard, who interpreted Pawnee and French, by whose means we were able to communicate freely with them. They offered some apology, for not receiving us at their village, saying, they could not have left their medicine feast, if the village had been on fire. We caused our intended route to be explained to them, with the objects we had in view, in undertaking so long a journey. To this they answered, that our undertaking was attended with great difficulty and danger, that the country about the head of the Platte, was filled with bands of powerful and ferocious Indians, who would lose no opportunity to attack and injure us, that in some parts of our route, we must suffer from want of water, in others there was no game. In short, said the Grand chief, "you must have long hearts, to undertake such a journey with so weak a force; hearts that would reach from the earth to the heavens." These representations would, it is probable, have had some effect upon our spirits, had we not supposed, they were made entirely for that purpose. The Pawnees undoubtedly hoped to alarm our fears to such a degree, that we should be induced to relinquish our proposed journey; their design being to deter us from passing through their hunting grounds, and perhaps hoping by these means to possess themselves of a larger share of the articles, we had provided for Indian presents.

Finding our determination was not to be shaken, they advised us to ascend the Loup Fork, instead of taking the route by the Platte, which we had mentioned. This advice, and the statement by which it was accompanied, that there were no bisons on the Platte, we suspected of originating from the same motive, which had induced them to make the representation above mentioned; it was not, therefore, allowed in any manner to influence our determination.

After collecting from them what information we could obtain, relative to the country to the west, we endeavoured to dismiss them with some presents. They were not, however, easily to be satisfied—they importuned us for tobacco, and other articles, which the limited nature of our supplies would not allow us to give, as we expected soon to meet with Indians, whose good will it would be more important for us to purchase.

Our camp was something more than a mile from the village. The intervening space, as well as the plain for a great extent on all sides, was covered with great numbers of horses, intermixed with men, women, and children. The men having no serious business, pass much of their time in the open air, either on horseback, or engaged at some game of hazard.

The Pawnees are expert horsemen, and delight in the exhibition of feats of skill and adroitness. Many of their horses are branded, but this is the case with such only as are taken in their predatory excursions against the Spaniards of New Mexico, or the south-western Indians; the branded horses all come originally from the Spaniards. It does not appear, that the Indians have any method of affixing distinctive marks to their animals. Each Indian has usually but a very limited number of horses, which are as well known, and as universally acknowledged to be his, as the children or other members of his family. Some of the finest horses which we observed, were ornamented with gaudy trappings, and furniture of Spanish manufacture.

We spent some time in attempting to explain to the chiefs, the nature and effects of the vaccine disease, and in endeavouring to persuade them to influence some of their people to submit to inoculation; but in this we were unsuccessful. It is now several years, since the ravages of the small pox have been experienced among them, and it is probable they feel an undue degree of security against its future visitations. We were, however, by no means confident, that they comprehended what we said on the subject of vaccination, if they did it is not probable their confidence in us was sufficient to induce them to receive it as truth. All we were able to effect, was to persuade the young Spanish interpreter, to allow us to make use of his arm, to show the Indians that the proposed operation was by no means a formidable one. With the same intention, the operation was performed upon Major Long's arm, and that of Mr. H. Dougherty.

We were not very solicitous to make the experiment among them, our virus, as before remarked, being unfit for use. We were accordingly afraid of impairing their confidence in the remedy.

In the plain about the village, we noticed several little groups of squaws, busily engaged in dressing the skins of the bison for robes. When the processes of tanning and dressing are completed, and the inner surface of the skin dry, figures are traced upon it with vermillion, and other showy colours.

These are designed as ornaments, but are sometimes a record of important facts. The story of a battle is often depicted in this way, and the robe of a warrior is frequently decorated with the narration in pictures, of some of his exploits.

During the afternoon our camp was somewhat thronged by the Indians, offering to trade horses, and squaws proposing barters, but at night they withdrew towards their village, and all remained quiet.

As the day began to dawn on the following morning, numerous parties of squaws, accompanied by their dogs, were seen on their way from the village to the corn patches, scattered at the distance of several miles.

At sunrise we mounted our horses, and arranging ourselves as on the preceding day, and carrying a white silk flag with a painted design, emblematic of peaceable intentions in the front, and the United States' flag in the centre of our party, we moved forward towards the second village, distant about three miles from our camp.

The bands which inhabit this village, are called Republican Pawnees. This name, it is said, has been applied to this band, in consequence of their having seceded from the parent stock or Grand Pawnees, some years since, and established themselves under a separate government.

They resided formerly on the Republican Fork of the Konzas river, to which they have given their name; whence they removed a few years since to their present situation, that they might enjoy the protection of their more powerful allies, the Grand Pawnees. Their village is distant four miles from that of the Grand Pawnees, and like it on the immediate bank of the river. *Fool Robe* their chief, received us with a little more attention than we had met on the preceding day, shaking us each by the hand. He afterwards conducted us to his lodge, within the village, but excused himself from feasting us, saying, his squaws were all absent at the cornfields.

It was a war party from this band, which had plundered the detachment from the steam boat, on the preceding summer near the Konza village. For this outrage they had been compelled by the prompt and vigorous interference of

Major O'Fallon, the Indian agent, to make ample restitution. Whether it was, that Fool Robe and his warriors were yet a little sore on account of this affair, or for some other reasons, it was evident, we were not welcome visitants. We had hitherto entertained exalted ideas, of the hospitality of the Pawnees, in their manner of receiving strangers, and were consequently a little disappointed at the reception we had met. We stayed but a short time with Fool Robe. Having briefly described to him the outline of our intended journey, and listened to his remarks and advice respecting it, we remounted our horses, and proceeded towards the Loup village.

On our way we were met by the Knife-chief, who, having heard of our intention to visit him, came out on horse-back, and met us more than a mile from the village. He gave us a very cordial and friendly reception, frequently rubbing his breast in token of the satisfaction he felt at seeing us. His frank and intelligent countenance, and his impressive gestures made him easily understood, without the aid of an interpreter. As our cavalcade passed by him, he appeared to examine with some attention, the physiognomy and appointments of the individuals composing it, but when his rapid eye alighted upon Julien, with whom he could use much freedom, he rode up to him and eagerly inquired by means of signs . . . if we had brought with us any whiskey, which, we were grieved to learn, by this intimation, that he was acquainted with, and would indulge in; Julien replied in the negative, by the exhibition of the proper sign . . . with which he did not betray any dissatisfaction, although it was evident from his subsequent conversation, that he believed it to be false. On the way to the village, he pointed out a convenient place for us to dispose of our horses and establish our camp. Here we dismounted, having our horses in the care of the guard, and followed the chief to his lodge. Soon after our arrival, a large dish was placed before us, according to the custom of the Indians, filled with boiled sweet corn. While we were eating, the Knife-chief with the principal men of his nation, were sitting silently behind us. Having finished our repast, we gave the Indians an account of ourselves, the occasion of our visit to them, our intended journey to the mountains at the head of the Platte, &c., as in the other villages. To all this the Knife-chief listened with great attention. He expressed himself satisfied with the account we had given of the objects of our enterprize, but feared we should be ill-treated by the savages we should meet. "Your heart must be strong," said he, "to go upon so hazardous a journey. May the Master of Life be your protector." The same benediction had been given us by the chiefs of the Republican and Grand Pawnees, probably with nearly the same degree of ingenuousness and sincerity. The Pawnees are at war with the Arrapahoes, Kaskaias, and other erratic bands, who wander about the sources of the Platte and Arkansa. Their war parties are often sent out in that direction, where they sometimes meet a spirited reception from their enemies. It may be on this account, that the Pawnees connect the idea of imminent danger, to an excursion into those parts of the country which we proposed to visit. It is, however, highly probable, their unwillingness to have us pass through their hunting grounds, was the most productive cause of all the anxiety, and all the fears they expressed on our account.

The chief addressed us for some time with great apparent earnestness, but his discourse as it came to our comprehension, by the aid of an interpreter, whom we obtained at this village, seemed directed solely to one object, the exciting our compassion for his poverty.

"Father—You see me here; I am very poor; my young men are very poor; we hope our great Father, will not forget the red-skins his children, they are poor," with a great deal more in the same strain. He, however, returned frequently to the subject of our journey to the west. "I will tell my young men," said he, (meaning the war parties which should be sent out in that direction,) "when they meet you, to take you by the hand, and smoke the peace pipe with you."

The Knife-chief, with his son Petalesharoo, celebrated for his filial affection, his valour and his humanity, visited us at our camp in the afternoon, and we were proud to entertain one whom we thought so worthy of our admiration. We also received a visit from a *Medicine-man*, who, having heard that there were great medicine-men belonging to our party, requested to be shown some of the mysteries of their profession. We accordingly displayed before him a pair of bullet-forceps, a small case of surgeons' instruments, and some similar articles, and began to explain to him the use of each. He attended for some time to our discourse, but apparently without comprehending any part of it, and at length turned abruptly away, with an air of dissatisfaction and contempt.

The Canadian, who had been engaged before we left the Missouri as a guide, now gave us to understand, that it was not his intention to accompany the expedition. Having been informed of other persons in the village, who were qualified for this undertaking, Major Long made application to several of these, who at first expressed a willingness to accompany him, but soon afterwards recalled their promises. Finding them disposed to trifle, in this manner, he at length assured them that unless some one was immediately procured to attend the expedition, as guide, their refusal, and the breach of engagement on the part of Bijeau, should be made known to the agent, and the whole corps of Canadian traders be deprived of the privilege of residing, or trading among the Pawnees. This representation had the desired effect. A ludicrous degree of consternation and alarm was depicted upon the faces of all the traders, and they immediately made a common concern of a subject which before they had treated with very little attention. Two were immediately selected from their number, and were in a short time ready to attend us. It is probable almost any other method of punishment would have appeared to them less terrible. Having been long resident among the Indians, they have conformed to their mode of life, which certainly is not without its charms to the uninformed and the idle. A tie not less powerful is that of conjugal and paternal affection, they having among the Indians wives and children relying upon their exertions for protection and maintenance.

About the village we saw several parties of young men eagerly engaged at games of hazard. One of these, which we noticed particularly, is played between two persons, and something is staked on the event of each game. The instruments used are a small hoop, about six inches in diameter, which is usually wound with thongs of leather, and a pole five or six feet long, on the larger end of which a limb is left to project about six inches. The whole bears some resemblance to a shepherd's crook. The game is played upon a smooth beaten path, at one end of which the gamester commences, and running at full speed, he first rolls from him the hoop, then discharges after it the pole, which slides along the path pursuing the hoop until both stop together, at the distance of about thirty yards from the place when they were thrown. After throwing them from him the gamester continues his pace, and the Indian, the hoop, and the pole arrive at the end of the path about the same time. The effort appears to be to place the end of the pole either in the ring, or as near as possible, and we could perceive that those casts were considered best when the ring was caught by the hook at the end of the pole. What constitutes a point, or how many points are reckoned to the game, we could not ascertain. It is, however, sufficiently evident that they are desperate gamesters, often losing their ornaments, articles of dress, &c. at play.

This game, like some of those described in a former part of this work, requires considerable exertion, and is well calculated for the exhibition of that gracefulness of figure, and that ease and celerity of motion in which the savages so far surpass their civilized neighbours. We saw many young men engaged at these diversions, who had thrown aside their robes, leggins, and all superfluous articles of dress, displaying a symmetry of proportion, and beauty of form, which we have rarely seen surpassed. They were so intent upon their diversion that in some instances our approach towards them, as we were rambling about the village, did not for a moment call off their attention from the game.

The population of the three Pawnee villages was estimated by Capt. Pike, in 1806, at 6,223, and they were at that time supposed to be able to call into the field 1,993 warriors. At present it is believed they would fall short of this estimate, particularly in the number of warriors. They are, however, still numerous, and are said to be increasing, and are respected by the Sioux, and other neighbouring nations, as warlike and powerful.

About the three villages are six or eight thousand horses, feeding in the plains during the day, but confined at night. These, with a breed of sharp-eared, meagre, wolf-like dogs, are their only domestic animals. On the approach of winter they conceal their stores of grain, dry pumpkins, beans, &c. and with their whole retinue of dogs and horses desert their villages. This they are compelled to do from the want of wood, not only for fuel, but for the support of their numerous horses.

They encamp in their lodges of skin wherever the cotton wood is found in sufficient quantities for their horses, and game for themselves. The horses, in the country bordering the Missouri, are fed, during the winter, in the extensive wooded bottoms of that river, and are not, therefore, confined exclusively to the cotton wood, having access to other timber, also to the rushes and coarse grass which abound in the bottoms. We are, however, well assured that the Indian horses, farther to the west, about the upper branches of the Platte, and Arkansa, subsist, and thrive, during the winter, with no other article of food than the bark and branches of the cotton wood. The winter at the Pawnee villages is said to be uncommonly severe, but is probably little, if any more so, than at Council Bluff, on the Missouri. Thermometric observations at Council Bluff, and at St. Peters on the Mississippi, prove that the climate of these two places does not very widely differ from that of the corresponding latitudes on the Atlantic coast, except that it is at times something colder. The vicissitudes of temperature appear to be equally great and sudden.

The climate at Council Bluff is beyond the influence of the south-western winds from the Gulf of Mexico, which have been supposed to have so perceptible an effect to soften the rigors of winter in the valley of the lower Mississippi. The three Pawnee villages, with their pasture grounds, and insignificant enclosures, occupy about ten miles in length of the fertile valley of the Wolf river. The surface is wholly naked of timber, rising gradually to the river hills, which are broad and low, and from a mile to a mile and an half distant. The soil of this valley is deep and of inexhaustible fertility. The surface, to the depth of two or three feet, is a dark coloured vegetable mould intermixed with argillaceous loam, and still deeper, with a fine siliceous sand. The agriculture of the Pawnees is extremely rude. They are supplied with a few hoes by the traders, but many of their labors are accomplished with the rude instruments of wood and bone which their own ingenuity supplies. They plant corn and pumpkins in little patches along the sides of deep ravines, and wherever by any accident the grassy turf has been eradicated. Sometimes these little plantations are enclosed with a sort of wicker fence, and in other instances are left entirely open. These last are probably watched by the squaws during the day time, when the horses run at large.

We slept on the night of the 12th at our encampment in front of the Pawnee Loup village. During the night all remained at rest except the dogs, who howled in concert, in the same voice, and nearly to the same tune, as the wolves, to whose nightly serenade we were now accustomed.

As soon as the day dawned we observed the surrounding plain filled with groups of squaws, with their small children, trooping to their cornfields in every direction. Some, who passed our encampment, lingered a moment to admire our novel appearance; but the air of serious business was manifest in their countenances, and they soon hurried away to their daily labors. Some of the groups of young females were accompanied by a jolly looking young man as a protector. Their corn is usually gathered before it is entirely ripe, it is then boiled, cut from the cob, and dried. Their cookery consists in boiling it, either with or without the tallow of the bison, according to the state of their supplies. The pumpkins are cut in slips, which are dried in the sun, and afterwards woven into mats for the convenience of carrying. They offered us these articles in exchange for tobacco, vermillion, beads, looking glasses, and various other trinkets. Also jerked bison beef, and the tallow of that animal, of which we purchased a small quantity. We saw among them the Pomme blanche, so called by the Canadian traders and boatmen, which is the root of the Psoralea *esculenta*. It is eaten either boiled or roasted, and somewhat resembles the sweet potatoe.

At ten o'clock, on the morning of the 13th, we commenced crossing the river, opposite the village. This we found an undertaking of some difficulty, as the current was rapid, and the bottom partook something of the nature of quicksands. Major Long, Mr. Say, and one or two others, who were riding at the head of our line, had nearly crossed, and were wading their horses about mid-sides deep in the water, when they were suddenly thrown from their saddles by the sinking of their horses feet in the sand; the horses, however, extricated themselves by their own exertion; and those of the party who had experienced this unexpected immersion, were greeted, upon their standing up in the water, by the shouts and acclamations of the Pawnees who lined the shore we had left. Major Long's gun and jacob-staff, as well as Mr. Say's gun, blanket, and other articles, were dropped into the river; all of these were, however, recovered except the blanket; and Mr. Say, having lost the greater part of his furniture at the river of Souls, by the ill-timed activity of his horse, was now, in a great measure, unencumbered with baggage. At length, by leading our horses, we arrived in safety on the opposite shore, where we encamped, intending to make some further barters with the Pawnees, and to dry some of our baggage, guns, &c. which had been wet in crossing.

The sand of this river, which in the aggregate has a very white appearance, consists principally of minute grains of transparent quartz, mixed with some which are red, yellow, and variously coloured. The shore, opposite the Loup village, is covered with shrubs and other plants, growing among the loose sands. One of the most common is a large flowering rose, rising to about three feet high, and diffusing a most grateful fragrance. The Symphoria *glomerata*, common in all the country west of the Mississippi thus far, is also a beautiful shrub very frequent at this place; the flowers are white, with a faint and delicate tinge of red, having the inside of the corrolla densely villous, like the Mitchilla, to which plant it is manifestly allied. On the hills, at a little distane from the river, we observed the Cactus fragilis. This plant, which was first detected on the Missouri by Lewis and Clark, has been accurately described by Mr. Nuttall. The articulations or joints of which it consists, are small, oblong, and tapering, but separate from each other with great readiness, and adhere by means of the barbed spines, with which they are thickly set, to whatever they may happen to touch. This has led to a saying among the hunters, that the plant grows without roots.

In the afternoon a young Indian belonging to the Arikara nation on the Missouri, but who resided among the Pawnees, stopped at our camp, on his return from a solitary excursion to the Arkansa. He had brought with him, from one of the upper branches of that river, two masses of salt, each weighing about thirty pounds. This salt is pure and perfect, consisting of large crystalline grains, so concentrated together as to form a mass about twenty inches in diameter and six in thickness. It had evidently been formed by the evaporation of water in some pond or basin, and that surface of the mass, which was its lower in its original position, was intermixed with red sand, indicating the sort of soil in which it is found. Mr. Peale procured some specimens in exchange for tobacco.

This Indian had been many days absent, on his excursion, and as he sat upon his horse before our encampment we had an opportunity to note a trait in the Indian character, which has been the subject of remark by many authors, and which we had previously observed in several instances ourselves; we allude to the apparent coolness which friends, and the nearest relatives, observe to each other when they meet after a long separation. Several of his fellow townsmen, who were about our encampment, hardly noticed him when he first appeared, and it was only after the lapse of a considerable interval that one of them spoke to him, but without any visible ceremony of greeting.

On the morning of the 14th, we left our encampment, opposite the village of the Pawnee Loups, and proceeded on our journey, taking the most direct course towards the Platte. Our party had here received an addition of two men, one named Bijeau, engaged as guide and interpreter, the other, Ledoux, to serve as hunter, farrier, &c. Both were Frenchmen, residing permanently among the Pawnees, and had been repeatedly on the head waters of the Platte and Arkansa, for the purpose of hunting and trapping beaver. Bijeau was partially acquainted with several Indian languages; in particular, that of the Crow nation, which is extensively understood by the western tribes, and, by frequent intercourse with the savages he had gained a complete knowledge of the language of signs, universally current among them. The great number, and the wide dissimilarity of the dialects of the aborigines render this method of communication necessary to them, and it is not surprising it should have arrived at considerable perfection among tribes who, from their situation and manner of life, must often find occasion to make use of it.

Besides these two men a young Spaniard, a refugee from some of the settlements of New Mexico, joined our party, intending to accompany us as far as his fear of his own countrymen would permit. He had probably been guilty of some misdemeanor, which made it necessary to avoid his former acquaintances, and, on this account, he could not be induced to accompany us into the neighbourhood of the Spanish settlements. The Frenchmen brought with them three horses and a mule, so that our party, which was now supposed to be made up for the journey, consisted, exclusive of the Spaniard, of twenty-two men, thirty-four horses and mules, and two dogs.

We were well armed and equipped, each man carrying a yauger or rifle gun, with the exception of two or three who had muskets; most of us had pistols, all tomahawks and long knives, which we carried suspended at our belts. We believed ourselves about to enter on a district of country inhabited by lawless and predatory bands of savages, where we should have occasion to make use, not only of our arms, but of whatever share of courage and hardihood we might chance to possess.

The country which we passed on the 14th, lying between the Loup fork and the Platte, has an undulating surface, except that portion of it which comprises the bottom lands of the two rivers. The ridges are of little elevation, destitute of stone of any kind, and irregular in direction; the soil is sandy and infertile. The high and barren parts of this tract are occupied by numerous communities of the Prairie dog or Louisiana marmot.

On arriving near the Platte we observed a species of prickly pear *(Cactus ferox. N.)* to become very numerous. It resembles the common prickly pear of New Jersey, *(C. opuntia,)* but is larger, and protected by a more formidable armature of thorns. Our Indian horses were so well acquainted with this plant, and its properties, that they used the utmost care to avoid stepping near it. The flowers are of a sulphur yellow, and when fully expanded are nearly as large as those of the garden pæony, and crowded together upon the summits of the terminal articulations of which the plant consists. These articulations, (or segments contained between the joints) are oblong and flattened, being longer and thicker than a man's hand. A second species, the *G. mamillaris N.* occurs on the dry sandy ridges between the Pawnee villages and the Platte. The beautiful cristaria *coccinnea. Ph.* (malva *coccinnea. N.*) is very frequent in the low plains along the Platte. Its flowers have nearly the aspects of those of the common wild rose, except that they are more deeply coloured.

We arrived at the Platte a little before sun-set, the distance from the Pawnees being, according to our computation, twenty-five miles. After entering the valley of the river we travelled several miles across an unvaried plain, and at length passing down by a gradual descent of a few feet, we came upon a second level tract, extending to the river.

The soil of the first of these portions is a bed of sand, intermixed with small water-worn pebbles and gravel, that of the latter is more fertile, and produces a luxuriant vegetation.

Our guide informed us that the Platte, opposite the point where we entered its valley, contains an island which is more than one day's journey across, and about thirty miles in length.

At no great distance from our camp, which was placed immediately on the brink of the river, we found the body of a horse lying dead in the edge of the water. The animal had, in all probability, been recently lost by a war party of Indians.

15th. Soon after leaving our camp we crossed a small stream tributary to the Platte, from the north. It is called Great Wood river, and has some timber along its banks.

Our provisions being nearly exhausted two of the hunters were sent forward in search of game, but after some time they rejoined the party, having killed nothing.

Shortly afterwards a single bison was discovered some miles ahead of the party, and travelling apparently in the same direction. Four of our hunters, having disencumbered their horses of all their baggage, spurred forward in the pursuit, but none of them were able to overtake the animal, except the young Spaniard, who came near enough to wound it with an arrow; but his horse being exhausted he was compelled to desist from the pursuit, and suffer the bison to escape.

Having ascended the Platte about sixteen miles we halted to make such a dinner as the condition of our stores would allow, and here the Spaniard took his leave of us to return to the Pawnees.

In the scenery of the Platte there is the utmost uniformity; a broad plain, unvaried by any object on which the eye can rest, lies extended before us; on our right are the low and distant hills which bound the valley; and on our left the broad Platte, studded with numerous small, but verdant islands. On these islands is usually a little timber, which is not met with in other situations. We were fortunate in finding, towards evening, an old Indian encampment, where were poles, stakes, &c. which had been brought from the islands, and here we placed our camp. Some antelopes were seen during the day, but so wild and vigilant that all our efforts to take them proved unsuccessful. Our supper, therefore, was not of the choicest kind, and, what was infinitely more vexatious to us, was limited in quantity.

On the following day we passed a number of prairie dog villages, some of them extending from two to three miles along the river. Though much in want of game, most of our exertions to take these animals were without success. A number were killed, but we were able to possess ourselves of no more than two of them. These we found to be in good condition and well flavoured. Their flesh nearly resembles that of the ground hog, or woodchuck (Arctomys Marylandica.)

In some small ponds near the Platte we saw the common species of pond weed (Potamogeton *natans* and P. *fluitans*. Ph.) also the Utricularia longirostris? of Leconte, and an interesting species of Myrlophillum.

By observations at morning and evening the magnetic variation was found thirteen and an half degrees east. In the middle of the day the heat was excessive, and we were under the necessity of halting at a place where no shade could be found to shelter us from the scorching rays of the sun, except what was afforded by our tents, which were set up for this purpose. Here we remained until 4 P.M. when we resumed our journey. We crossed towards evening a small creek, three miles beyond which we arrived at an old Indian camp where we halted for the night. We had not been long here before a tremendous storm of wind assailed our tents with such violence, that it was only by stationing ourselves outside, and holding the margin to the ground, that we were able to keep them standing.

Two of the hunters who had been sent out during the afternoon, returned to camp late in the evening, bringing in a buck antelope, a highly acceptable acquisition to us, as we had been for some time restricted to short commons. The flesh we found palatable, being very similar in every respect to that of the common deer.

We had proceeded but a few miles from our camp, on the following morning, when we perceived a number of antelopes at a little distance in the prairie. Being on the windward side of the party they were not able, by their sense of smelling, to inform themselves of the nature of the danger which was approaching. One of them, "the patriarch of the flock," leaving his companions came so near our line as to be within the reach of a rifle ball, and was killed by Lieutenant Swift.

The antelope possesses an unconquerable inquisitiveness, of which the hunters often take advantage to compass the destruction of the animal. The attempt to approach immediately towards them in the open plains, where they are always found, rarely proves successful. Instead of this the hunter getting as near the animal as is practicable without exciting alarm, conceals himself by lying down, then fixing a handkerchief, or cap, upon the end of his ramrod continues to wave it, still remaining concealed. The animal after a long contest between curiosity and fear, at length approaches near enough to become a sacrifice to the former.

In the afternoon a single bison was seen at the distance of several miles, being the second since we had left the Pawnee villages, which were now about a hundred miles distant, and we were beginning to fear that the representations of the Indians, in relation to the difficulty of procuring game to subsist so large a party as ours, would prove true. We found, however, that every part of the country, which we had recently passed, had, at no distant, period been occupied by innumerable herds of bisons. Their tracks, and dung, were still to be seen in vast numbers, and the surface of the ground was strewed with skulls, and skeletons, which were yet undecayed.

At 4 o'clock P.M. we arrived at an old Indian encampment, opposite an island, on which was some wood, and perceiving that none would be met with for many miles ahead, we determined to halt here for the night.

The 18th, being Sunday, we remained in camp. This indulgence was not only highly acceptable to the soldiers and men who accompanied us, they being much harassed and fatigued by their exertions during the week, but was necessary for our horses, which not being in good condition when we left the Missouri, were perceptibly failing under the laborious services they were made to perform. At our nightly encampments we found it necessary to confine them, as we had not always a plentiful supply of grass in the immediate vicinity of our camp, and if left at large they would wander in search of better pasture, and occasion us great trouble to collect them again in the morning. Accordingly long ropes had been provided, which were carried constantly on the necks of the horses, and by these they were made fast during the night to stakes driven into the ground. After having eaten all the grass within his reach the horse was removed to another place, and this was done several times during the night, by a guard kept constantly on duty, both for the performance of this service, and also to give timely notice in case of the approach of Indians to the camp. Notwithstanding this care, on our part, our horses were sometimes but poorly fed, as we were often compelled to encamp in places where little grass was to be found. When we remained in camp during the day they were suffered to range more at liberty, a watch being kept out to prevent their wandering too great a distance. Notwithstanding the Sabbath was devoted to the refreshment of our horses, and the relaxation of the men who accompanied us, some attention was given to the great objects of the Expedition. Astronomical observations for the correction of our time-piece, and for other purposes were made. At Engineer Cantonment we had furnished ourselves with port folios of paper to receive specimens of such plants as we might collect, but we found that the precautions which had been used to protect these from the weather had been insufficient, some of our collections being in part wet, and others having been made during the heavy rains which fell before we reached the Pawnee villages required much attention. The Sabbath also afforded us an opportunity to devote a little attention to the important objects of personal cleanliness and comfort. The plain about our encampment was strewed with the bones of the bison and other animals; and among the rest we distinguished some of men. We picked up a number of human skulls, one of which we thought it no sacrilege to compliment with a place upon one of our pack-horses. Our guides could give us no satisfactory information on the time and manner in which the several persons, to whom these bones formerly belonged, had been compelled to lay them down in this place; it is certain, however, that at no very distant period a battle had been fought, or a massacre committed, on this spot.

We had now arrived at a point about two hundred miles distant from the confluence of the Platte and Missouri, yet the character of the former river was but little changed. It was still from one to three miles in breadth, containing numerous islands, covered with a scanty growth of cotton wood willows, the Amorpha fruticosa, and other shrubs.

CHAPTER II

The Platte—Desert plains—Mirage—Arrival at the Rocky Mountains.

THE Platte, called by the Otoes Ne-braska, (Flat river, or water,) is, as its name imports, almost uniformly broad and shoal. It is fordable at almost any place, except when swollen by freshets, which occur in the Spring season, from the melting of snow, and occasionally during the other portions of the year, from excessive rain. Its bed is composed almost exclusively of sand, forming innumerable bars, which are continually changing their position, and moving downward, till at length they are discharged into the Missouri, and swept away to the ocean by that rapid and turbulent river.

The range of the Platte, from extreme low to extreme high water is very inconsiderable, manifestly not exceeding six or eight feet. This is about the usual height of its banks above the surface of the sand which forms its bed. The banks are sometimes overflowed, but evidently to no great extent. The rapidity of the current, and the great width of the bed of the river, preclude the possibility of any extensive inundation of the surrounding country. The bottom lands of the river rise by an imperceptible ascent, on each side, extending laterally to a distance of from two to ten miles, where they are terminated by low ranges of gravelly hills, running parallel to the general direction of the river. Beyond these the surface is an undulating plain, having an elevation of from fifty to one hundred feet, and presenting the aspect of hopeless and irreclaimable sterility.

The Missouri in compliance with the usage of boat-men, hunters, &c., has been usually considered under two divisions, the lower extending from the Mississippi to the confluence of the Platte; and the upper, comprehending all above that point. As might be expected, the influx of so large and so peculiar a river as the Platte, gives new character to the Missouri below. It is more rapid, more difficult of navigation, and the water more turbid than above.

Among other plants observed about our encampment, was the wild liquorice, (glycyrhiza *lepidota, N.)* which is believed to be the plant mentioned by Sir A. Mackenzie, which is used as food by the savages of the northwest. The root is large and long, spreading horizontally to a great distance. In taste it bears a very slight resemblance to the liquorice of the shops, but is bitter and nauseous. The leaves are frequently covered with a viscid exudation.

We were prevented from continuing our astronomical observations, in the afternoon, the weather becoming cloudy, and at evening a thunder storm commenced, which continued with short intermissions during the night. The lightning exhibited an incessant glare, and peals of thunder which seemed to shake the earth to its centre, followed each other in rapid succession.

On Monday 19th, we moved on, and ascending the Platte about thirty miles, arrived in the evening at a place where the hills on the north side close in, quite to the bed of the river. On both sides they became more broken and elevated, and on the north, they approached so near to the bed of the Platte, that we were under the necessity of travelling across them. We were glad, however, of any change of scene. The monotony of a vast unbroken plain, like that in which we had now travelled, nearly one hundred and fifty miles, is little less tiresome to the eye, and fatiguing to the spirit, than the dreary solitude of the ocean.

With this change of the surface, some change is observed in the vegetable products of the soil. Here we first saw a new species of prickly poppy, with a spreading white flower, as large as that of the common poppy of the gardens. The aspect of this plant is very similar to that of the common poppy, except that the leaves are covered with innumerable large and strong prickles. When wounded it exudes a thick yellowish sap, intensely bitter to the taste. On the summits of some of the dry sandy ridges, we saw a few of the plants called Adam's needles, (Yucca, *angustifolia)* thriving with an appearance of luxuriance and verdure, in a soil which bids defiance to almost every other species of vegetation. Nature has, however, fitted the yucca, for the ungenial soil it is destined to occupy. The plant consists of a large tuft of rigid spear-pointed leaves, placed immediately upon the root, and sending up in the flowering season, a stalk bearing a cluster of lilliaceous flowers as large as those of the common tulip of the gardens. The root bears more resemblance to the trunk of a tree, than to the roots of ordinary plants. It is two or three inches in diameter, descending undivided to a great depth below the surface, where it is impossible the moisture of the earth should ever be exhausted, and there terminates in numerous spreading branches. In some instances the sand is blown from about the root, leaving several feet of it exposed, and supporting the dense leafy head, at some distance from the surface.

Several bisons and other game, had been seen in the course of the day, but nothing taken. As our provisions were now exhausted, it was resolved to remain encamped where we were, while parties were sent out in different directions to hunt.

Being now at a place where, as our guide informed us, the Pawnees often cross the Platte, and as it was our intention to ascend on the other side of the river, Major Long rode across to ascertain the practicability of fording, but the summer freshet being now at its height, it was found the river could not be crossed without swimming, and the design was relinquished. Six of our party including the hunters, were sent out in pursuit of game.

At camp, observations were taken for ascertaining longitude and other purposes. At evening, Mr. Peale returned, having killed an antelope at the distance of ten miles from the camp, and brought it within about four, where being fatigued and hungry, he had made a fire, cooked and ate part of the animal, and left the remainder, suspending a handkerchief near it, to protect it from the wolves. Soon

Antelope, T.R. Peale, June 19, 1820, watercolor.

afterwards others returned, and when all were collected, it appeared there had been killed one bison, two antelopes, and a hare, all at a distance from camp. Horses were accordingly sent out to bring in the meat, a part of which we attempted to dry during the night, by cutting it in thin pieces and exposing it over a slow fire, but a storm of wind and rain which continued greater part of the night, prevented our success in this attempt.

21st. The storm continued throughout the night, and the following day was cold, with a heavy mist from the southeast.

After travelling this day our customary distance, which was about twenty-five miles, we were compelled to halt at a place where we could find no poles to set up our tents. We were fortunate in finding part of a tree which had drifted down the Platte, and which sufficed to make a fire for the cooking of our supper. An Indian dog who had made his appearance at the encampment on the preceding day, had followed us thus far, but kept aloof, not allowing us to come within one or two hunded yards of him.

On the following morning, six miles from our camp, we arrived at the confluence of the north and south fork of the Platte. We had halted here, and were making preparations to examine the north fork with a view of crossing it, when we saw two elk plunge into the river a little above us on the same side. Perceiving it was their design to cross the river, we watched them until they arrived on the other side, which they did without swimming. We accordingly chose the same place they had taken, and putting a part of our baggage in a skin canoe, waded across, leading our horses, and arrived safely on the other side; no accident having happened, except the wetting of such of our baggage as was left on the horses.

The North fork at its confluence is about eight hundred yards wide, is shoal and rapid like the Platte, and has a sandy bed. We were informed by our guide who had been repeatedly to its sources, that it rises within the Rocky Mountains, about one hundred and twenty miles north of the sources of the Platte.

It is probably the river which was mistaken by Captain Pike for the Yellow-stone, and has been laid down as such on his map, whence the mistake has been copied into several others. It has its source in numerous small streams, which descend from the hills surrounding a circumscribed valley within the mountains, called the Bull-pen. This basin is surrounded by high and rugged mountains, except at the place where the North fork passes into the plains. On each side of this strait, or pass, are high and abrupt rocky promontories, which confine the river to a narrow channel. The diameter of the circumscribed valley, called the Bull-pen, is one day's travel, about twenty miles. The upper branches of the North fork have some timber, mostly cotton-wood and willow, and abound in beaver.

From the limited information communicated to the public, on the subject of Mr. Hunt's Expedition to the mouth of the Columbia, commenced in the year 1811, it appears that a part of the men, engaged in that undertaking, in their return from the Pacific, crossed the Rocky Mountains from some one of the upper branches of Lewis' river, and falling upon the sources of the North fork of the Platte, descended thence to the Missouri.

On the 28th of June 1812, Mr. Robert Stewart, one of the partners of the Pacific Fur Company, with two Frenchmen, M'Clellan and Crooks, left the Pacific ocean with despatches for New York.

Having proceeded about seven hundred miles, they met Mr. Joseph Miller, on his way to the mouth of the Columbia. He had been considerably to the south and east, and had fallen in with the Black-arms, and Arrapahoes, who wander about the sources of the Arkansa. By the latter of these he had been robbed, in consequence of which, he was now reduced to starvation and nakedness.

Mr. Stewart and his companions had fifteen horses, but soon afterwards met with a band of the Crow Indians, near the Rocky Mountains, who behaved with the most unbounded insolence, and finally stole every horse belonging to the party.

They now found themselves on foot, with the Rocky Mountains, and a journey of two thousand miles before them; fifteen hundred of which was through a country wholly unknown, as their route lay considerably to the south of that of Lewis and Clark.

Putting the best face upon their prospects, they pursued their journey towards the Rocky Mountains, travelling east southeast, until they struck the "head waters of the great river Platte," which they followed to its mouth, having spent the winter upon it, six hundred miles from the Missouri.

The confluence of the North fork and the Platte is, according to our estimate of distances, one hundred and forty-nine miles by our courses, from the Pawnee Loup village.

Some of the upper branches of the Wolf river, head about thirty miles to the north of this point.

After fording the North fork, we crossed a narrow point of low prairie to the Platte, where, as it was now near night, we resolved to encamp, and attempt the passage of the river on the following day.

Our view of the opposite margin of the Platte, during this day's march, had been intercepted by an elevated swell of the surface, which extended along, parallel to the river, that we were now approaching. Immediately upon surmounting this undulation we saw before us, upon the broad expanse of the left margin of the river, immense herds of bisons, grazing in undisturbed possession, and obscuring, with the density of their numbers, the verdant plain; to the right

Bison, T.R. Peale, February, 1820, pencil.

and left, as far as the eye was permitted to rove, the crowd seemed hardly to diminish, and it would be no exaggeration to say, that at least ten thousand here burst on our sight in the instant. Small columns of dust were occasionally wafted by the wind from the bulls that were *pawing* the earth, and rolling; the interest of action was also communicated to the scene, by the unwieldy playfulness of some individuals, that the eye would occasionally rest upon, their real or affected combats, or by the slow and rapid progress of others to and from their watering places. On the distant bluffs, individuals were constantly disappearing, whilst others were presenting themselves to our view, until, as the dusk of the evening increased, their massive forms, thus elevated above the line of other objects, were but dimly defined on the skies. We retired to our evening fare, highly gratified with the novel spectacle we had witnessed, and with the most sanguine expectations of the future.

In the morning we again sought the living picture, but upon all the plain, which last evening was so teeming with noble animals, not one remained. We forded the Platte with less delay and difficulty, than we had encountered in crossing the North fork.

It is about nine hundred yards wide, and very rapid, but so shoal that we found it unnecessary to dismount from our horses, or to unpack the mules. We found the plains on the south side of the Platte, more closely depastured, than those we had before seen. The grass is fine and short, forming a dense and matted turf, as in the oldest pastures.

Meeting with wood at about three o'clock P.M., we resolved to encamp. On the two preceding evenings, we had found it difficult to collect as much wood as sufficed to kindle a fire, which was afterwards kept up with the dung of the bison, though not without some difficulty, as the weather was rainy.

The dung of the bison is used as fuel in many parts of the woodless country southwest of the Missouri, by the Indians, and by hunters, who often encamp where no wood is to be found. We learn from Sonini and others, that the excrement of the camel, mixed with chopped straw and afterwards dried, is similarly used in the woodless parts of Egypt.

The hills on the south side of the Platte, above the confluence of the north fork, become more abrupt and elevated, approaching in character those of the Missouri which are destitute of stone. There is here the same transcript of Alpine scenery, in miniature, which constitutes so striking a feature in the Missouri landscape, when viewed from the river bottom.

We had no sooner crossed the Platte, than our attention was arrested by the beautiful white primrose (Œnothera pinnatifida. N.) with its long and slender corrolla reclining upon the grass. The flower, which is near two inches long, constitutes about one half of the entire length of the plant.

The valley of the Platte, above the forks, is much narrower, and a little more irregular in direction than below, and is frequently interrupted by small hills running in towards the river. On ascending these hills, we found them of a coarse sand, and containing more gravel and small pebbles than below. Among the gravel stones small fragments of flesh-coloured feldspar are distinguished. About the summits of the hills we saw some detached pieces of fine carnelian, with agates and chalcedony.

We had often examined, with some anxiety, the turbid waters of the Platte, hoping thereby to gain information respecting the predominating rock formations of the mountainous district, from which that river descends.

It had been a received opinion, among some of the geologists of the United States, that the Rocky Mountains were not of primitive rocks; we had, hitherto, observed nothing which could either confirm or invalidate this opinion.

The great alluvial formation, which occupies the country on both sides of the lower portion of the river Platte, is an almost unmixed siliceous sand, in no manner distinguishable from the *debris* of the sandstones of transition mountains. Near the forks of the Platte, we first observed that the waters of that river bring down, among other matters, numerous small scales of mica. This also is a constituent of the sandstones of the lower secondary or transition formations. The fragments of unmixed and crystalline feldspar, which now began to be of frequent occurrence, were considered as the first convincing evidence of the primitive character of the Rocky Mountains. These fragments of feldspar, we believed, could have been derived from no other than primitive rocks.

During all the day on the 23rd, we travelled along the south side of the Platte, our course inclining something more towards the south west than heretofore.

Intermixed in the narrow fringe of timber, which marks the course of the river, are very numerous trees, killed by the action of the beaver or by the effects of old age, their decorticated and bleached trunks and limbs strongly contrasting with the surrounding objects, many of them rendered doubly interesting by affording a support to the nests of the bald eagle, elevated like a beacon in the horizon of the traveller.

Large herds of bisons were seen in every direction; but as we had already killed a deer, and were supplied with meat enough for the day, none of the party were allowed to go in pursuit of them. Prickly pears became more and more abundant as we ascended the river, and here they occurred in such extensive patches as considerably to retard our progress, it being wholly impracticable to urge our horses across them. The Cactus *ferox* is the most common, and, indeed, the only species which is of frequent occurrence. It has been stated by a traveller to the upper Missouri, that the antelope, which inhabits the extensive plains of that river and its tributaries, finds means to make this plant, notwithstanding its terrific armature of thorns, subservient to its necessities, "by cutting it up with his hoofs." We were able to discover no confirmation of this statement; it may, however, be applicable to some plains, more arid and sterile than any we have passed, where the antelopes may be driven by necessity to the use of this hard expedient.

Bison, T.R. Peale, undated, pencil.

On the following day, we saw immense herds of bisons, blackening the whole surface of the country through which we passed. At this time they were in their summer coat. From the shoulders backward, all the hinder parts of the animal are covered with a growth of very short and fine hair, as smooth and soft to the touch as a piece of velvet. The tail is very short and tufted at the end, and its services, as a fly-brush, are confined to a very limited surface.

The fore parts of the body are covered with long shaggy hair, descending in a tuft behind the knee, in a distinct beard beneath the lower jaw, rising in a dense mass on the top of his head as high as the tip of the horns, matted and curled on his front so thickly as to deaden the force of the rifle-ball, which rebounds from the forehead and lodges in the hair, causing the animal only to shake his head as he bounds heavily onward. The head is so large and ponderous, in proportion to the size of the body, that the supporting muscles, which greatly enlarge the neck, form over the shoulders, where they are imbedded on each side of the elongated vertebral processes distinguished by the name of hump ribs, a very considerable elevation called the hump, which is of an oblong form, diminishing in height as it recedes, so as to give considerable obliquity to the line of the back. The eye is small, black, and piercing; the horns, which are black and remarkably robust at base, curve outward and upward, tapering rapidly to the tip. The profile of the face is somewhat convexly curved, and the superior lip, on each side, papillous within, is dilated and extended downward so as to give a very oblique appearance to the lateral rictus or gape of the mouth, considerably resembling, in this respect, the ancient architectural bas reliefs representing the heads of the ox. The physiognomy is menacing and ferocious, and the whole aspect of the animal is sufficiently formidable to influence the spectator, who is, for the first time, placed near him on his native wilds, with certain feelings which indicate the propriety of immediate attention to personal safety.

The bison cow bears the same relation, as to appearance, to the bull, that the domestic cow does to her mate; she is smaller, with much less hair on the anterior part of her body, and though she has a conspicuous beard, yet this appendage is comparatively short; her horns also are much less robust and not partially concealed by hair.

The dun colour prevails on the coat of the bison, but the long hair of the anterior part of the body, with the exception of the head, is more or less tinged with yellowish or rust colour. The uniformity of the colour, however, amongst these animals is so steadfast, that any considerable deviation from the ordinary standard is regarded by the natives as effected under the immediate influence of the Divinity.

A trader on the Missouri informed us that he had seen a grayish-white bison, and that another, a yearling calf, was distinguished by several white spots on the side, and by a white frontal mark and white fore feet.

Mr. J. Dougherty saw in an Indian hut, a bison head, very well prepared, which had a white star on the front; the owner valued it highly, calling it his great medicine; he could not be tempted to part with it, "for," said he, "the herds come every season into the vicinity to seek their white-faced companion."

Indian bison hunt, T.R. Peale, February, 1820, pencil.

They are the skins of the cows, almost exclusively, that are used in commerce; those of the bulls being so large, heavy, and difficult to prepare, that this is, comparatively, seldom attempted.

That the bison formerly ranged over the Atlantic states there can be no doubt, and Lawson informs us that even in his time some were killed in Virginia, and Cumming, in his Sketches of a Tour to the western country, informs us that "long after the country (Kentucky) began to be generally settled, and ceased to be a hunting ground by the Indians," the "buffaloes, bears, and deer were so plenty in the country that little or no bread was used," and "the facility of gaining them prevented the progress of agriculture, until the poor innocent buffaloes were completely extirpated, and the other wild animals much thinned." This process of extirpation has not since been relaxed, and the bison is now driven beyond the lakes, the Illinois, and the southern portion of the Mississippi rivers, their range extending from the country west of Hudson's bay to the northern provinces of Mexico. They have not yet crossed the entire breadth of the mountains at the head of the Missouri, though they penetrate, in some parts, far within that range, to the most accessible fertile valleys, particularly the valley of Lewis' river. It was there that Mr. Henry and his party of hunters wintered, and subsisted chiefly upon the flesh of these animals, which they saw in considerable herds, but the Indians affirmed that it was unusual for the bisons to visit that neighbourhood.

All the mountains which we ascended were more or less strewed with the dung of these animals, about the lower parts, a conclusive evidence that this portion of the range had been traversed by the bisons.

The cows remain fat from July to the latter part of December. The rutting season occurs toward the latter part of July, and continues until the beginning of September, after which month the cows separate from the bulls, in distinct herds, and bring forth their calves in April. The calves seldom separate themselves from the mother under the age of one year, and cows are often seen accompanied by the calves of three seasons.

The meat of the bison has often been compared with that of the domestic ox, and the preference yielded to the latter, as an article of food. This decision, however, we cannot, from our experience confirm; it appeared to us that although of a somewhat coarser fibre, yet, after making due allowance for the situation in which we were placed, our appetites often increased by hunger and privation, that the flesh of the bison is in no degree inferior in delicacy and sweetness to that of the common ox. But that the flesh of those which we were accustomed to eat was more agreeably sapid than that which formed a subject of comparison to the authors alluded to, is altogether possible, as the grass upon which they usually fed was short, firm, and nutritious, considerably differing in its nature from the luxuriant and less solid grass nourished by a fertile soil. It was preferred by the party to the flesh of the elk or deer, which was thrown away when it could be substituted by the bison meat.

To the fat of the bison we conceded a decided superiority over that of the common ox, as being richer and sweeter to the taste.

As our stock of provisions was nearly exhausted, permission was given, when we had arrived near a suitable place of our mid-day halt, to the hunters to go out in pursuit of bisons, and in a short time two were killed. The choice parts of these were taken and placed upon pack-horses, to be carried forward to our next encampment, where some of it might be *jerked* on the ensuing day, which was Sunday.

Aside from the vast herds of bisons which it contains, the country along the Platte is enlivened by great numbers of deer, badgers, hares, prairie wolves, eagles, buzzards, ravens, and owls: these, with its rare and interesting plants, in some measure relieved the uniformity of its cheerless scenery. We found a constant source of amusement in observing the unsightly figure, the cumbrous gait, and impolitic movements of the bison; we were often delighted by the beauty and fleetness of the antelope, and the social comfort and neatness of the prairie dog.

This barren and ungenial district appeared, at that time, to be filled with greater numbers of animals than its meagre productions are sufficient to support. It was, however, manifest that the bisons, then thronging in such numbers, were moving towards the south. Experience may have taught them to repair at certain seasons to the more luxuriant plains of Arkansa and Red river. What should ever prompt them to return to the inhospitable deserts of the Platte, it is not, perhaps, easy to conjecture. In whatever direction they move, parasites and dependants fail not to follow. Large herds are invariably attended by gangs of meagre, famine-pinched wolves, and flights of obscene and ravenous birds.

We have frequently remarked broad shallow excavations in the soil, of the diameter of from five to eight feet, and greatest depth from six inches to eighteen. These are of rare occurrence near the Missouri, as far as Engineer Cantonment, and in other districts where the bison is seldom seen at the present day; and when they do exist there, they are overgrown by grass and nearly obliterated. As you approach the country, still the constant residence of these animals, the excavations become more numerous, and are less productive of grass. They now are so numerous as to be of constant recurrence, offering a considerable impediment to the traveller, who winds his way amongst them, and are entirely destitute of grass, their surface being covered with a deep dust. Until recently, we had no opportunity to observe the cause which gives rise to these appearances, but we were now convinced that they were the result of the habit which the bulls have, in common with the domestic bull, of scraping up the earth with their fore feet, in the process of dusting themselves; they serve also as places for rolling and wallowing, a gratification which the bison bull indulges in as frequently, and in the same manner as the horse.

Some extensive tracts of land along the Platte, particularly those portions which are a little elevated, with an undulating or broken surface, are almost exclusively occupied by a scattered growth of several species of wormwood, (Artemisia.) some of which are common to this country and that on the lower Missouri: we may enumerate the following—A. *Ludoviciana*, A. *longifolia*, A. *serrata*, A. *columbiensis*, A. *cernua*, A. *canadensis*; most of these species have simply or finely divided compound leaves, which are long and slender, and canescent, like those of the A. *absynthium*, the common wormwood of the gardens. The peculiar aromatic scent, and the flavor of this well known plant, is recognized in all the species we have mentioned. Several of them are eaten by the bisons, and our horses were sometimes reduced to the necessity of feeding upon them.

The intense reflection of light and heat from the surface of many tracts of naked sand, which we crossed, added much to the fatigue and suffering of our journey. We often met with extensive districts covered entirely with loose and fine sand, blown from the adjacent hills. In the low plains along the river, where the soil is permanent, it is highly impregnated with saline substances, and too sterile to produce any thing except a few stinted carices and rushes.

On the evening of the twenty-fourth, after we had encamped, several bull bisons, being on the windward side, came so near to us as to create a disturbance among our horses, who were not yet so familiarized to the formidable appearance of those animals, as to regard their near approach with indifference. The bulls, at length, became troublesome, approaching so near, to smell at the horses, that some of the latter broke the cords by which they were fastened and made their escape. A man was then sent to frighten away the bisons, who, in their turn, exhibited as much terror as they had occasioned to our horses.

On Sunday, the 25th, we remained encamped, and some of the men were employed in drying a part of the meat killed on the preceding day. This was done that we might be able to carry constantly with us a small supply of provisions, in reserve against any occasion when we might not meet with game.

The magnetic variation equated from two sets of observations, was found to be 14° east. Observations for longitude were made; it was also attempted to take the meridian altitude of Antares, for ascertaining the latitude, but the observation was commenced a few minutes too late, we having been longer occupied in making the preceding observations than we had anticipated.

26th. The weather had now been for some days fair. As we approached the mountains, we felt or fancied, a very manifest change in the character of the weather, and the temperature of the air. Mornings and evenings were usually calm, and the heat more oppressive than in the middle of the day. Early in the forenoon, a light and refreshing breeze often sprung up, blowing from the west or southwest, which again subsided on the approach of night. This phenomenon was so often observed that we were induced to attribute it to the operation of the same local cause, which in the neighbourhood of the sea, produced a diurnal change in the winds, which blow alternately to and from the shore. The Rocky Mountains may be considered as forming the shore of that sea of sand, which is traversed by the Platte, and extends northward to the Missouri, above the great bend.

The rarefaction of the air over this great plain, by the reverberation of the sun's rays during the day, causes an ascending current, which is supplied by the rushing down of the condensed air from the mountains. Though the sun's rays in the middle of the day, were scorching and extremely afflictive to our eyes, the temperature of the air as indicated by the thermometer, had hitherto rarely exceeded 80° Fah.

In the forenoon we passed a range of hills more elevated than any we had seen west of the Missouri. These hills cross the Platte from north to south, and though inconsiderable in magnitude, they can be distinguished extending several miles on each side of the river. They consist principally of gravel, intermixed with small, water-worn fragments of granite and other primitive rocks, but are based on a stratum of coarse friable sandstone, of a dark gray colour, which has been uncovered, and cut through by the bed of the Platte.

This range may perhaps be a continuation or spur from the black hills mentioned by Lewis and Clark, as containing the sources of the Shienne, and other tributaries to the Missouri, at no great distance to the north of the place where we now were.

At evening we arrived at another scattering grove of cotton-wood trees, among which we placed our camp, immediately on the brink of the river. The trees of which these insulated groves are usually composed, from their low and branching figure, and their remoteness from each other, as they stand scattered over the soil, they occupy, revived strongly in our minds the appearance and gratifications resulting from an apple orchard, for which from a little distance they might readily be mistaken, if seen in a cultivated region. At a few rods distant on our right hand, was a fortified Indian camp, which appeared to have been recently occupied. It was constructed of such broken half-decayed logs of wood as the place afforded, intermixed with some skeletons of bisons recently killed. It is of a circular form, enclosing space enough for about thirty men to lie down upon. The wall is about five feet high, with an opening towards the east, and the top uncovered.

At a little distance in front of the entrance of this breast-work, was a semicircular row of sixteen bison skulls, with their noses pointing down the river. Near the centre of the circle which this row would describe, if continued, was another skull marked with a number of red lines.

Our interpreter informed us that this arrangement of skulls and other marks here discovered, were designed to communicate the following informa- tion, namely, that the camp had been occupied by a war party of the Skeeree or Pawnee Loup Indians, who had lately come from an excursion against the Cumancias, Ietans, or some of the western tribes. The number of red lines traced on the painted skull indicated the number of the party to have been thirty-six; the position in which the skulls were placed, that they were on their return to their own country. Two small rods stuck in the ground, with a few hairs tied in two parcels at the end of each, signified that four scalps had been taken.

A record of facts which may be important and interesting to others, is thus left for the benefit of all who may follow. For our part we were glad to be in- formed, that one lawless and predatory band of savages had lately left the coun- try we were about to traverse. We were never without some anxiety on the subject of Indian war parties, who are known frequently to remunerate themselves for any discomfiture or loss they may have sustained, by making free booty of the property and the scalps of the first weak or unguarded party they may meet.

At a late hour in the night, after our camp had become quiet, we were suddenly awakened by a loud rushing noise, which in a moment seemed to reach the centre of our encampment; immediately a piercing exclamation of terror was heard, from one of our interpreters, which from the peculiarity of its tone, seemed to have escaped from a throat under the grasp of death. It became immediately apparent that the cause of the alarm proceeded from our horses, all of whom had broken loose from their stakes, near the Indian fort, and had run in a state of fright through our camp, with the apparent desire to gain our protection against something in their rear. We proceeded in a cautious manner to reconnoitre the environs of the camp, stooping low, in order that the eye might be directed along the level of the top of the grass, which was here of a very luxuriant growth, in order to detect in the gloom, any inimical object that might rise above it; having thus convinced ourselves that nothing dangerous to our safety remained very near to us, the horses were again secured, and we betook ourselves to our beds, with the reflection, that they had probably been alarmed by the too near approach of bisons.

We had scarce fallen asleep, when we were aroused the second time, by the discharge of a gun close to our tent. This was the signal which we had all understood was to be given by the sentinel, in case of the hostile approach of Indians to the camp. We therefore bestirred ourselves, being well assured we had other business at hand, than the security of horses. Several of the party went to reconnoitre the old fort above mentioned, but nothing was discovered and they returned.

After all were assembled at camp, Major Long informed us the alarm had been given by his order, and was intended to test the coolness and self-possession of the party, and to prepare us in some measure for an unpleasant occurrence, we all thought too likely to happen, which was no other than a serious attack from the Indians, to be made according to their custom at that highly unseasonable hour of the morning.

Since leaving the Missouri, we had never indulged a disposition to sluggishness, accustoming ourselves to rise every morning long before the sun, but we still found we left that small spot of earth, on which we had rested our limbs and which had become warm and dry by the heat of our bodies with as much reluctance, as we have felt at quitting softer beds.

The mode of rallying now prescribed, was the following: immediately after an alarm should be given, the party should seize their arms, and form in front of the tents, in the rear of the lines of packs, and await any orders that might be given. The sentinel giving the alarm, should proceed to the tent of the officers, in order to acquaint them with the cause. Major Long and Captain Bell should reconnoitre about the encampment, and if practicable ascertain the real occasion of the alarm. Farther movements be to regulated as the emergency might require.

This alarm was the occasion of our starting on the morning of the 26th at an earlier hour than usual. We rode on through the same uninteresting and dreary country as before, but were constantly amused at observing the motions of the countless thousands of bisons, by which we were all the time surrounded. The wind happening to blow fresh from the south, the scent of our party was borne directly across the Platte, and we could distinctly note every step of its progress through a distance of eight or ten miles, by the consternation and terror it excited among the buffaloe. The moment the tainted gale infected their atmosphere, they ran with as much violence as if pursued by a party of mounted hunters, and instead of running from danger, turned their heads towards the wind, eager to escape from the terrifying scent, they pushed forward in an oblique direction towards our party, and plunging into the river they swam and waded, and ran with the utmost violence, in several instances breaking through our line of march, which was immediately along the left bank of the Platte. One of the party perceiving from the direction taken by the bull, that preceded the extended column of his companions, that he intended to emerge from the low river bottom, at a particular point, where the precipitous bank was worn by much travelling, into a deep notch, urged his horse rapidly forward to gain this station, that he might have a near view of these interesting animals; he had no sooner arrived at this point, than the formidable leader, bounding up the steep, gained the summit of the bank, with his fore feet, and in this position abruptly halted from his full career, and glared fiercely at the horse, which now occupied his path. The horse, trembling violently from fear of this sudden apparition, would have wheeled and exerted his utmost speed, had he not been restrained by the greatest strength of his rider; he recoiled however a few feet, and sunk down upon his hams. The bull halted but a moment, then being urged forward by the irresistible impulse of the moving column behind, rushed onward by the half sitting horse. The multitude came swiftly on, crowding up the narrow defile. The party had now arrived, and extending along a considerable distance, the bisons ran in a confused manner in various directions to gain the distant bluffs; numbers were compelled to pass through our line of march, between the horses.

This scene added to the plunging and roaring in the river of those that were yet crossing, produced a grand effect, which was still heightened, by the fire opened upon them by our hunters. As they ascended the bank, innumerable opportunities offered of selecting and killing the fattest, and it was with difficulty, we restrained our hunters from slaughtering many more than we needed.

It is remarked by hunters, and appears to be an established fact, that the odour of a white man is more terrifying to wild animals, particularly the bison, than that of an Indian. This animal, in the course of its periodic migrations, comes into the immediate neighbourhood of the permanent Indian villages, on the Missouri and the Platte. One was seen by our hunters within six miles of the Grand Pawnee village, and immediately about the towns, we saw many heads and skeletons, of such as had been killed there the preceding spring. They had come in, while the Pawnees were absent on their winter's hunt, and at their return, we were informed they found the bisons immediately about their villages. They disappeared invariably from the neighbourhood of the white settlements within a few years. We are aware that another cause may be found for this, than the frightful scent of the white man, which is the impolitic, exterminating war, which he wages against all unsubdued animals within his reach.

Indians hunting bison, T.R. Peale, February, 1820, pencil.

It would be highly desirable, that some law for the preservation of game, might be extended to, and rigidly enforced in the country, where the bison is still met with: that the wanton destruction of these valuable animals, by the white hunters, might be checked or prevented. It is common for hunters to attack large herds of these animals, and having slaughtered as many as they are able, from mere wantonness and love of this barbarous sport, to leave the carcasses to be devoured by the wolves and birds of prey; thousands are slaughtered yearly, of which no part is saved except the tongues. This inconsiderate and cruel practice, is undoubtedly the principal reason why the bison flies so far and so soon from the neighbourhood of our frontier settlements.

It is well known to those in the least degree conversant with the Indians, that the odour which their bodies exhale, though very strong and peculiar, is by no means unpleasant at least to most persons. A negro in the employment of the Missouri fur company, and living at fort Lisa, was often heard to complain of the intolerable scent of the squaws; in like manner the Indians find the odour of a white man, extremely offensive. In the language of the Peruvian Indians, are three words to express their idea of the smell of the European, the Aboriginal American, and the negro. They called the first *Pezuna*, the second *Posco*, and the third *Grajo*.

After passing the range of hills, above mentioned, the surface subsides nearly to a plain, having however, manifestly a greater inclination than below. The velocity of the current of the river is much increased, the bed narrower, and the banks more precipitous. We passed several extensive tracts nearly destitute of vegetation. The surface of these consisted entirely of coarse sand and gravel, with here there an insulated mass of clay, highly impregnated with salt, and gnawed and licked into various singular shapes, exhibiting the forms of massive insulated columns, huge buttresses, prominent angles and profound excavations, fortuitously mingled, and which are now gradually diminishing, under the action of the cause which produced them. The present surface upon which they repose, seems to be a stratum of a different earth, which does not afford the condiment so attractive to the animals; the consequence is that the licking and chewing, principally, heretofore affecting the surface, on which the animal stood, is now directed against the upright portions of this singular grand excavation, and most remarkable of all known salt licks.

Some extensive portions of the immediate bottom land, along the river, were white with an effloresced salt; but this being impure and but imperfectly soluble, did not appear to have been licked.

Towards evening we passed two springs, of transparent, but impure and brackish water. They were the first we had met with on the Platte. Among a considerable number of undescribed plants collected on the 27th, are three referrible to the family of the rough-leaved plants, (asperifoliæ) one of them belonging to a genus not heretofore known in the United States. It has a salver-form corrolla, with a large, spreading, angular, plaited border. Another plant very conspicuously ornamental to these barren deserts, is a lactescent annual, belonging to the family of the convolvulacæ with a bright purple corrolla, as large as that of the common Strammonium. We also observed the white stalked primrose, (Œnothera *albicaulis,* N.) a very small white flowered species of Talinum, and some others. We observed in repeated instances, several individuals of a singular genus of reptiles (Chirotes. Cuv.) which, in form, resemble short serpents, but are more closely allied to the lizards, by being furnished with two feet. They were so active that it was not without some difficulty that we succeeded in obtaining a specimen. Of this (as was our uniform custom, when any apparently new animal was presented) we immediately drew out a description. But as the specimen was unfortunately lost, and the description formed part of the Zoological notes and observations, which were carried off by our deserters, we are reduced to the necessity of merely indicating the probability of the existence of the *Chirotes lumbricoides* of naturalists, within the territory of the United States.

At night we were again alarmed by a disturbance among our horses, of which we were not able to ascertain the cause. Some of the party had, on the preceeding day, reported that they had seen Indians at a distance, that they were on horse back, &c. but of this there could be no certainty, the imagination often representing a herd of antelopes, or other animals, seen at a distance, and perhaps distorted by the looming of the prairie, as so many mounted Indians. We had often found ourselves more grossly abused by our eye-sight, than is supposed in this instance, having mistaken turkeys for bisons, wolves for horses, &c.

28th. We breakfasted, and left our encampment before 5 o'clock. We had not proceeded far when we discovered about thirty wild horses at a distance before us. They had taken our scent, and run off in a fright, when we were a mile distant. Their activity and fleetness surpassed what we had expected from this noble animal in his savage state. In the course of the day we saw other herds, but all at a distance. The country south of the Platte contains, as we are informed, vast numbers of horses. They are of the domesticated stock introduced by the Spaniards, but they multiply rapidly in their present state of regained freedom, and are apparently wilder than any of the native occupants of this country. They are of various colours, and of all sizes, there being many colts, and some mules, among them. Their playfulness seemed to be excited, rather than their fears, by our appearance, and we often saw them, more than a mile distant, leaping and curvetting, involved by a cloud of dust, which they seemed to delight in raising.

About some sandy ridges, which we passed in the middle of the day, several miliary rattle snakes were seen, two of which were killed. These had been occasionally met with all along the Platte, but were by no means numerous. Mr. Peale killed a female antelope, without leaving our line. The animal had not been able to satisfy its curiosity, and stood at a little distance gazing at us, until it was shot down.

During the day we passed three small creeks discharging into the Platte from the northwest. One of these, called by the Indians Bat-so-ah, or Cherry creek, heads in the Rocky Mountains. On these creeks are a few small cotton-wood and willow trees. These trees, as well as all those along the Platte, are low, with very large and branching tops, as is the case with all trees which grow remote from each other.

In the afternoon hunters were sent forward, but it was not without some difficulty that a single bison was killed, those animals having become much less frequent.

Our small stock of bread was by this time so nearly exhausted, that it was thought prudent to reserve the remainder as a last resort, in case of the failure of a supply of game, or other accident. A quantity of parched maize, equal to a gill per day, to each man, was daily distributed to each of the three messes into which the party was divided. This was thrown into the kettle where the bison meat was boiled, and supplied the place of barley in the soup, always the first and most important dish. Whenever game was plenty we had a variety of excellent dishes, consisting of the choice parts of the bison, the tongue, the hump ribs, the marow bones, &c. dressed in various ways. The *hump ribs* of the bison, which many epicures prefer to any other part of the animal, are the spinous processes of the back bone, and are from eighteen to twenty-four inches in length. They are taken out with a small portion of the flesh adhering to each side, and whether roasted, boiled, or stewed, are certainly very far superior to any part of the flesh of the domestic ox.

29th. We had proceeded but a few miles from our camp when it was found that Mr. Say's horse was so far exhausted as to be unable to proceed at the same pace as the other horses. Mr. Say accordingly dismounted, and by driving his horse before him, urged the animal along for a few miles; but this being found too laborious, and as several of the horses were near failing, it was determined to halt, which we did at 10 o'clock, and remained in camp during the day.

The country, for several miles to the west of the range of hills mentioned above, is as uniformly plain as that on any part of the Platte. It differs from that further to the east only in being of a coarser sand, and in an aspect of more unvaried sterility. The cactus ferox reigns sole monarch, and sole possessor, of thousands of acres of this dreary plain. It forms patches which neither a horse nor any other animal will attempt to pass over. The rabbit's foot plantation, and a few brown and withered grasses, are sparingly scattered over the intervening spaces. In depressed and moist situations, where the soil is not so entirely unproductive, the variegated spurge, (Euphorbia *variegata,*) with its painted involucrum, and parti-coloured leaves is a conspicuous and beautiful ornament. The Lepidium virginicum, distributed over every part of northern and equinoctial America, from Hudson's Bay to the summit of the Silla of Caraccas, is here of such diminutive size that we were induced to search, though we sought in vain, for some character to distinguish it as a separate species.

At three o'clock P.M. the planet Venus was distinctly visible. Its distance from the sun at 3h. 45m. was east 36° 15'. There were a few broken cumulo-stratose clouds from the southwest, otherwise the sky was clear, and near the Zenith, where the star was seen, of a deep and beautiful azure. Our actual elevation, at this time, must have been considerable, and might be supposed to effect, in some degree, the transparency of our atmosphere.

Several magpies were seen about the islands in the river, where it is probable they rear their young.

On the 30th we left the encampment at our accustomed early
hour, and at 8 o'clock were cheered by
a distant view of the Rocky Mountains.
For some time we were unable to de-
cide whether what we saw were mountains, or banks of cumulous clouds
skirting the horizon, and glittering in
the reflected rays of the sun. It was only
by watching the bright parts, and ob-

Magpies, T.R. Peale, June 29, 1820, watercolor.

serving that their form and position remained unaltered, that we were able to satisfy ourselves, they were indeed mountains. They were visible from the lowest parts of the plain, and their summits were, when first discovered, several degrees above our horizon. They became visible by detaching themselves from the sky beyond, and not by emerging from beneath the sensible horizon, so that we might have seen them from a greater distance had it not been for the want of transparency in the atmosphere. Our first views of the mountains were indistinct, on account of some smokiness of the atmosphere, but from our encampment, at noon, we had a very distinct and satisfactory prospect of them. A small part only of the intervening plain was visible, the convexity of the surface intercepting the view, from the base of the mountains, and that portion of the plain adjacent to it.

Snow could be seen on every part of them which was visible above our horizon.

The thermometer immersed in the water of the river fell from 80° the temperature of the atmosphere, to 75°. Observations had been made daily to ascertain the temperature of the water of the Platte. Notwithstanding there were only about five degrees difference between the temperature of the air and that of the water, it was remarked by several of the party, that a sensation of extreme cold was felt on passing from the one to the other.

It is possible, that at the elevation we had now attained, the rapidity of evaporation, on account of the diminished pressure of the atmosphere, might be something greater than we had been accustomed to. For several days the sky had been clear, and in the morning we had observed an unusual degree of transparency in every part of the atmosphere. As the day advanced, and the heat of the sun began to be felt, such quantities of vapour were seen to ascend, from every part of the plain, that all objects, at a little distance, appeared magnified, and variously distorted. An undulating or tremulous motion in ascending lines was manifest over every part of the surface. Commencing soon after sunrise it continued to increase in quantity until the afternoon, when it diminished gradually, keeping an even pace with the intensity of the sun's heat. The density of the vapour was often such as to produce the perfect image of a pool of water in every valley upon which we could look down at an angle of about ten degrees. This effect was several times seen so perfect and beautiful as to deceive almost every one of our party. A herd of bisons, at the distance of a mile, seemed to be standing in a pool of water; and what appeared to us the reflected image was as distinctly seen as the animal itself. Illusions of this kind are common in the African and Asiatic deserts, as we learn from travellers, and from the language of poets. They are called by the Persians *sirraub*, "water of the desert;" and in the Sanscrit language *Mriga trichna* "the desire or thirst of the antelope." Elphinstone relates, that at Moujgur, in the kingdom of Caubul, towards evening many persons were astonished at the appearance of a long lake enclosing several little islands. Notwithstanding the well known nature of the country, which was a sandy desert, many were positive that it was a lake, and one of the surveyors took the bearings of it. "I had imagined," says he, "this phenomenon to be occasioned by a thin vapour which is spread over the ground in hot weather in India, but this appearance was entirely different, and on looking along the ground no vapour whatever could be perceived. The ground was quite level and smooth, and the weather very hot. It is only found in level, smooth, and dry places; the position of the sun, and the degree of heat, are not material, for it was afterwards seen in Damaun when the weather was not hotter than in England." On the frontier of Caubul Elphinstone saw what he calls a most magnificent mirage, which looked like an extensive lake, or a very wide river. The water seemed clear and beautiful, and the figures of two gentlemen, who rode along it, were *reflected as distinctly as in real water.* It is common in our own country, says the London Monthly Review, for ground-mists to assume the appearance of water, to make a meadow seem inundated, and to change a valley into a lake; but these mists never reflect the surrounding trees and hills. Hence the *mirage* must consist of a peculiar gas, of which the particles are combined by a stronger attraction of cohesion than the vapours of real water; the *liquor silicum* of the alchemists is described as exhibiting, in some circumstances, this glassy surface, yet as being equally evanescent. It is afterwards suggested, in the same paper, that the gas which occasioned these extraordinary reflections may probably be the substance of the pernicious wind called Simoom. The explanation here offered will not probably be thought satisfactory. It seems to belong to the epoch of great and brilliant discoveries in pneumatic chemistry, when "a peculiar gas" was thought the agent of every phenomenon.

The images of pools of water, which we saw in the deserts of the Platte, appeared to us similar to those mentioned by Elphinstone, likewise to those observed by Nieburgh in Arabia, where *inverted* images were seen.

To the more common effects of light passing through a medium charged with vapours we had become familiar. We had, for many days, seen the low bluffs of the valley of the Platte suspended over the verge of our apparent horizon, as distant capes are suspended over the sea; but in viewing these perfect images of lakes we could scarce believe they were occasioned by *refraction*, to which the phenomena of mirage have usually been attributed. The circumstance that these pools could only be seen when we looked down at a considerable angle upon some valley; the perfect manner in which the image of the sky was returned, from the surface, and the inverted position of the objects seen, induced us to inquire whether the effect might not be produced by reflection from the lower stratum of watery vapour. These appearances are sufficient to justify the conclusion that the quantity of evaporation is much greater here than in less elevated districts of country, where such things are not.

Towards evening the air became more clear, and our view of the mountains was more satisfactory, though as yet we could only distinguish their grand outline, imprinted in bold indentations upon the luminous margin of the sky. We soon remarked a particular part of the range divided into three conic summits, each apparently of nearly equal altitude. This we concluded to be the point designated by Pike as the Highest Peak. Its bearing was taken a short time before we halted for the evening, and found to be south, 73° west. As we were about to encamp some of the party went in pursuit of a herd of bisons, one of which they killed, and returned to camp a little before sunset.

July 1st. Although the temperature indicated by the thermometer for several days had been about 80°, in the middle of the day, the heat, owing to the cool breezes from the mountain, had been by no means oppressive. On the night of the 30th of June the mercury fell to 55°, and on the following morning the air was chilly, and a strong breeze was felt before sunrise, from the southeast. We left our camp at a very early hour, and travelling over a tract differing in no respect

Distant view of the Rocky Mountains, Samuel Seymour, engraving.

but its greater barrenness from that passed on the preceding day. We halted to dine at the distance of sixteen and an half miles. Many acres of this plain had not vegetation enough to communicate to the surface the least shade of green; a few dwarfish sunflowers and grasses, which had grown here in the early part of the summer, being now entirely withered and brown. In stagnant pools near the river we saw the common arrow head, (Saggittaria saggittifolia,) the alisma plantago, and the small lemna growing together, as in similar situations in the eastern States.

A striking feature of that part of the plain country, we were now passing, is formed by innumerable ant-heaps, rising from twelve to eighteen inches above the common level of the surface. They occur with some uniformity, at intervals of about twenty feet, and are all similar in size and dimensions. They consist so entirely of small grains of flesh-coloured feldspar, that they have all of them an uniform reddish aspect, and it is not without careful examination, that any other kind of gravel can be detected in them. The entrance to the interior of each of these little mounds, is uniformly on the eastward side, and very rarely occurs beyond the boundaries of N. E. and S. E. It is never at the top, nor on a level with the surface of the soil, but is a little elevated above it. It seems highly probable, that the active little architects, thus place the entrance to their edifice on the eastward side, in order to escape the direct influence of the cold mountain winds.

At three o'clock as we were about to resume our journey, there came on a gentle shower of rain, with rain at east, and low broken clouds. In the afternoon we passed some small ridges of sandstone crossing the river from north to south, but very inconsiderable in point of elevation and extent. We travelled this day twenty-seven miles, directly towards the base of the mountains, but they appeared almost as distant in the evening, as they had done in the morning. The bearing of the high peaks above mentioned, from our encampment was south, 75° west.

The ensuing day being Sabbath, was devoted to rest. About our camp which was in the most fertile spot we could select, in a ride of several miles, there was but a very insufficient supply of grass for our horses. A species of cone flower, (Rudbeckia *columnaris*, N.) was here beginning to expand. The showy R. *purpurea*, very common on the Missouri, and the lower part of the Platte, does not extend into the desolate regions. The common purslane (Portulacca *oleracea*) is one of the most frequent plants about the base of the Rocky Mountains, particularly in places much frequented, as licks by the bisons, and other animals.

From this encampment, we had a plain but still distant view of the mountains. No inequality occurs in the surface of the subjacent country on the east of the mountains, so that our view was wholly unobstructed. They stretched from north to south, like an immense wall occupying all that portion of the horizon, lying to the northwest, west, and southwest. We could now see the surface of the plain, extending almost unvaried to the base of the first ridge, which rises by an abrupt ascent above the commencement of the snow.

A set of observations for longitude was commenced in the morning, but the weather becoming cloudy, we were prevented from completing them. In the afternoon a storm came on from the north, which continued during the night. Much rain fell, accompanied with thunder, and high but variable winds. Between twelve o'clock and sunset, the mercury in Fahrenheit's thermometer, fell nineteen degrees, from 89° to 60°

3rd. Breakfast was despatched, and we had mounted our horses before five o'clock. We were enabled to have our breakfast thus early, as the sentinel on duty during the night, was directed to put the kettles over the fire at three o'clock, all the processes preparatory to boiling, having been finished on the preceding evening.

As we approached the mountains, wood became much more abundant along the Platte. We had often heard our guide, in speaking of the country, two or three days journey from the mountains, mention the *Grand Forest*, and were a little surprised on arriving at it, to find no more than a narrow but uninterrupted strip of timber, extending along the immediate banks of the river, never occupying the space of half a mile in width.

For several days the direction of our course in ascending the Platte, had inclined considerably to the south, varying from due west to south, 20° west.

In the course of the day, we passed the mouths of three large creeks, heading in the mountains, and entering the Platte from the northwest. One of these nearly opposite to which we encamped, is called Potera's creek, from a Frenchman of that name, who is said to have been bewildered upon it, wandering about for twenty days, almost without food. He was then found by a band of Kiawas, who frequent this part of the country, and restored to his companions, a party of hunters, at that time encamped on the Arkansa.

Throughout the day we were approaching the mountains obliquely, and from our encampment, at evening we supposed them to be about twenty miles distant. Clouds were hanging about all the higher parts of the mountains, which were sometimes observed to collect together, and descend in showers, circumscribed to a limited district. This state of the weather obstructed the clearness, but added greatly to the imposing grandeur of some of the views, which the mountain presented.

4th. We had hoped to celebrate our great national festival on the Rocky Mountains; but the day had arrived, and they were still at a distance. Being extremely impatient of any unnecessary delay, which prevented us from entering upon the examination of the mountains, we did not devote the day to rest, as had been our intention. It was not, however, forgotten to celebrate the Anniversary of our National Independence, according to our circumstances. An extra pint of maize was issued to each mess, and a small portion of whiskey distributed.

On leaving the camp in the morning, Major Long and Lieutenant Swift preceded the party, intending to select a suitable place for encampment, where they proposed to commence a set of observations, and to wait the arrival of the remainder of the party. But as they had gone forward about two miles, the point of the woods at which they had left the course, was mistaken by the main body, which moved on until about eleven o'clock. By this time much anxiety was felt on account of their absence, and persons were sent out to attempt to discover them, but returned unsuccessful. A circumstance tending to increase the anxiety we felt was, that Indians were reported to have been seen in the course of the morning, by several of the party. Captain Bell was about to despatch as large a force as it was thought prudent to spare from the camp, to search for them in all the distance which had been passed since they were seen—when they arrived at the encampment of the main body, at half past one P.M.

The observations which had been made, were of course lost, as the corresponding equal altitudes for the correction of time could not be had.

In the evening the meridional altitude of Antares, was taken for latitude. The party remained encamped during the afternoon, when the extra allowance of corn was cooked and eaten, and the whiskey drank in honor of the day.

Several valuable plants were here collected, and among others a large suffruticose species of Lupine. The long leaved cotton-wood of Lewis and Clark, which is according to their suggestion, a species of populus, is here of very common occurrence. It is found intermixed with the common cotton-wood, resembling it in size and general aspect. Its leaves are long and narrow, its trunk smoother, and its branches more slender and flexile, than those of the Populus *angulata*. Some of its fruit was fortunately still remaining, affording us an opportunity to be entirely satisfied of its relation to this genus.

Here we also observed both species of the splendid and interesting Bartonia, the B. *nuda* in full flower, the *ornata* not yet expanded.

These most singular plants are interesting on several accounts, particularly the regular expansion of their large and beautiful flowers, towards the evening of several successive days. In the morning the long and slender petals, and the petal-like *nectaries*, which compose the flower, are found accurately closed upon each other, forming a cone of about an inch in length. In this situation they remain if the weather be clear, until about sunset, when they gradually expand. If the weather is dark and cloudy, with a humid atmosphere, they are awakened from their slumbers at an earlier hour. We have, in some instances, seen them fully expanded early in the afternoon, but this has always been in stormy or cloudy weather. In this particular, the Bartonia bears some resemblance to the great night flowering cereus, to which it is closely allied, but the gaudy petals of the cereus once unfolded, fall into a state of irretrievable collapse, whereas the Bartonia closes and expands its flowers for many days in succession.

A number of young magpies were seen in the bushes about the river, also the nests and young of the mocking bird, (Turdus orpheus, Vieil.)

The prairie-dog villages we had observed to become more frequent and more extensive, as we approached the mountains, and we had now constant opportunities of contrasting the stupendous elevations of the Andes, with the humble mounds cast up by this interesting little animal. We observed in the numerous burrows, an appearance of greater antiquity, than in those more remote from the mountains. Many of the mounds occupy an extent of several yards in diameter, though of but inconsiderable elevation, and with the exception of the present entrance, overgrown with a scanty herbage, which always marks the area of the prairie-dog villages. Indeed we have observed several large villages, with scarce a trace of vegetation about them. The food of the marmot consisting of grasses and herbaceous plants, it is not perhaps easy to assign a reason for the preference which, in selecting the site of his habitation, he always shows for the most barren places, unless it be that he may enjoy an unobstructed view of the surrounding country, in order to be seasonably warned of the approach of wolves, or other enemies.

Rattle snakes of a particular species are sometimes seen in these villages. They are found between the Mississippi and the Rocky Mountains, and appear to prefer an unproductive soil, where their sluggish gait may not be retarded by the opposing obstacles of grass and weeds. Whilst exploring Boyer Creek, of the Missouri, in the Spring of 1820, our party met with six or eight of them during one day's march on the prairie, and on our subsequent journey to the Rocky Mountains we several times encountered equal or even greater numbers, in the same space of time. This is the species of serpent which travellers have observed to frequent the villages of the prairie dogs, and to which they have attributed the unnatural habit of voluntary domiciliation with that interesting animal. It is true that the *tergeminus*, like many other serpents, will secure a refuge from danger in any hole of the earth, rock, or fallen tree, that may present itself, regardless of the rightful occupant; but we witnessed no facts which could be received as proof that it is an acceptable inmate of the dwelling of the Arctomys.

From the disparity in the number of plates and scales, and from the greater size of the vertebral spots in this species than in the C. *miliaris*, we have been induced to consider this a distinct species. Specimens are in the Philadelphia museum.

On the 5th July we left our camp at an early hour, and ascended the Platte about ten miles. Here the party encamped for the day, and Dr. James and Mr. Peale with two riflemen, Verplank and Bernard, went out for an excursion on foot, intending to ascend the Cannon-ball creek to the mountains which appeared to be about five miles distant.

This creek is rapid and clear, flowing over a bed paved with rounded masses of granite and gneiss. It is from a supposed resemblance to these masses to cannon balls that the creek has received its name from the French hunters. The channel is sunk from fifty to one hundred feet below the common level of the plain.

This plain consists of a bed of coarse pebbles, gravel, and sand, and its surface is thinly covered with prickly pears and a scanty growth of starved and rigid grasses. Among these, the hygrometric stipas, [S. *juncea*, S. *barbata*] are extremely troublesome, their barbed and pointed seeds adhering and penetrating like the quills of the porcupine into every part of the dress with which they come in contact. The long and rigid awn is contorted or strait in proportion to the humidity or dryness of the atmosphere, indicating the changes in this respect with the precision of the nicest hygrometer.

The detached party extended their walk about eight miles without finding the apparent distance to the base of the mountain had very considerably diminished. They had unluckily forgotten to make any provision for dinner, and now found themselves fatigued and hungry at the distance of eight miles from the encampment or the main body, and so far from the mountains that it was evidently impossible to reach them and return on the same day. They therefore determined to relinquish the attempt, and Mr. Peale was fortunate enough to kill a couple of curliews, which were roasted and eaten without loss of time.

Near the place of this halt they observed some small sandstone ridges similar to those on the Platte below, and collected among other plants, the species of currant, [Ribes *aureum?*] so often mentioned by Lewis and Clark, the fruit of which formed an important article of the subsistence of their party while crossing the Rocky Mountains.

They also saw about the shelvings of the sandstone rocks, which formed for some distance the banks of the stream, innumerable nests of the cliff swallow, similar to those seen on the Missouri. In returning to the camp by a different route, they were much annoyed by the prickly pears, covering the ground so closely, that their feet were frequently wounded by the thorns, against which their mockasins presented but a very inadequate protection.

Having killed a young antelope, they re-crossed the Platte, which was here about three feet deep, clear, and rapid, and arrived at the camp after sunset.

Here a complete set of observations, for latitude, longitude, &c., had been taken. Major Long and Lieutenant Swift having preceded the party in the morning, and arrived before seven o'clock, for that purpose. In the evening, observations were attempted, but without success, as the sky soon became cloudy.

Robins, (Turdus migratorius.) which we had not seen since we left the Missouri, here occurred in great numbers.

On the following morning, soon after leaving the encampment, we crossed Vermillion creek, a considerable tributary from the south. In some part of its course, its valley is bounded by precipitous cliffs of red sand-rock, whence the name of the creek.

Our guide informed us that the Indians, a few years since, destroyed every individual of a large herd of bisons, by driving them over the brink of one of these precipices.

Opposite the mouth of Vermillion creek, is a much larger stream, from the northwest, which is called Medicine-lodge creek, from an old Indian medicine lodge, which formerly stood near its mouth. A few miles further, on the same side, is Grand-camp creek, heading also in the mountains. About four years previous to the time of our visit, there had been a large encampment of Indians and hunters on this creek. On that occasion three nations of Indians, namely, the Kiawas, Arrapahoes, and Kaskaias or Bad-hearts, had been assembled together, with forty five French hunters in the employ of Mr. Choteau and Mr. Demun of St. Louis. They had assembled for the purpose of holding a trading council with a band of Shiennes. These last had been recently supplied with goods by the British traders on the Missouri, and had come to exchange them with the former for horses. The Kiawas, Arrapahoes, &c., who wander in the extensive plains of the Arkansa and Red river, have always great numbers of horses, which they rear with much less difficulty than the Shiennes, whose country is cold and barren.

The British traders annually supply the Minnetarees or *Gros ventres* of the Missouri with goods; from these they pass to the Shiennes and Crow Indians, who, in their turn, barter them with remoter tribes: in this manner the Indians who wander near the mountains receive their supplies of goods, and they give a decided and well founded preference to those which reach them by this circuitous channel, over those which they receive from any other source.

Two miles beyond Grand Camp creek, is the mouth of Grape creek, and a little above on the opposite side, that of Defile creek, a tributary to the Platte, from the south, which has its course in a narrow defile, lying along the base of the mountains.

At eleven o'clock we arrived at the boundary of that vast plain, across which we had journeyed for a distance of near one thousand miles; and encamped at the base of the mountain. The woodless plain is terminated by a range of naked and almost perpendicular rocks, visible at a distance of several

View near the Base of the Rocky Mountains, Samuel Seymour, watercolor.

miles, and resembling a vast wall, parallel to the base of the mountain. These rocks are sandstone, similar in composition and character, to that on the Cannon-ball creek. They emerge at a great angle of inclination from beneath the alluvial of the plain, and rise abruptly to an elevation of one hundred and fifty, or two hundred feet. Passing within this first range, we found a narrow valley separating it from the second ridge of sandstone, of nearly equal elevation, and apparently resting against the base of a high primitive hill beyond. At the foot of the first range, the party encamped at noon, and were soon scattered in various directions, being eager to commence the examination of that interesting region.

CHAPTER III

Sandstone formation at the base of the Rocky Mountains—
The Platte within the mountains—Granite between the Platte and the Arkansa
—Birds—Plants, &c.

THE inclined sandstone at the base of the Rocky Mountains we found much wider and its summits incomparably more elevated than our previous opinions, or a distant view had led us to expect. This extensive range, rising abruptly from the plain, skirts the base of the mountain like a vast rampart, and from a person standing near it, intercepts the view of the still more grand and imposing features of the granite ridge beyond. It consists of rocks in which the comminuted fragments of primitive aggregates are intermixed with the reliquiæ of the animals of a former world, known to us only by the monuments which these remains exhibit. The stratifications, with which this rugged and precipitous wall of sandstone is distinctly seamed, penetrate the mass with various degrees of obliquity; not unfrequently the laminæ are entirely vertical, as if the whole had receded from its original position, and these immense rocky masses, had, by the operation of some powerful agent, been broken off from their former continuity, with the strata now found in a horizontal position in the plains.

It is difficult, when contemplating the present appearance and situation of these rocks, to prevent the imagination from wandering back to that remote unascertained period, when the billows of the primeval ocean lashed the base of the Rocky Mountains, and deposited, during a succession of ages, that vast accumulation of rounded fragments of rocks alternating with beds of animal remains, which now extend without interruption from the base of this range to the summits of the Alleghanies; and endeavouring to form some conception of that subsequent catastrophe which has so changed the relative elevation of the two great formations that the margin of the secondary has been broken off and thrown into an inclined or vertical position.

The valley between this parapet of sand-rock and the first granitic ridge is near a mile wide. It is ornamented with numerous isolated columnar rocks, often of a snowy whiteness, standing like pyramids and obelisks, interspersed among mounds and hillocks, which seem to have resulted from the disintegration of similar masses.

The range of sandstone appears to have been originally of uniform elevation and uninterrupted continuity, stretching along the base of the mountains from north to south, but it has been divided transversely by the bed of the Platte, and all the larger rivers in their descent to the plains.

From our camp, we had expected to be able to ascend the most distant summits then in sight, and return the same evening, but night overtook us and we found ourselves scarcely arrived at the base of the mountain. The lowest part of the sandstone stratum, exposed at the western declivities of the hills, and in the points nearest the granite, contains extensive beds of coarse conglomerate or pudding-stone, often of a reddish colour. The more compact parts of the rock present remains of terebratulæ and other submarine animals. Among these, few are entire or in good preservation. We observed here, several singular, scorpion-like animals, inhabiting under stones and dried bison's dung. They have a formidable appearance, and run actively. They belong to the class Arachnides, genus Galeodes, which has been heretofore observed only in warm climates; not one was known to inhabit this continent.

About the sandstone ledges we collected a geranium intermediate between the crane's bill and herb robert, the beautiful calochortus, [C. *elegans, Ph.*] and a few other valuable plants.

The Platte at the foot of the mountains is twenty-five yards wide, having an average depth of about three feet; its water clear and cool, and its current rapid. Its descent for twenty miles below cannot be less than eight feet per mile. Its valley is narrow and serpentine, bounded by steep and elevated hills, embosoming innumerable little lawns often of a semicircular form, ornamented by the narrow margin of shrubbery along the Platte.

The narrow valley, which intervenes' between the ridges of sandstone before mentioned, is a little more fertile than the plains along the river. It is covered with fine and short grasses, and varied with here and there a copse of small oaks or hazles. There are also some columnar masses of white sandstone, twenty or thirty feet high, standing remote from each other, having the debris around their bases covered with shrubby oaks.

We observed here the obscure wren, a bird more closely related to the great Carolina wren of Wilson than any other we have seen; but the characters drawn from the primaries, and from the marking of the tail sufficiently distinguish it from that species. The bill is somewhat longer, and the general tint of the plumage of a much more sombre hue. It frequents the arid country in the vicinity of the mountains, and is often seen hopping about upon the branches and singularly compressed semi-procumbent trunks, of a species of juniper.

The bill of this species approaches the form which characterizes the genus *Certhia*, in which Wilson has placed its kindred species, the Carolina wren.

On the morning of the 7th of July, the party remaining in the encampment of the preceding day, Dr. James and Mr. Peale, accompanied by two riflemen, were sent out to examine the mountains. These appeared most accessible on the north side of the river, which was opposite our encampment. The river was here about four feet deep, and the strength of the current such as to render it impossible for a man to keep on his feet, in the deepest part of the stream. As some of the party destined for the mountains could not swim, it was thought hazardous for them to attempt to cross by fording. To obviate this difficulty two men were sent with a long rope, which they were directed to stretch across the river, making the ends fast on either shore. This was readily accomplished, one of the men swimming across with an end of the rope in his teeth. By the aid of this the detachment were enabled to keep their feet in crossing, though with extreme difficulty as the bed of the river was uneven and rocky. They all however arrived in safety on the left bank about sunrise.

After passing the region of inclined sandstone, which is about two miles in width, they began to rise upon what may be considered the base of the mountain. As the day advanced the heat became oppressive, and they found themselves somewhat exhausted, before they had crossed the sandstone hills, which appeared so inconsiderable from our encampment, that the labour of crossing them had been almost forgotten in estimating the toils of the day. The first range of primitive rocks they found far more abrupt and rugged than the sandstone hills they had already passed. Its sides are destitute of vegetation, except a few prickly pears and yuccas, with here and there a stinted oak or juniper, and so steep that great exertion as well as the utmost caution are necessary in ascending.

The rock is an aggregate of feldspar and hornblend, approaching in character some of the common varieties of Sienite. On the eastern side, where the feldspar is in the greatest proportion, it is flesh-coloured and its structure crystalline, the fractured surface of the mass being uneven like that of coarse granite; advancing towards the west, hornblend was found more and more predominant, and so arranged as to have, in the mass, a laminated appearance. The natural fissures or cleavages between the laminæ run nearly in a perpendicular direction, giving the rock the columnar structure of trap, or greenstone. As they proceeded, a few interesting insects and plants occurred to reward their labors. But these impenetrable and naked rocks are the abodes of few living beings either animal or vegetable. In the crevices where a scanty soil has accumulated, is here and there planted, a hardy evergreen, whose short and gnarled trunk, and recurved inflexible branches, seem to proclaim the storms it has withstood, and the centuries during which it has vegetated.

The design of the party had been to cross the first range of the mountains and gain the valley of the Platte beyond, but this they found themselves unable to accomplish. After climbing successively to the summit of several ridges, which they had supposed to be the top of the mountain, they still found others beyond higher and more rugged. They therefore relinquished the intention of crossing, and began to look for the best way to descend to the bed of the river, which lay on their left hand. Here they halted to rest for a few moments, and exposed a thermometer in the shade of a large rock. The mercury fell to 72°; in camp, at the same hour, it stood at 86°. They were so much elevated above the river, that although they could see it plainly, it appeared like a small brook of two or three yards in width, white with foam and spray caused by the impetuosity of its current and the roughness of its channel. They could distinguish two principal branches of the Platte, one coming from the northwest, the other from the south. A little below the confluence of these branches the river turns abruptly to S. E., bursting through a chasm in a vast mural precipice of naked columnar rocks.

About noon the detachment commenced their descent, which cost them no less exertion than their ascent in the morning. Their fatigue was aggravated by thirst, as they met with no water nor any shade except that of projecting rocks in the higher parts of the mountains. They chose a different route from that which they had taken in ascending, intending to descend to the river, with the hope of being able to travel along its bed. They were obliged to assist each other in lowering themselves down precipices, which they would have found it impossible to pass singly. On the southern declivity of the mountain they met with a few ripe currants, but these were hard and juiceless, of a sweetish taste, and aggravated instead of alleviating their thirst, and were probably the cause of a violent headache with which several of the party were affected soon after eating them. There were also found a few large and delicious raspberries, of a species approaching the flowering raspberry, [Rubus *odoratus*] but with smaller leaves and a more branching stem.

After descending from the more precipitous parts about the summit of the mountain, they crossed a long and rugged tract, buried, and rendered almost impassable by boulders and fragments which had fallen from above, and were at length so fortunate as to find a spring of cool water, and a shade in a narrow ravine, where they sat down to rest, and dine on the provision they had brought.

The men who were with them stopped in the same ravine, a few rods below. One of these, immediately after drinking the water, was violently attacked with headach, vomiting, and purging, which increased to such an alarming degree that he was presently unable to stand upon his feet. As it was feared he would not soon recover strength enough to walk, Mr. Peale undertook to return alone to camp, and give notice of his situation, and return with medicine and assistance.

He descended along a rough and obstructed ravine until he arrived at the Platte, but found the valley so confined as to be impassable, and again directed his course across the mountains, towards the northeast, and after a most rugged and fatiguing march of about six miles, arrived at camp late in the afternoon. Here he found several of the party suffering in a similar manner, but not so severely as the man he had left in the mountains. Two men were immediately despatched with some medicines in search of the disabled party.

The spot where they halted was several miles within the mountains, and elevated nearly to the limit of phænogamous vegetation. The common hop, [H. *lupulus*] was growing in perfection, also the box elder, [Acer *negundo, Ph*] the common sarsaparilla of the Eastern states, [Aralia *nudicaulis*] the spikenard [A. *racemosa*,] and mamy other plants common to the Alleghanies and Green mountains. After waiting about two hours, the sick man had so far recovered as to be able to stand upon his feet, and to walk a little. They therefore relieved him of his gun and other luggage, and moved by short stages towards camp, where they arrived at a late hour of the night.

The men, who had been sent out to their assistance, returned some time afterwards, having sought for them without success. In the morning of the same day, soon after the departure of Dr. James' detachment, two of the party passed into the mountains, on the left side of the river; they experienced much difficulty, and underwent much labour in scaling the steep ascents, and some hazard in descending the precipitous declivities, which marked their course. The timber was small, scrubby, and scattered in the most favoured situations, and many of the solitary pines, which occupied an elevated position, had evidently been the sport of furious tempests, being rived and seamed by lightning.

To the right, and easy of access, was a projecting rock, supporting a single humble cedar in one of its fissures, from which a stone let fall was received into the torrent of the river which washed its base. The huge rampart of naked rocks, which had been seen from below to stretch across the valley, was now in nearer view, the river whirling abruptly around the acute angle of its extremity, and offering, at its superior edge, an embattled outline. They ascended a primitive mountain which seemed to be of superior elevation, in order to overlook the western ranges, but they here found their horizon bounded by the succeeding mountain, towering majestically above them. To the east, over the tops of a few inferior elevations, lay expanded, like an ocean, the vast interminable prairie, over which we had so long held our monotonous march. The undulations which vary its surface now disappeared, and the whole lay like a map before the observer. They could trace the course of the Platte, and number the streams they had crossed, and others which they had before passed near, by the slight fringing of timber or bushes which margined their banks, and by an occasional glimpse of their streams, shining like quicksilver, and interrupting and varying the continuity of the plain, as they pursued their serpentine course. The atmosphere was remarkably serene, and small clouds were coursing over the surface of the heavens, casting their swiftly-moving shadows upon the earth, and enhancing the beauty of the contrast, which the long lines of timber afforded, to the general glare of light. After contemplating for some time the beauty and extent of the scene, their attention was attracted by a moving point, rendered occasionally visible by reflecting the rays of the retiring sun. This object was our white flag waving in a gentle breeze and revealing the position of our camp, the only spot in the boundless landscape, where the eye could rest on the work of human hands.

Astronomical observations were attempted at camp, but in the middle of the day the moon was too near the sun, and in the evening the sky was cloudy.

The sickness experienced by almost all the party, was, probably, occasioned by eating currants, which were abundant about the camp. It is not to be supposed, this illness was caused by any very active deleterious quality in the fruit, but that the stomach, by long disuse, had, in a great measure, lost the power of digesting fruits. Several continued unwell during the night.

On the morning of the 9th, we resumed our journey, travelling somewhat east of south, along a small tributary of the Platte.

The bed of this stream lies from south to north, along a narrow valley, bounded on each side by high cliffs of sandstone. The rock is similar to that already mentioned, its strata having, however, less inclination than is observed nearer the base of the mountain. It is the margin of that great formation of secondary which occupies the plains, and appears as if broken off and thrown into an inclined position, by some convulsion which changed the relative elevation of the stratum. It is of great thickness, its laminæ in an almost vertical position, occupying a surface of two or three and sometimes many miles in width. On the eastern declivities of the first ranges of hills, in places which may be supposed to have been the surface of the stratum in its original position, the rock is usually of a close grain and compact texture, and of a yellowish-white or light gray colour.

We saw many masses of sandstone bearing a striking resemblance to colossal ruins, also some insulated hills with perpendicular sides and level summits. These seem to be the remains of an extensive portion of the sandstone stratum which formerly covered the country to the level of their highest summits. They occur at considerable distance from the base of the primitive mountains, and their summits are occupied by horizontal strata. For a small portion of the upper part of their elevation their sides are nearly perpendicular, but their bases are surrounded by an extensive accumulation of debris, sometimes rising nearly to the summit. After ascending the small stream, before mentioned, to its source, we crossed an inconsiderable ridge, which separates it from the valley of Defile creek: this we ascended to the place where its principal branch descends from the mountain, where we encamped.

Several of the tributaries to Defile creek appear to discharge as much water as is seen in the stream below their junction. This appearance is common to many of the larger creeks, their broad and sandy beds allowing much of the water to sink and pass through the sand. In the evening a favorable opportunity, the first for several days, presented, and observations for latitude were taken.

In that part of Defile creek, near which we encamped, are numerous dams, thrown across by the beaver, causing it to appear rather like a succession of ponds than a continued stream. As we ascended farther towards the mountains, we found the works of these animals still more frequent. The small willlows and cotton-wood trees, which are here in considerable numbers, afford them their most favorite food.

In visiting one of those peculiar tabular hills which mark the border of the secondary region, we crossed a ridge of sandstone about three hundred feet in height, with strata inclined to the west. To this succeeds a valley about one mile wide, having a scanty growth of pine and oak. The ascent of the hill is steep and rugged; horizontal strata of sandstone and coarse conglomerate are exposed on its sides, and the summit is capped by a thin stratum of compact sandstone surmounted by a bed of greenstone. The loose and splintery fragments of this rock sometimes cover the surface and make a clinking noise under the feet like fragments of pottery.

The summit of the hill is of an oval form, about eight hundred yards in length and five hundred in breadth. The elevation is about one thousand feet, and the height of the perpendicular precipice, from the summit of the debris to the top of the hill, about fifty.

From this hill the High Peak mentioned by Capt. Pike was discovered, and its bearing found to be S. 50° W.

Several of the party ascended Defile creek until they arrived at the mountains, into which they penetrated as far as was found practicable. As they travelled along the bed of this stream, they found the several rock formations beautifully exposed, and in the following order, commencing from the alluvial of the plain on the east.

First—Horizontal sandstone, embracing extensive beds of coarse conglomerate, and commonly of a light gray or reddish-yellow colour.

Second—Fine compact gray sandstone, containing a few impressions of organic remains, resembling those in the sandstones of coal formations. This rock is inclined at an angle of near twenty degrees towards the west. It forms continuous ranges of hills, not difficult of ascent from the east, but their western declivities are abrupt and precipitous.

Third—Lofty and detached columns of sandstone of a reddish or deep brown colour. These are irregularly scattered throughout a narrow woodless valley. Some of them rise probably three hundred feet above the common level of the plain, and are so steep on all sides as to preclude the possibility of ascent; others are accessible at some points, and one of these we ascended.

Fourth—Coarse white pudding-stone, or conglomerate and sandstone of a deep red colour, alternating with each other, and with beds of fine white sandstone, and resting against the granite in a highly inclined position. This rock contains well preserved remains of terebratula, productus, and other bivalve shells. These are usually found on or near the surface of large nodules of a fine flinty stone, closely resembling petrosilex. The same rock also contains an extensive bed of iron ore, and from its eastern side flows a copious brine spring.

About this spring, which had evidently been much frequented by animals, we saw the skulls of the male and female Big-horn, the bones of elk, bisons, and other animals.

The granite, which succeeds the sandstone last mentioned, is of a dark reddish-brown colour, containing a large proportion of feldspar of the flesh coloured variety, and black mica. The crystalline grains or fragments of the feldspar are large and detached easily; consequently, the rock is in a state of rapid disintegration. This granite rises abruptly in immense mountain masses, and, undoubtedly, extends far to the west.

The little river, on which we encamped, pours down the side of this granitic mountain through a deep, inaccessible chasm, forming a continued cascade of several hundred feet. From an elevation of one or two thousand feet, on the side of the mountain, we were able to overlook a great extent of secondary region at its base. The surface appeared broken for several miles, and in many of the vallies we could discern columnar and pyramidal masses of sandstone, sometimes entirely naked, and sometimes bearing little tufts of bushes about their summits.

In the evening, a thunder-cloud rose in the east, which appeared for some time to approach, the thunder being loud and frequent, but at length moved off towards the southeast, continuing visible in the horizon during great part of the night.

11th. From our encampment, we travelled nearly south, and, crossing a small ridge dividing the waters of the Platte from those of the Arkansa, halted to dine on a tributary of the latter. In an excursion from this place we collected a large species of columbine, somewhat resembling the common one of the gardens. It is heretofore unknown to the Flora of the United States, to which it forms a splendid acquisition. If it should appear not to have been described, it may receive the name of Aquilegia *coerulea*. Our road, during the morning, lay for about twelve miles, along the foot of the primitive mountains, having on our left hand some of the sandstone ridges and hills already described. On our right the brown and naked granite rose in shapeless masses far above our heads, and, occasionally, as we passed the deep fissures worn by the descending torrents, we caught a view of the distant summits, glittering with perpetual frost. In the vallies, towards the east, were many lofty insular hills with perpendicular sides and level table-like summits. They are sometimes disposed in parallel but interrupted ranges, and sometimes irregularly scattered without any appearance of order. In every instance they appeared to be the remains of extensive beds of sandstone, portions of which had been preserved from disintegration while the contiguous parts had crumbled down and been washed away.

One of these singular hills, of which Mr. Seymour has preserved a sketch, was called the Castle rock, on account of its striking resemblance to a work of art. It has columns, and porticoes, and arches, and, when seen from a distance, has an astonishingly regular and artificial appearance. On approaching it, the base is found enveloped in an extensive accumulation of soil intermixed with fragments of rapidly disintegrating sandstone. The lower portions of the perpendicular sides of the rock are of loosely cemented pudding-stone, but the summit is capped by a compact and somewhat durable sandstone. This is surmounted by a scanty soil in which grow a few stinted oaks and junipers.

We had seen no bisons for several days, but in the afternoon a few were discovered at a distance from our course, and three men despatched in pursuit of them. They were grazing on the side of a hill near a mile distant. As provisions had become scarce, we watched the progress of the hunters with some anxiety. At length the firing commenced, and we enjoyed a distinct, though distant view, of the animating spectacle of a bison hunt. In a short time the hunters joined us, their horses loaded with meat.

In the afternoon we moved on, descending the little stream on which we had halted for dinner. Like the small branches of the Platte it is inhabited by great numbers of beaver, but has more timber and a more fertile soil than any stream of similar magnitude we had lately passed. Some light showers occurred in the middle of the day, and at evening a thunder storm was observed, in the same manner as on the preceding day, to collect in the east, and after we had listened to its thunders for some time it moved off in the direction of the Arkansa, but no rain fell where we were. In the course of the day several elk were seen, and at evening we killed an antelope. Robins are here frequent, and a Jerboa was seen resembling the *Gerbillus canadensis*. Many fine plants were collected, several of which are hitherto undescribed.

Towards evening our guide discovered we had already passed considerably beyond the base of the Peak, near which it had been our intention to halt. As we were particularly desirous of visiting the mountains at the point designated in many maps as the *"Highest Peak,"* we resolved to return upon our course, but as it was now near sunset we thought it advisable to encamp for the night.

Our journey had been pursued in a bison path, and although not in the direction of our proper course, serving only to prolong our march without advancing us towards the end of our pilgrimage, yet brought us nearer to that romantic scenery which for many days we had chiefly contemplated with a distant eye. We entered the secondary range along the margin of a deep ravine, which wound with a serpentine course towards the base of the mountain. Our progress was sometimes impeded by huge rocky masses, which had been precipitated from some neighbouring height, and sometimes a dense forest of very limited extent, or an immense impending wall, or oblique buttress of rock, which, by its proximity to the eye, vied with the grandeur of the ascending piles beyond. We retraced our path of the preceding day until a small stream running towards the northeast offered us a change of scenery, and a course more in the direction we wished to pursue. The great inequalities of the surface, and the precipitous character of several of the passes, thoroughly tested our confidence in our sure-footed Indian horses and mules. The rude pathway skirted along the base of a high cliff, on whose side, far above our heads, projected a narrow ledge of rocks, frowning defiance to all attempts to ascend. This ledge declined gradually as we proceeded, until it terminated abruptly on the edge of a profound gulf. Here appeared to be the only spot at which the ridge could be ascended. On the brow of the cliff a fragment of rock, and a small portion of earth were suspended, by the binding roots of a solitary pine, offering a frail and precarious foothold. This we chose to ascend, startling and hazardous as the attempt appeared, rather than retrace our steps for several miles, and search for a passage in some other direction. The projecting ledge by which we ascended, had barely sufficient width to admit the passage of a single individual at a time. When we had gained the summit, we allowed our horses a moment's rest, in the partial shade of some straggling oaks; and contemplated, not without a feeling of terror, the danger we had passed. We thus pursued the route marked out for us by the bisons, which always trace the most direct and best course, until turning the side of a mountain of moderate elevation, the ocean of prairie again spread before us. This monotonous plain, of which we had been hitherto so weary, now burst upon the sight, and for a moment exhibited a cheerful and pleasant contrast to the rude mountain ruins, we had, with such toil and hazard, been clambering over. This charm was, however, soon to be dispelled. On descending to the plain, it became, as usual, desirable to find a good situation for an encampment, abounding with grass for the horses, and convenient to a water course. For this purpose, one of the party rode to a small line of timber, about a mile on our left, which ran in a parallel direction to our line of march. He overtook us again at the distance of two or three miles, having discovered a copious stream of water. It was about three miles below the point at which the water had been discovered, that we gained the line of timber, only to experience the mortification of disappointment, in finding a naked bed of sand, the stream having no doubt sunk into the earth, some distance above. We had therefore to undergo the pains of abstinence still longer, until we again sought the timber farther below, where the water had reappeared on the surface.

Near this encampment we first observed the great shrubby cactus, which forms so conspicuous a feature in the vegetable physiognomy of the plains of the Arkansa. Its trunk is six or eight feet in height, and at the root five or six inches in diameter. It is much branched, the ultimate divisions, consisting of long cylindric articulations. The flowers are as large as those of C. *ferox*, of a purple colour, and are on the ends of the articulations. These last are arranged somewhat in whorls, about the ends of the smaller branches. The surface of every part of the plant, aside from its terrific armature of thorns, is marked by little prominences of near an inch in length, and about one fourth of an inch in breadth, rising considerably and bearing a cluster of radiating spines. At their insertion, these thorns are surrounded by pungent setæ, as in C. *ferox*. The whole plant is so thickly beset with strong spines pointing in every direction, that no animal of any considerable size, can approach it unharmed. It does not form thickets, but each plant is a cluster by itself, and when first seen at a distance, they are mistaken for bisons. We were informed by one of our engagees, who had travelled into the Spanish provinces as far as Monterey, that this plant is common there, and its fruit much esteemed.

The Cacti are considered characteristic of warm and dry climates, like those of Egypt and California. Perhaps there is no part of the world, where plants of this family, constitute so large a proportion of the vegetable products of the soil, as in the arid plains of the Arkansa. These plains are sufficiently dry, but like those of the Platte and Upper Missouri, where *cacti* are almost equally abundant, they are visited by severe cold in winter.

Another highly interesting plant, which occurs in the most barren and desolate parts of the plain, is a cucurbitaceous vine, resembling some of our common squashes, bearing a small fruit, which is round and smooth, and as large as an orange. It is perennial, having a somewhat ligneous root, four or five inches in diameter, and descending often more than four feet into the earth. We were so fortunate as to meet with it in flower, and also with ripened fruit. It has the acutely margined seed of the Genus *Cucumis*, but in other respects, is closely allied to cucurbita. In addition to these we collected the Zygadenus *elegans, Ph.*, Asclepias *tuberosa*, and some others.

From an elevated ridge, which we passed in the morning, some bisons had been seen at the distance of five miles; and as we were in want of game, Mr. Peale with two hunters, rode forward in pursuit of them. They overtook the herd near a small creek, and attacked one of the largest, which was at length killed. On examining the body, twenty balls were found to have entered in different parts, before the animal fell. They arrived at camp, bringing the meat, at a little after noon.

From this camp we had a distinct view of "the Highest Peak." It appeared about twenty miles distant, towards the northwest; our view was cut off from the base, by an intervening spur of less elevation, but all the upper part of the Peak was visible, with patches of snow, extending down to the commencement of the woody region.

At about one o'clock P.M., a dense black cloud was seen to collect in the southwest, and advancing towards the Peak, it remained nearly stationary over that part of the mountains, pouring down torrents of rain. The thunder was loud and frequent, and though little rain fell near our camp, the creek soon began to swell, and before sunset it had risen about six feet, and again subsided nearly to its former level. When the stream began to rise, it was soon covered with such a quantity of bison's dung, suddenly washed in from the declivities of the mountains and the plains at its base, that the water could scarcely be seen.

As one of the objects of our excursion was to ascertain the elevation of the Peak, it was determined to remain in our present camp for three days, which would afford an opportunity for some of the party to ascend the mountain.

CHAPTER IV

Excursion to the summit of the Peak—Mineral Springs—
Coquimbo Owl—Encampment on the Arkansa.

AT an early hour on the morning of the 13th, Lieutenant Swift, accompanied by the guide, was despatched from camp, to measure a base near the
Peak, and to make there a part of the observations requisite for calculating its
elevation. Dr. James being furnished with four men, two to be left at the foot of
the mountain to take care of the horses, and two to accompany him in the
proposed ascent to the summit of the Peak, set off at the same time.

This detachment left the camp before sunrise, and taking the most direct
route across the plains, arrived at eleven o'clock, at the base of the mountain.
Here Lieutenant Swift found a place suited to his purpose, where also was a
convenient spot for those who were to ascend the mountain, to leave their horses
in a narrow valley, dividing transversely several sandstone ridges, and extending
westward to the base of the Peak.

After establishing their horse camp, the detachment moved up the valley
on foot, arriving about noon at the Boiling spring, where they dined on a saddle
of venison, and some bison ribs, they had brought ready cooked from camp.

The Boiling spring is a large and beautiful fountain of water, cool and transparent, and highly ærated with carbonic acid. It rises on the brink of a small stream, which here descends from the mountain, at the point where the bed of this stream divides the ridge of sandstone, which rests against the base of the first granitic range.

The water of the spring deposits a copious concretion of carbonate of lime, which has accumulated on every side, until it has formed a large basin overhanging the stream. This basin is of a snowy whiteness, and large enough to contain three or four hundred gallons, and is constantly overflowing. The spring rises from the bottom of the basin, with a rumbling noise, discharging about equal volumes of air and of water, probably about fifty gallons per minute, the whole being kept in constant agitation. The water is beautifully transparent, and has the sparkling appearance, the grateful taste, and the exhilarating effect of the most strongly ærated artificial mineral waters.

Distant a few rods from this, is another spring of the same kind, which discharges no water, its basin remaining constantly full, and air only escaping from it. We collected some of the air from both of these springs, in a box we had carried for the reception of plants, but could not perceive it to have the least smell, or the power of extinguishing flame, which was tested by plunging into it lighted splinters of dry cedar.

The temperature of the water of the larger spring at noon was 63°, the thermometer at the same time in the shade, stood at 68°; immersed in the small spring, at 67°. This difference in temperature, is owing to the difference of situation, the higher temperature of the small spring, depending entirely on its constant exposure to the rays of the sun, and to its retaining the same portion of water, while that in the large spring is constantly replaced by a new supply.

After we had dined, and hung up some provisions in a large red cedar tree, near the spring, intending it for a supply on our return, we took leave of Lieutenant Swift and began to ascend the mountain. We carried with us, each a small blanket, ten or twelve pounds of bison meat, three gills of parched-corn meal, and a small kettle.

The sandstone extends westward from the springs, about three hundred yards, rising rapidly upon the base of the mountain. It is of a deep red colour, usually compact and fine, but sometimes embracing angular fragments of petrosilx and other silicious stones, with a few organic impressions. The granite which succeeds it, is coarse, and of a deep red colour. Some loose fragments of gneiss, were seen lying about the surface, but none in place. The granite at the base of the mountain, contains a large proportion of feldspar of the rose-coloured variety, in imperfect cubic crystals, and disintegrating rapidly under the operation of frost and other causes, crumbling into small masses of half an ounce weight or less.

In ascending, we found the surface in many places, covered with this loose and crumbled granite, rolling from under our feet, and rendering the ascent extremely difficult. We began to credit the assertions of the guide, who had conducted us to the foot of the Peak; and left us with the assurance, that the whole of the mountain to its summit, was covered with loose sand and gravel, so that though many attempts had been made by the Indians and by hunters to ascend it, none had ever proved successful. We passed several of these tracks, not without some apprehension for our lives, as there was danger when the foot-hold was once lost of sliding down, and being thrown over precipices.

After clambering with extreme fatigue over about two miles, in which several of these dangerous places occurred, we halted at sunset in a small cluster of fir trees. We coud not, however, find a piece of even ground large enough to lie down upon, and were under the necessity of securing ourselves from rolling into the brook, near which we encamped, by means of a pole placed against two trees. In this situation we passed an uneasy night, and, though the mercury fell only to 54°, felt some inconvenience from cold.

On the morning of the 14th, as soon as daylight appeared, having suspended in a tree, whatever articles of clothing could be dispensed with, our blankets and provisions, except about three pounds of bison flesh, we continued the ascent, hoping to be able to reach the summit of the Peak, and return to the same camp in the evening. After passing about half a mile of rugged and difficult travelling, like that of the preceding day, we crossed a deep chasm, opening towards the bed of the small stream we had hitherto ascended, and following the summit of the ridge between these, found the way less difficult and dangerous.

Having passed a level tract of several acres, covered with the aspen poplar, a few birches and pines, we arrived at a small stream running towards the south, nearly parallel to the base of the conic part of the mountain, which forms the summit of the Peak. From this spot, we could distinctly see almost the whole of the Peak, its lower half thinly clad with pines, junipers, and other evergreen trees; the upper a naked conic pile of yellowish rocks, surmounted here and there with broad patches of snow; but the summit appeared so distant, and the ascent so steep, that we despaired of accomplishing the ascent, and returning on the same day.

In marshy places about this part of the mountain, we saw an undescribed white flowered species of caltha, some Spediculariæ, the shrubby cinquefoil, (Potentilla *fruticosa, Ph.*) and many alpine plants.

The day was agreeably bright and calm. As we ascended rapidly, a manifest change of temperature was perceptible, and before we reached the outskirts of the timber, a little wind was felt from the northeast. On this part of the mountain, the yellow flowered stone-crop, (Sedum *stenopetalum, Ph.*) is almost the only herbaceous plant which occurs. The boundary of the region of forests, is a defined line encircling the peak in a part which, when seen from the plain, appeared near the summit, but when we arrived at it, a greater part of the whole elevation of the mountain, seemed still before us. Above the timber the ascent is steeper, but less difficult than below, the surface being so highly inclined, that the large masses when loosened roll down, meeting no obstruction, until they arrive at the commencement of the timber. The red cedar, and the flexile pine, are the trees which appear at the greatest elevation. These are small, having thick and extremely rigid trunks, and near the commencement of the woodless part of the mountain, they have neither limbs nor bark on the side exposed to the descending masses of rocks. These trees have not probably grown in a situation so exposed, as to be unable to produce or retain bark or limbs on one side; the timber must formerly have extended to a greater elevation on the sides of this peak, than at present, so that those trees, which are now on the outskirts of the forest, were formerly protected by their more exposed neighbours.

A few trees were seen above the commencement of snow, but these are very small and entirely procumbent, being sheltered in the crevices and fissures of the rock. There are also the roots of trees to be seen at some distance, above the part where any are now standing.

A little above the point where the timber disappears entirely, commences a region of astonishing beauty, and of great interest on account of its productions; the intervals of soil are sometimes extensive, and are covered with a carpet of low but brilliantly flowering alpine plants. Most of these have either matted procumbent stems, or such as including the flower, rarely rise more than an inch in height. In many of them, the flower is the most conspicuous and the largest part of the plant, and in all, the colouring is astonishingly brilliant.

A deep blue is the prevailing colour among these flowers, and the Pentstemon *erianthera*, the mountain Columbine, (Aquilegia *cœruea*) and other plants common to less elevated districts, were here much more intensely coloured, than in ordinary situations.

It cannot be doubted, that the peculiar brilliancy of colouring, observed in alpine plants, inhabiting near the utmost limits of phænogamous vegetation, depends in a great measure on the intensity of the light transmitted from the bright and unobscured atmosphere of those regions, and increased by reflection from the immense impending masses of snow. May the deep cœrulean tint of the sky, be supposed to have an influence in producing the corresponding colour, so prevalent in the flowers of these plants?

At about two o'clock we found ourselves so much exhausted, as to render a halt necessary. Mr. Wilson who had accompanied us as a volunteer, had been left behind some time since, and could not now be seen in any direction. As we felt some anxiety on his account, we halted and endeavoured to apprize him of our situation; but repeated calls, and the discharging of the rifleman's piece produced no answer. We therefore determined to wait some time to rest, and to eat the provisions we had brought, hoping in the meantime he would overtake us.

Here, as we were sitting at our dinner, we observed several small animals, nearly of the size of the common gray squirrel, but shorter and more clumsily formed. They were of a dark gray colour, inclining to brown, with a short thick head, and erect rounded ears. In habits and appearance, they resemble the prairie dog, and are believed to be a species of the same genus. The mouth of their burrow is usually placed under the projection of a rock, and near these we afterwards saw several of the little animals, watching our approach and uttering a shrill note, somewhat like that of the ground squirrel. Several attempts were made to procure a specimen of this animal, but always without success, as we had no guns but such as carried a heavy ball.

After sitting about half an hour, we found ourselves somewhat refreshed, but much benumbed with cold. We now found it would be impossible to reach the summit of the mountain, and return to our camp of the preceding night, during that part of the day which remained; but as we could not persuade ourselves to turn back, after having so nearly accomplished the ascent, we resolved to take our chance of spending the night, on whatever part of the mountain, it might overtake us. Wilson had not yet been seen, but as no time could be lost, we resolved to go as soon as possible to the top of the Peak, and look for him on our return. We met, as we proceeded, such numbers of unknown and interesting plants, as to occasion much delay in collecting, and were under the disagreeable necessity of passing by numbers which we saw in situations difficult of access. As we approached the summit, these became less frequent, and at length ceased entirely. Few cryptogamous plants are seen about any part of the mountain, and neither these nor any others occur frequently on the top of the Peak. There is an area of ten or fifteen acres, forming the summit, which is nearly level, and on this part scarce a lichen is to be seen. It is covered to a great depth with large splintery fragments of a rock, entirely similar to that found at the base of the Peak, except, perhaps, a little more compact in its structure.

By removing a few of these fragments, they were found to rest upon a bed of ice, which is of great thickness, and may, perhaps, be as permanent and as old as the rocks, with which it occurs.

It was about 4 o'clock P. M., when we arrived on the summit. In our way we had attempted to cross a large field of snow, which occupied a deep ravine, extending down half a mile from the top, on the south-eastern side of the Peak. This was found impassable, being covered with a thin ice, not sufficiently strong to bear the weight of a man. We had not been long on the summit, when we were rejoined by the man, who had separated from us near the outskirts of the timber. He had turned aside and lain down to rest, and afterwards pursued the ascent by a different route.

From the summit of the Peak, the view towards the north, west, and south-west, is diversified with innumerable mountains, all white with snow; and on some of the more distant, it appears to extend down to their bases. Immediately under our feet on the west, lay the narrow valley of the Arkansa, which we could trace running towards the northwest, probably more than sixty miles.

On the north side of the Peak, was an immense mass of snow and ice. The ravine, in which it lay, terminated in a woodless and apparently fertile valley, lying west of the first great ridge, and extending far towards the north. This valley must undoubtedly contain a considerable branch of the Platte. In a part of it, distant probably thirty miles, the smoke of a fire was distinctly seen, and was supposed to indicate the encampment of a party of Indians.

To the east lay the great plain, rising as it receded, until, in the distant horizon, it appeared to mingle with the sky. A little want of transparency in the atmosphere, added to the great elevation from which we saw the plain, prevented our distinguishing the small inequalities of the surface. The Arkansa with several of its tributaries, and some of the branches of the Platte, could be distinctly traced as on a map, by the line of timber along their courses.

On the south the mountain is continued, having another summit (probably that ascended by Captain Pike,) at the distance of eight or ten miles. This, however, falls much below the High Peak in point of elevation, being wooded quite to its top. Between the two lies a small lake, about a mile long and half a mile wide, discharging eastward into the Boiling-spring creek. A few miles farther towards the south, the range containing these two peaks terminates abruptly.

The weather was calm and clear, while we remained on the Peak, but we were surprised to observe the air in every direction filled with such clouds of grasshoppers, as partially to obscure the day. They had been seen in vast numbers about all the higher parts of the mountain, and many had fallen upon the snow and perished. It is perhaps difficult to assign the cause, which induces these insects to ascend to those highly elevated regions of the atmosphere. Possibly they may have undertaken migrations to some remote district, but there appears not the least uniformity in the direction of their movements. They extended upwards from the summit of the mountain, to the utmost limit of vision, and as the sun shone brightly, they could be seen by the glittering of their wings, at a very considerable distance.

About all the woodless parts of the mountain, and particularly on the summit, numerous tracks were seen resembling those of the common deer, but they most probably have been those of the big-horn. The skulls and horns of these animals we had repeatedly seen near the licks and saline springs at the foot of the mountain, but they are known to resort principally about the most elevated and inaccessible places.

The party remained on the summit only about half an hour. In this time the mercury fell to 42°, the thermometer hanging against the side of a rock; which in all the early part of the day, had been exposed to the direct rays of the sun. At the encampment of the main body in the plains, a corresponding thermometer stood, in the middle of the day, at 96°, and did not fall below 80°, until a late hour in the evening.

Great uniformity was observed in the character of the rock about all the upper part of the mountain. It is a compact, indestructible aggregate of quartz and feldspar, with a little hornblend in very small particles. Its fracture is fine granular or even, and the mass exhibits a tendency to divide when broken into long, somewhat splintery fragments. It is of a yellowish-brown colour, which does not perceptibly change by long exposure to the air. It is undoubtedly owing to the close texture and the impenetrable firmness of this rock, that so few lichens are found upon it. For the same reason it is little subject to disintegration by the action of frost. It is not improbable that the splintery fragments which occur in such quantities on all the higher parts of the Peak, may owe their present form to the agency of lightning; no other cause seems adequate to the production of so great an effect.

Near the summit, some large detached crystals of feldspar, of a pea-green colour, were collected; also large fragments of transparent, white and smoky quartz, and an aggregate of opake white quartz, with crystals of hornblend.

About five in the afternoon we began to descend, and a little before sunset arrived at the commencement of the timber, but before we reached the small stream at the bottom of the first descent, we perceived we had missed our way. It was now become so dark, as to render an attempt to proceed extremely hazardous, and as the only alternative, we kindled a fire, and laid ourselves down on the first spot of level ground we could find. We had neither provisions nor blankets; and our clothing was by no means suitable for passing the night in so bleak and inhospitable a situation. We could not, however, proceed without imminent danger from precipices, and by the aid of a good fire, and no ordinary degree of fatigue, we found ourselves able to sleep during a greater part of the night.

At day-break on the following morning the thermometer stood at 38°; as we had few comforts to leave, we quitted our camp as soon as the light was sufficient to enable us to proceed, and had travelled about three hours, when we discovered a dense column of smoke rising from a deep ravine on our left. As we concluded this could be no other than the smoke of the encampment where we had left our blankets and provisions, we descended directly towards it. The fire had spread and burnt extensively among the leaves, dry grass, and small timber, and was now raging over an extent of several acres. This created some apprehension lest the smoke might attract the notice of any Indians, who should be at that time in the neighbourhood, and who might be tempted by our weakness to offer some molestation. But we soon discovered a less equivocal cause of regret, in the loss of our *cache* of provisions, blankets, clothing, &c. which had not escaped the conflagration. Most of our baggage was destroyed, but out of the ruins we collected a scanty breakfast, of the half consumed fragments of the bison's meat. We chose a different route for the remaining part of the descent, from the one we had taken in going up, and by that means avoided a part of the difficulty arising from the crumbled granite; but this was nearly counterbalanced by the increased numbers of yuccas and prickly pears.

We arrived, a little after noon, at the Boiling spring, where we indulged freely in the use of its highly ærated and exhilarating waters. In the bottom of both these springs a great number of beads and other small articles of Indian ornament were found, having unquestionably been left there as sacrifices or presents to the springs, which are regarded with a sort of veneration by the savages. Bijeau assured us he had repeatedly taken beads and other ornaments from these springs and sold them to the same savages, who had thrown them in.

A large and much frequented road passes the springs and enters the mountains, running to the north of the high Peak. It is travelled principally by the bisons, sometimes also by the Indians who penetrate here to the Columbia.

The men who had been left at the horse camp, about a mile below the springs, had killed several deer, and had a plentiful supply of provisions. Here we dined; then mounting our horses proceeded towards the encampment of the main body, where we arrived a little after dark, having completed our excursion within the time prescribed.

Among the plants collected in this excursion, several appear to be un-described. Many of them are strictly alpine, being confined to the higher parts of the mountain, above the commencement of the snow.

Most of the trees which occur on any part of the mountain are evergreen, consisting of several species of abies, among which may be enumerated the balsam fir, (A. *balsamea, Ph.*) the hemlock, white, red, and black spruce, (A. *canadensis*. A. *alba*. A. *rubra* and A. *nigra*,) the red cedar, and common juniper, and a few pines. One of these, which appears to have been hitherto unnoticed in North America, has, like the great white or Weymouth pine, five leaves in a fascicle, but in other respects there is little resemblance between them. The leaves are short and rather rigid, the sheathes which surround their bases, short and lacerated; the strobiles erect, composed of large unarmed scales, being somewhat smaller than those of P. *rigida*, but similar in shape, and exuding a great quantity of resin. The branches which are covered with leaves chiefly at the ends, are numerous and recurved, inclining to form a dense and large top: they are also remarkably flexile, feeling in the hand somewhat like those of the Dirca *palustris*. From this circumstance, the specific name *flexilis*, has been proposed for this tree, which is in several respects remarkably contrasted with the P. *rigida*. It inhabits the arid plains subjacent to the Rocky Mountains, and extends up their sides to the region of perpetual frost. The fruit of the Pinus flexilis is eaten by the Indians and French hunters about the Rocky Mountains, as is that of another species of the same genus by the inhabitants of some parts of Europe.

The creek, on which the party encamped during the three days, occupied in making the excursion above detailed, is called Boiling-spring creek, having one of its principal sources in the beautiful spring already described. It is skirted with a narrow margin of cotton-wood and willow trees, and its banks produce a small growth of rushes on which our horses subsisted, while we lay encamped here. This plant, the common rush, (Equisetum *hiemale, Ph.*) found in every part of the United States, is eaten with avidity by horses, and it is often met with in districts where little grass is to be had. When continued for a considerable time, its use proves deleterious.

The recent tracks of a grizzly bear were observed near the camp, and at no great distance one of those animals was seen and shot at, by one of the hunters, but not killed.

In the timber along the creek, the sparrow hawk, mocking bird, robin, red-head woodpecker, dove, winter wren, towhebunting, yellow-breasted chat, and several other birds were seen.

Orbicular lizards were found about this camp, and had been once or twice before noticed near the base of the mountains.

A smoke supposed to be that of an Indian encampment was seen, rising from a part of the mountains at a great distance towards the northwest. It had been our constant practice since we left the Missouri, to have sentinels stationed about all our encampments, and whenever we were not on the march by day, and until nine o'clock in the evening it was the duty of one of the three Frenchmen, to reconnoitre at a distance from camp in every direction, and to report immediately when any thing could be discovered, indicating that Indians were in the vicinity. Precautions of this kind are highly necessary to prevent surprisal, and are invariably practised by the Indians of the west, both at their villages and on their march.

On the 14th, Lieutenant Swift returned to camp, having performed the duties on which he was sent.

A base was measured near the camp, and observations taken for ascertaining the elevation of the Peak. . . . The entire elevation of the Peak above the level of the ocean . . . is eleven thousand five hundred feet.

Complete sets of observations for latitude and longitude were taken, which gave 38° 18' 9" north, and 105° 39' 49" west from Greenwich, or 28° 39' 45" from Washington, as the position of our camp. The bearing of the Peak from this point is north, 67° west, and the distance about twenty-five miles.

In all the prairie-dog villages we had passed, small owls had been observed moving briskly about, but they had hitherto eluded all our attempts to take them. One was here caught, and on examination found to be of the species denominated Coquimbo, or burrowing owl, (Strix *cunicularia.*)

This fellow citizen of the prairie dog, unlike its grave and recluse congeners, is of a social disposition, and does not retire from the light of the sun, but endures the strongest mid-day glare of that luminary, and is in all respects a diurnal bird. It stands high upon its legs, and flies with the rapidity of the hawk. The Coquimbo owl, both in Chili and St. Domingo, agreeably to the accounts of Molina and Viellot, digs large burrows for its habitation and for the purposes of incubation; the former author gives us to understand that the burrow penetrates the earth to a considerable depth, whilst Viellot informs us, that in St. Domingo the depth is about two feet.

With us the owl never occurred but in the prairie-dog villages, sometimes in a small flock, much scattered and often perched on different hillocks, at a distance, deceiving the eye with the appearance of the prairie dog itself, in an erect posture. They are not shy, but readily admit the hunter within gunshot, but on his too near approach, a part or the whole of them rise upon the wing, uttering a note very like that of the prairie dog, and alight at a short distance, or continue their flight beyond the view.

The burrows, into which we have seen the owl descend, resembled in all respects those of the prairie dog, leading us to suppose either that they were common, though, perhaps, not friendly occupants of the same burrow, or that the owl was the exclusive tenant of a burrow gained by the right of conquest. But it is at the same time probable, that, as in Chili, the owl may excavate his own tenement.

From the remarkable coincidence of note, between these two widely distinct animals, we might take occasion to remark, the probability of the prairie dog being an unintentional tutor to the young owl, did we not know that this bird utters the same sounds in the West Indies, where the prairie dog is not known to exist.

It may be, that more than a single species of diurnal owl has been confounded under the name of cunicularia, as Viellot states his bird to be somewhat different from that of Molina, and we cannot but observe that the eggs of the birds described by the latter are spotted with yellow, whilst those of the former are immaculate. . . .

The general colour is a light burnt brown, spotted with white; the larger feathers five or six banded, with white, each band more or less widely interrupted by the shaft, and their immediate margins, darker than the other portions of the feather; the tips of these feathers are white or whitish; the exterior primary feather is serrated, shorter than the three succeeding ones, and equal in length to the fifth; the bill is tinged with yellow on the ridges of both mandibles; the tarsi and feet distinctly granulated, the former naked behind, furnished before near the base with dense short feathers, which towards the toes become less crowded, and assume the form of single hairs, these on the toes are abruptly setaceous and scattered; the lobes beneath the toes are large and granulated.

In the plains about our encampment, were several natural mounds, greatly resembling some of the artificial works so common in the central portions of the great valley of the Mississippi. About the summits of these mounds were numerous petrifactions, which were found to be almost exclusively casts of bivalve shells, approaching the genus Cytherea, and usually from one half to one and an half inches in diameter.

On the evening of the fifteenth, finding all our stock of meat injured by too long keeping, four men were sent out on horseback to hunt. At the distance of six miles from camp, they found a solitary bison, which they killed, but concluding from its extreme leanness and the ill savour of the flesh, that the animal was diseased, they took no part of it. On the following morning they returned unsuccessful. We were now reduced to the necessity of feeding on our scanty allowance of a gill of parched maize per day to each man, this being the utmost our limited stores would afford.

On the sixteenth of July, we moved from our encampment on Boiling-spring creek, in a south-western direction to the Arkansa. This ride of twenty-eight miles, which we finished without having once dismounted from our horses, occupied about ten hours of a calm sultry day, in every respect like the preceding, in which the thermometer in the shade had ranged from 90 to 100°. Our route lay across a tract of low, but somewhat broken sandstone of an uncommonly slaty structure. It is fine-grained with an argillaceous cement, and of a light gray or yellowish-white colour. It contains thin beds of bituminous clay slate, and we saw scattered on the surface some small crystals of Selenite. It is traversed by numerous deep ravines in which at this time not a drop of water was to be found.

The soil is scanty and of incurable barrenness. The texture of the rock is so loose and porous, as to unfit it for retaining any portion of the water which falls upon it in rains. A few dwarfish cedars and pines are scattered over a surface of loose dusty soil intermixed with thin lamellar fragments of sandstone, and nearly destitute of grass or herbage of any kind. Our sufferings from thirst, heat, and fatigue were excessive, and were aggravated by the almost unlimited extent of the prospect before us, which promised nothing but a continuation of the same dreary and disgusting scenery. Late in the afternoon we arrived at the brink of the precipice which divides the high plains from the valley of the Arkansa. This is here narrow, and so deeply sunk in the horizontal sandstone, that although there are trees of considerable size growing along the river, they do not rise to the level of the surface of the great plain, and from a little distance on either side the valley is entirely hid. Here our thirst and impatience were for some time tantalized with the view of the cool and verdant valley and copious stream of the Arkansa, while we were searching up and down for a place where we could descend the precipice.

At length, a rugged ravine was discovered, down which we with some difficulty wound our way to the base of the cliff, where lay a beautiful level plain, having some scattered cotton-wood and willow trees, and affording good pasture for our horses. Here we encamped, and the remainder of the afternoon was spent in making preparations to despatch a small party up the Arkansa to the mountains on the succeeding day.

A small doe was killed near camp, which, though extremely lean, proved an important addition to our supply of provisions.

The place where we encamped was supposed to have been near where Pike's block house formerly stood, but we sought in vain for the traces of any thing resembling the work of a white man. . . .

CHAPTER V

A detachment from the exploring party ascend the Arkansa to the Rocky Mountains—
Bell's Springs—Descent of the Arkansa—Grizzly Bear.

ON the morning of the 17th, Captain Bell, with Dr. James and two men, left the encampment of the party proposing to ascend the Arkansa to the mountains. They were furnished with provisions for two days, according to the scanty allowance to which now we were reduced.

The river valley was found so narrow and so obstructed by the timber and the windings of the stream as greatly to obstruct the travelling. We therefore resolved to leave it, and pursue our journey in the open plain at a distance from the river. The course of the Arkansa for the first twenty miles from the mountain is but little south of east. It enters the plain at one extremity of an extensive amphitheatre formed by the continued chain of the mountains on the west and northwest and by the projecting spur which contains the High Peak on the east. This semicircular area is about thirty miles in length from north to south and probably twenty wide at its southern extremity. The mountains which bound it on the west are high, and at this time were partially covered with snow.

The surface of the area is an almost unvaried plain, based on a stratum of argillaceous sandstone. Near the foot of the mountain the same sandstone is observed resting in an inclined position against the primitive rocks. It forms a range like that already mentioned when speaking of the mountains at the Platte separated from the primitive, by a narrow valley. On entering this valley, we found the recent trace of a large party of Indians travelling with skin lodges, who appeared to have passed within a very short time. This trace we followed until we found it entered the mountains in the valley of a small stream which descends to the Arkansa from the northeast. This we left on the east, and traversing a rough and broken tract of sandstone hills, arrived after a toilsome journey of about thirty miles at the spot where the Arkansa leaves the mountains.

Here we found several springs whose water is impregnated with muriate of soda and other salts. They rise near each other in a small marshy tract of ground occupying the narrow valley of the river at the point where it traverses the inclined sandstone ridge. Very little water flows from them, and the evaporation of this has left a crystalline incrustation whitening the surface of the surrounding marsh. The springs are small excavations, which may perhaps have been dug by the Indians or by white hunters. They appear to remain constantly full; they all contain muriate of soda, and the smell of sulphuretted hydrogen is perceptible at a considerable distance from them. They differ in taste a little from each other; hence the account given of them by hunters that one is sour, another sweet, a third bitter, and so on. One contains so much fixed air as to give it considerable pungency, but the water of all of them is unpalatable. The sweetish, metallic taste observed in the water of one or two, appears to depend on an impregnation of sulphate of iron.

The sulphates of magnesia and soda will probably be found to exist in these springs, if their water should hereafter be analyzed; they may also be found to possess some active medicinal properties. They are seven in number, and have received the name of Bell's springs, in compliment to their discoverer. Though the country around them abounds with bisons, deer, &c., they do not appear to be frequented as most saline springs are, by these, or other herbivorous animals.

It was near sunset when Capt. Bell and his party arrived at the springs, and being very much exhausted by their laborious march, they immediately laid themselves down to rest, under the open sky, deferring their examinations for the following morning.

The sandstone near the springs is hard, though rather coarse, and of a dark gray, or brownish-yellow colour.

In ascending the Arkansa on the ensuing morning, we found the rock to become more inclined, and of a redder colour; as we approached the primitive, until at about half a mile from the springs, it is succeeded by the almost perpendicular gneiss rock, which appears here at the base of the first range of the mountains. We have noticed, that this particular spot is designated in the language of hunters, "as the place where the Arkansa *comes out* of the mountains," and it must be acknowledged the expression is not entirely inapplicable. The river pours with great impetuosity and violence through a deep and narrow fissure in the gneiss rock, which rises abruptly on both sides to such a height, as to oppose an impassable barrier to all further progress. According to the delineation of Pike's route on the map which accompanies his work, he must have entered the mountains at this place, but no corroboration can be derived from his journal. It appears almost incredible that he should have passed by this route and neglected to mention the extreme difficulty which must have attended the undertaking. Captain Bell and his party returned to the encampment of the main body, on the 18th.

The immediate valley of the Arkansa, near the mountains, is bounded by high cliffs of inclined sandstone; at a short distance below, these disappear, and a sloping margin of alluvial earth extends on each side to the distance of several miles. Somewhat farther down, horizontal sandstone appears, confining the valley to a very narrow space, and bounding it within perpendicular precipices on each side. Seven miles from the mountains, on the left bank of the Arkansa, is a remarkable mass of sandstone rocks, resembling a huge pile of architectural ruins. From this point, the bearing of James' Peak was found to be due north.

The Arkansa valley between our encampment of the 18th and the mountains, a distance of about thirty miles, has a meagre and gravelly soil sustaining a growth of small cotton-wood trees, rushes, and coarse grass. Above the rocky bluffs on each side spreads a dreary expanse of almost naked sand, intermixed with clay enough to prevent its drifting with the wind, but not enough to give it fertility. It is arid and sterile, bearing only a few dwarfish cedars, and must forever remain desolate.

Observations were made at camp, for ascertaining the latitude, longitude, &c. and all the party were occupied in their appropriate pursuits. Among the animals taken here, was the four-lined squirrel, (S. 4-vittatus) a very small and handsome species, very similar in its dorsal markings, to the *getulus, L.*; but as far as we can judge from the description and figures of the latter species by Buffon, our animal is distinguished by its striped head, less rounded ears, and much less bushy, and not striated and banded tail, and by its smaller size. The getulus is also said to have no thumb warts.

It is an inhabitant of the Rocky Mountains, about the sources of the Arkansa and Platte. It does not seem to ascend trees by choice, but nestles in holes and on the edge of the rocks. We did not observe it to have cheek pouches.

Its nest is composed of a most extraordinary quantity of the burrs of the Xanthium, branches and other portions of the large upright cactus, small branches of pine trees, and other vegetable productions, sufficient in some instances to fill the body of an ordinary cart. What the object of so great and apparently so superfluous an assemblage of rubbish, may be, we are at a loss to conjecture, we do not know what peculiarly dangerous enemy it may be intended to exclude by so much labour.

Their principal food, at least at this season, is the seeds of the pine which they readily extract from the cones.

There is also another species, inhabiting about the mountains, where it was first observed by those distinguished travellers Lewis and Clark, on their expedition to the Pacific ocean. It is allied to the *Sc. striatus*, and belongs to the same subgenus, (Tamias, Illig.) but it is of a somewhat larger stature, entirely destitute of the vertebral line, and is further distinguished by the lateral lines, commencing before the humerus where they are broadest, by the longer nails of the anterior feet, and by the armature of the thumb tubercle. It certainly cannot with propriety be regarded as a variety of the *striatus*, and we are not aware that the latter species is subject to vary to any remarkable degree in this country. But the species, to which, in the distribution of its colours, it is most closely allied, is unquestionably, the *Sc. bilinatus* of Geoffroy. A specimen is preserved in the Philadelphia Museum.

The *cliff swallow*, is here very frequent, as well as in all the rocky country near the mountains.

Cliff swallows, T.R. Peale, July 17, 1820, ink.

A very beautiful species of emberiza was caught, rather smaller than the indigo bunting, (Emberiza cyanea) with a note entirely dissimilar. It was observed to be much in the grass, rarely alighting on bushes or trees.

We also captured a rattlesnake, which like the *tergeminus*, we have found to inhabit a barren soil, and to frequent the villages of the Arctomys of the prairie, but its range appeared to us confined chiefly to the vicinity of the Rocky Mountains. Its rattle is proportionally much larger than that of the species just mentioned, and the head is destitute of large plates. It seems by the number of plates and scales, to be allied to the *atracaudatus* of Bosc and Daud, but their description induces the conclusion that their species is entirely white beneath. It is also allied to the Crotalus *durissus, L.* (C. rhombifer Beauv.) but is smaller, and the dorsal spots are more rounded. A specimen is placed in the Philadelphia Museum. A new species of Coluber also occurred.

The only specimens of organic reliquiæ from this vicinity, which we have been so fortunate as to preserve, are very indistinct in their character, and are only impressions on the gray sandstone. One of them appears to have been a phytoid *Millepore*, and the other a subequilateral bivalve, which may possibly have been a *Mactra*. It is suborbicular, and its surface is marked by concentric grooves or undulations. At a previous encampment, numerous fragments of shells of a dusky colour, occurred in the same variety of sandstone, and amongst these is an entire valve of a small species of Ostrea, of a shape very like that of a *Pinna*, and less than half an inch in length.

We have a specimen, from another locality, of a very dark coloured, compact, and very impure limestone, containing still more blackish fragments of bivalves, one of which presents the form of a much arquated Mytillus, but as the back of the valves only is offered to examination, it may be a *Chama*, but it seems to be perfectly destitute of sculpture.

Another specimen, from the mountains near the Platte is a reddish brick coloured petrosilicious mass, containing casts and impressions of a grooved Terebratula.

Hunters were kept out during the day on the 17th, but killed nothing. At evening they were again sent out on horseback, but did not return until three P.M. on the following day. They had descended the river twelve miles, finding little game. They had killed one deer, one old turkey with her young brood of six. This supply proved highly acceptable, as we had for some time been confined almost entirely to our small daily allowance of corn meal.

At the commencement of our tour, we had taken a small supply of sea biscuit. At first these were distributed, at the rate of three per day to each man; afterwards two, then one, then one for two days, then one for three, till our stock of bread was so nearly exhausted that it was thought proper to reserve the little that remained, for the use of the sick, should any unfortunately require it. We then began upon our parched maize, which proved an excellent substitute for bread. This was issued, at first, at the rate of one pint per day for four men, no distinction being made in this or any other case between the officers and gentlemen of the party, and the citizens and soldiers attached to it. When we arrived at the Arkansa, about one third part of our supply of this article was exhausted, and no augmentation of the daily issues could be allowed, although our supplies of meat had for some time been inadequate to the consumption of the party.

We had a little coffee, tea, and sugar, but these were reserved as hospital stores: our three gallons of salt were expended. We now depended entirely upon hunting for subsistence, as we had done for meat ever since we left the Pawnee villages, our pork having been entirely consumed before we arrived at that place. We, however, apprehended little want of meat, after we should have left the mountains, as we believed there would be plenty of bisons and other game in the plains, over which we were to travel.

At 2 o'clock P.M. on the 18th, rain began to fall, which continued during the remainder of the day, and made it impossible for us to complete the observations we had begun.

The Arkansa, from the mountains to the place of our encampment, has an average breadth of about sixty yards; it is from three to five feet deep, and the current rapid. At the mountains the water was transparent and pure, but soon after entering the plains it becomes turbid and brackish.

19th. This morning we turned our backs upon the mountains, and began to move down the Arkansa. It was not without a feeling of regret, that we found our long contemplated visit to these grand and interesting objects, was now at an end. More than one thousand miles of dreary and montonous plain lay between us and the enjoyments and indulgences of civilized countries. This we were to traverse in the heat of summer, but the scarcity of game about the mountains rendered an immediate departure necessary.

A large and beautiful animal of the lizard kind, (belonging to the Genus Ameiva,) was noticed in this day's ride. It very much resembles the Lacerta Ameiva, as figured and described by Lacepede, but the tail is proportionably much longer. Its movements were so extremely rapid, that it was with much difficulty we were able to capture a few of them.

We had proceeded about eight or ten miles from our camp, when we observed a very considerable change in the character, both of the river and its valley; the former becoming wider, less rapid, and filled with numerous islands; the latter, bounded by sloping sand hills, instead of perpendicular precipices. Here the barren cedar ridges, are succeeded by still more desolate plains, with scarce a green, or a living thing upon them, except here and there a tuft of grass, an orbicular lizard, basking on the scorching sand, a solitary Pimelia, a Blaps, or a Galeodes; among the few stinted and withered grasses, we distinguished a small cæspitose species of Agrostis, and several others, which are thought to be undescribed. Near the river and in spots of uncommon fertility, the unicorn plant, (Martynia *proboscidea, Ph.*) was growing in considerable perfection. This plant, which is sometimes cultivated in the gardens, where it is known by the name of Cuckold's horns, is a native of the Platte and Arkansa, and is occasionally seen in every part of the open country from St. Louis, westward to the mountains.

A little before noon, we crossed a small stream, which was called Castle Rock creek, from a remarkable pile of naked rocks, and halted for dinner on the bank of the river.

In the morning, Mr. Peale and two hunters, had taken a different route from the remainder of the party, hoping to meet with game. They arrived at a small grove of timber, where it was thought deer might be found. They therefore left their horses in care of one of the hunters, and entered the wood on foot. The man had been left alone but a short time, when he discovered a large grizzly bear approaching rapidly towards him, and without staying to make himself acquainted with the intentions of the animal, mounted his horse and fled.

The grizzly bear is widely distinct from any known species of bear, by the essential character of the elongated anterior claws, and rectilinear or slightly arquated figure of its facial profile. In general appearance, it may be compared to the Alpine bear, (U. *arctos,*) and particularly the Norwegian variety. The claws, however, of these appear to be of the usual form, and not elongated, and the facial space, included between the eyes is deeply indented; they also differ in their manners, and climb trees, which the grizzly bear is never known to do.

Lewis and Clark frequently saw and killed these bears, during their celebrated expedition across the continent. They mention one which was nine feet long, from the nose to the tip of the tail. The fore foot of another, was nine inches across, its hind foot eleven and three quarter inches long, exclusive of the talons, and seven inches wide. The talons of a third, were six and one-fourth inches long.

They will not always attack even when wounded.

"As they fired, he did not attempt to attack, but fled with a most tremendous roar, and such was its extraordinary tenacity of life, that although he had five balls passed through his lungs, and five other wounds, he swam more than half across the river to a sand bar, and survived twenty minutes. He weighed between five and six hundred pounds at least, and measured 8 feet 7 1-2 inches, from the nose to the extremity of the hind feet."—*Lewis and Clark.*

One lived two hours, after having been shot through the centre of his lungs, and whilst in this state, he prepared for himself a bed in the earth, two feet deep, and five feet long, after running a mile and a half. The fleece and skin were a heavy burden for two men, and the oil amounted to eight gallons.

Another, shot through the heart, ran at his usual pace nearly a quarter of a mile, before he fell.

This species, they further inform us, in all its variations of colouring, is called *Hohhost*, by the Chopunnish Indians.

These travellers mention another species of bear, which seems to be related to the Alpine bear, and which is most probably a new species. It climbs trees, and is known to the Chopunnish Indians, by the name of *Yackah*.

They also inform us, that the copulating season occurs about the 15th June.

The Indians of the Missouri, sometimes go to war in small parties against the grizzly bear, and trophies obtained from his body are highly esteemed, and dignify the fortunate individual who obtains them. We saw on the necks of many of their warriors, necklaces composed of the long fore claws, separated from the foot, tastefully arranged in a radiating manner, and one of the band of Pawnee warriors, that encountered a detachment of our party near the Konza village, was ornamented with the entire skin of the fore foot, with the claws remaining upon it, suspended on his breast.

It is not a little remarkable, that the grizzly bear, which was mentioned at a very early period by Lahontan, and subsequently by several writers, is not even at this day, established in the Zoological works, as a distinct species; that it is perfectly distinct from any described species, our description will prove. From the concurrent testimony of those who have seen the animal in its native haunts, and who have had an opportunity of observing its manners, it is without doubt, the most daring and truly formidable animal, that exists in the United States. He frequently pursues and attacks hunters, and no animal whose swiftness or art is not superior to his own, can evade him. He kills the bison, and drags the ponderous carcase to a distance, to devour it at leisure, as the calls of hunger may influence him.

The grizzly bear is not exclusively carnivorous, as has by some persons been imagined, but also, and perhaps in a still greater degree, derives nourishment from vegetables, both fruits and roots; the latter he digs up by means of his long fore claws.

That they formerly inhabited the Atlantic states, and that they were then equally formidable to the Indians, we have some foundation for belief, in the tradition of the Delaware Indians, respecting the Big Naked bear, the last one of which they believe formerly existed east of the Hudson river, and which Mr. Heckewelder assures us, is often arrayed by the Indians, before the minds of their crying children, to frighten them to quietness.

Governor Clinton in the notes appended to his learned *Introductory Discourse*, says, "Dixon, the Indian trader, told a friend of mine, that this animal has been seen fourteen feet long; that notwithstanding its ferocity, it has been sometimes domesticated, and that an Indian belonging to a tribe on the head waters of the Mississippi, had one in a reclaimed state, which he sportively directed to go into a canoe belonging to another tribe of Indians, then about returning from a visit: the bear obeyed, and was struck by an Indian; being considered one of the family, this was deemed an insult, was resented accordingly, and produced a war between these nations."

A half grown specimen was kept chained in the yard of the Missouri Fur Company, near Engineer Cantonment, last winter; he was fed chiefly on vegetable food, as it was observed, that he became furious when too plentifully supplied with animal fare. He was in continual motion during the greater part of the day, pacing backward and forward to the extent of his chain. His attendants ventured to play with him, though always in a reserved manner, fearful of trusting him too far, or of placing themselves absolutely within his grasp; he several times broke loose from his chain, on which occasions he would manifest the utmost joy, running about the yard in every direction, rearing up on his hind feet, and capering about. I was present at one of these exhibitions; the squaws and children belonging to the establishment ran precipitately to their huts, and closed the doors: he appeared much delighted with his temporary freedom, he ran to the dogs, which were straying about the yard, but they avoided him. In his round he came to me, and rearing up, placed his paws on my breast; wishing to rid myself of so rough a play fellow, I turned him around, upon which he ran down the bank of the river, plunged into the water, and swam about for some time.

Mr. John Dougherty had several narrow escapes from the grizzly bear. He was once hunting with a companion, on one of the upper tributaries of the Missouri, he heard the report of his companion's rifle, and looking round, he beheld him at a little distance, endeavouring to escape from one of these bears, which he had wounded as it was advancing on him. Mr. Dougherty, attentive only to the preservation of his friend, immediately hastened to divert the attention and pursuit of the bear to himself, and arrived within rifle shot distance, just in time to effect his generous object; he lodged his ball in the animal, and was obliged to fly in his turn, whilst his friend, relieved from imminent danger, prepared for another onset by charging his piece, with which he again wounded the bear, and relieved Mr. Dougherty from pursuit. In this most hazardous encounter, neither of them were injured, but the bear was fortunately destroyed.

Several hunters were pursued by a grizzly bear, that gained rapidly upon them; a boy belonging to the party, who possessed less speed than his companions, seeing the bear at his heels fell with his face to the soil; the bear reared up on his hind feet over the boy, looked down for a moment upon him, then bounded over him in pursuit of the fugitives.

A hunter just returned from a solitary excursion to the Qui Court river, informed me at Engineer Cantonment, that going one morning to examine his traps, he was pursued by a bear, and had merely time to get into a small tree, when the bear passed beneath him, and without halting or even looking up, passed on at the same pace.

Another hunter received a blow from the fore paw of one of these animals, which destroyed his eye and cheek bone.

In proof of the great muscular power with which this animal is endowed, a circumstance related to us by Mr. John Dougherty, may be stated. He shot down a bison, and leaving the carcass, went to obtain assistance to butcher it, but was surprised on his return to find, that it had been dragged entire, to a considerable distance, by one of these bears, and was now lodged in a concavity of the earth, which the animal had scooped out for its reception.

Notwithstanding the formidable character of this bear, we have not made use of any precautions against their attacks, and although they have been several times prowling about us in the night, they have not evinced any disposition to attack us, at that season.

They appear to be more readily intimidated by the voice, than by the appearance of men.

CHAPTER VI

Natural mounds—Kaskaia Indian and squaw—
Preparations for a division of the party—
Sandstones of the high plains south of the Arkansa—Floetz Trap Formation.

IN the afternoon of the 19th of July, we passed the mouth of the river St. Charles, called by Pike the Third fork, which enters the Arkansa from the southwest. It is about twenty yards wide, and receives, eight miles above its confluence, the Green-horn, a small stream from the southeast. The Green-horn rises in the mountains, and passes between the Spanish Peaks into the plains. These two peaks had been for several days visible, standing near to each other, and appearing entirely insulated. If they are not completely so, the other parts of the same range must fall far below them in elevation; they are of a sharp, conic form, and their summits white with snow, at midsummer.

We travelled twenty-five miles, the general direction of our course being a little south of east, and encamped at five P. M. in a grassy point on the north side of the river. The soil of the islands and the immediate valley of the river were found somewhat more fertile than above. Immediately after encamping the hunters were sent out, who soon returned with two deer and a turkey.

In the evening, the altitude of Antares was taken. Throughout the night we were much annoyed by mosquitoes, the first we had met for some weeks in sufficient numbers to be troublesome.

We left our encampment on the following morning at five, the weather warm and fair. Soon afterwards we passed the mouth of a creek on the south side, which our guide informed us, is called by the Spaniards Wharf creek, probably from the circumstance of its washing perpendicular precipices at moderate height, which is said to be the case. It is the stream designated in Pike's map as the Second fork. A party of hunters in the employ of Mr. Choteau, who were taken prisoners by the Spaniards in the month of May, 1817, were conducted up this creek to the mountains, thence across the mountains, to Santa Fe.

Near the place where we halted to dine, a large herd of elk were seen, but unfortunately they took the wind of us, and disappeared, giving us no opportunity to fire upon them.

Along the river bluffs, we saw numerous conic mounds, resembling those of artificial formation, so frequently met with near the Ohio and Mississippi, but differing from them by their surface, from the apex to the base, being terminated by a strait or concave, instead of a convex curve, which is usual in those of artificial origin. The natural mounds of which we speak, appear usually to contain a nucleus of sandstone, which is sometimes laid bare on the summit or on the sides, and sometimes entirely concealed by the accumulated debris resting upon it. This stone often contains petrified remains of marine animals.

At the end of this day's ride of twenty-six miles, we found the river valley more than a mile in width, and the distant bluffs which bound it, low, and of gradual ascent. The boulders, pebbles, and gravel, so abundant near the base of the mountain, had been growing gradually less prevalent, and diminishing in size till they had now almost entirely disappeared, their place being supplied by a fine sand intermixed with clay, which here composed the surface. The soil is extremely barren, the islands, and the immediate margin of the river, bearing an inconsiderable growth of cotton-wood and willows, the great mass of the country being almost destitute of vegetation of any kind.

Hunters were sent out, immediately on encamping, and returned at dark, bringing a wild cat, an old turkey, and five of her chickens.

A bird was taken, closely resembling in point of colouring, a species preserved in the Philadelphia museum under the name of *ruby-crowned flycatcher*, said to be from the East Indies, but the bill differs in being much less dilated. We can hardly think it a new species, yet in the more common books we do not find any distinct description of it. It is certainly allied to the Tyrannus *griseus*, and *sulphuratus* of Vieillot, but in addition to other essential characters, it is distinguished from the former, by its yellow belly, and from the latter, by the simplicity of the wing and tail feathers, and the absence of bands on the side of the head; the bill is also differently formed from either of those species, if we may judge from Vieillot's figures.

21st. We left our encampment at five A. M. and having descended six or eight miles along the river, we met an Indian and squaw, who were, as they informed us, of the tribe called Kaskaias, by the French, Bad-hearts. They were on horseback, and the squaw led a third horse, of uncommon beauty. They were on their way from the Arkansa below, to the mountains, near the sources of the Platte, where their nation sometimes resides. They informed us that the greater part of six nations of Indians were encamped about thirteen days' journey below us, on the Arkansa. These were the Kaskaias, Shiennes, Arrapahoes, Kiawas, the Bald-heads, and a few Shoshones, or Snakes. These nations, the Kaskaia informed us, had been for some time embodied, and had been engaged on a warlike expedition against the Spaniards on Red river, where a battle was fought, in which the Spaniards were defeated with considerable loss.

We now understood the reason of a fact which had appeared a little remarkable; namely, that we should have traversed so great an extent of Indian country, as we have done since leaving the Pawnees, without meeting a single savage. The bands above enumerated, are supposed to comprise nearly the whole erratic population of the country about the sources of the Platte and Arkansa, and they had all been absent from their usual haunts, on a predatory excursion against the Indians of New Mexico.

At our request, the Kaskaia and his squaw returned with us several miles, to point out a place suitable for fording the Arkansa, and to give us any other information or assistance in their power to communicate. Being made to understand it was the design of some of the party to visit the sources of Red river, he pretended to give us information and advice upon that subject; also to direct us to a place where we might find a mass of rock-salt, which he described as existing on one of the upper branches of Red river.

At ten o'clock we arrived at the ford, where we halted to make a distribution of the baggage and other preparations requisite to the proposed division of the party which was here to take place. Our Kaskaia visitor, with his handsome and highly ornamented wife encamped near us, having erected a little tent covered with skins. They presented us some jerked bison meat, and received in return a little tobacco and other inconsiderable articles. A small looking-glass, which was among the presents given him, he immediately stripped of the frame and covering, and inserted it with some ingenuity into a large billet of wood, on which he began to carve the figure of an alligator. Capt. Bell bought of him the horse which they had led with them, and which, according to their account, had recently been caught from among the wild horses of the prairie. This made some new arrangement of their baggage necessary, and we were surprised to witness the facility and despatch with which the squaw constructed a new pack-saddle. She felled a small cotton-wood tree, from which she cut two forked sticks. These were soon reduced to the proper dimensions, and adapted to the ends of two flat pieces of wood about two feet in length, and designed to fit accurately to the back of the horse, a longitudinal space of a few inches in width being left between them to receive the ridge of the back. The whole was fastened together without nails, pins, or mortises, but by a strong covering of dressed horse-hide sewed on wet with fibres of deer's sinew.

The Indian informed us he was called "The Calf." He appeared excessively fond of his squaw, and their caresses and endearments they were at no pains to conceal. It was conjectured by our guide, and afterwards ascertained by the detachment that descended the Arkansa, that this mutually fond couple had married in violation of the laws and usages of their tribe; she being already the wife of another man, had stolen the horse they sold us, and deserted their band to escape punishment.

The low grounds, on the upper part of the Arkansa, have a sandy soil, and are thinly covered with cotton-wood, intermixed with the aspen poplar (P. *tremuloides. Mx.*) and a few willows. The undergrowth is scattering and small, consisting principally of the Amorpha *fruticosa* and a syngeneceous shrub, probably a vernonia. Along the base of the mountains and about this encampment, we had observed a small asclepias, not easily distinguished from A. *verticillata*, but rarely rising more than two or three inches from the ground. Here we saw also the A. *longifolia* and A. *viridiflora* of Pursh. The scanty catalogue of grassy and herbaceous plants comprises two sunflowers (H. *gigantus* and H. *petiolaris*.) the great Bartonia, the white argemone, the Cactus *ferox*, the Andropogon *furcatum* and A. *ciliatum*, Cyperus *uncinatus*, Elymus *striatus*, and a few others.

Soon after arriving at this encampment, we commenced the separation of our baggage, horses, &c., preparatory to the division of the party. It was now proposed, pursuant to the plan already detailed, that one division, consisting of Mr. Say, Mr. Seymour, Lieutenant Swift, the three Frenchmen, Bijeau, Le Doux, and Julien, with five riflemen, the greater part of the pack-horses, and heavy baggage under the direction of Capt. Bell, should proceed down the Arkansa, by the most direct route, to Fort Smith, there to wait the arrival of the other division, while Major Long, accompanied by Dr. James, Mr. Peale, and seven men, should cross the Arkansa, and travel southward in search of the sources of the Red river.

While several of the party were engaged in making these preparations, hunters were sent out, who were so far successful that they soon returned, bringing two deer, one antelope, and seven turkeys. The opportunity of an unoccupied moment was taken to collect from Bijeau an account of some parts of the Rocky mountains which we had not seen.

Joseph Bijeau (or Bessonet, which is his hereditary name, the former having been derived from a second marriage of his mother,) had performed in a very adequate and faithful manner the services of guide and interpreter, from the Pawnee villages to this place. He had formerly been resident in these regions, in capacity of hunter and trapper, during the greater part of six years.

He had traversed the country lying between the north fork of the Platte and the Arkansa, in almost every direction. His pursuits often led him within the Rocky Mountains, where the beaver are particularly abundant. He appears possessed not only of considerable acuteness of observation, but of a degree of candour and veracity which gives credibility to his accounts and descriptions. To him we are indebted for the following account of the country within the mountains.

The region, lying west of the first range of the Rocky Mountains and between the sources of the Yellow-stone, on the north, and Santa Fe, on the south, consists of ridges of mountains, spurs, and vallies. The mountains are usually abrupt, often towering into inaccessible peaks, covered with perpetual snows. The interior ranges and spurs are generally more elevated than the exterior: this conclusion is at least naturally drawn from the fact that they are covered with snow to a greater extent below their summits. Although that point which we have denominated James' Peak has been represented as higher than any other part of the mountains, within one hundred or one hundred and fifty miles, we are inclined to believe it falls much below several other peaks, and particularly that which was for many days observed by the party, when ascending the Platte.

The vallies within the Rocky Mountains are many of them extensive, being from ten to twenty or thirty miles in width, and are traversed by many large and beautiful streams. In these vallies, which are destitute of timber, the soil is frequently fertile and covered with a rich growth of a white flowering clover, upon which horses and other animals feed with avidity. The vallies have an undulated surface and are terminated on all sides by gentle slopes, leading up to the base of the circumjacent mountains. Timber may be had, on the declivities of the hills, in sufficient quantity to subserve the purposes of the settlement. The soil is deep, well watered, and adapted to cultivation.

The Indians, who inhabit within the mountains, are roving bands, having no permanent places of residence, and subsisting entirely on the products of the chase. The people called Padoucas have been often represented as residing in the district now under consideration, but are not at this time to be found here, unless this name be synonymous with that of the Bald-heads or some other of the six nations already enumerated.

On the morning of the 22nd, one of two hunters, who had been sent out on the preceding day, but had not returned, came into camp to give notice that a bison had been killed at the distance of eight miles on the other side of the river. Men were accordingly despatched with pack-horses to bring in the meat. Astronomical observations were resumed, and all the party were busily employed in the discharge of their ordinary duties, or in preparations for the approaching separation. A vocabulary of the Kaskaia language was filled up with words obtained from the Calf, who still remained with us.

This encampment was about eighteen miles above the confluence of that tributary of the Arkansa, called in Pike's maps "The First fork," and, by our computation, near one hundred miles from the base of the mountain. James' Peak was still visible, bearing north, 68° west, and the Spanish peaks, the westernmost of which bore south, 40° west. The observations made here received the most minute and careful attention. The moon was at this time too near the sun to admit of taking her distance from that luminary, and too near Antares for an observation. The distance of Spica Virginis was too great, and the star was too near the horizon, yet we trust accurate deductions may be made from the distances, which are given at the end of the volume.

On the evening of both days, which our Kaskaia guest spent with us, we observed him to commence soon after sunset, a monotonous and somewhat melancholy chant, which he continued for near an hour. He gave us some account of a battle, which had lately been fought between the Tabbaboos, (Anglo-Americans,) and the Spaniards, in which great guns were used, and when the Spaniards, though superior in number, had been beaten. He appeared well acquainted with the use of fire arms, and challenged one of the party to a trial of skill, in shooting at a mark with the rifle. He had a fusee, kept very carefully in a case of leather, and carried when travelling by his squaw. He was also armed with a bow and some light arrows for hunting, which he carried constantly in his hand. He took leave of us, on the morning of the 23d, having received several presents, with which he appeared highly pleased.

The Arkansa, between this point and the mountains, has a rapid current, whose velocity, probably, varies from four to six miles per hour. It may be forded at many places, in a moderate stage of water. The average breadth of the river is from sixty to seventy-five yards. At many places, however, it is much enlarged, including numerous islands. It pursues a remarkably serpentine course within its valley, forming a succession of points on both sides of the river, which, together with the islands, are usually covered with cotton-wood. The bed of the river is gravelly, or composed of water-worn stones, which diminish in size, as you recede from the mountains. The water is turbid, but in a less remarkable degree, than that of the Platte. The bed of the river, has, in many instances, changed its place, and the old channel is sometimes occupied by stagnant water, and sometimes by a small stream, which is rendered transparent by passing through the sand and gravel, forming the recently raised bank of the river.

On the 24th, the movements of the party were resumed; Major Long with the division destined for Red river, crossed the Arkansa, at five A.M. On arriving at the opposite bank, three cheers were given, which our late companions returned, from the other side. We lost sight of them as they were leaving the camp, to descend the Arkansa.

Major Long's division of the party consisting of ten men, took with them six horses and eight mules, most of them in good condition for travelling. A few had sore backs, but one horse only was unfit for service.

Our course, which was a little to the east of south, was nearly at right angles to the direction of the Arkansa. It was our intention to cross to, and ascend the First Fork, a considerable stream entering the Arkansa, eighteen miles below our last encampment. After leaving the river, we found the surface to rise gradually, till at the distance of six or eight miles, it is broken by a few small gravelly ridges; these are of little elevation, and their summits overlook an extensive waste of sand, terminated towards the south and east, only by the verge of the sky, towards the north and nothwest, by the snowy summits of the Spanish mountains. As our way led across the general course of the streams, we met with no water, except such as was still standing in puddles, which had been filled by the late rains. Near one of these we halted to dine. The thermometer hanging in the shade of our tent, which was the most perfect, and indeed the only shade we could find, stood at 100°. The little water we could procure was thick with mud, and swarming with the larvæ of mosquitoes, but this we regretted the less, as we had no cooking to perform. We dined upon jerked meat from our packs. Some animals seen at a distance, were at first mistaken for bisons, but were found by the hunters sent in pursuit of them, to be horses, and too wild and vigilant to be taken.

A species of cone flower (Rudbeckia *tagetes*,) with an elongated receptacle, and large red brown radial florets, was observed, about the margin of the stagnant pool, near which we halted.

We also collected the Linum *rigidum?* and a semiprocumbent species of Sida, which appears to be undescribed. It is a little larger than the S. *spinosa*, to which it has some general resemblance.

The whole tract, passed in this day's journey of twenty-seven miles, is sterile and sandy. At sunset we were so fortunate as to meet with another small pool of water, at which we pitched our tent, and kindled a fire with the dung of the bison. Since leaving the Arkansa, we had scarcely seen as much wood, as might have supplied us with fuel for a single night. We passed in the course of the day, not less than four or five paths, leading southwest towards the Spanish settlements. Some of them appeared to have been recently travelled by men with horses, such paths being easily distinguished from those of bisons or wild horses.

Our camp was near the head of a dry ravine, communicating towards the southeast, with a considerable stream, which we could distinguish at the distance of eight or ten miles, by a few trees along its course. Continuing our journey on the ensuing day, we soon found ourselves in a tract of country, resembling that on the Arkansa near the mountains. A similar horizontal slaty sandstone occurs, forming the basis of the country. There is also a variety of this stone, somewhat crystalline, resembling that of St. Michael's, in the lead mine district, but exhibiting no trace of metallic ores. These rocks are deeply channelled by the water courses, but at this time the streams contain little water. These ravines are, the greater number of them, destitute of timber, except a few cedars, attached here and there in the crevices of the rock. The larger vallies which contain streams of water, have a few cotton-wood and willow trees. The box elder, the common elder, (Sambucus *canadensis*,) and one or two species of Viburnum, are seen here.

It was perhaps owning to our having followed more carefully than they deserved, the directions of the Calf, that we did not arrive as early as we had expected, upon the stream we designed to ascend. In the middle of the day on the 25th, we fell in with a smaller river, at the distance of thirty-six miles from the point where we had left the Arkansa, this we concluded, could be no other than that tributary, whose mouth is said to be distant eighteen miles from the same spot. This stream, where we halted upon it to dine, is about ten yards wide, and three feet deep, but appeared at this time considerably swollen. Its immediate valley is about three hundred yards in width, bounded on both sides by perpendicular cliffs of sandstone, of near two hundred feet elevation. A very large part of the area included between these showed evidence in the slime and rubbish, with which its surface was covered, of having been recently inundated. This stream, like all others of similar magnitude, having their sources in high mountains, is subject to great and sudden floods.

A short time before we halted, our two hunters, Verplank and Dougherty, were sent forward to hunt, and joined us with a deer, soon after we had encamped.

After dinner we moved on, ascending the creek, whose valley was sufficiently wide for a little distance, to afford us an easy and unobstructed passage. The stream runs nearly from south to north, in a deep but narrow and tortuous valley, terminated on both sides, by lofty and perpendicular precipices, of red sand rock. This sandstone, appears entirely to resemble that before described, as occuring in an inclined position, along the base of the mountains, on the Arkansa and the Boiling-spring creek. Here it is disposed in horizontal strata of immense thickness. It varies in colour from a bright brick red, to a dark brown, and is sometimes gray, yellow, or white. It consists essentially of rounded particles of quartz and other silicious stones, varying in size from the finest sand to gravel stones, and large pebbles. Extensive beds of pudding stone occur in every part of it, but are abundant somewhat in proportion, to the proximity of the high primitive mountains. In the lower parts of the stratum, these beds of coarse conglomerate, appear to have the constituent gravel and pebble stones more loosely cemented, than in portions nearer the upper surface. Wherever we have met with them in immediate contact with the granite of the Rocky Mountains, they are nearly destitute of cement, and of a colour approaching to white. This remark, it is highly probable, may not be applicable to many extensive beds of pudding stone, which lie near the base of the mountains. In the instances which came under our notice, the absence of colour and the want of cement, may very probably have been accidental. The finer varieties of the sandstone are often met with in the immediate neighbourhood of the granite, and are of a compact structure, and an intense colour. Red is the prevailing colour in every part of the stratum, but stripes of yellow, gray, and white, are frequently interspersed. In hardness and other sensible properties, it varies widely at different points. In many instances it is entirely similar to the sandstone about New Brunswick, in New Jersey, at Nyac, and along the Tappan bay in New

York, and particularly the variety of it which is quarried at Nyac, and extensively used in the cities of New York and Albany, for building. It contains a little mica in small scales. Oxide of iron predominates in the cement, and the ore denominated the brown oxide, occurs in it, in reniform, botryoidal and irregular masses.

A few miles above our mid-day encampment, we entered the valley of a small creek, tributary from the southeast to the stream we had been ascending, but this we found so narrow and so obstructed by fallen masses of rocks, and almost impenetrable thickets of alders and willows, as to render our progress extremely tedious and painful. We were several times induced to attempt passing along the bed of the stream, but as the mud was in many places very deep, this was done at the cost of the most violent and fatiguing exertions, on the part of our horses, and the risk to ourselves of being thrown with our baggage into the stream. With the hope of finding an easier route across the hills, we ascended with much difficulty a craggy and abrupt ravine, until we had attained nearly the elevation of the precipitous ramparts, which hemmed in the narrow valley of the creek; but all we gained by this ascent, was the opportunity of looking down upon a few of our companions, still lingering below, diminished to the stature of dwarfs by the distance, and by contrast with the rude and colossal features of the scene. The surface of the country, extending on both sides from the summit of the precipices, consisted of abrupt conic piles, narrow ridges, and shapeless fragments of naked rocks, more impassable than the valley below. Counselled therefore by necessity, we resumed our former course, ascending along the bed of the creek.

Among other birds, which occured in this day's march, we noticed the *yellow-bellied fly-catcher*, and the *obscure wren*.

One of the small striped ground squirrels already noticed, was killed, and an individual belonging to another species distinguished by the extraordinary coarseness and flattened form of the fur, and by three black lines on each side of the tail. These lines at their tips, are of course, united over the surface of the tail, as in the Barbary squirrel. It nestles in holes and crevices of the rocks, and does not appear to ascend trees voluntarily.

It inhabits frequently about the naked parts of the sandstone cliffs, or where are only a few cedar bushes. In the pouch of the specimens killed, we found the buds and leaves of a few small plants common among the rocks.

Following up the bed of the creek, we ascended by a gradual acclivity, to the surface of the stratum of red sandstone. It is separated by a somewhat distinct boundary from the finer and more compact gray variety which rests upon it. This gray sandstone appears from the organic relicts it contains, as well as from its relative position, to have been of more recent deposition than the red. Its prevailing colours are gray or yellowish white, its stratifications distinct, and its cement often argillaceous.

After entering upon this variety, we found the valley of the creek less serpentine in direction, but narrower and more obstructed by detached fragments than below. The impaling cliffs on each side were also more uniformly perpendicular, putting it out of our power to choose any other path than the rugged one which lay before us. As with every step of our advance upon this route we were gaining a little in point of elevation, we hoped by following it, to reach at length, its termination in the high and open plain which we had no doubt existed, extending over the greater part of the surface of the country wherever the strata of sandstone were still unbroken. At five P. M., supposing we had arrived very near this wished-for spot, and finding an indifferent supply of grass for our horses, we halted for the night, having travelled fifteen miles.

26th. The water of the large stream we had crossed and ascended for some distance on the preceding day, was turbid, and so brackish, as to be nauseous to the taste. The same was observed, though in a less remarkable degree, of the little tributary we had followed up to our encampment. After leaving the region of red sandstone, we found the water perceptibly purer. In the districts occupied by that rock, we have observed several copious springs, but not one whose waters were without a very manifest impregnation of muriate of soda, or other saline substances. In the gray, or argillaceous sandstone, springs are less frequent, but the water is not so universally impure.

A beautiful Dalea, two or three Euphorbias, with several species of Eriogonum, are among the plants collected about this encampment. Notwithstanding the barrenness of the soil, and the aspect of desolation which so widely prevails, we are often surprised by the occurrence of splendid and interesting productions springing up under our feet, in situations that seemed to promise nothing but the most cheerless and unvaried sterility. Operating with unbounded energy, in every situation, adapting itself with wonderful versatility, to all combinations of circumstances; the principle of life extends its dominion over inhospitable tracts, which seem as if designed for the perpetual abode of inorganic desolation; distributing some of its choicest gifts to the most ungenial regions, fitting them, by peculiarity of structure, for the maintenance of life and vigor, in situations apparently the most unfavored.

At nine o'clock in the evening of the 25th, a fall of rain commenced. We were now ten in company, with a single tent, large enough to cover half the number. In order, however, to make the most equal distribution of our joint possessions, it was so arranged that about the half of each man was sheltered under the tent, while the remainder was exposed to the weather. This was effected, by placing all our heads near together in the centre of the tent, and allowing our feet to project in all directions, like the radii of a circle.

On the ensuing morning, we commenced our ride at an early hour, being encouraged still to pursue the course up the ravine, by a bison path, which we believed, would at length conduct us to the open plain. Our progress was slow, and laborious, and our narrow path so hemmed in with perpendicular cliffs of sandstone, that our views were nearly as confined, and the surrounding objects as unvaried, as if we had been making our way in a subterranean passage. Two black-tailed deer, with a few squirrels, and some small birds, were all the animals seen in the course of the day. Some enormous tracks of the grizzly bear, with the recent signs of bisons, afforded sufficient proof, that these animals, though unseen, were near at hand.

Our courses were nearly south, during the day, and the distance we travelled, estimated on them, fifteen miles. The actual distance passed, must have been much greater, as our real course was extremely circuitous, winding from right to left, in conformity to the sinuosities of the valley.

At four o'clock, we arrived at the head of the stream, which we had hitherto ascended. As we were conscious, that after leaving this, and emerging into the open country, we could not expect to meet with water again, in a distance of several miles, it was resolved to halt for the night, and the hunters were sent out. Soon afterwards, it began to rain. At sunset, the hunters returned, having killed a female of the black-tailed, or mule deer. The flesh of this, we found in tolerable condition, and extremely grateful to our hungry party.

On the morning of the 27th, we rose at three o'clock, and hastened our preparations for an early start. The morning was clear and calm, and the copious dew, which was beginning to exhale from the scanty herbage of the valley, gave the air a delightful freshness. The mercury, as on several of the preceding mornings, stood at about 55°.

At sunrise, we resumed our toilsome march, and, before ten o'clock, had arrived at a part of the valley beyond which it was found impossible to penetrate. The distance we had travelled would have been, in a direct line, about three miles. In passing it, we had followed no less than ten different courses, running in all possible directions. This fatiguing march had brought us to a point where the valley was so narrow and so obstructed with large detached fragments of rocks, as to be entirely impassable on horseback: we were therefore under the necessity of halting, and, as the place afforded some grass, our horses were turned loose to feed, while several persons were sent to discover, if possible, some passage by which we might extricate ourselves from the ravine. At length one returned, having found, at the distance of a mile and a half below, a pass where, it was thought, our horses could be led up the cliff.

On the preceding day, we had commenced our accustomed march in a valley bounded by perpendicular cliffs of red sandstone, having an elevation of at least two hundred feet from the surface of the valley. As we ascended gradually along the bed of the stream, we could perceive we were arriving near the surface of this vast horizontal stratum and, at night, we pitched our tent at the very point where the red sandstone began to be overlaid, in the bed of the creek, by a different variety. This second variety, the gray sandstone, was in a horizontal stratum, evidently more than two hundred feet in thickness. It is usually a more compact and imperishable stone than the red, its fragments remaining longer entire and retaining the angles and asperities of the surface, which in the other variety are soon softened down by the rapid progress of disintegration. It is easy to perceive that the sandstone formation, including the two varieties above mentioned, must be, at this point, of immense thickness; fifteen hundred feet is probably a very moderate estimate for the aggregate elevation of some extensive portions of the gray sandstone, above that part of the valley at which the red first appears. From this point downwards the extent of the latter variety may be very great; but no estimate can be formed which would be in any measure entitled to confidence.

After we had dined, we retraced our two last courses, and succeeded in ascending the cliff, at the place which one of the hunters had pointed out, taking, without the least regret, our final leave of the "Valley of the souls in Purgatory."

From the brow of the perpendicular precipice, an ascending slope of a few rods conducted us, through scattering groves of junipers, to the border of the open plain. Here, the interminable expanse of the grassy desert burst suddenly upon our view. Instead of a narrow crooked avenue, hedged in by impending cliffs and frightful precipices, a boundless and varied landscape lay spread before us. The broad valley of the Arkansa, studded with little groves of timber, and terminated, in the back ground, by the snowy summit of James' Peak, lay in our rear. The Spanish Peaks and numerous spurs of the Rocky Mountains, with the shining pinnacles of the more distant ranges, limited our view on the right. On our left and before us, lay the extended plain diversified with vast conic mounds, and insular table-like hills, while herds of bisons, antelopes, and wild horses, gave life and cheerfulness to the scene.

After travelling one and a half miles, into the plain, on a due south course, we halted to take the bearing of several remarkable points. Due east, was a solitary and almost naked pile of rocks, towering to a very considerable elevation above the surface of the plain. James' Peak bore north 71° west; the west Spanish Peak south, 87° west; magnetic variation, 13 1/2° east. As we proceeded, we were surprised to witness an aspect of unwonted verdure and freshness, in the grasses and other plants of the plain, and in searching for the cause of this change, discovered we had arrived at a region differing, both in point of soil and geological features, from any portion of the country we had before seen. Several circumstances had induced us to conjecture that rocks of the newst floetz trap formation existed in some portion of the secondary region, along the eastern declivity of the Rocky Mountains, but, until this time, we had met with no positive confirmation of the opinion. We were glad to be at length relieved from the tiresome sameness of the sand formation, and promised ourselves, in the treasures of new and more fertile variety of soil, the acquisition of many important plants.

At five P. M. we met with a little stagnant water, near which we encamped, having travelled about ten miles nearly due south from the point where we had left the valley of the creek. The hunters went out on foot, in pursuit of bisons, several herds being in sight, but returned at dark, having effected no more than to break the shoulder of a young bull, who ran off pursued by a gang of wolves. Several of the party, being informed of the route the animal had taken, and instigated, in common with the wolves, by the powerful incitement of hunger, resolved to join the chase, and to dispute with their canine competitors the possession of the prey. When they had nearly overtaken the bison, they saw him several times thrown to the ground by the wolves, and afterwards regaining his feet. They soon came near enough to do execution with their pistols, and frightened away the wolves, only to make a speedier end of the harassed animal. It was now past nine o'clock, but the starlight was sufficient to enable them to dress the meat, with which they returned loaded to camp, and spent the greater part of the night in regaling on the choice pieces.

28th. From an elevated point, about eight miles south of our encampment, the high peak at the head of the Arkansa was still visible. From a computation of our courses and distances, we found we could not be less than one hundred and thirty miles distant from its base, but the air, at that time, was remarkably clear, and our elevation above the common level of the plain very considerable. By referring to Pike's "Journal of a voyage to the sources of the Arkansa," it will be seen that this peak is the most prominent and conspicuous feature in a great extent of the surrounding country. "It is indeed so remarkable as to be known to all the savage nations for hundreds of miles around, and to be spoken of, with admiration, by the Spaniards of New Mexico, and was the bounds of their travels northwest. Indeed, in our wanderings in the mountains, it was never out of sight, except when in a valley, from the 14th November to the 27th January." See page 171.

Notwithstanding this representation, and that the peak in question was seen by ourselves, at the distance of one hundred and thirty miles, we are inclined to think, that, in point of elevation, it falls far below many portions of the interior ridges of the mountains, which are visible from its summit, and from the plains of the Platte, and that it is, by standing a little detached from the principal group of the mountains, it acquires a great portion of the imposing grandeur of its appearance.

We passed, in the morning, some tracts of gray sandstone, having, however, met with several inconsiderable conic hills, belonging to that interesting formation, called by Werner the Floetz Trap rocks. We perceived before us a striking change in the aspect and conformation of the surface; instead of the wearisome uniformity, the low and pointless ridges, which mark the long tract of horizontal sandstone we had passed, we had now the prospect of a country varied by numerous continued ranges of lofty hills, interspersed with insulated cone-like piles, and irregular masses of every variety of magnitude and position. This scenery is not to be compared, in point of grandeur, with the naked and towering majesty of the great chain of the Andes, which we had lately left, but, in its kind, it is of uncommon beauty. The hills, though often abrupt and high, are sometimes smooth and grassy to their summits, having a surface unbroken by a single rock or tree, large enough to be seen at the distance of a mile.

At noon, we halted near the base of a hill of this description. It is of greenstone, and the sand-rock on which it rests is disclosed at the bottom of a ravine, which commences near the foot of the hill. This latter rock is of a slaty structure, and embraces narrow beds of bituminous clay slate, which contains pieces of charcoal or the carbonized remains of vegetables, in every possible respect resembling the charcoal produced by the process of combustion in the open air. In the ravines, and over the surface of the soil, we observed masses of a light, porous, reddish-brown substance, greatly resembling that so often seen floating down the Missouri, by some considered a product of pseudo-volcanic fires, said to exist on the upper branches of that river. We also saw some porphyritic masses with a basis of greenstone, containing crystals of feldspar.

In the afternoon, several magpies, shore-larks, and cow-buntings were seen. One of the cow-buntings followed us five or six miles, alighting on the ground near the foremost of our line, and within a few paces of the horses' feet, where he stood gazing at the horses until all had passed him, when he again flew forward to the front, repeating the same movements many times in succession.

We had now arrived near that part of the country where, according to the information of the Kaskaia, we expected to find the remarkable saline spring, from which, we were told, the Indians often procured large masses of salt. The Kaskaia had, by the aid of a map traced in the sand, given us a minute account of the situation of the spring, and of the surrounding country, stating that the salt existed in masses at the bottom of a basin-like cavity, which contained about four and a half feet of reddish water. Thus far we had not found a single feature of the country to correspond, in the slightest degree, to his descriptions, and as we had been careful to follow the general direction of the course pointed out to us, it was probably his intention to deceive.

Our course, which was a little east of south, led us across several extensive vallies, having a thin dark-coloured soil, closely covered with grasses and strewed with fragments of greenstone. Descending, towards evening, into a broad and deep valley, we found ourselves again immured between walls of gray sandstone, similar in elevation and all other particulars to those which limit the valley of Purgatory creek. It was not until considerable search had been made, that we discovered a place where it was possible to effect the descent, which was at length accomplished, not without danger to the life and limbs of ourselves and horses. The area of the valley was covered with a sandy soil, in which we again saw the great cylindric Cactus, the Cucumis, and other plants common to the sandy districts, but rarely found in the scanty soils of the Trap formation. Pursuing our way, along this valley, we arrived, towards evening, at an inconsiderable stream of transparent and nearly pure water descending along a narrow channel, paved with black and shapeless masses of amygdaloidal and imperfectly porphyritic greenstone. This was the first stream we had, for a long time, seen traversing rocks of secondary formation, whose waters were free from an impregnation of muriate of soda and other salts. From the very considerable magnitude of the valley, and the quantity of water in the creek, it is reasonable to infer that its sources were distant at least twenty miles to the west, and the purity and transparency of its waters afford sufficient evidence that it flows principally from a surface of Trap rocks.

Having crossed the creek, with some difficulty, we halted on the bank to set up our tent and prepare ourselves for a thunder-shower, which was already commencing. After the rain, the sky became clear, and the sun, which was near setting, gilded with its radiance the dripping foliage of a cluster of oaks and poplars which stood near our tent. The grassy plain, acquiring unwonted verdure from the shower, and sparkling with the reflection from innumerable suspended rain drops, disclosed here and there a conic pile or a solitary fragment of black and porous Amygdaloid. The thinly wooded banks of the creek resounded to the loud notes of the robin, and the more varied and melodious song of the mocking bird; the stern features of Nature seemed to relax into a momentary smile to cheer us on our toilsome journey.

On the morning of the 29th, our course (S. 35° E.) brought us at the distance of three miles from our camp to the foot of the cliff, which separates the valley from the high plain. This mural barrier, has an elevation of about two hundred feet, and is impassable except at particular points, where it is broken by ravines. One of these we were fortunate in finding without being compelled to deviate greatly from our course, and climbing its rugged declivity, we emerged upon the broad expanse of the high plain. Turning with a sort of involuntary motion towards the west, we again caught a view of the distant summits of the Andes, appearing on the verge of our horizon. The scene before us was beautifully varied with smooth valleys, high conic hills, and irregular knobs scattered in every direction as far as the eye could comprehend. Among these singular eminences nothing could be perceived like a continuous unbroken range; most of them stand entirely isolated, others in groups and ranges, but all are distinct hills, with unconnected bases. The surface of the country generally, and more especially in the immediate vicinity of these hills, is strewed with fragments of compact or porphyritic greenstone. These are in some places accumulated in such quantities as greatly to retard the traveller.

At half past eleven A. M., a violent storm with high and cold wind, came on from the northeast, and continued for two hours. Soon after its commencement we halted to dine, but were unable to find a spot affording wood, until so much rain had fallen as to wet our clothing and baggage. Fire was almost the only comfort we could now command, our provision being so nearly exhausted, that about an ounce of jerked bison meat was all that could be allowed each man for his dinner.

The rain ceasing, we again resumed our march, but had not proceeded far, when we were overtaken by a second storm from the N. E., still more violent than the first, and attended with such pelting hail, that our horses refused to proceed in any direction, except that of the wind, so that rather than suffer ourselves to be carried off our course, we were compelled to halt and sit patiently upon our horses; opposing our backs to the storm, we waited for its violence to abate. As soon as the hail ceased, we moved on; the water pouring in streams from our mockasins and every part of our dress. The rain continued until dark, when being unable to find wood, and having no occasion for water, we halted, and without the delay of cooking supper or eating it, we set up our tent, and piled ourselves together under it in the most social manner imaginable. During the day, the mercury had fallen from 70° to 47°, indicating a change of temperature, which was the more severely felt as we were hungry, wet, and much fatigued. As we had neither dry clothing nor blankets, we could find no other method of restoring the warmth to our benumbed bodies than by placing them together in the least possible compass. We spent a cheerless night, in the course of which Mr. Peale experienced an alarming attack of a spasmodic affection of the stomach induced probably by cold and inanition. He was somewhat relieved by the free use of opium and whiskey.

We left our comfortless camp at an early hour on the ensuing morning, and traversing a wide plain strewed with fragments of greenstone, amygdaloid, and the vessicular substance already mentioned as the pumice stone of Bradbury, we arrived in the middle of the day, in sight of a creek, which like all water courses of this region, occupies the bottom of a deep and almost inaccessible valley; with the customary difficulty and danger, we at length found our way to the stream, and encamped.

We were much concerned, but by no means surprised, to discover that our horses were rapidly failing under the severe services they were now made to perform; we had been often compelled to encamp without a sufficiency of grass, and the rocky ways, to which we had for some time accustomed them, were destroying their hoofs. Several were becoming lame, and all much exhausted and weakened.

Verplank, our faithful and indefatigable hunter, was so fortunate, as to kill a black-tailed deer, at a distance from our course. A horse was, however, sent for the remainder of the meat, (Verplank having brought the greater part of it on his shoulders) and we once more enjoyed the luxury of a full meal.

CHAPTER VII

Sufferings of the party from stormy weather and want of provisions—
Indications of an approach towards settlements—Inscribed rocks—
Cervus Macrotis—Volcanic origin of Amygdaloid.

THE valley in which we halted is narrow, and bounded on both sides by cliffs of greenstone, having manifestly a tendency to columnar or polyedral structure. It falls readily into large prismatic masses, but obstinately resists that further disintegration, which must take place before it can be removed by the water. For this reason the valley is much obstructed by the fallen masses retaining their angular form, and a little intermixed with soil.

The stream which exists in this valley, for a part of the year at least, but which was now dry, runs towards the southeast. Having arrived at that part of the country which has by common consent, been represented to contain the sources of the Red river of Louisiana, we were induced by the general inclination of the surface, and the direction of this creek to consider it as one of those sources, and accordingly resolved to descend along its course, hoping it would soon conduct us to a country abounding in game, and presenting fewer obstacles to our progress, than that in which we now were. Our sufferings from the want of provisions, and from the late storm, together with the enfeebled condition of our horses, had discouraged us from prolonging, farther than was necessary, our journey towards the southwest.

The country between the sources of Purgatory creek, and the stream on which we were encamped, is a wide and elevated formation of trap rocks, resting upon horizontal sandstone. It has a loose and scanty soil, in which sand, gravel, and rolled pebbles are rarely seen, except in the vicinity of some points, where the sandstone appears to have been uncovered by the action of currents of water. In traversing it we had collected many new and interesting plants, among these were a large decumbent mentzelia, an unarmed rubus, with species of astragalus, pentstemon, myosotis, helianthus, &c. Beside the common purslane, which is one of the most frequent plants about the mountains, we had observed on the Arkansa a smaller species, remarkably pilose about the axils of the leaves, which are also narrower than in P. *oleracea*. A very small cuscuta also occurs almost exclusively parasitic on the common purslane.

31st. In attempting to descend the creek from our last encampment, we found the valley so obstructed with fragments of greenstone, as to be wholly impassable. We accordingly ascended into the plain, and continuing along the brink of the precipice, arrived in a few hours at a point where the substratum of sandstone emerges to light, at the base of an inconsiderable hill. It is a fine gray sandstone, having an argillaceous cement, and its laminæ are so nearly horizontal, that their inclination is not manifest to the eye. It is smooth and fissile, and in every respect remarkably contrasted to the massive and imperfectly columnar greenstone, which it supports.

The greenstone of this district is not universally marked by any tinge of green in the colouring, but often, as in the instance of which we are now speaking, its colour is some shade of gray, varying from light gray to grayish black. The hornblend and feldspar which enter into its composition, are minutely and intimately blended. Its minute structure is rarely, if ever, distinctly crystalline; most frequently it is compact, and the fracture nearly even.

The hunters were kept constantly in advance of the party, and, in the course of the morning, they killed a small fawn and a heron. At one o'clock, we arrived at the confluence of a creek, tributary from the east to the stream we were following, and descending into its valley, by a precipitous declivity of about four hundred feet, encamped for the remainder of the day. This valley is bounded by perpendicular cliffs of sandstone, surmounted by extensive beds of greenstone. The fragments of the latter have fallen down into the valley, and, being less perishable than the sandstone, they constitute the greater part of the debris accumulated along the base of the cliffs.

The sand-rock, which in some places is exposed in perpendicular precipices, is soft and friable, being very readily scratched with the point of a knife, and has been rudely inscribed, probably by the Indians, with emblematical figures commemorative of some past event. Several of the figures, intended to represent men, are distinguished by the sign of the cross inscribed near the head; some are represented smoking, and some leading horses, from which we infer, that the inscriptions are intended to commemorate some peaceful meeting of the Indians with the Spaniards of New Mexico, for the purposes of trade, where horses were either given as presents or bartered for other articles. Some meeting of this kind has, probably, happened here at no very distant period, as corn-cobs were found near our encampment: from this circumstance, it would appear that the distance to the Spanish settlements cannot be very great.

Mr. Peale, who had been unwell since the cold storm of the 28th, now found some little relief in the opening of an abscess which had formed on his jaw.

As several of our horses had been lamed in descending into the valley, and by the rough journey to the preceding day, it was thought necessary to allow ourselves a day of rest. Since arriving in the country inhabited by the hitherto undescribed animal, called the black-tailed or mule deer, we had been constantly attentive to the important object of procuring a complete specimen for preservation and description. Hitherto, though several had been killed, none had been brought to camp, possessing all the characters of the perfect animal. Supposing we soon should pass beyond their range, a reward had been offered to the hunter who should kill and bring to the camp an entire and full grown buck.

Verplank killed one of this description, on the afternoon of the first of August, near enough our camp to call for assistance and bring it in entire. They did not arrive until dark, and we had such pressing necessity for the flesh of the animal, that we could not defer dressing it until the next morning. The dimensions were accordingly taken, and a drawing made by Mr. Peale, by the light of a large fire. Verplank informed us that in company with the buck which he killed, were five does, two of the common red deer, (C. Virginianus,) and three of the other kind.

We observed about this camp a yellow flowering sensitive plant, apparently a congener to the saw brier (Schranika *uncinata.*) of the Platte and Arkansa. Its leaves are twice pinnated, and manifestly irritable. We also added to our collection two new species of Gaura, much smaller than G *mollis*, which is also found here.

Several rattlesnakes were seen and many orbicular lizards. These are evidently of two distinct species, differing from each other in the length of the spines, and the position of the nostrils. Scarce any two of either species are precisely similar in colour, but the markings are permanent. Both species possess, in a slight degree, the power of varying the shades of colour. We could find no conspicuous difference marking the different sexes in the species with long spines; the other we have not had sufficient opportunity to examine.

Aug. 2d. The rain which had fallen during great part of the preceding day and night, had considerably raised the water in the small creek, on which we were encamped. At sunrise we collected our horses, and proceeded down the valley, the direction of our course, being south, 80° east. At the distance of two or three miles we found the valley much expanded in width, and observed a conspicuous change in the sandstone precipices, which bound it. This change is the occurrence of a second variety of sand-rock, appearing along the base of the cliff, and supporting the slaty argillaceous stratum above described. These rocks have the same relative position, and nearly the same aggregate elevation, as the two very similar varieties in the valley of Purgatory creek: indeed the conclusion, that they are the continuation of the same strata, can scarcely be avoided. The lower-most or red sand-rock, is here very friable and coarse. Its prevailing colour is a yellowish gray or light brown. It often consists almost exclusively of large rounded particles of white or transparent quartz, united by a scanty cement, which usually contains lime, and sometimes, but not always, oxide of iron. In some instances the cement seems to be wanting. Its stratifications are very indistinct, compared to those of the gray sandstone, and like them disposed horizontally.

On entering the wider part of the valley, we perceived before us, standing alone in the middle of the plain, an immense circular elevation, rising nearly to the level of the surface of the sandstone table, and apparently inaccessible on all sides. On its summit is a level area of several acres bearing a few cedar bushes, probably the habitation of birds only.

Leaving this we passed three others in succession, similar in character, but more elevated and remarkable.

After passing the last of these, the hills ceased abruptly, and we found ourselves once more entering on a vast unvaried plain of sand. The bed of the creek had become much wider, but its water had disappeared. Meeting at length with a stagnant pool, we halted to dine, but found the water more bitter and nauseous to the taste, than that of the ocean, as it could neither be used for cooking or to drink; we made but a short halt, dining on a scanty allowance of roasted venison, which we ate without bread, salt, water, or any thing else. Some fragments of amygdaloid, were strewed along the bed of the stream, but we saw no more of that rock, or of the other members of the Floetz Trap formation in place. They may extend far towards the southwest, but of this we have no conclusive evidence. The aspect of these rocks particularly of the amygdaloid or toadstone, is so peculiar, and its disposition so remarkably dissimilar to that of the sandstones, with which it is associated, as strongly to suggest the idea of a different origin.

In the midst of one of the violent storms, we encountered in passing this trap formation, we crossed the point of a long but low ridge of amygdaloid, so singularly disposed as to suggest to every one of the party, the idea, that the mass had once been in a fluid state, and that when in that state it had formed a current, descending along the bed of a narrow ravine, which it now occupied, conforming to all the sinuosities and inequalities of the valley, as a column of semi-fluid matter would do. Its substance was penetrated with numerous vessicular cavities, which appeared in some instances elongated in the direction of the ridge. Its colour is nearly black; and when two masses are rubbed together, they emit a smell somewhat like the soot of a chimney. These appearances are so remarkable, that it is not surprising these rocks should have been considered of volcanic origin, and it is this supposition, unquestionably, from which has originated the statement contained in the late map of the United States, by Melish, that the district about the sources of Red river, is occupied by volcanic rocks; this information having probably been derived from the accounts of hunters.

The vallies which penetrate into the sandstone, supporting the trap rocks, have usually a sandy soil, while that of the more elevated portions, though inconsiderable in quantity, is not sandy not intermixed with pebbles or gravel. Among the few scattered and scrubby trees, met with in this district, are oaks, willows, and the cotton-wood; also a most interesting shrub or small tree, rising sometimes to the height of twelve or fourteen feet. It has dioiceous flowers, and produces a leguminous fruit, making in several particulars a near approach to Gleditschia, from which, however, it is sufficiently distinguished by the form of the legume, which is long and nearly cylindiric, and by the seeds, which are enclosed in separate cells, immersed in a saccharine pulp, but easily detached from the valves of the legume. In these particulars it discovers an affinity to the tamarind of the West Indies. The legume or pod, which is from six to ten inches long, and near half an inch in diameter, contains a considerable quantity of sugar-like pulp, very grateful to the taste when ripe. The leaves are pinnated, and the trunk beset with spines, somewhat like the honey locust, but the spines are simple. Our Spanish interpreter, informed us that it is found about Monterey, and in other parts of the internal provinces, where it must have been noticed by Humboldt; but we have not been able to have access to his account of it.

In the afternoon, we travelled thirteen miles, descending along the valley in a southeast direction. We extended our ride farther than we had wished; finding no suitable place to encamp. After sunset we found a small puddle of stagnant water in the bed of the creek, which though extremely impure, was not as bitter as that near which we halted in the middle of the day. Neither wood nor bison dung could be found, so that being unable to kindle a fire, we were compelled to rest satisfied with the eighth part of a sea biscuit each for supper, that being the utmost our supplies would allow. In the afternoon one of our hunters had killed a badger, which was all the game we had, and this we were compelled to reserve until we could make a fire to cook it.

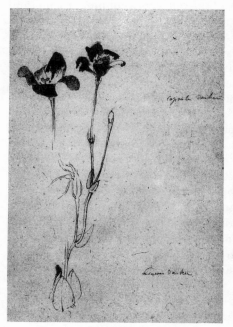

Flowers, T.R. Peale, August 3, 1820, watercolor and pencil.

3d. Little delay was occasioned by our preparations for breakfast. The fourth part of a biscuit, which had been issued to each man on the preceding evening, and which was to furnish both supper and breakfast, would have required little time had all of it remained to be eaten, which was not the case. We were becoming somewhat impatient on account of thirst, having met with no water which we could drink, for near twenty-four hours. Accordingly getting upon our horses at an early hour, we moved down the valley, passing an extensive tract, whose soil is a loose red sand, intermixed with gravel and small pebbles, and producing nothing but a few sunflowers and sand-cherries still unripe. While we should remain upon a soil of this description, we could scarcely expect to meet with water or wood, for both of which we began to feel the most urgent necessity, and as the prospect of the country before us promised no change, it is not surprising we should have felt a degree of anxiety and alarm, which, added to our sufferings from hunger and thirst, made our situation extremely unpleasant. We had travelled greater part of the day enveloped in a burning atmosphere, sometimes letting fall upon us the scorching particles of sand which had been raised by the wind, sometimes almost suffocating by its entire stagnation, when we had the good fortune to meet with a pool of stagnant water, which though muddy and brackish, was not entirely impotable, and afforded us a more welcome refreshment, than is often in the power of abundance to supply. Here was also a little wood, and our badger, with the addition of a young owl, which we had the good fortune to take, was very hastily cooked and eaten.

4th. We were still passing through a barren and desolate region, affording no game, and nearly destitute of wood and water. Its soil is evidently the detritus of a stratum of red sandstone, and coarse conglomerate, which is still the basis and prevailing rock. It appears to contain a considerable proportion of lime, and fragments of plaister-stone and Selenite are often seen intermixed with it.

Our morning's ride of sixteen miles, brought us to a place where the water of the river emerges to view, rising to the surface of that bed of sand, beneath which it had been concealed for a distance of more than one hundred miles. The stream was still very inconsiderable in magnitude, the water brackish and mixed with so large a quantity of red earth, as to give it the colour of florid blood. The general direction of its course inclining still towards the southeast, we were now induced to believe it must be one of the most considerable of the upper tributaries of Red river. A circumstance tending to confirm this opinion, was our falling in with a large and much frequented Indian trace crossing the creek, from the west, and following down along the east bank. This trace consisted of more than twenty parallel paths, and bore sufficient marks of having been recently travelled, affording an explanation of the cause of the alarming scarcity of game we had for some time experienced. We supposed it to be the road leading from the Pawnee Piqua village, on Red river to Santa Fe.

Two shrubby species of Cactus, smaller than the great cylindric prickly pear, noticed near the Rocky Mountains, occur in the sandy plains, we were now traversing. One of these which is about four feet high, and very much branched, has long and solitary spines, a small yellow flower, and its fruit, which is about as large as the garden cherry, is very pleasant to taste. The fruit of the C. *ferox,* which is also found here, was now ripe, being nearly as large as an egg, and of a deep purple colour. The jatropha stimulosa, a congener to the manihot or

Cassada of the West Indies, a cassia, an amorpha, and many new plants were here added to our collections.

A few wild horses had been observed in the course of the day, and towards evening one was seen following the party, but keeping at a distance. At night, after our horses had been staked in the usual manner near the camp, we perceived him still lingering about, and at length approaching the tent, so closely, that we began to entertain hopes of capturing him alive. In attempting this, we stationed a man with a noosed rope, in the top of a cotton-wood tree, under which we tied a few of our horses, but this plan did not succeed.

On the following morning, one of our hunters fortunately discovered the same horse standing asleep under the shade of a tree, and having shot him, returned immediately to camp with the intelligence. We had all suffered so severely from hunger, and our present want of provisions was so great, and we ate indiscriminately and greedily of this unaccustomed food, and congratulated each other on the acquisition of so seasonable a supply. We felt a little regret at killing so beautiful an animal, who had followed us several miles on the day before, and had lingered with a sort of confidence about our camp; but all our scruples yielded to the admonitions of hunger.

The day being Sunday, and the plain about our camp affording a supply of grass for our jaded horses, we resolved to remain encamped, seizing the opportunity of making observations for latitude, &c. The morning was calm and clear, the mercury at 69° Fah. For five mornings preceding, it had been at 58° and in the middle of each day rose above 90°. The moon was now too near the sun to admit of observations by lunar distances, but the meridional altitude of the sun's lower limb, taken with great care, and under circumstances favorable to accuracy, gave 35° 16' 19" for the latitude of our encampment.

The river bed, at this place, was found by admeasurement, sixty yards in width, twenty of which were naked sand-bar, the remaining forty covered with water, having an average depth of about ten inches. The current is moderate, the water intensely red, having nearly the temperature and the saltness of new milk. It suspends a very considerable quantity of clay, derived from the cement of the sand-rock, but notwithstanding its impurities, it is more grateful to the taste than any we had met with since leaving the mountains, and though drank in large quantities, produced no unpleasant effect.

Some spots in the low plains had here considerable fertility, depending probably in some degree on the intermixture of a large porportion of calcareous matter, with the soil resulting from the disintegrated sand-rock. Though no extensive formation of limestone appears, yet the sandstone has not only in many instances a calcareous cement, but is traversed by numerous veins, both of Gypsum and carbonate of lime.

The occurrence of the elm and the diospyros indicated a soil at least approaching towards one adapted to the purposes of agriculture. Among great numbers of interesting plants, we found here a gentiana, with a flower much larger than g. *crinita*, an orobanche, probably the *o. ludoviciana, N.,* a new croton, an ipomopsis and many others. Notwithstanding the scarcity of game, which we had so long felt, we daily saw numbers of antelopes, with some signs of bear, deer, and turkies; but these animals had acquired all the vigilance which results from the habit of being often hunted, and the entire want of thick forests, and even of solitary trees or inequalities of the surface to cover the approach of the hunter, rendered abortive most of our attempts to take them.

The common partridge, (Perdix *virginianus*) was seen near this encampment; also the dove, which had never disappeared entirely in all the country we had passed.

Rising at the customary hour on the morning of the 7th, we perceived that a part of our horses were missing. As we were apprehensive they had been stolen by Indians, a small party was immediately sent to discover the route they had taken. Pursuing along their path, the men overtook them at the distance of two or three miles, as they were straying on in search of pasture.

On leaving our camp we endeavoured to regain the trace, on which we had for several days travelled; but though we spent much time in the search, and travelled several miles off our course we were not able to find it. This we had occasion to regret, as the surface of the country is mostly of a loose sand, bearing tufts of wormwood, and other plants, rendering the travelling difficult where there is no road. In order to shun the numerous ravines which now began to occur, we chose our route at some distance from the bank of the river, where we found the vallies deeper and more abrupt, though less frequent.

In the course of our morning's ride of twenty miles, we saw several gangs of wild horses, and with these we distinguished numbers of colts and some mules. In passing through a village of prairie dogs, of which we saw great numbers, Mr. Peale killed a burrowing owl. The bird, though killed instantly, had fallen into one of the marmot's burrows, but had luckily lodged within the reach of the arm. On opening it, the intestines were found filled with the fragments of grasshoppers' wings, and the hard parts of other insects. We have never been able from examination to discover any evidence, that these owls prey upon the marmots, whose villages they infest.

After proceeding near twenty miles, we directed our course towards the

Burrowing owl, T.R. Peale, August 7, 1820, ink.

river, which we had kept at some distance on our left. Arriving at it at two o'clock, we encamped, and sent out the hunters, as we had some hope of procuring a supply of provisions, less repugnant to our prejudices than horseflesh; the hunters, however, as well as others of the party, spent the remaining part of the afternoon in an unavailing search for game.

The hills, which bound the immediate valley of the river at this place, have an elevation of from one to two hundred feet above the surface of the water. They are usually covered with a deep sandy soil, but disclose in their sides, points and precipices of red sandstone, containing large quantities of very beautiful Selenite. The other more common varieties of sulphate of lime, are also of frequent occurrence. Crystals of carbonate of lime, are met with in veins traversing the sandstone.

In this region, the cenchrus tribuloides, a most annoying grass, supplies the place of the Cactus *ferox,* and the troublesome stipas of the Platte. The cenchrus bears its seed in small spikelets, which consist of a number of rigid radiating spines. These clusters of barbed thorns are detached at the slightest touch, falling into our mockasins, adhering to our blankets and clothing, and annoying us at every point. The clott-bur, (Xanthium *strumiarum*) which had occurred in every part of our route, began now to ripen and cast off its muricated fruit, adding one more to the sources of constant molestation.

A formidable centipede, (Scolopendra) was caught near the camp, and brought in alive by one of the engagees. It was about eight inches in length, and nearly three-fourths of an inch in breadth, being of a flattened form, and of a dark brown colour. While kept alive, it showed great viciousness of disposition, biting at every thing which came within its reach. Its bite is said to be venomous.

On the morning of the 8th, we continued our journey, crossing and recrossing the river several times. This we found necessary, as the occurrence of steep and rocky ravines made it impossible to pass along the bank parallel to the course of the river, which here became more meandering, winding about the points of rocky and impassable promontories.

Few trees occur along this part of the valley, but grapevines were becoming numerous, and some of them loaded with fruit. Among these we saw signs of the black bear, and one of these animals was shot at but not killed. We also saw some recent tracks of bisons, reviving us with the hope of a return of the days of plenty. We constantly met with the remains of Indian encampments; trees which had been felled with the tomahawk, and other evidences that the country had been recently occupied by savages.

We passed in the afternoon, to a more plain and fertile country than that we had for some days been traversing. The river valley became wide, and bounded on both sides by low and rounded hills, instead of abrupt and perpendicular precipices. The general surface of the country is but little elevated above the river, and is nearly unbroken.

We crossed the beds of several creeks, apparently large streams in the wet season, but now entirely destitute of water. As yet we had not crossed a single tributary discharging any water into the river, nor had we been able to discover any augmentation of the volume of water, which appeared to have been derived from tributaries entering on the other side. The channels of all the creeks, hitherto observed, were beds of sand without water. Several of these "dry rivers," which we passed in the course of the day, have broad vallies, which, if we may judge from a comparison with that we were descending, must have an extent of more than one hundred miles, draining a wide expanse of country of the surplus water in the rainy season, but remaining dry during great part of the year. At five o'clock we encamped, having travelled twenty-six miles due east. The hunters were immediately sent out, but returned without game, having seen nothing.

A beautiful white flowered Gaura, had been for several days observed along the bank of the river. It is undescribed, and has, before flowering, a very distinct resemblance to common flax.

View of the Chasm through which the Platte issues from the Rocky Mountains, Samuel Seymour, engraving.

CHAPTER VIII

Band of Kaskaias—Indian encampment—Unfriendly behavior of the Kaskaias—Some account of their persons and manners—Salt plains—Camancias.

ON the 9th we breakfasted on the last of the horse-beef, which, having been killed on the 5th, and the weather being unusually warm, had suffered from long keeping. We ate it cheerfully, only regretting we had not the prospect of any thing as good for dinner. All the marksmen of the party were kept constantly out in search of game, but for several days had met with no success in hunting.

Our sufferings from want of provisions, and from the apprehension of still more distressing extremities, were now so considerable, that we gave little attention to any object except hunting. Unfortunately for us, the wind had been high during the morning, and had blown from west to east, nearly in the direction of our route, so that whatever animals might have been in the way, had received early intimation of our approach, and made their escape. We were glad to observe considerable numbers of prairie wolves, and carrion birds, as they afforded an almost certain indication of the proximity of bisons. The recent tracks of a herd of these animals had been discovered, from which we learned that they had crossed the river within a day or two, in a crowded and hurried manner, as if pursued by hunters. We pursued nearly the same course during the day, and halted for the night at a late hour, having travelled twenty-eight miles, and being much exhausted with fatigue, hunger, and the heat of the day, the mercury at noon having stood at 96°.

At about ten o'clock on the morning following, the hunters, who had preceded the party, discovered on the opposite side of the river, a solitary bison, of which they went immediately in pursuit. The party had made their breakfast of about two ounces of sugar and some grapes, which had been found near camp, and having been for several days reduced to a scanty allowance of provision, they encamped immediately, and awaited with great anxiety the return of the hunters, who soon joined us bringing in the greater part of the carcass of the bison, so extremely lean and ill-flavored that nothing but the most urgent necessity could have induced us to taste it. It was evident that the animal was diseased, and had lingered behind the herd for want of strength to travel. Our situation, however, afforded us not the power of choosing, and from the occurrence of this one we were induced to hope we should soon meet with others in better condition.

We had passed on the preceding day for the first time a small creek discharging some water into the river, and shortly afterwards the sandy bed of another, sixty yards in width, with an extensive valley, but having no water visible above the sand. This morning we also crossed a tributary affording a little water, and a dry channel communicating opposite to our encampment with the bed of the river, which is here paved with small stones, occasioning an inconsiderable fall. Throughout the day the weather was extremely warm, and at sunrise on the following morning the mercury was standing at 71°.

We had not proceeded far on our way, when we discovered on the opposite side of the river, a large party of Indians, approaching in an irregular and interrupted line, which extended more than a mile, from the opposite bank. They had, as was evident, already discovered us, and their outriders were seen plunging into the river at various points, and several soon came up to shake hands with us. The foremost scarcely allowed themselves time to finish this hasty ceremony of salutation, when they rode to reconnoitre some points of bushes and patches of low grape vines on our left, manifestly to ascertain if the whole strength of our party was collected. The main body of the Indians crossed the river more slowly, and as we halted on an elevation near the point where they ascended the bank, the whole passed in review before us. They were all on horseback, and the squaws and children, composing by far the greatest part of the cavalcade, passed us without halting. Every squaw appeared to have under her care a greater or less number of horses, which were driven before her, some dragging lodge-poles, some loaded with packs of meat, and some carrying children. We were amused at observing many small children, too young to be able by their own strength to sit on a horse, lashed by their legs to the saddle, and riding on in entire unconcern. As they passed the deepest part of the river, many of the squaws stooped to fill their vessels with water. These were of the most primitive kind, being formed almost without exception of the stomach or bladder of a bison or other animal.

At length the chief, who was one of the last to cross the river, came up, and shaking us each by the hand, with some appearance of cordiality, invited us to accompany him a short distance on his route, to a place where his party would encamp for the remainder of the day and the ensuing night. The chief was accompanied by an old man, who could speak a little Spanish, by which language we communicated with him. He informed us, his band were a part of the tribe of Kaskaias or Bad-hearts, as they are called by the French, that they had been on a hunting excursion to the sources of the Rio Brassis and the Rio Colorado of Texas, and were now on their way to meet the Spanish traders, at a point near the sources of the river we were descending. They in their turn demanded who we were, whence and whither we were travelling, and were apparently satisfied with our answers, though as afterwards appeared, they did not entirely credit what we had told them of the purposes of our journey.

To our inquiries concerning the river, they answered without hesitation, that it was Red river; that at the distance of ten days travelling, in the manner of Indians with their lodges, (about one hundred miles) we should meet with the permanent village of the Pawnee Piquas; that a large band of Camancias were hunting on the river below, whom we should fall in with in two or three days. Having described to them the route we had pursued, and the great and frequented road on which we had travelled, they said that when we were at the point where the road first crosses the river, we were three days ride from Santa Fe, which was situated behind a low and distant range of hills, that we remembered to have seen from that place.

We hesitated a little to comply with the request of the chief, enforced as it was with some insolence, that we would return and encamp with his party; but as we wished to purchase horses and provisions, and to make the best use of an opportunity to become acquainted with the savages, we at length consented. The ground they chose for their encampment, was a beautiful open plain, having the river in front and a small creek on the left. We were somewhat surprised to witness the sudden manner in which this plain became covered with their tall conic lodges, raised by the squaws, in perfect silence and good order.

For our accommodation a lodge was spread, enclosing as much space as possible in a semi-circular area, in such a manner, that the skin covering afforded a shade, which was all the shelter needed. In order to enlarge this tent as much as possible, the covering was raised so high upon the poles that its lower margin did not extend to the ground by a space of several feet. To remedy this the squaws brought bushes from a neighbouring thicket, which they placed around the base of the lodge, in such a manner as effectually to exclude the sunshine. We were sorry to find afterwards that this had been done not more from motives of hospitality, than to aid them in their design of pilfering from our baggage.

These skin lodges, are the only habitations of the wandering savages, during all seasons of the year. Those of the Kaskaias differ in no respect from those we have already described, as used by the Otoes and others of the Missouri Indians. The poles, which are six or eight to each lodge, are from twenty to thirty feet in length, and are dragged constantly about in all their movements, so that the trace of a party with lodges is easily distinguished from that of a war party. When they halt to encamp, the women immediately set up these poles, four of them being tied together by the smaller ends, the larger resting on the ground, are placed so far apart as to include as much space as the covering will surround. The remaining poles are added to strengthen the work and give a circular form.

The covering is then made fast by one corner to the end of the last pole, which is to be raised, by which means it is spread upon the frame with little difficulty. The structure when completed is in the form of a sharp cone. At the summit is a small opening for window, chimney, &c., out of which the lodge poles project some distance, crossing each other at the point where the four shortest are tied together. The skin lodge, of which a drawing by Mr. Peale is annexed, is greatly inferior in point of comfort, particularly in winter season, to the spacious mud cabins of the settled Indians.

The poles, necessary for the construction of these moveable dwellings, are not to be found in any part of the country of the Kaskaias, but are purchased from the Indians of the Missouri, or others inhabiting countries more plentifully supplied with timber. We were informed by Bijeau, that five of these poles are, among the Bad-hearts, equal in value to a horse.

The chief of this band is called the Red Mouse. He is of large stature, is somewhat past the middle age of life, and no way deficient in his person, and countenance of those indications of strength, cunning, and ferocity, which form so important a part of greatness in the estimation of the Indians.

Immediately after he had dismounted, on the halting of his party, a small wooden dish was brought him, containing some water. He had received a wound some time before apparently from an arrow, which had passed through the arm. Placing the dish on the ground before him, he dipped his hand repeatedly in the water, then seizing a small image of an alligator, profusely ornamented with white and blue beads, he pressed it in his hand with all the strength of his wounded arm. This we saw him repeat a great number of times. The alligator appeared to be the *great medicine*, on which he relied for the curse of his wound; no dressing or application of any kind was made immediately to the affected part.

As soon as we had placed our baggage in the tent provided for us, we commenced negotiations with Red Mouse, for the purchase of horses. When the articles we proposed to barter were exhibited, he appeared dissatisfied, supposing probably, we had still others in reserve, which he would be able by a little obstinacy to extort from us. He accordingly insisted that more of the packs should be opened, and, at last, undertook to extend his inquiries to our private baggage. This we found it necessary to resist, and a little scuffle ensued, at which many of the Indians, with a throng of women and children, who surrounded us, took fright and ran off with the utmost despatch. They all appeared somewhat surprised and intimidated, and the few who remained in our lodge, entreated us not to be angry at the insolence they had shown, saying we should frighten their women, and that they had mistaken us for traders. We had good reasons for wishing not to carry our resentment farther than was necessary, and accordingly relinquished the attempt to trade with them, informing them, at the same time, that we were hungry. Having received us in a friendly manner, we expected they would, according to the custom of most Indians, have shown their good will by inviting us to a feast. We had, therefore, waited with some impatience for their good cheer, so long that hope began to fail us. It will be recollected we had for some days been almost in a starving condition, and we perceived that the Indians had very plentiful supplies of jerked meat. In compliance with our repeated requests the wife of Red Mouse at length brought us a little half boiled bison meat, from which we had observed her to select the best pieces, and give them to the children. After we had eaten this we returned the wooden dish on which it had been brought, at the same time asking her for more. This second demand procured us a little more jerked meat, which came so reluctantly, that our hunger was now somewhat appeased, we resolved to ask them for no more.

One of the party having asked for water, the paunch of a bison was brought, containing three or four quarts, from which we all managed to drink, though with some difficulty. Little care or labour had been bestowed on the preparation of this vessel. The papilous coat, which formed the internal surface of the stomach of the animal, had not been removed; nor had it lost from long use its peculiar smell. The organ is suffered to retain its original form, as far as is consistent with the uses to which it is applied; one of the orifices is brought nearly in contact with the other, where it is retained by a stick passed through the margin, the depending part is a sack, sometimes large enough to contain six or eight gallons. It may well be supposed, practice is required to enable a person to drink with ease and adroitness from one of these vessels, and the Indians appeared somewhat amused, at the awkwardness of our attempts, in which we spilt more water in our bosoms, than was conveyed into our mouths.

When filled, these sacks cannot be set upon the ground without suffering the loss of their contents. To remedy this the Kaskaias carry with them, as an indispensable article of furniture, a sort of tripod consisting of three light poles tied together at one end and sharpened at the other, by which they are driven into the ground, and the water-sack is suspended between them. One of these was placed near the entrance of almost every lodge in this encampment.

We had scarcely finished our scanty repast, when the wife of the Red Mouse, showing her trencher to signify that we were her debtors, began to beset us for presents; as we were, however, little pleased with her hospitality, we treated her demands, as she had done ours. A number of small articles were pilfered from us, and the Indians seemed determined to show us little respect, until they perceived we were putting our guns in order for immediate use; at this they expressed some apprehension, and behaved afterwards with less rudeness.

They had thirty-two lodges, and were probably about two hundred and fifty in number, including men, women, and children. Among these we could number only twenty-two armed men, and these kept constantly about us. They were armed, exclusively, with bows and arrows, and, as we believed, had some fear of us, though we were less than half their number. It was, probably, owing to our preceiving, or at least appearing to perceive this, that we escaped from them uninjured. They had many horses, probably more than five hundred and some of them very good.

Towards evening, the chief withdrew from our lodge, when we observed his squaw prepare some food for him, pounding the jerked meat to a powder, with a stone pestle, using a piece of skin instead of a mortar. When reduced to very fine fragments, it was mixed with bison tallow, a little water added, and the whole boiled together.

After the chief had finished his meal, a council was held between all the men of the band. They met behind the chief's lodge, and we were not greatly pleased to perceive that they seemed anxious to conceal their meeting from us. At night we determined to collect all our horses, and placing them as near as we could around our lodge, to watch them until morning, but, upon examination, a few of them only could be found, the remainder, as we believed, having been secreted by the Indians. The crowd, which had been assembled about us during the day, dispersed, as the evening advanced, and, at dark, all became still in and about the encampment. At this time, the chief, whose lodge was near ours, standing at the entrance of his dwelling, harangued with great vehemence, in a voice sufficiently loud and clear to be heard by all his people, who had now retired to their several lodges. As we had no interpeter of their language, we could understand nothing of the import of his speech. Every thing remained quiet during the night, and as soon as day dawned on the following morning, a loud harangue, similar to that in the evening, was pronounced by the chief, and immediately afterwards the whole camp was in motion. The lodges were taken down, the packs placed upon the horses, and the whole body were in a short time ready to move off. As several of our horses, our kettles, and other articles of the greatest importance were missing, we were unwilling to part from our hosts in the hasty manner they seemed to intend. We accordingly summoned the old Indian interpreter, and made our complaint and remonstrance to the chief. He told us our horses had strayed from the camp, and that several of his people were then out, searching for them, and made other excuses, evidently designed to gain time until his band could move off. Perceiving we had no time to lose, Major Long ordered horses and other articles to be seized, corresponding to those we had lost. This timely measure produced the desired effect. Their whole camp had been some time in motion: the women and children, with all their baggage, except what we had detained, had moved to a considerable distance, and we found ourselves, at this unpleasant state of the dispute, surrounded by their whole armed force. We observed greater numbers of arrows in their hands than on the preceding day, and were not without our fears that they intended to carry the dispute, respecting our horses and kettles, to greater lengths than we could wish. We were, however, agreeably disappointed to learn that all our lost property had been found. It was accordingly restored to us and we parted from the Kaskaias as friends.

The time we spent with this band of savages was so short, as to afford little opportunity of becoming acquainted with their manners. Their dress is nearly similar to that of the Pawnees, but consists more exclusively of leather. The women, instead of the robe, wear a loose frock without sleeves. It has an opening for the neck, large enough to admit the head, and descends from the shoulders, hanging like a bag about the body, and reaching below the knees. When eagerly engaged in their employments this inconvenient article of dress is thrown aside, and the squabbish person of the female savage is exposed to view, disfigured only by a small apron of leather worn round the waist. The young females appear in some measure, exempted from the laborious services performed by the married women, and consequently, possess a degree of lightness and elasticity in their persons, which they soon lose after they begin to bear children, and subject themselves to the severe drudgeries of a married life. Their breasts become so flaccid and pendulous that we have seen them give suck to their children, the mother and child at the same time standing erect upon the ground. This fact is sufficient to prove that they do not, at least in some instances, wean their children at a very early age.

Like all savages, they suffer themselves to be covered with filth and vermin, and as among many northern tribes, lice are sought for and eaten with avidity, at least by the women; notwithstanding which, some of the young females are far from disgusting in their appearance. They have well turned features, aquiline noses, large and regular teeth, and eyes which, though usually rather small, are clear and brilliant. In the general structure of their features, and in the complexion of their skins, they resemble the Missouri tribes, being of a clearer and brighter red, than many of the eastern Indians. In stature and in symmetry of body they are inferior to the Otoes, Pawnees, and most of the Missouri Indians who reside in permanent villages.

They seemed to have had little intercourse with the whites, as some among them appeared to take great pleasure in exhibiting to their friends the skin of our arms, which they requested us to show them for that purpose. It was probably by means of a mistake, on the part of one of the interpreters, that we received the intimation that they had never before heard of such a people as that to which we belonged. We saw among them few articles of foreign production; these they had, probably, received from Spanish traders. In the whole encampment we saw but one kettle, which belonged to the chief, and their great eagerness to steal our tin cups and other similar articles, sufficiently evinced that such things are scarce, and of great value among them. They have some beads, most of which are bestowed in ornamenting the dress of the children; also some pewter and brass rings, worn principally by the women. They are acquainted with the use of tobacco, and smoked with us according to the universal custom of the Indians, but expressed, by signs, that they found the smoke of unmixed tobacco too strong for them. One of their young men, who was in his ordinary dress when we met the party, visited us soon after we had encamped, dressed in leggings and breech-cloth, with a striped worsted vest and a silver-headed bamboo.

A child was shown us, who spoke Spanish, and who was said to be a prisoner from the Spanish settlements; he was not, however, distinguished from the Kaskaias by any difference of colour or of features. He spoke frequently of the Christians, which convinced us that he had, at least been among the half civilized Indians of New Mexico, who have some acquaintance with the Spanish language, and have been taught enough of the Christian religion to make use of the sign of the cross.

This band of Kaskaias frequent the country about the sources of the Platte, Arkansa, and Rio Del Norte, and extend their hunting excursions to Red river and the sources of the Brassis. The great numbers of images of the Alligator, which they wear, either as ornaments, or as amulets for the cure or prevention of disease and misfortune, afford sufficient proof of their extending their rambles to districts inhabited by that reptile. These images are of carved wood, covered with leather, and profusely ornamented with beads. They are suspended around the neck, and we saw several worn in this manner by the children as well as by adults. It was observed, likewise, that the rude frames of the looking-glasses carried by several of the men, were carved so as to approximate towards the same form.

It is, perhaps, owing to their frequent exposures to the stormy and variable atmosphere of the country about the Rocky Mountains, that these Indians are subjected to numerous attacks of rheumatic and scrofulous diseases. We saw one old woman with a distorted spine, who had, probably, suffered when young from rickets. A young man of a fine athletic frame, had his neck covered with scrofulous ulcers. While he was with us, he was constantly endeavouring to conceal with his robe this afflicting spectacle. He remained but a short time amongst us, and did not make his second appearance.

An old man came frequently to us with a diseased leg, informing us by signs that it had repeatedly formed large abscesses, which had discharged much matter, and afterwards healed. His frequent applications to us were made with the hope that we would do something for his relief.

The men of this band wear the hair long, and suffer it to hang negligently about the shoulders. Some of them have a braid behind which is garnished with bits of red cloth, small pieces of tin, &c., and descends nearly to the ground, being sometimes eked out with the hair of a horse's tail. Among the old men, were several who had suffered a number of scattering hairs on the face to become of considerable length, a violation of good manners, and a neglect of personal neatness, not often met with among the Indians, and excusable only in the old. In their conduct towards us they were guilty of more rudeness and incivility than we had been accustomed to meet with among the savages of the Missouri.

Though we saw much to admire among this people, we cannot but think them among the most degraded and miserable of the uncivilized Indians on this side of the Rocky Mountains. Their wandering and precarious manner of life, as well as the inhospitable character of the country they inhabit, precludes the possibility of advancement from the profoundest barbarism. As is common among other of the western tribes, they were persevering in offering us their women, but this appeared to be done from mere beastliness and the hope of reward, rather than any motive of hospitality or a desire to show us respect. We saw among them no article of food, except the flesh of the bison; their horses, their arms, lodges, and dogs, are their only wealth.

In their marches they are all on horseback, the men are expert horsemen, and evince great dexterity in throwing the rope, taking in this way many of the wild horses which inhabit some parts of their country. They hunt the bison on horseback with the bow and arrow, being little acquainted with the use of fire arms. One of them, who had received a valuable pistol, from a member of our party, soon afterwards returned and wished to barter it for a knife. They begged for tobacco, but did not inquire for whiskey. It is probable they have not yet acquired a fondness for intoxicating liquors.

At eight o'clock on the morning of the 12th, we took our leave of the Kaskaias, having recovered from them all the articles they had stolen, except a few ropes, halters, and other small affairs, which, not being indispensably necessary to us, we chose to relinquish, rather than submit to a longer delay, among a people we had so much reason to dislike.

They had shown a disposition, so far from friendly toward us, that we were surprised to have escaped without having found it necessary to use our arms in self-defence, and as we thought it by no means improbable some of their young men might follow us to steal our horses, we moved on rather briskly, intending to travel as far in the course of the day as we conveniently could.

The river valley spread considerably a little below the point where we had encamped. In many places we found the surface a smooth and naked bed of sand, in others covered by an incrustation of salt, like a thin ice, and manifestly derived from the evaporation of water, which had flowed down from the red sandstone hills bounding the valley. These hills were here of moderate elevation, the side towards the river being usually abrupt and naked. The sandstone is fine, of a deep red colour, indistinctly stratified, and traversed in various directions by veins, filled principally with sulphate of lime.

We had seen among the Indians, on the preceding day, quantities of salt, in large but detached crystalline fragments, resembling the common coarse salt of commerce. It had evidently been collected from some place like the one above mentioned, where it had been deposited from solution in water. When we inquired the particular locality, the Indians pointed to the south, and said, it was found near the sources of a river, rising in that direction.

At the place of our evening encampment, we saw the red-necked avoset, (Recurvirostra *americana*) the minute tern, (Sterna *minuta)* and several other strand birds, which we could not approach near enough to distinguish the species. There is also a very evident similarity between the plants found here, and many of those growing in saline soils along the sea coast. We see here several species of atriplex, chenopodium, salsola, kochia, and anabasis, all delighting in a saline soil, and affording on analysis a greater proportion of soda, than most inland plants.

The day had been unusually warm. During all our midday halt, protracted on account of the sultriness of the weather, to an unaccustomed length, the mercury had remained at 100°, the thermometer being suspended in the closest shade we could find. It is to be remarked, however, that in almost every one of the numerous instances, when the mercurial column had indicated so high a temperature, a fair exposure could not be had. We often found it necessary to halt upon the open plain, where the intensity of light and heat were much increased by the reflection of the sun's rays from the sand. The temperature indicated by the thermometer suspended in the imperfect shade of our tent, or of a small tree, was, however, somewhat lower than that to which our bodies were exposed, and it will be believed, our sufferings from this source were great, both on our marches and while encamped in the middle of the day. Our tent being too small to afford its imperfect shade to the whole party, we sometimes suspended blankets, using instead of poles our rifles and gunsticks, but the protection these could afford against the scorching glare of a vertical sun, was found extremely inadequate.

At sunset we crossed, what appears to be, at some seasons of the year, the bed of a large river, at least two hundred yards wide, but at this time not a drop of water was found in it. It has a wide valley, and in every respect, but the occasional want of water, is a large stream. A little beyond this we encamped for the night, having travelled twenty-eight miles.

13th. The course of the river had here become considerably serpentine, so that our route along its valley, was of necessity somewhat circuitous. Wishing to avoid the unnecessary travelling thus occasioned, we turned off from the river, and ascended the hills, hoping to meet with an Indian trace, leading across the country by the most direct route. Our search was, however unavailing, only affording us an opportunity of examining a portion of the country remote from the river. This we found much broken with irregular hills, abrupt ravines, and deep vallies. At 10 o'clock we met with a small stream of water, running towards the river we had left, and crossing it, perceived the trace of a large party of mounted Indians, which had ascended the creek within a few hours previous. We supposed them to have been the band of Camancias spoken of by the Bad-hearts, and notwithstanding we had reason to entertain some fear, that they would have treated us no better than the Kaskaias had done, we considered ourselves unfortunate, in not having met them. Much confusion and uncertainty attends the limited information, hitherto before the public, concerning the wandering bands of savages, who occupy the country between the frontiers of New Mexico and the United States. Some who have spoken of these Indians, seem to have included several of the erratic hordes already enumerated, under the name of Hietans or Camancias. From their wandering mode of life, it un-avoidably happens, that the same band is met by hunters and travellers, in different parts of the country, at different times, consequently they receive different appellations, and the estimate of their numbers becomes much exaggerated. Of this band, we have no other information to communicate, than that they appeared, from the tracks of their horses and lodge poles, to have been rather more numerous than the party of Bad-hearts we had lately met. A recent grave was discovered by one of our hunters, at no great distance from the river, in which it was supposed one of this band had been buried. At one end of the grave was erected a pole about ten feet in length, crossed near the top by another two feet long. To the foot of this rude cross was tied a pair of mockasins, newly soaled and carefully prepared for the use of the departed, in that long journey, on the *road of the dead*, to which the good wishes of some friend had accompanied him.

Where we halted at noon, were some trees, and several of these were covered with grape vines, loaded with ripe and delicious fruit. The Osage plum was also common, and now beginning to ripen. The temperature of the air within our tent, partially shaded by some small trees, was sufficiently high to keep the mercury at 105° Fah. From twelve o'clock to three P.M. a suffocating stillness prevailed in the air, and we could find no relief from the painful glare of light, and the intense heat, which seemed about to reduce the scanty vegetation to ashes.

In the afternoon, a thick grove of timber was descried at a distance below, and on the opposite side of the river. This cheering sight was like the discovery of land to the mariner, reminding us of the comparative comfort and plenty, which we had learned to consider inseparable from a forest country, and exciting in us the hope that we should soon exchange our desolate and scorching sands for a more hospitable and more favoured region. As this little grove of trees, appearing to us like the commencement of an immense forest, gave reason to expect we should soon find some small game, Mr. Peale, with one man, went forward to hunt. Soon after arriving at the wood, they discovered a flock of turkies, and the rifleman, dismounting to shoot, left his mule for a moment at liberty. The animal taking a sudden advantage of the opportunity, turned about and made the best of his way out of the wood, pursued by Mr. Peale. This chase continued about five miles, and ended in putting the mule on the recent trace of the party, which there was no reason to fear he could be induced to leave until he had rejoined his companions. Mr. Peale who was exhausted with the pursuit, followed slowly, and neglecting to pursue carefully the path of the party, passed us, after we had turned aside to encamp, still travelling on in the direction of our course. At dark, believing we were still before him, and knowing we must encamp near the river, he betook himself to the sandbars, which were now naked, occupying the greater part of what was sometimes the bed of the stream. Along these he travelled, occasionally discharging a pistol, and looking about, in constant expectation of seeing the blaze of our evening fire, until the moon began to sink behind the hills, when finding the light insufficient to enable him to continue his search, he tied his horse to a tree and laid down to wait for the return of daylight.

At camp guns were discharged, as large a fire kindled as we could find the means of making, and other measures taken to give him notice of our position, and late in the evening, the man, whose mule had been the occasion of the accident, joined us, but was unable to give any account of Mr. Peale, or the mule, which had, however, arrived before him. At seven o'clock, on the morning following, Mr. Peale returned to us, having convinced himself, by a careful examination of the river valley, that we were still above. He accordingly retraced his course, until he discovered the smoke of our encampment. He had been much harassed, in the night, by mosquitoes; and bisons having recently occupied the shade of the tree under which he slept, the place afforded as little refreshment for the horse as for himself. Delaying a little to allow him time to make amends for his long abstinence, we left our camp at a later hour than usual, and moving along a wide and somewhat grassy plain, halted to dine near an old Indian breast-work, by the side of a grove of cottonwood trees, intermixed with a few small-leaved elms. This breast-work is built like that discovered on the Platte, a few days march above the Pawnees. We have met with the remains of similar works in almost every grove of trees about the base of the mountains. Near some of them, we noticed holes dug a few feet into the ground, probably as *caches* or depositaries of provision, the earth which was raised having been removed to a distance, or thrown into the river that it might not lead to discovery of the concealed articles. We sometimes saw large excavations of this kind, having an entrance comparatively small, and so placed as to be easily concealed, made by white hunters, to hold their furs, and whatever else they might wish to deposit in safe keeping.

The occurrence of the elm, the phytolacca, the cephalanthus, and other plants, not met with in a desert of sand, gave us the pleasing assurance of a change we had long been expecting in the aspect of the country. The blue jay, the purple martin, a deer, and some turkies were also seen near this encampment. The bed of the river is here, eight hundred yards wide, but the quantity of water visible is much less than in some places above. The magnetic variation, ascertained at this camp, was 12° 30' east.

CHAPTER IX

Sand plains—Mississippi hawk—Small-leaved elm—Wild horses—Hail storm—
Climate—Bisons—Grapes—Red-sand formation—Gypsum.

EXTENSIVE tracts of loose sand, so destitute of plants and so fine as to be driven by the winds, occur in every part of the saline sandstone formation southwest of the Arkansa. They are, perhaps, invariably the detritus of the sand-rock, deposited in vallies and depressions where the rapidity of the currents of water has been checked by permanent obstacles. This loose sand differs in colour from the sandstone, which is almost invariably red. The difference may have been produced simply by the operation of water suspending and removing the light colouring matter, no longer retained by the aggregation of the sandstone. These fields of sand have most frequently an undulated surface, occasioned, probably, not less by the operation of winds than by the currents of water. A few plum bushes, almost the only woody plants found on them, wherever they take root form points, about which the sand accumulates, and, in this manner, permanent elevations are produced. The yucca *angustifolia* and the shrubby cactus, the white argemone, and the night-flowering Bartonia, are the most conspicuous plants in these sandy wastes.

Our course, on the 15th, led us twice across the bed of the river, which we found one thousand and four hundred paces in width, and without water, except in a few small pools where it was stagnant. This wide and shallow bed is included between low banks, sometimes sloped gradually and sometimes, though rarely, perpendicular, and rising scarcely more than four feet from the common level of the bottom of the channel. Driftwood is occasionally seen without these banks, at an elevation of a few feet above them, affording evidence that they are, at times, not only full but overflowed. Whenever they are but partially filled it is easy to see that, what for a great part of the year is a naked sand-beach, then becomes a broad and majestic river. It must flow with a rapid current, and, in floods, its waters cannot be otherwise than of an intense red colour. The immediate valley of the river had now become little less than two miles in width, and had, in some places, a fertile soil. This happens wherever places occur having little elevation above the bed of the river, and which have not recently been covered with drifted sand.

Several species of locust were extremely frequent here, filling the air by day with their shrill and deafening cries, and feeding with their bodies great numbers of that beautiful species of hawk, the Falco *Mississippiensis* of Wilson. It afforded us a constant amusement to watch the motions of this greedy devourer, in the pursuit of the locust his favorite prey. The insect being large and not very active is easily taken; the hawk then poises on the wing, suspending himself in the air, while with his talons and beak he tears in pieces and devours his prey.

Prairie wolves, and vultures, occurred in unusual numbers, and the carcasses of several bisons, recently killed, had been seen. We could also distinguish the recent marks of a hunting party of Indians, the tracks of horses and men being still fresh in the sand. At four P.M. several bisons were discovered at a distance, and, as we were in the greatest want of provisions, we halted and sent the hunters in pursuit, and, being soon apprised of their success, the requisite preparations were made for jerking the meat. Near our camp was a scattering grove of small leaved elms. This tree (the Ulmus *alata, N.*) is not known in the Eastern States, but is common in many parts of Tennessee, Missouri, and Arkansa. When found in forests intermixed with other trees, it is usually of a smaller size than the Ulmus *Americana*, and is distinguished from it by the smallness of the leaves and the whiteness of the trunk. On the borders of the open country, where large trees often occur entirely isolated, the Ulmus *alata* has decidedly a more dense and flattened top than any other tree we have seen. When standing entirely alone, it rarely attains an elevation of more than thirty or thirty-five feet, but its top, lying close to the ground, is spread over an area of sixty or seventy feet in diameter, and is externally so close and smooth as to resemble, when seen from a distance, a small grassy hillock.

Near our camp was a circular breast-work, constructed like those already mentioned, and large enough to contain eighty or an hundred men. We were not particularly pleased at meeting these works so frequently, as they indicate a country subject to the incursions and ravages of Indian war parties.

16th. The greater part of the flesh of the bison, killed on the preceding evening, had been dried and smoked in the course of the night, so that we had now no fear of immediate suffering from hunger, having as much jerked meat as was sufficient to last several days.

The sky continued clear, but the wind was high, and the drifting of the sand occasioned much annoyance. The heat of the atmosphere became more intolerable, on account of the showers of burning sand driven against us, with such force as to penetrate every part of our dress, and proving so afflictive to our eyes, that it was with the greatest difficulty we could see to guide our horses. The sand is carried from the bed of the river, which is here a naked beach, of more than half a mile wide, and piled in immense drifts along the bank. Some of these heaps we have seen covering the trunk and a portion of the upper branches, of what appeared to be large trees. Notwithstanding we were now three hundred miles distant from the sources of the river, we found very little water, and that being stagnant and frequented by bisons and other animals, was so loathsome, both to sight and smell, that nothing but the most incontrollable thirst, could have induced us to taste it.

At a short distance below the place of our encampment, we passed the confluence of a large creek, entering from the southwest. Though like all the streams of this thirsty region its waters were entirely hid in the sand, yet it is evidently the bed of a large tributary; from its direction, we conclude it can be no other than the one on which the Kaskaias informed us they had encamped the night before we met them. Its name, if it have any among the Indians or Spaniards, we have not learned.

We had for some days observed a few wild horses, and they, as well as the bisons, were now becoming numerous. In the habits of the wild horse, we find little unlike what is seen in the domestic animal. He becomes the most timorous and watchful of the inhabitants of the wilderness. They show a similar attachment to each others' society, though the males are occasionally found at a distance from the herds. It would appear from the paths we have seen, that they sometimes perform long journies, and it may be worthy of remark, that along these paths are frequently found very large piles of horse-dung of different ages, affording sufficient evidence that this animal in a wild state, has, in common with some others, an inclination to drop his excrement where another has done so before him. This habit is sometimes faintly discovered in the domestic horse.

As we were about to halt for dinner, a male bison which had lingered near our path was killed, but the flesh was found in too ill a conditon to be eaten, as is the case with all the bulls at this season.

Soon after we had mounted our horses in the afternoon, a violent thunder storm came on from the northwest. Hail fell in such abundance as to cover the surface of the ground, and some of the hailstones, which we examined, were near an inch in diameter. Falling with a strong wind, these heavy masses struck upon our bodies with considerable violence. Our horses, as they had done on a similar occasion before, refused to move, except before the wind. Some of the mules turned off from our course, and had run more than half a mile before they could be overtaken. For ourselves, we found some protection, by wrapping our blankets as loosely as possible around our bodies, and waited for the cessation of the storm, not without calling to mind some instances on record, of hailstones, which have destroyed the lives of men and animals. It is not improbable, that the climate of a portion of country, within the range of the immediate influence of the Rocky Mountains, may be more subject to hailstorms in summer, than other parts of the continent, lying in the same latitude. The radiation of heat from so extensive a surface of naked sand, lying along the base of this vast range of snowy mountains, must produce great local inequalities of temperature: the diminished pressure of the atmosphere, and the consequent rapidity of evaporation, may in these elevated regions also be supposed to have an important influence on the weather. We have not spent sufficient time in the country near the eastern border of the Rocky Mountains, to enable us to speak with confidence of the character of its climate. It is, however, sufficiently manifest that in summer it must be extremely variable, as we have found it; the thermometer often indicating an increase of near fifty degrees of temperature, between sunrise and the middle of the day. These rapid alternations of heat and cold must be supposed to mark a climate little favourable to health, though we may safely assert that this portion of the country is exempt from the operation of those causes, which produce so deleterious an atmosphere in the lower and more fertile portions of the Mississippi basin. If the wide plains of the Platte, the upper Arkansa, and the Red river of Louisiana, should ever become the seat of a permanent civilized population, the diseases most incident to such a population, will probably be fevers attended with pulmonary and pleuritic inflammations, rheumatism, scrofula, and consumption. It is true that few if any instances of pulmonary consumption, occur among the Indians of this region; the same remark is probably as true of the original native population of New York and New England.

Though much rain fell during this storm, it was so rapidly absorbed by the soil, that little running water was to be seen. The bed of the river was found smooth and unobstructed, and afforded us for several days the most convenient path for travelling. As we descended, we found it to expand in some places to a width of near two miles. Bisons became astonishingly numerous, and in the middle of the day countless thousands of them were seen, coming in from every quarter to the stagnant pools, which filled the most depressed places in the channel of the river. The water of these was of course too filthy to be used in cooking our meat, and though sometimes compelled to drink it, we found little alleviation to our thirst. At our encampments we were able to furnish ourselves with water of a better quality by digging in the sand, where we seldom failed to meet with a supply at a few feet from the surface.

On the 17th we halted in the middle of the day to hunt, as, although we had killed several bisons on our marches of the preceding days, none of them had been found in good condition. The flesh of the bulls in the months of August and September, is poor and ill-flavoured; but these are much more easily killed than the cows, being less vigilant, and sometimes suffering themselves to be overtaken by the hunter without attempting to escape. As the herds of cows were now seen in great numbers, we halted and the hunters went out and killed several. Our camp was on the southwest side of the river, under a low bluff, which separates the half wooded valley from the open and elevated plains. The small elms along this valley were bending under the weight of innumerable grape vines, now loaded with ripe fruit, the purple clusters crouded in such profusion as almost to give colouring to the landscape. On the opposite side of the river was a range of low sand hills, fringed with vines, rising not more than a foot or eighteen inches from the surface. On examination we found these hillocks had been produced, exclusively by the agency of the grape vines arresting the sand, as it was borne along by the wind, until such quantities had been accumulated as to bury every part of the plant except the ends of the branches. Many of these were so loaded with fruit, as to present nothing to the eye but a series of clusters so closely arranged as to conceal every part of the stem. The fruit of these vines is incomparably finer than that of any other, either native or exotic, which we have met with in the United States. The burying of the greater part of the trunk, with its larger branches, produces the effect of pruning, in as much as it prevents the unfolding of leaves and flowers on the parts below the surface, while the protruding ends of the branches enjoy an increased degree of light and heat from the reflection of the sand. It is owing undoubtedly to these causes that the grapes in question are so far superior to the fruit of the same vines in ordinary circumstances.

The treatment here employed by nature to bring to perfection the fruit of the vine may be imitated, but without the same peculiarities of soil and exposure, can with difficulty be carried to the same magnificent extent. Here are hundreds of acres covered with a surface of moveable sand, and abounding in vines, placed in more favorable circumstances, by the agency of the sun and the winds, than it is in the power of man, to afford to so great an extent. We indulged ourselves to excess, if excess could be committed in the use of such delicious and salutary fruit, and invited by the cleanness of the sand, and a refreshing shade, we threw ourselves down, and slept away with unusual zest, a few of the hours of a summer afternoon.

Our hunters had been as successful as could be wished, and at evening we assembled around a full feast of "marrow bones," a treat whose value must forever remain unknown to those who have not tried the adventurous life of the hunter. We were often surprised to witness in ourselves a proof of the facility, with which a part at least of the habits of the savage could be adopted. Having been in several instances compelled to practice a tedious abstinence, the return of plenty found us well disposed to make amends for these temporary privations, and we lingered almost involuntarily at every meal, as if determined not only to make amends for the deficiency of the past, but to secure so ample a supply as would enable us to defy the future.

The grapes and plums, so abundant in this portion of the country, are eaten by turkies and black bears, and the plums by wolves, as we conclude from observing plumstones in the excrement of these animals. It is difficult to conceive whence such numbers of predatory animals and birds, as exist in every part of the country where the bisons are present, can derive sufficient supplies for the sustenance of life; it is indeed sufficiently evident, their existence is but a protraction of the sufferings of famine.

The great flowering hibiscus is here a conspicuous and highly ornamental plant, among the scattering trees in the low ground. The occurrence of the black walnut for the first time, since we left the Missouri, indicated a soil somewhat adapted to the purposes of agriculture. Portions of the river valley, which are not covered with loose sand, have a red soil, resulting from the disintegration of the prevailing rocks, red sandstone and gypsum, intermixed with clay, and are covered with a dense growth of fine and nutritious grasses. Extensive tracts of the great woodless plain, at a distance from the river, appear to be based on a more compact variety of sandstone, usually of a dark gray colour, and less pervious to water than the red. For this reason some copious springs are found upon it, and a soil by no means destitute of fertility, yielding sustenance to inconceivable numbers of herbivorous animals, and through them to innumerable birds and beast's of prey. It must be supposed, however, that the herds of bisons, daily seen about the river, range over a much greater extent of the country than was comprised within our limited views; the want of water in many places, may compel them to resort frequently to the river in dry weather, though at other times they may be dispersed in the high plains.

18th. In speaking of a country, whose geography is so little known, as that of the region southwest of the Arkansa, we feel the want of ascertained and fixed points of reference. Were we to designate the locality of a mineral or any other interesting object, as twenty or thirty days' journey from the Rocky Mountains, we should do nearly all in our power; yet this sort of information would probably be thought vague and useless. The smaller rivers of this region have as yet received no names from white hunters; if they have names among the Indians, these are unknown to us. There are no mountains, hills, or other remarkable objects, to serve as points of *reckoning*, nearer than the Rocky Mountains and the Arkansa. The river itself, which we supposed to be the Red river of Natchitoches, is a permanent land mark, but it is a line, and aids us only in one direction in our attempts to designate locality. The map accompanying this work was projected in conformity to the results of numerous astronomical observations for latitude and longitude, but many of these observations were made at places, not at present to be known by any names we might attempt to fix upon them. More extensive and minute examination, than we have been able to bestow, might establish something like a sectional division, founded on the distribution of certain remarkable plants. The great cylindric cactus, the American colycinth, (Cucumis *perennis*,) and the small-leaved elm, might be used in such an attempt, but it is easy to see that the advantages resulting from it, would be for the most part imaginary.

Discussions of this sort have been much insisted on, and may be important as aiding in the geography of climates and soils, but can afford little assistance to topography.

The geological features of the region under consideration, afford some foundation for a natural division, but this division must be so extremely general, as to afford little satisfaction. We could only distinguish the red sandstone, the argillaceous sandstone, and the trap districts, and though each of these have distinctive characters, not easy to be mistaken, they are so irregular in form and position, as to be in no degree adapted to aid in the description, and identifying of particular places. On the contrary it is to be regretted, there are no established points, to which we might refer, in communicating what we have observed of the position of these formations, and indicating the particular localities of some of the valuable minerals they contain.

The red sandstone, apparently the most extensive of the rocky formations of this region, shows, wherever it occurs, indications of the presence of muriate of soda, and almost as commonly discloses veins and beds of sulphate of lime. This substance had been growing more and more abundant, since we left the region of the trap rocks at the sources of the river. It was now so frequent as to be conspicuous in all the exposed portions of the sand-rock, and was often seen from a distance of several miles. It occurs under various forms; sometimes we met with the most beautiful selenite, disposed in broad reticulating veins, traversing the sandstone. The granular and fibrous varieties, whose snowy whiteness contrasts strongly with the deep red and brown of the sandstone, are sometimes seen in thin horizontal laminæ, or scattered about the surface, sometimes included in larger masses of the common amorphous plaister stone. This last is usually of a colour approaching to white, but the exposed surfaces are more or less tinged with the colouring matter of the sand-rock, and all the varieties are so soft as to disintegrate rapidly, when exposed to the air. Recent surfaces show no ferruginous tinge, in other words, this colour does not appear to have been contemporaneous to the formation of the sulphate of lime, but derived from the cement of the sandstone, and to have penetrated no farther than it has been carried by the infiltration of water.

We left our encampment at five o'clock; the morning fair; thermometer at 62°. Our courses, regulated entirely by the direction of the river, were north, fifty-five east, eleven miles, then north, ten east, seven miles, in all eighteen miles before dinner. The average direction of our course, for some days, had been rather to the north than south of east. This fact did not coincide with our previous ideas of the direction of Red River, and much less of the Faux Ouachitta or False Washita, which, being the largest of the upper branches of Red River from the north, we believed might be the stream we were descending. From observations taken at several points along the river we had ascertained that we must travel three or four days' journey to the south, in order to arrive at the parallel of the confluence of the Kiamesha with the Red river, and we were constantly expecting a change in the direction of our courses. The confident assurance of the Kaskaias, that we were on Red River, and but a few days' march above the village of the Pawnee Piquas, tended to quiet the suspicions we began to feel on this subject. We had now travelled, since meeting the Indians, a greater distance than we could suppose they had intended to indicate by the admeasurement of ten "lodge days," but we were conscious our communications with them had been made through inadequate interpreters, and it was not without reason we began to fear we might have received erroneous impressions. In the afternoon, however, the river inclined more to the direction we wished to travel; and we had several courses to the south of east. At sunset we pitched our tent on the north side of the river, and dug a well in the sand, which afforded a sufficient supply of wholesome, though brackish water. Throughout the night the roaring of immense herds of bisons, and the solemn notes of the hooting owl, were heard, intermixed with the desolate cries of the prairie wolf, and the screech owl. The mulberry and the guilandina growing near our camp, with many of the plants and birds we had been accustomed to see in the frontier settlements of the United States, reminded us of the comforts of home, and the cheering scenes of social life, giving us, at the same time, the assurance that we were about to arrive at the point where we should take leave of the desert.

19th. The mercury at sunrise stood at 71°. The morning was calm, and the sky tinged with that intense and beautiful blue which marks many of our summer skies, and is seen with greater pleasure, by those who know that home, or a good tavern, is near, than by such as have no prospect of shelter, save what a tent or a blanket can afford. We were now looking, with much impatience, for something to indicate an approach towards the village of the Pawnee Piquas; but instead of this the traces of Indians seemed to become less and less frequent. Notwithstanding the astonishing numbers of bison, deer, antelopes, and other animals, the country is less strewed with bones than almost any we have seen, affording an evidence that it is not a favourite hunting ground of any tribe of Indians. The animals also appeared wholly unaccustomed to the sight of men. The bisons and wolves moved slowly off to right and left, leaving a lane for the party to pass; but those on the windward side often lingered for a long time almost within the reach of our rifles, regarding us with little appearance of alarm. We had now nothing to suffer, either from the apprehension or the reality of hunger, and could have been content that the distance between ourselves and the settlements should have been much greater than we supposed it to be.

In the afternoon, finding the course of the river again bending towards the north, and becoming more and more serpentine, we turned off on the right side, and choosing an east course, travelled across the hills, not doubting but we would soon arrive again at the river. We found the country, at a distance from the bed of the river, somewhat elevated and broken; but, upon climbing some of the highest hills, we again saw the landscape of the unbounded and unvaried grassy plain spread out before us. All the inequalities of the surface have evidently been produced by the excavating operation of currents of water, and they are consequently most considerable near the channels of the large streams. This remark is applicable to the vallies of all the large rivers in the central portions of the great horizontal formation west of the Alleganies. We find, accordingly, that on the Ohio, the Missouri, the Platte, the Konzas, and many of the rivers tributary to the Mississippi, the surface becomes broken in proportion as we proceed from the interior towards the bed of the river; and all the hills bear convincing evidence that they have received their existence and their form from the action of the currents of water, which have removed the soil and other matters formerly occupying the vallies, and elevating the whole surface of the country nearly to a common level. Regarding in this view the extensive vallies of the Mississippi, and its tributaries, we naturally inquire how great a length of time must have been spent in the production of such an effect, the cause operating as it now does? It is scarce necessary to remark that where the vallies of the rivers in question are bounded on both sides, as they often are, by perpendicular cliffs of sandstone or limestone in horizontal strata, the seams and markings on one side correspond with those of the other, indicating the stratifications to have been originally continuous.

A ride of a few miles, in a direction passing obliquely from the river, brought us to a point which overlooked a large extent of the surrounding country. From this we could distinguish the winding course of a small stream uniting numerous tributaries from the ridge we occupied, and pursuing its way towards the southeast along a narrow and well wooded valley. The dense and verdant foliage of the poplars and elms contrasted faintly with the bright red of the sandstone cliffs, which rose on both sides, far surpassing the elevation of the tallest trees, and disclosing here and there masses of sulphate of lime of a snowy whiteness. Looking back upon the broad valley of the river we had left, the eye rested upon insulated portions of the sandy bed, disclosed by the inflections of its course, or the opening of ravines, and resembling pools of blood rather than wastes of sand. We had been so long accustomed to the red sands that the intensity of the colouring ceased to excite attention, until a distant view afforded us the opportunity of contrasting it with the general aspect of the country.

The elevated plains we found covered with a plenteous, but close fed crop of grasses, and occupied by extensive marmot villages. The red soil is usually fine, and little intermixed with gravel and pebbles, but too sandy to retain moisture enough for the purposes of agriculture. The luxuriance and fineness of the grasses, as well as the astonishing number and good condition of the herbivorous animals of this region clearly indicate its value for purposes of pasturage. There can be no doubt that more valuable and productive grasses than the native species can, with little trouble, be introduced. This may easily be effected by burning the prairies, at a proper season of the year, and sowing the seeds of any of the more hardy cultivated graminæ. Some of the perennial plants common in the prairies, will, undoubtedly, be found difficult to exterminate; their strong roots penetrating to a great depth, and enveloping the rudiments of new shoots placed beyond the reach of a fire on the surface. The soil of the more fertile plains is penetrated with such numbers of these as to present more resistance to the plough than the oldest cultivated pastures.

We had continued our march until near sunset, expecting constantly to come in view of the river, which we were persuaded must soon make a great bend to the south; but perceiving the night would overtake us in the plains, we began to search for a place to encamp. The bison paths in this country are as frequent, and almost as conspicuous, as the roads in the most populous parts of the United States. They converge from all directions to the places where water is to be found, and by following their guidance we were soon led to a spot where was a small spring, dripping from the side of a cliff of sandstone. The water collected in a little basin at the foot of the cliff, and flowing a few rods down a narrow ravine disappeared in the sand. Having established our camp, we travelled down this ravine, searching for plants, while any daylight remained. The rocks were beautifully exposed, but exhibited no appearance unlike what we had been accustomed to see along the river; the red indistinctly stratified sand-rock, spotted and veined with plaister stone and selenite. About the shelvings and crevices of the rocks the slender corrolla of the Oenothera macro*carpa* and the purple blossoms of the Pentstemon *bradburii* lay withering together, while the fading leaves and the ripening fruit reminded us that the summer was drawing to a close.

On the morning following we resumed our march, alternating our course from S.E. to N.E. The want of water in the hills compelled us again to seek the river. Falling in with a large bison path which we knew would conduct us by the easiest and most direct route, we travelled about fifteen miles, and encamped at noon on the bank of the river. In returning to the low grounds we passed some grassy pastures carpeted with the densest and finest verdure, and sprinkled with herds of deer, antelopes, and bisons. In some places the ground was covered with a purple mat of the prickly leaves and branches of a procumbent Eryngo intermixed with the tall and graceful Centaurea *speciosa*, with here and there a humble Dalea, or an ascending Petalostemon. As we approached the river we discovered a fine herd of bisons in the grove where we intended to place our camp, some lying down in the shade, others standing in the pool of water which extended along under the bank. Dismounting from our horses and approaching under cover of the bushes we shot two of the fattest, but before we had time to reload our pieces, after the second fire, we perceived a bull running towards us, evidently with the design to make battle; we, however, gave him the slip, by escaping into the thick bushes, and he turned off to follow the retiring herd.

It is only in the rutting season that any danger is to be apprehended from the strength and ferocity of the male bison. At all other times, whether wounded or not, their efforts are, to the last, directed solely towards an escape from their pursuers, and at this time it does not appear that their rage is provoked, particularly by an attack upon themselves, but their unusual intrepidity is directed indiscriminately against all suspicious intruders.

We had now, for some days, been excessively annoyed with large swarms of blowing flies, which had prevented our carrying fresh game along with us for more than a single day. It had been our custom at meals to place our boiled or roasted bison meat on the grass, or the broken boughs of a tree, in the middle of our circle; but this practice we now found it inexpedient to continue, as before we could finish our repast our table often became white with the eggs deposited by the flies. We were commonly induced to dispense with our roast meats, unless we chose to superintend the cooking ourselves; and afterwards it required the exertions of one hand to keep away the flies while with the other we helped ourselves to what we wished to eat. Our more common practice was to confine ourselves to the single dish of hunters' soup, suffering the meat to remain immersed in the kettle until we were ready to transfer it to our mouths.

Gnats had been rather frequent, and we began to feel once more the persecutions of the ticks, the most tormenting of the insects of this country.

The little pool near our tent afforded all the water that could be found within a very considerable distance. The bisons came in from every direction to drink, and we almost regretted that our presence frighted away the suffering animals with their thirst unslaked.

21st. The day was warm and somewhat rainy. Soon after leaving our camp we saw three black bears and killed one of them. This is the first animal of the kind we had eaten since we left the Missouri, and the flesh, though now not in the best condition, we found deserving the high encomiums commonly lavished upon it. Experienced hunters prefer it to that of the bison, and indeed to almost every thing, except the tail of the beaver.

Black bears had been frequent in this country passed since the 15th. At this season they feed principally upon grapes, plums, the berries of the cornus *alba* and c. *cirunata* and the acorns of a small scrubby oak common about the sand hills.

They also eat the flesh of animals, and it is not uncommon to see them disputing with the wolves and buzzards for their share of the carcasses of bisons, and other animals, which have been left by the hunters, or have died of disease. Grapes had evidently been very abundant here, but had been devoured, and the vines torn in pieces by the bears and turkies.

In the middle of the day we found the heat more oppressive, with the mercury at 96°, than we had known it in many instances when the thermometer had indicated a higher temperature by six or eight degrees. This sultry calm was, however, soon succeeded by thunder showers, attended with their ordinary effects upon the atmosphere. In the afternoon, the country we passed was swarming with innumerable herds of bisons, wild horses, deer, elk, &c., while great numbers of minute sandpipers, yellow-shanked snipes, kill-deer plovers (charadrius *vociferus*) and tell-tale godwits, about the river, seemed to indicate the vicinity of larger bodies of water than we had been accustomed of late to see. During the afternoon and the night, there was a continual and rapid alternation of bright, calm, and cloudless skies, with sudden and violent thunder storms. Our horizon was a little obscured on both sides by the hills and the scattered trees which skirted along the sides of the valley. As we looked out of our tent, to observe the progress of the night, we found sometimes a pitchy darkness veiling every object; at others, by the clear light of the stars, and the constant flashing from some unseen cloud, we could distinguish all the features of the surrounding scene; our horses grazing quietly about our tent, and the famished prairie wolf prowling near, to seize the fragments of our plentiful supper. The thunder was almost incessant, but its low and distant mutterings were, at times, so blended with the roaring of the bisons, that more experienced ears than ours might have found a difficulty in distinguishing between them. At a late hour in the night some disturbance was perceived among the horses, occasioned by a herd of wild horses, which had come in and struck up a hasty acquaintaince with their enslaved fellow-brutes. As it was near daylight we forbore to do any thing to frighten away the intruders, hoping, to have an opportunity to prove our skill in the operation of *creasing*, as soon as the light should be sufficient. A method sometimes adopted by hunters for taking the wild horse is to shoot the animal through the neck using the requisite care not to injure the spine. A horse may receive a rifle ball through a particular part of the neck without sustaining any permanent injury; the blow is, however, sufficient to occasion a temporary suspension of the powers of life, during which the animal is easily taken. This is called creasing; and requires for its successful performance a very considerable degree of skill and precision in the use of the rifle. A valuable but rather refractory mule, belonging to our party escaped from the cantonment near Council Bluff, a few days before we left that place. He was pursued by two men through the prairies of the Papillon, across the Elkhorn, and finally to the Platte, where, as they saw no prospect of taking him by other means, they resolved upon creasing. The ball however swerved an inch or two from its aim and broke the neck of the animal.

CHAPTER X

Inconveniences resulting from want of water—Wood-ticks—Plants—
Loss of one of the Party—Honey bees—Forests—
Gray sandstone—Indications of coal—Limestone.

AUGUST 22. So much rain had fallen during the night that soon after commencing our morning march we enjoyed the novel and pleasing sight of a running stream of water. It had been only two weeks since the disappearance of running water in the river above, but during this time we had suffered much from thirst, and had been constantly tantalized with the expectation of arriving at the spot where the river should emerge from the sand. By our computation of distances we had travelled more than one hundred and fifty miles along the bed of this river, without once having found it to contain running water. We had passed the mouths of many large tributaries, but they, like the river itself, were beds of naked sand. These *dry rivers*, at least the more considerable of them, are constantly conveying away, silent and unseen, in the bottom of their deep beds, streams of water of no trifling magnitude. This is probably the case with all such as have their sources in the primitive country of the Rocky Mountains, likewise with those which traverse any great extent of the floetz trap district, as both of these formations afford a more abundant supply of water than the sandstone tracts.

In the afternoon we saw a dense column of smoke, rising suddenly from the summit of a hill, at some distance on the right side of the river. As at the moment, the air happened to be calm, the smoke rose perpendicularly in a defined mass, and after continuing, for a few minutes, ceased suddenly. Having recently observed signs of Indians, we took this as a confirmation of our suspicions, that an encampment or a village was not far distant. We had observed that parties of Indians, whether stationary or on their marches, are never without *videttes*, kept constantly at a distance from the main body, for the purpose of giving timely notice of the approach of enemies. Several methods of telegraphic communication are in use among them, one of which is this, of raising a sudden smoke, and for this purpose, they are said to keep in constant readiness, a supply of combustibles. During the remainder of this, and the day following, we were in constant expectation of falling in with Indians. Towards evening on the 23d, we saw an unusual number of horses, probably four or five hundred, standing among the scattered trees along the river bottom. We discovered them while more than a mile distant, and from their dispersed manner of feeding, and the intermixture of various colours among them, we concluded they must be the horses belonging to a band of Indians. We accordingly halted, and put our guns in order for immediate use, and then approaching cautiously, arrived within a few rods of the nearest, before we discovered them to be wild horses. They took flight, and dispersing in several directions, disappeared almost instantly.

At eleven P.M., the double meridian altitude of the moon's lower limb, observed for latitude, was 72° 18' 15"; index error, minus 4'. For the two last days, our average course had inclined considerably to the south. The water visible in the river had increased rapidly in quantity, and the apparent magnitude of the stream was nearly equal to what it had been four hundred miles above.

24th. Our supply of parched corn-meal was now entirely exhausted. Since separating from our companions on the Arkansa, we had confined ourselves to the fifth part of a pint per day, to each man, and the discontinuance of this small allowance, was at first sensibly felt. We, however, became gradually accustomed to the hunter's life in its utmost simplicity, eating our bison or bear meat, without salt or condiments of any kind, and substituting turkey or venison, both of which we had in the greatest plenty, for bread. The few hungry weeks we had spent about the sources of the river, had taught us how to dispense with superfluous luxuries, provided the demands of nature could be satisfied.

The inconveniences resulting from another cause, were more serious. All our clothing had become so dirty, as to be offensive both to sight and smell. Uniting in our own persons, the professions of traveller, hostler, butcher, and cook, sleeping on the ground by night, and being almost incessantly on the march by day, it is not to be supposed, we could give as much attention to personal neatness, as might be wished. Notwithstanding this, we had kept ourselves in comfortable condition, as long as we had met with water, fit for washing our clothes. This had not now been the case for some weeks. The sand of the river bed approaches in character so near to a fluid, that it is in vain to search for, or to attempt to produce any considerable inequalities on its surface. The utmost we had been able to accomplish, when we had found it necessary to dig for water, was to scoop a wide and shallow excavation, in the bottom of which a very small quantity would collect, but not more than a pint could be dipped up at a time, and since water had appeared above the sand, it was rare to find it more than an inch or two in depth, and so turbid as to be unfit for use. The excessive heat of the weather, aggravated the inconvenience resulting from the want of clean clothing, and we were not without fears that our health might suffer.

The common post oak, the white oak, and several other species, with the gymnocladus, or coffee bean tree, the cercis, and the black walnut, which indicate a soil of very considerable fertility, now began to occur, and game grew so abundant, that we had it at any time in our power, to kill as many bisons, bear, deer, and turkies, as we might wish.

25th. Our daily journies over desolate and uninhabited plains, could afford little to record, unless we were to set down the names of the trees we passed, and of the plants and animals which occured to our notice. Our horses had become so exhausted by the great fatigues of the tour, that we found it necessary to content ourselves with a slower progress than formerly. According to our expectations, when we first commenced the descent of the river, we should some time since have arrived near the settlements; these, however, we could plainly perceive, were still far distant. The country we were traversing, had a soil of sufficient fertility to support a dense population, but the want of springs and streams of water, must long oppose a serious obstacle to its occupation of permanent residents. A little water was to be seen in the river, but that was stagnant, the rise occasioned by the late rains having subsided.

Leaving our camp at an early hour, we moved down the valley towards the southeast, passing some large and beautiful groves of timber. The fox squirrel which we had not seen since we left the Missouri, the cardinal and summer red-bird, the forked-tail tyrant, and the pileated woodpecker, with other birds and animals, belonging to a woody country, now became frequent. The ravens, common in all the open plains, began to give place to crows, now first noticed. Thickets of oak, elm, and nyssa, began to occur on the hills, and the fertile soil of the low plains to be covered with a dense growth of ambrosia, helianthus, and other heavy weeds. As we were riding forward at a small distance from the river, two bucks and a fawn happpened to cross our path, a few rods in front of the party. As the wind blew from them to us, they could not take our scent, but turned to gaze at us, without the least appearance of alarm. The leader was shot down by one of the party, when his companion and the fawn, instead of taking fright, came nearer to us, and stood within pistol shot, closely watching our movements, while the hunters were butchering the one we had killed. This unusual degree of tameness we could discover more or less, in all the animals of this region, and it seems to indicate that man, the enemy and destroyer of all things, is less known here, than in other portions of the country we had passed. In some parts of our route, we had seen the antelopes take fright, when we were more than a mile to the windward of them, when they could have received no intimation from us, except by sight, yet it does not appear, that their powers of vision are, in any degree, superior to those of most other ruminant animals.

27th. We were able to select for this day's rest, a delightful situation at the estuary of a small creek from the south. The wide valley of the river here presented a pleasing alternation of heavy forests, with small but luxuriant meadows, affording a profuse supply of grass for our horses. The broad hills swelling gently one above another, as they recede from the river, are diversified with nearly the same intermixture of field and forest, as in the most highly cultivated portions of the Eastern States. Herds of bisons, wild horses, elk, and deer, are seen quietly grazing in these extensive and fertile pastures, and the habitations and the works of men, alone seem wanting, to complete the picture of rural abundance.

We found, however, the annoyance of innumerable multitudes of minute, almost invisible seed ticks, a sufficient counterpart to the advantages of our situation. These insects unlike the mosquitoes, gnats, and sandflies, are not to be turned aside by a gust of wind, or an atmosphere surcharged with smoke, nor does the closest dress of leather afford any protection from their persecutions. A person no sooner sets foot among them than they commence in countless thousands, their silent and unseen march; ascending along the feet and legs, they insinuate themselves into every article of dress, and fasten, unperceived, their fangs upon every part of the body. The bite is not felt until the insect has had time to bury the whole of his beak, and in the case of the most minute and most troublesome species, nearly his whole body seems hid under the skin. Where he fastens himself with such tenacity that he will sooner suffer his head and body to be dragged apart than relinquish his hold. It would, perhaps, be well when they are once thoroughly planted to suffer them to remain unmolested, as the beaks left under the skin produce more irritation than the living animal; but they excite such intolerable itching, that the sufferer cannot avoid aggravating the evil by his efforts to relieve himself from the offending cause. The wound which was at first almost imperceptible, swells and inflames gradually, and being enlarged by rubbing and scratching, at length discharges a serous fluid, and finally suppurates. If the insect is sufferer to remain unmolested, he protracts his feast for some weeks, when he is found to have grown of enormous size, and to have assumed nearly the colour of the skin on which he has been feeding. His limbs do not enlarge, but are almost buried in the mass accumulated on his neck, which extending forward, bears against the skin, and at last pushes him from his hold.

Nothing is to be hoped from becoming accustomed to the bite of these wood-ticks. On the contrary, by long exposure to their venomous attacks the skin acquires a morbid irritability, which increases in proportion to the frequency and continuance of the evil, until at length the bite of a single tick is sufficient to produce a large and painful phlegmon. This may not be the case with every one, but it was so with us. The burning and smarting of the skin prompted us to bathe and wash whenever we met with water: but we had not long continued this practice when we perceived it only to augment our suffering, by increasing the irritation it was meant to allay.

It is not on men alone that these blood-thirsty insects fasten themselves. Horses, dogs, and many wild animals are subject to the attacks of a tick that sometimes attains a very large size. It is nevertheless sufficiently evident, that like mosquitoes and other blood-sucking insects, by far the greater number of wood-ticks must spend their lives without ever establishing themselves as parasites on any animal, and even without a single opportunity of gratifying that thirst for blood, which, as they can exist and perform all the common functions of their life without its agency, would seem to have been given them merely for the annoyance of every animal that may fall in their way.

Among many other plants common to the low and fertile parts of the United States, we observed the acalypha and the splendid lobelia *cardinalis*, also the cardiospermum *helicacabum*, sometimes cultivated in the gardens, and said to be a native of the East Indies. It is a delicate climbing vine, conspicuous in its large inflated capsules. The acacia, [robinea *pseudacacia*] the honey locust, and the Ohio æsculus are among the forest trees, but are confined to the low grounds. The common black haw [viburnum *lentago*] the persimmon or date plum, and a vitis unknown to us, occurred frequently and were all loaded with unripe fruit. The misseltoe, whose range of elevation and latitude seems to correspond very nearly with that of the miegia and the cypress, occurs here, parasitic on the branches of elms. In the sandy soils of the hills, the formidable jatropha *stimulosa* is sometimes so frequent, as to render the walking difficult. It is covered with long and slender prickles, capable of inflicting a painful and lasting wound, which is said to prove ruinous to the feet of the blacks in the West Indies. The cacti and the bartonias had now disappeared, as also the yucca, the argemone, and most of the plants which had been conspicuous in the country about the mountains. The phytolacca *decandra*, an almost certain indication of a fertile soil, the diodia *tetragona*, a monarda, and several new plants were collected in an excursion from our encampment. The red sand-rock is disclosed in the sides of the hills, but appears less frequently, and contains less gypsum than above, though it still retains the same peculiar marks distinguishing it as the depository of fossil salt. Extensive beds of red argillaceous soil occur, and are almost invariably accompanied by saline efflorescences, or incrustations. We search in vain, both in the rocks and the soils for the remains of animals, and it is rare in this salt formation to meet with the traces of organic substances of any kind; the rock, itself, though fine and compact, disintegrates rapidly, producing a soil which contains so much alumine as to remain long suspended in water, tinging with its peculiar colour all the rivers of this region. It has been remarked that the southern tributaries of the Arkansa, particularly the Canadian, the Negracka, and the Ne-sew-ke-tonga, discharge red waters, at the time of high freshets in such quantity as to give a colouring to the Arkansa quite to its confluence with the Mississippi. From this it is inferred that those rivers have their sources in a region of red sandstone, whose north-eastern limit is not very far removed from the bed of the Arkansa. We attempted to take sets of equal altitudes, but failed on account of a trifling inaccuracy in our watch. The variation of the magnetic needle was found to be the same as on the 25th; namely, 11° 30' east.

Our hunters had been sent out in quest of game, as notwithstanding the plenty we had enjoyed and the great number of animals we had killed we found it impossible, on account of the heat of the weather and the multiplicity of the blowing flies, to keep a supply of meat for more than one day. At evening they returned, having killed a large black bear. The animal finding himself wounded had turned with great fury upon the hunter, who, being alone, was compelled to seek his safety by climbing into a tree. It is well known that the black bear will sometimes turn upon his pursuers, and this, it is probable, is more frequently the case at this season than at any other, as they are now unincumbered with that profusion of fat which, for a part of the year, renders them clumsy and inactive, and the males are, morover, excited by that uncommon ferocity which belongs to this season of their lives.

We had observed that the sand-drifts, extending along all that part of the river we had passed in the three last weeks, were, almost exclusively on the northern bank. The country we were now passing is too fertile and too closely covered with vegetation, to admit the drifting of the sand, except from the uncovered bed of the river; yet along the northern side of the valley we frequently saw naked piles of sand, which had been wafted to considerable distance by the winds. From the position of these sand banks, as well as from our experience, we were induced to believe that the high winds of this region, are mostly from the south, at least during the dry season.

We left our encampment at half past five on the morning of the 28th, and following the river, the aggregate of our courses for the day was about east, and the distance twenty-one miles. Our last course led us out of the valley of the river, and for a few miles across the open plain. Here we passed a large and uncommonly beautiful village of the prairie marmots, covering an area of about a mile square, having a smooth surface and sloping almost imperceptibly towards the east. The grass on this plain was fine, thick and close fed. As we approached, it happened to be covered with a herd of some thousands of bisons; on the left were a number of wild horses, and immediately before us twenty or thirty antelopes and about half as many deer. As it was near sunset the light fell obliquely upon the grass, giving an additional brilliancy to its dark verdure. The little inhabitants of the village were seen running playfully about in all directions, and as we approached, they perched themselves on their burrows and proclaimed their terror in the customary note of alarm. A scene of this kind comprises most of what is beautiful and interesting to the passing traveller in the wide unvaried plains of the Missouri and Arkansa.

In the course of the day we passed two large creeks, one entering from the south, the other from the north; also several springs on the south side, along the base of a rocky hill, rising abruptly from the bed of the river; but notwithstanding all these tributary supplies, no running water appeared above the sands.

We passed great numbers of carcases of bisons recently slaughtered, and the air was darkened by flights of carrion birds, among which we distinguished the vultur *aura* and the V. *atrata*, the black vulture of the Southern States. From the great number of carcases and skeletons, we were induced to believe ourselves near the hunting ground of some nation of Indians, and our expectations of seeing the Pawnees of Red River began to revive.

29th. Finding the valley of the river somewhat contracted in width and extremely serpentine, we ascended into the open country on the north side and made our way across the hills, taking a course a little south of east. At the distance of a mile or two from the river we enjoyed a delightful view of the elevated country beautifully varied with gentle hills, broad vallies, fertile pastures, and extensive woodlands. The soil we found of a superior quality, the timber more abundant than in any region we had passed since we left the Missouri. Extensive forests appeared in the distant horizon, and the prairies in every direction were intersected by creeks and ravines, fringed by lines of timber. The aspect of the country is very similar to that of Grand river and the lower part of the Missouri, but the soil is more fertile. The first elevations rise from forty to fifty feet above the bed of the river, and these are succeeded by others ascending by an almost imperceptible slope towards the interior. Among the trees on the uplands are the black cherry, the linden, and the honey locust all indicating a fertile soil.

A little before we halted to dine, Adams, our interpreter of Spanish, having dropped some article of baggage returned on the track for the purpose of recovering it, and as he did not join us again we concluded he must have missed his way.

At evening we returned to the valley of the river and placed our camp under a small cottonwood tree, upon one of whose branches was a swarm of bees. These useful insects reminded us of the comforts and luxuries of life among men, and at the same time gave us the assurance that we were drawing near the abodes of civilization. Bees, it is said by the hunter and the Indians, are rarely if ever seen more than two hundred and fifty or three hundred miles in advance of the white settlements.

On receiving the first intimation of the absence of Adams, who had been following in the rear of the party, a man was sent back to search for, and bring him to our encampment; but as he could not be found we concluded that he had missed our path, and probably gone forward. We were confirmed in this belief, when on the following morning we discovered the track of a solitary mule, which had passed down along the bed of the river. This we accordingly followed, not doubting but Adams must soon perceive he had passed us, and would wait until we should overtake him.

The loose soft sands of the river bed, yielding to our horses' feet, made the travelling extremely laborious; and the intense reflection of the rays of the sun almost deprived us of the use of our eyes. Mr. Peale's horse soon became unable to proceed at an equal pace with the remainder of the party; but, as no suitable spot for encampment appeared, he dismounted and, by great exertions, was able to urge his animal along in the rear. The travelling in the bed of the river became so extremely inconvenient, that we resolved upon attempting to penetrate the thick woods of the bottom, and ascend to the open plains. We found, however, the woods so close and so interlaced with scandent species of Smilax, Cissus, and other climbing vines as greatly to retard our progress, and we were soon induced to wish ourselves again upon the naked sands. Notwithstanding the annoyance they gave us, we took a pleasure in observing the three American species of Cissus growing almost side by side. The C. q*uinquefolia*, the common woodbine, cultivated as an ornament about yards and summer-houses, grows here to an enormous size, and as well as the C. *hederacea*, seems to prefer climbing on elms. The remaining species, the C. *bipinnata*, is a smaller plant, and though much branched, is rarely scandent. They all abound in ripe fruit, which, notwithstanding its external resemblance, and its close affinity to the grape, is nauseous to the taste, and does not appear to be sought with avidity even by the bears.

In ascending the hills, we found them based upon a variety of sandstone, unlike the red rock of the salt formation, to which we had been so long accustomed. We observed that a corresponding change also takes place in the conformation of the surface and the general aspect of the country. The hills are higher and more abrupt; the forests more extensive; the streams of water more copious, and more serpentine in direction; in other words, we here begin to recognize the features of a mountainous region. The sandstone, which appears in the beds of the streams and the sides of the hills, is coarse and hard, of a dark gray colour, and a horizontally laminated structure. It is deeply covered with a soil of considerable fertility, sustaining heavy forests of oak. Among these trees, the upland white oak is common, but is of rather diminutive size, and often hollow. In a tree of this description we observed as we passed the habitation of a swarm of bees, and, as it was not convenient at that time to stop, we fixed a mark upon it and proceeded to make the best of our way towards the river. On descending the hills, we found the valley of the river much contracted in width; and the bed itself occupying less space by half than where we had left it above.

On the following day, the party remained encamped, to take observations, and afford an opportunity for rest to the horses. Some of the men went back about six miles to the bee-tree we had passed on the preceding day, and brought in a small quantity of honey, inclosed in the skin of a deer recently killed. About our camp we examined several ledges of sandstone of the coarse dark gray variety above mentioned. In some instances, we found it nearly approaching in character the glittering crystalline variety of the lead mine district, but we sought in vain for an opportunity to observe the manner of its connexion with red sandstone.

As we were now at the western base of that interesting group of hills, to which we have attempted to give the name of the almost extinct tribe of the Oarks, and, as we believed ourselves near the extreme southern bend of the river we were descending, we thought it important to ascertain our latitude and longitude by as complete sets of observations as circumstances allowed us to make, and this, the favourable position of the moon enabled us to do in the most satisfactory manner. . . .

During the extreme heat of the day the mercury stood at 99° in a fair exposure. This extraordinary degree of heat may have been, in some degree, occasioned by the stagnation of the air between the hills, and, possibly, by the reverberation of the sun's rays from the naked sands; but the instrument was one of an approved character, and was exposed in the deep shade of an extensive grove of trees.

As yet no running water appeared in the river, but, as the pools were large, and some of them little frequented by the bisons, we were no longer under the necessity of digging.

Sept. 1st. The sycamore, the æsculus, the misseltoe, and the parroquet, are conspicuous objects in the deep and heavy forests of the Ohio and Mississippi: with these we now found ourselves surrounded. Bisons were comparatively scarce along this part of the river; but whether this was owing to the near approach of inhabited countries, or to the great extent and almost impenetrable density of the forests on each side of the river, we were unable to determine. At night we still heard the growling of the herds in the distant prairies, and occasionally saw bisons in small bodies crossing the river.

The Kaskaia Indians had told us that before we arrived at the village of the Pawnee Piquas, we should pass a range of blue hills. These we concluded could be no other than hills whose sides were covered with forests, like those we were now passing, and, accordingly, we watched with some anxiety for the appearance of something to indicate the vicinity of an Indian village.

As we pursued our way along the serpentine bed of the river, the valley became narrower, the hills more elevated, and, as we crossed the rocky points of their bases, we observed that the sandstone was of a different character from any we had before seen. It contains more mica than that of the Alleghanies, and that of the secondary hills along the base of the Rocky Mountains. It glitters conspicuously like mica slate when seen in the sunshine, and this, as we found by examination, does not depend entirely on the great proportion of mica it contains, but also, in some degree, on the crystalline structure of the minute particles. Its cement is often argillaceous, and this, as well as the impressions of Strobilaria and other organic relics we observed in it, induced us to expect the occurrence of coal beds.

On ascending the hills, from the place of our mid-day encampment, we found this sandstone at an elevation of about two hundred feet, according to our estimate, from the bed of the river, succeeded by a stratum of limestone of the common compact blue variety, abounding in casts of anomias, encrinites, &c. This rests horizontally on the summits of the hills, and as it disintegrates less rapidly than the sandstone which forms their bases, it is sometimes left projecting in such a manner as to render access impossible. Climbing to the summit of some of the hills near the river, we had the view, towards the south and east, of a wild and mountainous region, covered with forests, where, among the bright verdure of the oak, the nyssa, and the castanea pumila, we distinguished the darker shade of the juniper, and others of the coniferæ.

A little before arriving at the place of our evening encampment, we observed the track of a man who had passed on foot, and with bare feet, down the river. This we were confident could be no other than the track of our lost interpreter, Adams. What accident could have deprived him of his mule we were at a loss to conjecture. We found it equally difficult to account for his pushing forward with such perseverance, when he must have had every reason to believe we were behind him.

2d. The morning was fair, and we commenced our journey by sunrise. At a little distance below our encampment, we passed the mouth of a large tributary from the south. It was about sixty yards wide, and appeared to contain considerable water which was absorbed in the sands immediately at its junction with the larger stream. About the mouth of this creek we saw the remains of several gar fish [Esox *osseus*]. This fish is protected by a skin so flinty and incorruptible, as to be invulnerable to the attack of birds and breasts of prey, and even when the internal soft parts have been dissolved and removed by putrefaction, the bony cuticle retains its original shape like that of the trunk and limbs of the canoe birch, after the wood has rotted away. The gar is usually found in deep water, lying concealed in the places where the small fish resort, and seizing them between his elongated jaws, which are armed with numerous small and sharp teeth. This fish, though not held in high estimation as an article of food, is little inferior, as we have often found by experiment, to the sturgeon of the Hudson. Its unsightly aspect produces a prejudice against it, and in countries of such abundance as those watered by the Mississippi and its tributaries, a creature so disgusting in appearance, and of so unpromising a name, is rarely eaten.

We had passed the mouth of the creek about a mile, when we discovered a little column of smoke ascending among some scattered oaks on the right bank of the river. Approaching the spot, we perceived our lost interpreter, who had parted from us five days before, sitting a few feet in advance of his fire. When we discovered him, his appearance indicated the deepest despondency. He had kindled a fire upon a little rocky eminence, projecting to the verge of the river, and seated himself near it upon the ground with his face turned towards the river, as if in expectation of relief from that quarter. His elbows rested upon his knees, and his hands supported his head. Having sat in long expectation of seeing us, he had fallen asleep, and on being waked, some minutes elapsed before he recovered entire self-possession and consciousness. His long, sunburnt hair hung loosely about a face, it could scarcely be said to shade, and on which famine and terror had imprinted a frightful expression of ghastliness. Perhaps some consciousness of having acted an imprudent and reprehensible part, prevented any demonstrations of joy he might otherwise have shown at sight of us. Under the apprehension that accidents of this kind might occur it had repeatedly been enjoined upon all the party, never to lose sight of the main body when on the march. But on this occasion, no regard was paid to this necessary regulation.

From his statement, we learned, that after separating from us on the morning of the 29th August, he had returned a mile or two, to search for his canteen, but not finding it, in his hurry to rejoin the party, he had missed the trace, and presently found himself bewildered. Taking the bed of the river as his guide, he urged on his mule without allowing it time to rest, or to feed, till on the third day it refused to proceed, and he left it. He then took his baggage, musket, &c. and pushed forward on foot, evidently with the hope of arriving at the Pawnee village; but by the end of the day, found his strength so exhausted that he could go no farther, and was compelled to encamp. Having expended his ammunition in unsuccessful attempts to shoot turkies, he had been trying to make a substitute for fish hooks by bending up some needles; but this project he had not brought to perfection, and assured us he had not tasted food since the breakfast of the 29th, a period of more than five days.

The Small leaved and the White elm, the Nettle tree or Hackberry, the Cotton-wood, Mulberry, Black walnut, Pecan, Ash, Sycamore, and most of the trees common to the low grounds of the Mississippi, are intermixed here to form the dense forests of the river valley; while in the more scattered woods of the highlands, the prevailing growth is Oak, with some species of Nyssa, the Dyospiros and a few other small trees.

At evening a large flock of white pelicans passed us on their way up the river.

On the morning of the 3d, not having been able to select a suitable place for a Sunday encampment, we moved on, searching for a supply of grass, that we might halt for the day. The hunters preceded the party, and meeting with a herd of bisons, and good pasturage in the same place, killed a bull of a most gigantic stature, and waited until the remainder of the party came up, and encamped near the carcass.

Having arranged our camp, and performed in the way of washing, dressing, &c., the little in our power to do, we made an excursion into the adjoining forest, to collect plants, and to search for honey, which, from the great numbers of bees we had seen, we were conscious must be abundant. Since leaving the open country, we had remarked a very great change in the vegetation. The dense shade, and perhaps, the somewhat confined air of the forest, are unfavorable to the growth of many of those grasses, and those robust perennials, which seem to delight in the arid soils, and the scorching winds of the sandy desert. The sensitive cassia (C. *nictitans.*) the favorite food of the bees, some species of Hedysarum and a few other leguminæ, are however, common to both regions.

A considerable part of the day we spent in unavailing contest with the ticks. The torment of their stings increased upon us if we were a moment idle, or attempted to rest ourselves under the shadow of a tree. We considered ourselves peculiarly fortunate, when we could find the shade of a tree extending some distance on the naked sands of the river bed, for there the ticks were less numerous. In the middle of the day, the mercury again rose to 97°, and the blowing flies swarmed in such numbers about our blankets and clothing, as to allow us no rest.

Above the pools near our camp, we saw the little white Egret; the snowy Heron had been common for some days. Great numbers of cranes, ducks, pelicans, and other aquatic birds, induced us to believe, that larger bodies of water than we had recently seen, must be near.

Bears and wolves were still frequent. Among the latter, we observed a black one of a small size, which we believed to be specifically different from any of those we had seen above. All our attempts to capture this watchful animal, were without success. Since entering the region of forests, we had found the number of small animals, birds, and insects, considerably increased. An enormous, black, hairy spider, resembling the mygale *avicularia* of South America, was often seen, and it was not without shuddering, that we sometimes perceived this formidable insect, looking out from his hole, within a few feet of the spot, on which we had thrown ourselves down to rest.

On the 4th, we met with nothing interesting, except the appearance of running water in the bed of the river. Since the 13th of the preceding month, we had travelled constantly along the river, and in all the distance passed in that time, which could not have been less than five hundred miles, we had seen running water in the river, in one or two instances only; of those, one in it had evidently been occasioned by recent rains, and had extended but a mile or two, when it disappeared.

CHAPTER XI

Maclura auran tiaca—Birds—Falls of the Canadian—
Green argillaceous sandstone—Northern and Southern tributaries of the Canadian—
Cotton-wood—Arrival at the Arkansa—Cane-brakes—Cherokees—Belle Point.

THE region we were now traversing, is one of great fertility, and we had daily occasion to regret that our visit to it had not been made earlier in the season. Many unknown plants were observed, but their flowering season being past, the fruit of many of them having ripened and fallen, we were deprived of the means of ascertaining the name and place of such as had been heretofore described, and of describing such as were new. We had, however, the satisfaction to recognize some interesting productions, among which we may enumerate a very beautiful species of Bignonia, and the bow-wood or Osage orange. The rocky hills abound in trees of a small size, and the cedars are sometimes so numerous, as to give their peculiar and gloomy colouring to the landscape.

We listened, as we rode forward, to the note of a bird, new to some of us, and bearing a singular resemblance to the noise of a child's toy trumpet. This we soon found to be the cry of the great ivory billed woodpecker, (Picas *principalis*) the largest of the North American species, and confined to the warmer parts. The P. *pileatus* we had seen on the 28th August, more than one hundred miles above, and this, with the P. *erythrocephalus*, were now common. Turkies were very numerous. The paroquet, chuck-wills-widow, wood robin, mocking bird, and many other small birds, filled the woods with life and music. The bald eagle, the turkey-buzzard and black vulture, raven, and crow, were seen swarming like the blowing flies, about any spot where a bison, an elk, or a deer had fallen a prey to the hunter. About the river were large flocks of pelicans, with numbers of snowy herons, and the beautiful ardea egretta.

Soon after we had commenced our morning ride, we heard the report of a gun, at a distance of a mile, as we thought, on our left. This was distinctly heard by several of the party, and induced us to believe that white hunters were in the neighbourhood. We had recently seen great numbers of elk, and killed one or two, which we had found in bad condition.

6th. Numerous ridges or rocky hills traverse the country from northeast to southwest, crossing the direction of the river obliquely. They are of a sandstone which bears sufficient evidence of belonging to a coal formation. At the spot where we halted to dine, one of these ranges, crossing the river, produces an inconsiderable fall. As the whole width of the channel is paved with a compact horizontal sandstone, we believed all the water of the river must be forced up to view, and were surprised to find the quantity something less than it had been almost six hundred miles above in the same stream. It would appear, that all the water, which falls in rains, or flows from springs in an extent of country far greater than Pennsylvania, is not sufficient to supply the evaporation of so extensive a surface of naked and heated sands.

If the river, of which we speak, should, at any season of the year, contain water enough for the purposes of navigation, it is probable the fall, occasioned by the rocky traverse above mentioned, will be sufficient to prevent the passage upwards. The point is a remarkable one as being the locality of a rare and beautiful variety of sandstone. The rock which appears in the bed of the river is a compact slaty sandstone of a deep green colour resembling some varieties of chloritic slate. Whether the colour depends upon *epidote chlorite*, or some other substance, we were not able to determine. The sandstone is micaceous, but the particles of mica, as well as those of the other integrant minerals, are very minutely divided. The same rock, as we found by tracing it to some distance, becomes of a light gray colour, and contains extensive beds of bituminous clay slate. Its stratifications are so little inclined that their dip cannot be estimated by the eye. This point, though scarce deserving the name of a cataract, is so marked by the occurrence of a peculiar bed of rocks crossing the river, and by the rapid descent of the current, that it may readily be recognized by any who shall pass that way hereafter. In this view we attach some importance to it, as the only spot, in a distance of six hundred miles, we can hope to identify by description. In ascending, when the traveller arrives at this point, he has little to expect beyond but sandy wastes, and thirsty inhospitable steppes. The skirts of the hilly and wooded region extend to a distance of fifty or sixty miles above; but even this district is indifferently supplied with water. Beyond, commences the wide sandy desert stretching westward to the base of the Rocky Mountains. We have little apprehension of giving too unfavorable an account of this portion of the country. Though the soil is, in some places, fertile, the want of timber, of navigable streams, and of water for the necessities of life, render it an unfit residence for any but a nomade population. The traveller who shall, at any time, have traversed its desolate sands will, we think, join us in the wish that this region may forever remain the unmolested haunt of the native hunter, the bison, the prairie wolf, and the marmot.

One mile below this point, (which we call the falls of the Canadian, rather for the sake of a name than as considering it worthy to be thus designated,) is the entrance from the south of a river fifty yards wide. Its banks are lined with tall forests of cotton-wood and sycamore, and its bottoms are wide and fertile. Its bed is less choked with sand than that of the river to which it is tributary. Six or eight miles farther down, and on the other side, is the confluence of the Great North Fork, discharging at least three times as much water as we found above it. It is about eighty yards wide. The beds of both these tributaries are covered with water from shore to shore; but they have gentle currents, and are not deep, and neither of them have, in any considerable degree, that red tinge which characterises the Canadian. We have already mentioned, that what we consider the sources of the North Fork are in the floetz trap country, nearly opposite those of Purgatory creek of the Arkansa. Of one of its northern tributaries we have received some information from the recent work of Mr. Nuttall, who crossed it in his journey to the Great Salt river of Arkansa, in 1819. "Still proceeding," says he, "a little to the north of west, about ten miles further, we came to a considerable rivulet of clear and still water, deep enough to swim our horses. This stream was called the Little North Fork (or branch) of the Canadian, and emptied into the main North Fork of the same river nearly two hundred miles distant, including its meanders, which had been ascended by the trappers of beaver." From his account it appears that the banks of this stream are wooded, and that the "superincumbent rock" is a sandstone, not of the red formation, but probably belonging to a coal district.

Its water, like that of the Arkansa and its northern tributaries, when not swelled by rains, is of a greenish colour. This colouring is, sometimes, so intense in the river of this region as to suggest the idea that the water is filled with minute confervas, or other floating plants; but when we see it by transmitted light, as when a portion of it is held in a glass vessel, the colour disappears.

Three and an half miles below the confluence of the North Fork is a remarkable rock, standing isolated in the middle of the river, like the Grand Tower in the Mississippi. It is about seventy-five feet high, and fifty or sixty in diameter, and its sides so perpendicular as to render the summit inaccessible. It appears to have been broken from a high promontory of gray sandstone overhanging the river on the north side.

Not being able to find grass for pasture, we rode later than usual, and were finally compelled to encamp on a sandy beach, which afforded nothing but rushes for our horses.

8th. The quantity of water in the river, had now become so considerable, as to impede our descent along the bed, but the valley was narrow and so filled with close and entangled forests, and the uplands so broken and rugged, that no other path appeared to remain for us. We therefore continued to make our way, though with great difficulty, and found our horses much incommoded, by being kept almost constantly in the water, as we were compelled to do, to cross from the point of a sand bar on one side of the river, to the next on the other. Quicksands also occurred, and in places where we least expected it, our horses and ourselves were made to *bite the dust*, without a moment's notice. These sudden falls, occasioned by sinking in the sand, and the subsequent exertions necessary to extricate themselves, proved extremely harrassing to our jaded horses, and we had reason to fear, that they would fail us, in our utmost need.

Above the falls the width of the river, that is, of the space included between its two banks, varies from three hundred yards, to two miles; below, it is uniformly narrower, scarce exceeding four hundred yards. The beaches are sloping, and often covered with young cotton-wood or willow trees. In the Missouri, Mississippi, and to some extent in the Arkansa, and its tributaries, the islands, sand-bars, and even the banks are constantly shifting place. In the progress of these changes, the young willows and cotton-wood trees, which spring up wherever a naked beach is exposed, may be supposed to have some agency, by confining the soil with their roots, and arresting the dirt and rubbish in times of high water. In the Missouri, the first growth which springs up in these places, is so commonly the willow, that the expressions "willow bar," and "willow island," have passed into the language of the boatmen, and communicate the definite idea of a bar or an island, recently risen from the water. These willows become intermixed with the cotton-wood, and these trees are often almost the exclusive occupants of extensive portions of the low grounds. The foliage of the most common species of willow, (S. *angustata*,) is of a light green colour, and when seen under certain angles, of a silvery gray, contrasting beautifully with the intense and vivid green of the cotton-wood. Within a few rods of the spot where we halted to dine, we were so fortunate as to find a small log canoe, made fast on shore. From its appearance, we were assured it had been some months deserted by its rightful owner, and from the necessity of our situation, thought ourselves justified in seizing, and converting it to our own use. Our pack-horses had become much weakened, and reduced by long fatigue, and in crossing the river, as we had often to do, we felt that our collections, the only valuable part of our baggage, were constantly exposed to the risk of being wetted. We accordingly made prize of the canoe, and putting on board our packs and heavy baggage, manned it with two men, designing that they should navigate it down to the settlements. Not far from this canoe, we discovered in the adjoining woods, the remains of an old camp, which we perceived had been occupied by white men, and saw other convincing proofs, that we were coming near some inhabited country.

We halted at evening in a small prairie, on the north side of the river, the first we had seen for some time. The difficulties of navigation, arising from the shallowness of the water, prevented the arrival of the canoe and baggage, until a late hour. The men had been compelled to wade a great part of the way, and drag the canoe over the sand.

9th. We had proceeded a mile or two from our encampment, when we discovered a herd of twenty or thirty elk, some standing in the water, and some lying upon the sand beach, at no great distance before us. The hunters went forward, and singling out one of the finest bucks, fired upon him; at which the whole herd plunged into the thicket, and disappeared. We had, however, too much confidence in the skill of the hunter, to doubt but his shot had been fatal, and several of the party dismounting, pursued the herd into the woods, where they soon overtook the wounded buck. The noble animal, finding his pursuers at his heels, turned upon the foremost, who saved himself by springing into a thicket, which the elk could not penetrate, but in which he soon became entangled by his enormous antlers, and fell an easy victim. His head was enveloped in such a quantity of cissus, smilax, and other twining vines, that scarce the tips of his horns could be seen: thus blindfolded, he stood until most of those, who had followed into the woods, had discharged their pieces, and did not finally yield to his foes, until he was stabbed to the heart with a knife. He was found in excellent condition, having more than two inches of fat on the brisket. The meat was carried to the river, and deposited on a projecting point of rocks, with a note addressed to the men who were behind with the canoe, directing them to add this supply of provisions to their cargo.

At this point, and again at an inconsiderable distance below, a soft green slaty sandstone forms the bed of the river, and occasions a succession of rapids.

At noon an observation by the meridian altitude of the sun's lower limb gave us 35° 80' as an approximation to our latitude. This was much greater than we had anticipated, from the position assigned to Red river on the maps, and tended to confirm the unpleasant fears we had entertained of having mistaken some tributary of the Arkansa for the Red river.

Thick and extensive cane brakes occurred on all sides, and though the bottoms were wide and covered with heavy forests, we could see, at intervals, the distant sandstone hills with their scattered forests of cedar and oak.

10th. We left our camp at the usual hour, and, after riding eight or ten miles, arrived at the confluence of our supposed Red river with another of a much greater size, which we at once perceived to be the Arkansa. Our disappointment and chagrin, at discovering the mistake we had so long laboured under, was little alleviated by the consciousness that the season was so far advanced, our horses and our means so far exhausted, as to place it beyond our power to return and attempt the discovery of the sources of Red river. We had been misled by some little reliance on the maps, and the current statements concerning the position of the upper branches of Red river, and more particularly by the confident assurance we had received from the Kaskaia Indians, whom we did not suspect of a wish to deceive us in an affair of such indifference to them. Knowing there was a degree of ambiguity and confusion in the nomenclature of the rivers, we had insisted particularly on being informed whether the river we were descending, was the one on which the Pawnee Piquas had their permanent residence, and this we were repeatedly assured was the case. Several other circumstances, which have been already mentioned, led us to the commission of this unfortunate mistake.

According to our estimate of distances on our courses, it is seven hundred ninety-six and a half miles from the point where we first struck the Canadian to its confluence with the Arkansa. If we make a reasonable allowance for the meanders of the river, and for the extension of its upper branches some distance to the west of the place where we commenced our descent, the entire length of the Canadian will appear to be about one thousand miles. Our journey upon it had occupied a space of seven weeks, travelling with the utmost diligence the strength of our horses would permit.

On arriving at the Arkansa, we waited a short time for our canoe, in which we carried across our heavy baggage, and then swimming our horses, ascended the bank in search of a place to encamp, but soon found ourselves surrounded by a dense and almost impenetrable cane brake, where no vestige of a path could be found. In this dilemma, no alternative remained but to force our way forward, by the most laborious exertions. The canes were of a large size, and stood so close together, that a horse could not move forward the length of his body without breaking, by main force, a great number of them. Making our way, with excessive toil, among these gigantic gramina, our party might be said to resemble a company of rats traversing a sturdy field of grass. The cane stalks, after being trod to the earth, often inflicted, in virtue of their elasticity, blows as severe as they were unexpected. It is not to be supposed, that our horses alone felt the inconvenience of this sort of travelling. We received frequent blows and bruises on all parts of our bodies, had our sweaty faces and hands scratched by the rough leaves of the cane, and, oftentimes, as our attention was otherwheres directed, we caught with our feet, and had dragged across our shins the flexible and spiny stalks of the green briar.

This most harassing ride was commenced at eleven in the morning, and continued, without a moment's intermission, till sunset, when finding we were not about to extricate ourselves, we returned near a mile and a half on our track, to a spot where we had passed a piece of open woods, large enough to spread our blankets on. Here we laid ourselves down at dark, much exhausted by our day's journey.

Our fatigue was sufficient to overcome the irritation of the ticks, and we slept soundly until about midnight, when we were awakened by the commencement of a heavy fall of rain, from which, as we had not been able to set up our tent, we had no shelter.

On the following morning, after several hours spent in most laborious travelling, like that of the preceding day, we found ourselves emerging from the river bottom, and, to our great satisfaction, exchanging the cane-brakes for open woods. At the foot of the hill, lay a deep morass, covered with the Nelumbo and other aquatic plants. It had, probably, been the former bed of the Arkansa. Observing water in some parts of it, several of the party attempted to penetrate to it, to drink, but the quaking bog was found so deep and soft as to be wholly impassable.

After ascending the hills, we pursued our course nearly due north, through open woods of oak and nyssa, until we reached the prairie, and soon after discovered a large and frequented path, which we knew could be no other than that leading to Fort Smith. On emerging from the low grounds, we had no longer the prospect of boundless and monotonous plains. We were in a region of mountains and forests interspersed with open plains, but these were of limited extent.

12th. We resumed our journey at sunrise. The weather was cool and the morning fair. The wide and densely wooded valley of the Arkansa lay on our right. The course of the river was marked by a long and undulating line of mist, brightening in the beams of the rising sun. Beyond, rose the blue summits of the Point Sucre and Cavaniol mountains, "in the clear light, above the dews of morn." Though the region about us had all the characters of a mountain district, we could discover little uniformity in the direction of the ranges. The Cavaniol and Point Sucre mountains stand on opposite sides of the Poteau, near the mouth of the Meline fork, and are parts of low ridges running from southwest and northeast. On the north side of the Arkansa is a ridge of considerable elevation, nearly parallel in direction to the general course of the river.

In the path we were travelling, we observed tracks indicating that men on horseback had recently passed, and in the course of the morning we met a party of six or eight Indians who informed us they were of the Cherokee nation, and that we should be able to arrive at the military post at Belle Point on the following morning. They were on horseback, carrying guns, kettles, and other articles suited to a hunting excursion, which it was their purpose to make in the territory of the Osages. Two or three of them had round hats; all had calico shirts, or some other article of foreign fabric, as part of their dress, and, in all, a mean and squalid appearance, indicated that they had been in habits of frequent intercourse with the whites. They were unable to speak or understand our language, but communicated with considerable ease by means of signs.

At eleven o'clock we halted, and as our provisions were nearly exhausted, most of the party went out to hunt, but were not fortunate in meeting game. We found, however, some papaw trees, with ripe fruit of an uncommon size and delicious flavor, with which we were able to allay our hunger. The papaw tree attains a much larger size, and the fruit arrives at greater perfection in the low grounds of the Arkansa than on the Missouri, Ohio, and upper Mississippi, where it is also common. The papaws fall to the ground as soon as fully ripe, and are eagerly sought after by the bears, racoons, opossums, &c.

In the afternoon one of our mules failed so far, that the undivided attention, and the most active exertions of two men were required to keep him moving at the rate of a slow walk. This made it necessary we should encamp, and we accordingly selected a spot in a fine open grove, where we pitched our tent. Among other interesting plants, we collected here the beautiful vexillaria *virginica* of Eaton, which has the largest flower of any of the legumina of the United States, as is remarked by Mr. Nuttall. We saw also the menispermum lyoni Hieracium *marianum*, Rhexia *virginica*, &c.

As we encamped at an early hour, the party dispersed in various directions in search of game. Nothing was found except a swarm of bees affording as much honey as we chose to eat for supper. While engaged in felling the tree, we heard several guns, at a distance, and by sending persons to examine, we learned that they were those of a party of men accompanying Mr. Hugh Glen on his way from Fort Smith, to the trading house at the mouth of the Verdigris. In the evening we received a visit from Mr. Glen, whose camp was distant only about a mile from ours. He was the first white man, not of our own party, whom we had seen since the 6th of the preceding June. From him we received a highly acceptable present of coffee, biscuits, a bottle of spirits, &c.; also the welcome intelligence that Captain Bell, with his division of the exploring party, had arrived at Fort Smith some days previous.

Early on the 13th, we took up our march in a heavy fall of rain, which continued until we arrived at the little plantation opposite Belle Point. Here we emerged from the deep silence and twilight gloom of the forest, and found ourselves once more surrounded by the works of men. The plantation consisted of a single enclosure covered with a thick crop of maize intermixed with gigantic stalks of the phytolacca *decandra*, and Ricinus *palma-christi*, forming a forest of annual plants, which seemed almost to vie with miegias and annonas, occupying the adjacent portions of the river bottom.

Urged by our impatience to see human faces, we called out to the people in the cottage to direct us to Belle Pointe, although we knew the path could not be mistaken, and that we were not ten rods from the ferry. Notwithstanding our inquiries might have been thought impertinent, we were very civilly answered by a young woman, who came to the door, and attempted to silence the clamours of the dogs. We were not surprised to find our uncouth appearance a matter of astonishment both to dogs and men.

On arriving at the beach opposite Fort Smith, and making known our arrival by the discharge of a pistol, we perceived the inhabitants of the garrison and our former companions, coming down to the ferry to give us welcome: and being soon carried over, we met with Major Bradford and Captain Ballard, a most cordial reception. Captain Bell, with Mr. Say, Mr. Seymour, and Lieutenant

Swift, having experienced numerous casualties, and achieved various adventures, having suffered much from hunger, and more from the perfidy of some of their soldiers, had arrived on the 9th, and were all in good health. The loss most sensibly felt, was that of the manuscript notes of Mr. Say and Lieutenant Swift. Measures for the apprehension of the deserters, and the recovery of these important papers were taken immediately, and a reward of two hundred dollars offered. Mr. Glen had kindly volunteered his assistance, and his influence, to engage the Osages in the pursuit. But these efforts were unavailing.

We arrived at Fort Smith at about nine o'clock, and were soon afterwards invited to a bountifully furnished breakfast-table at Major Bradford's. Our attentive host, knowing the caution necessary to be used by men in our situation, restrained us from a too unbounded indulgence in the use of bread, sweet potatoes, and other articles of diet, to which we had been long unaccustomed. The experience of a few days taught us that we should have been fortunate had we given more implicit heed to his cautions.

It is now necessary to return, and attend Captain Bell's detachment of the party, in their progress down the Arkansa.

CHAPTER XII

The party proceed upon their route—Thunder storm—
Some account of the Kiawa, Kaskaia, Arrapaho, and Shienne Indians—
New species of toad.

24TH. After the departure of so great a portion of our number, combined with whom, we could hardly be regarded as sufficiently powerful to contend successfully with a force which we were daily liable to encounter, we were well aware of the necessity of exerting an increased vigilance, and of relying still more implicitly upon our individual means of defence than we had hitherto done. Our small band now consisted of Captain Bell, Lieutenant Swift, Mr. Seymour, Mr. Say, and the interpreters Bijeau, Ledoux, and Julien, with five soldiers.

We were cheered by the reflection that we had successfully performed a very considerable and most important part of our expedition, harmonizing well with each other, and unassailed by any urgent visible dangers, such as had been anticipated by ourselves, and predicted by others. We could not, however, look forward to the trackless desert which still separated us from the uttermost boundary of civilization, and which we had no reason to believe was less than one thousand miles in breadth, traversed, in many portions of its extent, by lawless war parties of various nations of Indians, without an emotion of anxiety and of doubt, as to the successful termination of our enterprize.

We were this afternoon assailed by a very severe thunder storm; and Julien, who had skirted the timber for the purpose of hunting, was electrified by a flash of lightning which entered the earth within a few yards of him.

The wind was violent, and blew the drops of rain with so much force into our faces, that our horses refused to proceed, constantly endeavouring to turn themselves about from the storm; we at length yielded to their obstinacy, and halted upon the plain. The storm did not abate until we were thoroughly drenched to the skin, when, after being delayed some additional space of time until a straggler had joined us, we continued our journey.

The striped and spotted ground squirrel, a beautiful little animal, occurred to our notice several times in the course of the day.

Mr. T. Nuttall long since obtained specimens of this species, near the Mandan village, on the Missouri, and in the year 1814 he presented skins of it to several of his scientific friends in London.

He informs me that he has seen tippets worn by the Indians of the Upper Missouri, which were made of the skins of this elegant species, sewn together.

They burrow in the earth, and do not voluntarily climb trees. They inhabit an extensive portion of North America, extending at least from the more northern lakes to the Arkansa river, and most probably in that direction into Mexico, and westward to the Rocky Mountains. They were not uncommon in the vicinity of Engineer Cantonment.

26th. Late in the afternoon we saw, at a great distance before us, evident indications of the proximity of Indians, consisting of conic elevations, or skin lodges, on the edge of the skirting timber, partially concealed by the foliage of the trees. On our nearer approach we observed their horses peacefully grazing; but becoming suddenly frightened, probably by our scent, they all bounded off towards the camp, which was now full in view. Our attention was called off from horses by the appearance of their masters, who were now seen running towards us with all their swiftness. A minute afterwards we were surrounded by them, and were happy to observe, in their features and gestures, a manifestation of the most pacific disposition; they shook us by the hand, assured us by signs that they rejoiced to see us, and invited us to partake of their hospitality. We, however, replied that we had brought our own lodges with us, and would encamp near them. We selected for this purpose a clear spot of ground on the bank of the river, intending to remain a day or two with this little known people, to observe their manners and way of life. We had scarcely pitched our tents, watered and staked our horses, before presents of jerked bison meat were brought to us by the squaws, consisting of selected pieces, the fattest and the best, and in sufficient quantity for the consumption of two or three days. After the usual ceremony of smoking, they were informed to what nation we belonged; and that further communication would be made to their principal men to-morrow, whom we wished summoned for that purpose. About sundown they all retired, and left us to our repose. The Indians were encamped on both sides of the river, but the great body of them was on the opposite bank, their skin lodges extending in a long single line, the extremities of which were concealed from our view by the timber of the islands in the river, whilst about ten lodges only were erected on the side we occupied, and within a quarter of a mile of our camp.

Soon after our arrival, an Indian, well stricken in years, inquired if we had seen a man and squaw within a day or two on our route; we described to him the appearance of the Calf and his squaw; that is my wife, said he, who has eloped away from me, and I will instantly go in pursuit of them. He accordingly procured a companion, and both were soon on their way, well armed and mounted.

27th. Notice having been sent to the opposite party of our arrival, and of our wish to see the principal men, four chiefs presented themselves at our camp this morning at an early hour, as representatives of the several bands, of the same number of different nations here associated together, and consisting of Kiawas, Kaskaias, or Bad-hearts, Shiennes (sometimes written Chayenne,) and Arrapahoes; several distinguished men accompanied them. We had made some little preparation for their reception by spreading skins for them to sit on, hoisting our flag, and selecting a few presents from our scanty stores. They arranged themselves with due solemnity, and the pipe being passed around, many of them seemed to enjoy it as the greatest rarity, eyeing it as it passed from mouth to mouth, and inhaling its fragrant smoke into their lungs with a pleasure which they could not conceal. One individual, of a tall, emaciated frame, whose visage was furrowed with deep wrinkles, evidently rather the effect of disease than of age, after filling his lungs and mouth top full of smoke, placed his hands firmly upon his face and inflated cheeks as in an ecstasy, and unwilling to part with what yielded the utmost pleasure, he retained his breath until suffocation compelled him to drive out the smoke and inhale fresh air, which he effected so suddenly, and with so much earnestness and singular contortion of countenance, that we restrained ourselves with some effort from committing the indecorum of a broad laugh. We had the good fortune to find one of them who could speak the

Kiowa Encampment, Samuel Seymour, watercolor.

Pawnee language tolerably well; he had acquired it in his early youth, whilst residing in a state of captivity in that nation, so that by means of our interpreters we experienced no difficulty in acquainting them, that we belonged to the numerous and powerful nation of Americans, that we had been sent by our great chief, who presides over all that country, to examine that part of his territories, that he might become acquainted with its features, its produce, and population; that we had been many moons on our journey, and had passed through many red nations, of whose hospitality we largely partook, &c. This was translated into French, then into Pawnee, and afterwards into Kiawa and the other languages, by their respective interpreters. In reply a chief expressed his surprise that we had travelled so far, and assured us that they were happy to see us, and hoped that as a road was now open to our nation, traders would be sent amongst them.

We assured them that traders would be soon amongst them, provided we could report, on our return, that we had been hospitably treated while travelling through their country.

A few presents, such as knives, combs, vermillion, &c. were then laid before the chiefs, who in return presented us with three or four horses, which terminated the proceedings of the council. We afterwards understood that our guests thought we gave but little, and it is perhaps true that the value of their presents was far greater than ours, yet our liberality was fully equal to our means.

The whole population had now deserted their edifices, and crowded about us, and agreeably to our wishes, which were announced in the council, the women brought jerked meat, and the men skin and hair ropes for halters, to trade with us for trinkets, and we were enabled to obtain a sufficient quantity of each, at a very moderate price. The trading being completed, we expected the crowd to diminish, but it seemed rather to augment, both in magnitude and density, until becoming a very serious inconvenience, we requested the chiefs to direct their people to retire, which they immediately complied with; but, with the exception of the Shienne chief, were not obeyed. All the Shiennes forthwith left us in compliance with the peremptory orders of their chief, who seemed to be a man born to command, endowed with a spirit of unconquerable ferocity, and capable of inflicting exemplary punishment upon any one who should dare disobey his orders. He was tall and graceful, with a highly ridged aquiline nose, corrugated forehead, mouth with the corners drawn downward, and rather small, but remarkably piercing eye, which when fixed upon your countenance, appeared strained in the intenseness of its gaze, and to seek rather for the movements of the soul within, than to ascertain the mere lineaments it contemplated. The other chiefs seemed to possess only the dignity of office, without the power of command; the result, probably, of a deficiency of that native energy with which their companion was so preeminently endowed; they scarcely dared to reiterate their admonitions to their followers not to press so closely upon the white people, but to limit their approaches to the line of our baggage; still our tents were filled, and our persons hemmed in by the ardent and insatiable curiosity of the multitude of both sexes, and of all ages, mounted and on foot. To an observer of mankind the present scene was abundantly fruitful and interesting. We could not but remark the ease and air of security, with which the equestrians preserved their equipoise on the naked backs of their horses in their evolutions beyond the crowd, nor could we restrain a smile, in the midst of vexatious circumstances, at the appearance of the naked children mounted on horses, sometimes to the number of three or four on each, fearlessly standing erect, or kneeling upon their backs to catch a glance over the heads of the intervening multitude, at the singular deportment, costume, and appearance of the white strangers.

In the rear of our tent a squaw, who had become possessed of a wooden small-toothed comb, was occupied in removing from her head a population as numerous as the individuals composing it were robust and well fed; she had placed a skin upon her lap to receive the victims as they fell; and a female companion, who sat at her feet, alternately craunched the oily vermin between her teeth, and conversed with the most rapid and pleasant loquacity as she picked them up from the skin before her.

Our attention was now arrested by a phenomenon, which soon relieved us from the crowd that pressed upon us. A heavy and extensive cloud of dust was observed in the north obscuring the horizon, and bounding the range of vision in that direction; it moved rapidly towards us. An animated scene ensued. The Indians forded the river with as much rapidity of movement as they could exert towards their encampment, horse and foot, the water foaming before them. It soon became obvious that the dust ascended into the atmosphere under the influence of a violent current of air; we, therefore employed a few moments of interval, in strengthening our feeble tenements, to resist the influence of the approaching tempest. They were so nearly filled with our red brethren, that it was with no little difficulty we wedged ourselves into shelter. It soon became necessary to exert our strength in holding down our tents, and supporting the poles, which bowed and shook violently under the pressure of the blast; thunder, lightning, rain, and hail succeeded. During this play of the elements our guests sat in stillness, scarcely articulating a word during the prevalence of the electrical explosions.

Our tents were much admired, and previously to the fall of rain, which exposed their imperfection, in admitting the water modified into the form of a mist, one of the natives offered to exchange an excellent mule for that in which he was sitting. And, as the commonalty could not distinguish us in their minds from traders, another offered two mules, valued equal to four horses, for a double barrelled gun; and a third would willingly have bartered a very good horse for an old and almost worn out camp kettle, which we could by no means part with, though much in want of horses.

These Indians differ, in many particulars, from those of the Missouri, with whose appearance we had been, for some time, familiar. Their average stature appeared to us less considerable, and although the general appearance of the countenance was such as we had been accustomed to see, yet their faces have, perhaps, somewhat more latitude, and the Roman nose is obviously far less predominant; but still, the direction of the eye, the prominence of the cheek bones, the form of the lips, teeth, chin, and retreating forehead, are precisely similar. They have also the same habit of plucking the hair from various parts of the body; but that of the head, in the female, is only suffered to attain to the shoulders, whilst the men permit theirs to grow to its full extent. They even regard long hair as an ornament; and many wear false hair fastened to their own by means of an earthy matter, resembling red clay, and depending, in many instances, particularly in the young beaux, to their knees, in the form of queues, one on each side of the head, variously decorated with ribbon-like slips of red and blue cloth, or coloured skin. Others, and by no means an inconsiderable few, had collected their long hair into several flat masses of the breadth of two or three fingers, and less than the fifth of an inch in thickness, each one separately annulated with red clay, at regular intervals. The elders wore their hair without decoration, flowing loosely about their shoulders, or simply intermixed with slender plaited queues. In structure and colour it is not distinguished from that of the Missouri Indians, though in early youth it is often of a much lighter colour; and a young man, of perhaps fifteen years of age, who visited us today, had hair decidedly of a flaxen hue, with a tint of dusky yellow.

Their costume is very simple, that of the female consisting of a leathern petticoat, reaching the calf of the leg, destitute of a seam, and often exposing a well formed thigh, as the casualties of wind, or position, influence the artless foldings of the skirt; the leg and foot are often naked, but usually invested by gaiters and mockasins; a kind of sleeveless short gown, composed a single piece of the same material, loosely clothes the body, hanging upon the shoulders, readily thrown off, without any sense of indelicacy, when suckling their children, or under the influence of a heated atmosphere, displaying loose and pendent mammæ. A few are covered by the more costly attire of coarse red or blue cloth, ornamented with a profusion of blue and white beads; the shortgown of this dress has the addition of wide sleeves descending below the elbow; its body is of a square form with a transverse slit in the upper edge for the head to pass through; around this aperture, and on the upper side of the sleeves, is a continuous stripe, the breadth of the hand, of blue and white beads, tastefully arranged in contact with each other, and adding considerable weight, as well as ornament, to this part of the dress; around the petticoat, and in a line with the knees, is an even row of oblong conic bells, made of sheet copper, each about an inch and a half in length, suspended vertically by short leathern thongs as near to each other as possible, so that when the person is in motion they strike upon each other and produce a tinkling sound. The young unmarried females are more neatly dressed, and seem to participate but little in the laborious occupations, which fall chiefly to the lot of their wedded companions.

The dress of the men is composed of a breech-cloth, skin leggings, mockasins, and a bison robe. In warm weather, the three latter articles of dress are sometimes thrown aside as superfluous, exposing the limbs and body to view and to the direct influence of the most ardent rays of the sun. Such are the habiliments that necessity compels the multitude to adopt; but the opulence of a few has gained for themselves the comfortable, as well as ornamental, and highly esteemed Spanish blanket, from the Mexican traders, and of which we had previously seen two or three in the possession of Pawnee warriors, worn as trophies. Another species of garment, in their estimation equally sumptuous with the blanket, is the cloth robe, which is of ample dimensions, simple in form, one half red and the other blue, thrown loosely about the person, and at a little distance, excepting the singular arrangement of colours, resembling a Spanish cloak.

Some have, suspended from the slits of their ears, the highly prized nacre, or perlaceous fragments of a marine shell, brought probably from the northwest coast.

The Shienne chief revisited us in the afternooon. He informed us that one of his young men, who had been sent to ascertain the route which the bison herds had taken, and their present locality, had observed the trail of a large party of men, whom, by pursuing the direction, he had discovered to be Spaniards on their way towards the position we then occupied, where they must very soon arrive. As we were now in a region, claimed by the Mexican Spaniards as exclusively their own, and as we had for some days anticipated such an event as highly probable, we involuntarily reposed implicit confidence, in the truth of the intelligence communicated by the chief, who regarded that people as our natural enemies. Nevertheless, his story was heard by our little band, as it was proper that it should have been in our situation, and in the presence of Indians, with the appearance of absolute apathy. The chief seemed not to have accomplished some object he had in view, and departed evidently displeased. When he was out of hearing, the Indian interpreter who had become our friend, told us that the story was entirely false, and was without a doubt the invention of the chief, and designed to expedite the trade for a few additional horses, that we were then negociating.

Mr. Say, accompanied by an interpreter, who made a short visit to the small group of lodges near us, was kindly received, though hooted at by the children, and of course snarled and snapped at by the dogs. The skin lodges of these wandering people, are very similar to those of the Missouri tribes, but in those to which he was introduced, he experienced the oppression of an almost suffocating heat, certainly many degrees above the temperature of the very sultry exterior atmosphere. A very portly old man, whose features were distinguished by a remarkably wide mouth and lengthened chin, invited him to a small ragged lodge, to see the riches it contained. These consisted of habiliments of red and blue cloth, profusely garnished with blue and white beads, the product of the industry and ingenuity of his squaw, from materials obtained last winter from some white traders, who made their appearance on Red river. The present members of his family, were the old man, one wife and four children, the latter as usual in a state of nudity. The baggage was piled around the lodge, serving for seats and beds, and a pile of jerked meat near the door, served also for a seat, and was occasionally visited by the dirty feet of the children. A boy was amusing himself with that primitive weapon, the sling, of an ordinary form, which he used with considerable dexterity, the effect of which he appeared disposed to try upon the stranger, and was not readily turned from his purpose, by a harsh rebuke and menacing gesture.

He was informed that the party of traders, who had last winter ascended Red river to their country, were *Tabbyboos*, a name which they also applied to us, and which appears to be the same word which, according to Lewis and Clark, in the language of the Snake Indians, means white men, but it was here applied particularly to the Americans. These traders offered various articles, such as coarse cloths, beads, vermillion, kettles, knives, guns, powder, lead, &c.; in exchange for horses and mules, bison robes, and parchment or *parfleche*. Such was the anxiety to obtain the merchandise thus displayed before them, that those enterprising warriors, whose stock of horses was but small, crossed the mountains into Mexico, and returned with a plentiful supply of those animals for exchange, captured from the Spanish inhabitants of that country. This illicit trade in horses was conducted so extensively by that party of traders, that he was told of a single Indian, who sold them fifty mules, besides a considerable number of horses from his own stock.

At his return to camp, he was informed that an old Indian had been there, who asserted that he never before had seen a white man, and on being permitted to view a part of the body, usually covered by the dress, he seemed much surprised at its whiteness.

These Indians seem to hold in exalted estimation, the martial prowess of the Americans. They said that a battle had lately been fought in the country, which lay very far down Red river, between a handful of Americans, and a great war party of Spaniards; that the latter were soon routed, retreating in a dastardly manner, "like partridges running through the grass." They were at present at war with the Spaniards themselves, and had lately killed many individuals of a party of that nation, near the mountains.

In the evening, squaws were brought to our camp, and after we had retired to our tent at night, a brother of the grand chief, Bear's-tooth, continued to interrupt our repose, with solicitations in favour of a squaw he had brought with him, until he was peremptorily directed to begone, and the centinel was ordered to prevent his further intrusion.

The Bear-tooth is the grand chief of the Arrapahoes, and his influence extends over all the tribes of the country in which he roves: he was said to be encamped at no great distance, with the principal body of these nations. He is said to be very favorably disposed towards the white people, and to have afforded protection, and a home in his own lodge, to a poor and miserable American, who had had the good fortune to escape from the barbarity and mistaken policy of the Mexican Spaniards, and from the horrors of a Spanish prison, to find an asylum amongst those whom they regard as barbarians, but to whose commiseration his wretchedness seemed to have been a passport.

28th. This morning at sunrise, we were called from our tents by the cry of *Tabbyboo*, proceeding from two handsome mounted Arrapahoes, who appeared delighted to see us; they had passed our camp in the night, on their way from the camp of the Bear-tooth, with a message from that chief to our neighbours. In consequence of this information or order, the lodges on both sides of the river were struck at six o'clock, and the whole body of Indians, commenced their march up the river, notwithstanding the threatening aspect of the heavens, which portended a storm. We could not but admire the regularity, with which the preparations for their journey seemed to be conducted, and the remarkable facility with which the lodges disappeared, and with all their cumbrous and various contents, were secured to the backs of the numerous horses and mules. As the long drawn caravan proceeded onward, a military air was imparted to the whole, at the distance at which we contemplated it, by the activity of the young warriors, with their lances and shields, galloping or racing along the line for caprice or amusement.

The Kiawa chief and a few attendants, called to make his parting visit. He is an old man, rather short, inelegantly formed, destitute of any remarkable physiognomical peculiarity, and like other chiefs, without any distinction of personal ornament. In common with many of his tribe, his system was subject to cutaneous eruptions, of which several indications, besides a large ulcer, near the angle of the mouth, exhibited the proof. We were soon all driven into our flimsy and almost worn out tents, which afforded us but a very partial shelter from the fall of a heavy shower of rain from the N.W. There we obtained some additional information from the chief, who was disposed to be communicative, to augment the considerable mass, which we had already collected from other Indians, and particularly from Bijeau, respecting those wandering hordes. The chief seemed to take a pleasure in pronouncing to us words of the Kiawa language, and smiled at our awkward attempts to imitate them, whilst we were engaged in committing them to paper. This vocabulary, as well as that of the Kaskaia language, which we had previously obtained from the Calf, had been for some time the objects of our wishes, as Bijeau persuaded us, that they were more difficult to acquire than any other language, and that, although formerly he resided three years with those nations, he never could understand the meaning of a single word, not even their expressions for *Frenchman* or *tobacco*. Nor does this observation, though, perhaps unintentionally exaggerating the ideas of the abstruse nature of the language, appear absolutely destitute of foundation, since these nations, although constantly associating together, and united under the influence of the Bear-tooth, are yet totally ignorant of each others language, insomuch that it was no uncommon occurrence, to see two individuals of different nations, sitting upon the ground, and conversing freely with each other, by means of the language of signs. In the art of thus conveying their ideas, they were thorough adepts, and their manual display was only interrupted at remote intervals by a smile, or by the auxiliary of an articulated word of the language of the Crow Indians, which to a very limited extent, passes current amongst them.

These languages abound with sounds strange to our ears, and in the noisy loquacity of some squaws, who held an animated debate near our tent yesterday, we distinguished preeminently, sounds which may be expressed by the letters koo, koo, koo.

The Shiennes or Shawhays, who have united their destiny with these wanderers, are a band of seceders from their own nation, and some time since on the occurrence of a serious dispute with their kindred on Shienne river of the Missouri, flew their country, and placed themselves under the protection of the Bear-tooth.

These nations have been for the three past years, wandering on the head waters and tributaries of Red river, having returned to the Arkansa, only the day which preceded our first interview with them, on their way to the mountains, at the sources of the Platte river. They have no permanent town, but constantly rove, as necessity urges them, in pursuit of the herds of bisons, in the vicinity of the sources of the Platte, Arkansa, and Red rivers.

They are habitually at war with all the nations of the Missouri; indeed martial occurrences in which they were interested with those enemies, formed the chief topic of their conversation with our interpreters. They were desirous to know of them the names of particular individuals whom they had met in battle, and whom they described; how many had been present at a particular engagement, and who were killed or wounded. The late battle which we have before spoken of, with the Loup Pawnees, also occupied their inquiries; they denied that they were on that occasion aided by the Spaniards, as we understood they had been, but admitted their great numerical superiority, and the loss of many in killed and wounded. Their martial weapons are bows and arrows, lances, war clubs, tomahawks, scalping knives, and shields.

Tobacco being very scarce, they do not carry with them a pouch, for the convenience of having it always at hand, an article of dress invariably attendant on the Missouri Indian. Bijeau informed us that the smoking of tobacco was regarded as a pleasure so sacred and important, that the females were accustomed to depart from the interior of a lodge when the men indulged themselves with the pipe. The Shienne chief, in consequence of a vow he had made against using the pipe, abstained from smoking while at our council, until he had the good fortune to find a small piece of paper which some one of our party had rejected; with this he rolled up a small quantity of tobacco fragments in the form of a segar, after the manner of the Spaniards, and thus contented himself with infringing the spirit of his vow, whilst he obeyed it to the letter.

The rain having ceased, our guest and his attendants took their leave.

These Indians might readily be induced to hunt the beaver, which are so extremely abundant in their country, but as yet, these peltries seem not to have entered amongst the items of their trade.

In the afternoon we struck our tents, and continued our journey; we were soon overtaken by a thunder storm, which poured down upon us a deluge of rain, and continued, with partial intermissions, during the night.

For the elucidation of what we have said respecting the form and arrangement of the skin, or travelling lodges of the Indians, we subjoin an engraving, representing an encampment of Oto Indians, which Mr. Seymour sketched near the Platte river. In this plate, the group of Indians on the left is intended to represent a party of Konza Indians approaching to perform the calumet dance in the Oto village. It may be proper to remark, that this party when still distant from the Otoes, had sent forward a messenger, with the offer of a prize to the first Oto that should meet them. This circumstance was productive of much bustle and activity among the warriors and young men, who eagerly mounted their horses, and exerted their utmost speed.

Since we have mentioned the Otoes, we will notice the ceremony of marking a distinguished squaw, which was in part witnessed by some of our party at the Oto village. This marking, which we have elsewhere alluded to, consists in picking into the forehead, with a small fascicle of needles, or other small pointed instruments, a portion of minute particles of carbon, from a solution of gun powder, or comminuted and moistened wood coal, so as to form upon the part a small blue spot. On the approach of our party, however, to the group of Indians in which this ceremony was performed, each individual sat perfectly still, with his head inclined, as if indisposed to proceed whilst observed by strangers. In the centre of the group was a piece of wood supported at each end by an upright crotchet, and holding suspended various articles of merchandize, intended to compensate the operator; consisting of red and blue strouding, and many other articles of much value. The squaw, with her family and friends; accompanied by the individual who was to perform the operation, sat in the form of a semicircle, in front of these valuables, and a large decorated pipe was laid on the soil before them. Our party supposed that the value of the merchandize thus offered in exchange for the distinction of a small spot on the forehead, was, in that country, and particularly after having passed through the hands of the traders, estimable at one hundred dollars.

We will further interrupt our narrative in this place, to mention a circumstance, that has been omitted in our account of the manners and habits of the Indians of the Missouri. It serves to show that their attention is not limited to the larger and more imposing objects of the creation, but that it is directed to the "watches, as well as the clocks of nature."

The Oto warrior, *Little black bear*, when looking at our collections of insects at Engineer cantonment, recognised a considerable number of them, told which inhabited the water, and which the land, and noticed many little anecdotes of their manners with much accuracy; with respect to some, however, which he pointed out, he entertained strange notions, doubtless in common with his countrymen. Our largest species of dytiscus, he said, sometimes entered the womb of a pregnant squaw, and destroyed the foetus. The large green grasshopper with a pointed head, (Truxalis) he said, would seize the nipple of a squaw with its mouth, and would not quit its hold until the body was torn from the head.

29th. The sun arose with renewed splendour, and ushered in another sultry day. Two of the horses, which had been presented by the chiefs, ran off, and were observed to rise the bluffs and disappear; men were despatched in pursuit of them, who after a long and fatiguing chase, returned about noon, unsuccessful. We reconciled ourselves as we might to this privation, and after dining, proceeded onward. The alluvial margins of the river are gradually dilating as we descend, and the mosquitoes, which have of late visited our camp but sparingly, are now increasing in number.

A fine species of toad (Bufo) inhabits this region. It resembles the common toad (B. *musicus.* Daud.) but differs in the arrangement of the olours, and in the proportional length of the groove of the head, which in that species extends to the nose; it is destitute of large verrucose prominences intervening between the verrucæ behind the eyes, and of the large, irregular, black dorsal spots edged with white, observable upon the *musicus.* In the arrangement of the cinereous lines it presents a general resemblance to B. *fuscus.* Laur. as represented on pl. 96. of the Encyc. Method.

It resides in a country almost destitute of timber, where, with a variety of the *musicus,* it is very much exposed to the direct rays of the sun.

CHAPTER XIII

Arrapaho war-party—Cowhunting—Rattlesnakes—Burrowing-owl—
Departure of Bijeau and Ledoux for the Pawnee villages—
Scarcity of timber—Great herds of bisons—wolves.

ON the 30th, about sunrise, a dense fog intercepted the view of the surrounding scenery, which was soon dissipated as we moved on, exhibiting all the variety of partially revealed, and unnaturally enlarged objects, so familiar to observers of rural sights. At noon, a beautiful natural grove of cottonwood, lining a ravine in which was some cool but stagnant water, near the bank of the river, invited us to repose during the oppressive mid-day heat. We had hardly stripped our horses of their baggage, and betaken ourselves to our respective occupations, when a voice from the opposite bank of the river warned us of the proximity of Indians, who had been until now unseen. Nine Indians soon appeared, and crossed the river to our camp. They proved to be an Arrapaho war party of eight men and a squaw, of whom one was a Kiawa. This party informed us that they had left the Bear-tooth's party on a tributary of this river, at the distance of half a day's journey from us, moving upwards. As no apprehension of mischief was entertained from so small a party, they were invited to encamp near us for the remainder of the day, to which, urged by curiosity, and perhaps by the hope of receiving some presents, they readily assented. The squaw busied herself in erecting a little bowery of sufficient size to contain herself and her husband, who we afterwards discovered to be a personage of some eminence in their mystic arts.

Having supplied our guests with a pipe and some tobacco, we resumed our occupations. Our attention was however diverted to the young Kiawa warrior, who had the presumption to seize the Kaskaia horse, which was purchased of the Calf Indian, loose him from the stake around which he was grazing, and having the further audacity to lead him near to our tent, proceeded to make a noose in the halter; which he placed over the mouth of the animal, that patiently submitted to his operations. This sudden subjection of the horse was a subject of more surprise to us, than the outrageous attempt of the Indian, as he had hitherto resisted all our endeavours to accomplish the same object, whether conciliatory or forcible. It seeed to corroborate the truth of the observation, that the horse readily distinguishes the native from the white man, by his acute sense of smelling. The intention of the Indian to take possession of the horse was now manifest, and one of our party stepped forward and seized the halter near the head of the animal; but the Indian who held the other extremity of the halter, betrayed no symptoms of fear, or of an intention to relinquish a possession which he had thus partially gained. He looked sternly at his antagonist, and asserted his right to the horse, inasmuch as he had, he said, formerly owned him, and meant now to repossess him. Supposing that this altercation might eventuate unpleasantly, the remainder of our party stood prepared to repulse any attempt which the other Indians might make to support the claim of their companion, whilst Bijeau advanced with a manly decision and jerked the halter out of the hands of the Indian. His companions sat enjoying themselves with their pipe, and did not appear disposed to take any part in the transaction. He fortunately made no further exertions to obtain possesion of the horse, but immediately mounted his own horse, and rode off in high dudgeon, saying he would remain no longer with us, for fear we would kill him. Contrary to our expectations, the other Indians loudly condemned his conduct; they said that the horse had never been his property, that they all knew the animal well, that he was a very bad Kiawa, and would either assemble a party to return against us, or he would return himself that night, to accomplish his purpose. "If he does come," said they, "you need not give yourselves any trouble, for we will watch for him, and kill him ourselves."

When the excitement of this incident had subsided, we felt desirous to examine the contents of the medicine bag of the man of mysteries, who was at once a magician and the leader of the party. At our solicitation he readily opened his sacred depository, and displayed its contents on a skin before us, whilst he politely proceeded to expatiate on their powers and virtues in the occult art, as well as their physical efficacy. They consisted of various roots, seeds, pappus, and powders, both active and inert, as respects their action on the human system, carefully enveloped in skins, leaves, &c.; some of which, to his credulous faith, were invested with supernatural powers. Similar qualities were also attributed to some animal products, with which these were accompanied, such as claws of birds, beaks, feathers, and hair. But the object that more particularly attracted our attention, was the intoxicating bean, as it has been called, of which he possessed upwards of a pint. Julien recognised it immediately. He informed us that it is in such high request amongst the Oto Indians, that a horse has been exchanged for eight or ten of them. In that nation they are only used by a particular society, who, at their nocturnal orgies, make a decoction of the bean, and, with much pomp and ceremony, administer the delightful beverage to each member. The initiation fees of this society are rather extravagant, and the proceeds are devoted principally to the purchase of the bean. That old sensualist, Shongotonga (Big-horse), is the principal or presiding member of the society, and the bean is obtained, in some circuitous manner, from the Pawnee Piquas of Red river, who, probably, receive it from the Mexican Indians. With some few trinkets, of little value, we purchased the principal portion of our medicine-man's store of beans; they are of an oval form, and of a light red, sometimes yellowish colour, with a rather deeply impressed oval cicatrix, and larger than a common bean. A small number of a differently coloured, and rather larger bean was intermixed with them.

The squaw had in her possession, a quantity of small, flat, blackish cakes, which, on tasting, we found very palatable. Having purchased some of them, we ascertained that they were composed of the wild cherry, both pulp and stone pounded together, until the latter is broken into fragments, then mixed with grease, and dried in the sun.

Not choosing to rely implicitly on the good faith of the strangers, however emphatically expressed, the sentinel was directed to look well to them, and also to keep the horse in question constantly in view during the night, and to alarm us upon the occurrence of any suspicious movements. All, however, remained quiet during the night, and in the morning, the 31st., we resumed our journey.

The river now considerably dilates, and is studded with a number of small islands, but the timber and shrubs that skirt it are still less abundant and more scattered. The alluvial formation affords a moderate growth of grass, but the general surface of the country is flat, sterile, and uninteresting. The day was cloudy, with an E.S.E. wind, which at night brought some rain.

Aug. 1st. Set out late, and after having travelled about two miles, a horseman armed with a spear was seen on the Bluffs, at the distance of about a quarter of a mile, who, after gazing at our line for a short time, disappeared. Our Pawnee interpreters being at a considerable distance in the rear, Julien was sent forward to reconnoitre. He mounted the Bluff to the general level of the country, and abruptly halted his horse within our view, as if appearances before him rendered precaution necessary. The Indian again came in sight, and, in full career, rushed towards him, passed him, and wheeling halted his horse. Many other Indians then appeared, who surrounded Julien, and, after a short and hurried conference, they dashed at full speed down the steep bank of the Bluff to meet us, the whole in concert singing the scalp song. So adventurous and heedless was this movement, that one of the horses stumbled, and fell with great violence, and rolled to the bottom. His rider, no doubt, prepared for such an accident, threw himself in the instant from his seat, so as to fall in the most favorable manner, and avoid the danger of being crushed by the horse. Not the slightest attention was bestowed upon him by his companions, and, indeed, the disaster, however serious it at first appeared, hardly interrupted his song. His horse being but little injured, he almost immediately regained his saddle, and came on but little in the rear of the others, who now had mingled with our party, shaking us by the hand with a kind of earnest familiarity, not the most agreeable. We needed no additional information to convince us that this was a war party; their appearance was a sufficient evidence of the nature of their occupation. One of us asked an individual, if they were Kiawas, and was answered in the affirmative; he asked a second if they were Kaskaias, and a third if they were Arrapahoes, who both also answered affirmatively. This conduct, added to their general deportment, served to excite our suspicions and redouble our vigilance. Two or three other little detached squads were now seen to approach, also singing the scalp-song.

Our interpreters having joined us, it was proposed that we should avail ourselves of the shade of a large tree, which stood near the river, to sit down and smoke with them. They reared their spears against the tree, with apparent carelessness and indifference, and took their seats in the form of a semicircle on the ground. Having staked our horses in the rear, and stationed the men to protect them and the baggage, we seated ourselves, and circulated the pipe as usual. But as the party opposed to us was nearly quadruple our number, we did not choose to follow their example, in relinquishing our arms, but grasped them securely in our hands, and retained a cautious attitude.

Bijeau ascertained that they were a Shienne war party on their return from an expedition against the Pawnee Loups. They had killed one squaw, whose scalp was suspended to the spear of the partizan or leader of the party, the handle of which was decorated with strips of red and white cloth, beads, and tail-plumes of the war-eagle. He also informed us that he recognized several of them, particularly a chief who sat next to him, whose person, himself and party had formerly seized upon, and detained as a hostage for the recovery of some horses that had been stolen. The chief, however, did not now betray any symptoms of a disposition to retaliate for that act, though, without doubt, he regarded us as in his power.

Our interpreter readily conversed with them, through the medium of a Crow prisoner, whose language he partially understood.

The partizan, who killed the victim of this excursion, and two others, one of whom first struck the dead body, and the other who took off the scalp, were painted deep black with charcoal, and almost the entire body being exposed, rendered the effect more impressive. One of the latter, a tall athletic figure, remained standing behind us, and refused to smoke when the pipe was offered to him, alledging as an excuse, the obligation of a vow he had made against the use of tobacco on the decease of his late father.

We now drew upon our little stores of merchandize for two or three twists of tobacco and a few knives, which, being laid before the partizan, excited from his politeness, the return of thanks. He was of an ordinary stature, and had exceeded the middle age; his face much pitted with the smallpox, his nostrils distended by a habitual muscular action, which, at the same time, elevated the skin of the forehead and forcibly drew downward that part which corresponds with the inner extremity of the eyebrows, into a kind of gloomy frown. This singular expression of countenance, added to the contrast of the whites of his large eyes, with the black colour, with which his features and body were overspread, seemed to indicate the operations of a mind hardened to the commission of the most outrageous actions. He, however, behaved with much propriety. During these scenes, Mr. Say succeeded in ascertaining and recording many of the words of his language, from an Indian who had seated himself behind him.

The party was armed with spears, bows and arrows, war-clubs, tomahawks, scalping knives, &c.

As many of them now began to ask for tobacco, and for paper to include fragments of it, in the form of segars, for smoking, and not finding it convenient to gratify them in this respect, we thought it prudent to withdraw, lest a quarrel might ensue. We, therefore, mounted our horses, without molestation, having been detained an hour and a half, and proceeded on our journey, with the agreeable reflection, that our deportment had not warranted a supposition that we were conscious of any inferiority in force, but rather that it was dictated by a high courtesy.

A few bisons varied the landscape, which is fatiguing to the eye by its sameness, and, after travelling twenty-three miles, we encamped for the night.

A large green-headed fly (Tabanus.) has made its appearance in great numbers, which exceedingly annoys our already sufficiently miserable horses. Their range seems to be in a great measure restricted to the luxuriant bottoms, and, like the Zimb of Egypt, they appear to roam but little beyond their proper boundaries. If we traversed these fertile portions of the low grounds, which yield a profuse growth of grasses, we were sure of being attacked by them, seizing upon the necks of the horses and dying them with blood; but the refuge of the more elevated surface, and arid barren soil, afforded speedy relief, by banishing our assailants.

Scarcely were our tents pitched, when a thunder-storm, which had been approaching with a strong west wind, burst over us, but was of short continuance.

2nd. After moving a few miles, we halted, and sent out hunters to kill a bison. The *confluent rattlesnakes* are very abundant, particularly in and about the prairie-dog villages; but neither their appearance, nor the sound of their rattle excites the attention of our horses. The sagacity of Mr. Seymour's mule, however, seems superior to that of his quadruped companions. He appears to be perfectly aware of the dangerous qualities of these reptiles, and when he perceives one of them near him, he springs so abruptly to one side as to endanger his rider. Fortunately none of us have been bitten by them, during our pedestrian rambles.

A recent trail of some war party was this morning observed leading across the river.

The hunters returned unsuccessful, and we proceeded on until sunset, to a distance of twenty miles. Great numbers of bisons were seen this afternoon, and some antelopes.

3rd. The morning was clear and fine, with a temperature of 57 degrees. The antelopes became more numerous as we proceeded; one of them trotted up so near to our line, as to fall a victim to his curiosity. A considerable number of the coquimbo or burrowing-owl occurred in a prairie-dog village of moderate extent. They readily permitted the hunter to approach within gunshot, and we were successful in obtaining a specimen of the bird in good order. On examining the several burrows, at which the owls had been observed to be perched, we remarked in them a different aspect from those at which the prairie dog had appeared; they were often in a ruined condition, the sides, in some instances, fallen in, sometimes seamed and grooved by the action of the water, in its course from the surface to the interior, and, in other respects, presenting a deserted aspect, and, like dilapidated monuments of human art, were the fit abode of serpents, lizards, and owls.

The burrows, at which we saw the prairie dog, were, on the contrary, neat, always in repair, and evinced the operations of industrious tenants. This contrast, added to the form and magnitude of the dwelling, leads us to the belief that the coquimbo owl does not, in this region, excavate its own burrow, as it is said to do in South America and in the West India islands. But, rather, that it avails itself of the abandoned burrows of this species of marmot, for the purposes of nidification and shelter.

On our arrival at our mid-day resting place on the bank of the Arkansa, the water of the river was potable, but in a few minutes it became surcharged with earthy and stercoraceous matter, from the sweepings of the prairie by the late rain, to such a degree, that our horses would hardly drink it. There remained, however, a short distance below, a small stream of beautifully pellucid water, which rapidly filtrated through a fortuitous embankment of sand and pebbles, and strongly contrasted with the flood, with which it was soon again to intermingle. Our travelled distance to-day was twenty-three miles.

4th. Proceeded about six miles, when we forded a small portion of the river to an island, which supported a growth of low and distant trees. Here the tents were pitched, with the intention of halting a day or two, to recruit our miserable horses, and to supply ourselves with a store of jerked meat. The hunters were accordingly sent to the opposite side of the river, and in a short time they succeeded in killing four fat cows, which gave employment to all the men, in preparing the meat for transportation.

A brisk southerly wind prevailed, that rendered the atmosphere less oppressive than usual.

The wind ceased during the night, and the lowing of the thousands of bisons that surrounded us in every direction, reached us in one continual roar. This harsh and guttural noise, intermediate between the bellowing of the domestic bull, and the grunting of the hog, was varied by the shrill bark and scream of the prairie wolves, and the howling of the white wolves, (Canis Mexicanus Var?) which were also abundant. These wild and dissonant sounds, were associated with the idea of the barren and inhospitable wastes, in the midst of which we were then reposing, and vividly reminded us of our remoteness from the comforts of civilized society. Completed the operation of jerking the meat, of which we had prepared two packs, sufficient in weight to constitute a load for one of our horses, and disposed every thing for an early departure to-morrow.

6th. An unusual number of noisy wolves hovered around our encampment of last night, attracted probably by the smell of the meat. Resumed our journey on a fine cloudless morning, with a strong and highly agreeable breeze from the south. We were now traversing the great bend of the river. Travelled twenty-three miles this day, and shot two bulls which were now lean, and their flesh of a disagreeable rank taste, and scarcely eatable; we therefore contented ourselves with the tongues and marrow-bones.

7th. The mercurial column of the thermometer at sunrise, for a few days past, has ranged between 42 and 67 degrees, and the atmosphere is serene and dry. The services of the two French Pawnee interpeters, Bijeau and Ledoux, had terminated agreeably to their contract at Purgatory creek. But having been highly serviceable to us on our route, it became desirable, particularly on the departure of our companions for Red river, that they should accompany us still farther, until we should have passed beyond the great Indian war path, here so widely outspread. This they readily consented to, as they regarded a journey from that point to their home at the Pawnee villages, as somewhat too hazardous to be prudently attempted by only two individuals, however considerable their qualifications, and intimate their familiarity with the manners of those whom they would probably meet.

But as we now supposed ourselves to have almost reached the boundary of this region, and they again expressed their anxiety to return to their village, in order to prepare for their autumnal hunt, we no longer attempted to induce their further delay. They departed after breakfast, on a pathless journey of about three hundred miles, the supposed distance from this point to the Pawnee villages of the Platte; apparently well pleased with the treatment they had received, and expressing a desire again to accompany us, should we reascend the Missouri.

We cannot take leave of them, without expressing our entire approbation of their conduct and deportment, during our arduous journey; Bijeau particularly, was faithful, active, industrious, and communicative. Besides the duties of guide and interpreter, he occasionally and frequently volunteered his services as hunter, butcher, cook, veterinarian, &c., and pointed out various little services, tending to our comfort and security, which he performed with pleasure and alacrity, and which no other than one habituated to this mode of life would have devised. During leisure intervals, he had communicated an historical narrative of his life and adventures, more particularly in as far as they were relative to the country which we have been exploring. He particularized the adventures of Choteau and Demun's hunting and trading party, their success in beaver hunting, the considerable quantity of merchandise they took with them, their adventures with the natives, and the singular circumstances attendant on their capture by the Mexican Spaniards, and the transfer of the merchandise to Santa Fe, without, however, venturing to express any conjectures relative to the latter transaction. Much still more important information was derived from him, concerning the manners and habits of these mountain Indians, their history, affinities, and migrations.

A copious addition to our vocabulary of words of the Pawnee language, was obtained from Ledoux, together with an account of the manners and habits of that nation.

All these, however, composed a part of the manuscripts of Mr. Say, that were subsequently carried off by deserters from our camp.

Travelled this day twenty-seven miles. The soil is becoming in many districts more exclusively sandy, the finer particles of which, driven by the wind, have formed numerous large hillocks on the opposite side of the river, precisely resembling those which are accumulated on our sea coast. On the northern side, or that which we are traversing, the prairie still offers its unvaried flatness, and cheerless sterility, so that during a portion of the day's journey, not a solitary bush seen on the river bank, relieved the monotonous scene before us.

Proceeded early on the following morning, and at the distance of twelve miles crossed a creek of clear running water, called by Bijeau, Demun's creek, from the circumstance of that hunter losing here a fine horse. At a considerable distance above, its stream was slightly fringed with timber, but at our crossing place, it was like the neighbouring part of the river, to which it contributed, entirely destitute of trees. Our journey this day was a distance of twenty-four and a half miles; towards evening, we crossed another creek, over which, being much backed up by the river, we experienced some difficulty in effecting a passage, and were obliged with this view to ascend its stream some distance. It was moderately wooded, and amongst other trees we observed the elm, (Ulmus *alata,*) and some plum trees, bearing fruit nearly ripe.

9th. During these few days past, the bisons have occurred in vast and almost continuous herds, and in such infinite numbers, as seemed to indicate the great bend of the Arkansa, as their chief and general rendezvous. As we passed along, they ran in an almost uninterrupted line before us. The course of our line being parallel to that of the Arkansa, when we travelled at the distance of a mile or two from the river, great herds of these animals were included between us and it; as the prevailing wind blew very obliquely from our left towards the river, it informed them of our presence, by the scent which it conveyed. As soon as the odour reached even the farthest animal, though at the distance of two miles on our right, and perhaps a half a mile in our rear, he betrayed the utmost alarm, would start into a full bounding run, to pass before us to the bluffs, and as he turned round the head of our line, he would strain every muscle to accelerate his motion. This constant procession of bulls, cows, and calves of various sizes, grew so familiar to us at length, as no longer to divert our view from the contemplation of other objects, and from the examination of the comparatively more minute, but certainly not less wonderful works of nature.

The white and prairie wolves more intelligent than their associates, judging by the eye of the proximity of danger, as well as by their exquisite sense of smelling, either dashed over the river, or unhesitatingly crossed our scent in the rear, and at an easy pace, or dog-trot, chose the shortest route to the bluffs.

The soil during the afternoon's ride was a deep, fine, white sand, which rendered the travelling very laborious, under the debilitating influence of an extreme temperature of 94 degrees of Fahrenheit's scale, and affected the sight by the glare of light, which it so freely reflected. The chief produce of these tracts of unmixed sand, is the sunflower, often the dense and almost exclusive occupant.

The evening encampment was formed at the junction of a small tributary with the river, at the distance of about twenty-four miles from the last mentioned creek. The very trifling quantity of timber, supported by the immediate bank of the river in this region, is almost exclusively the cottonwood; we are therefore gratified to observe on this creek, besides the elm, the walnut, mulberry and ash, which we hail with a hearty welcome, as the harbingers of a more productive territory.

CHAPTER XIV

Termination of the great bend of the Arkansa—Ietan war party—
Little Arkansa—Red rivers fork—Little Neosho and Little Verdigris.

AUGUST 10th. The great bend of the Arkansa terminates here, and as our horses have fed insufficiently for several days past, we lay by for the day, to give them an opportunity of recruiting. S.S.E. winds prevailed, and at noon exerted a considerable force; the extreme heat was 96 degrees. The hunters brought in a deer and bison.

11th. Having jerked our meat, and our horses being refreshed, we set forward at an early hour. The sandy soil and growth of sunflowers, still continues on the river bottoms, and the surface of the opposite bank, still swells into occasional hillocks of naked sand. The rice bird, (Emberiza *oryzivora*, L.) was feeding on the seeds of the sunflower, and the bald eagle was seen sailing high in the air.

We have, hitherto, generally been able to procure a sufficient supply of small drift wood for our culinary purposes, but at this noon-day halting place, we were obliged to dispatch a man across the river, to collect enough to kindle a fire. From our evening encampment, not a tree was within the range of sight.

This day was extremely warm, the mercury at three o'clock indicating 96 degrees, a temperature not decreased by a nimbus in the west, pouring rain with some thunder. In the evening, lightning played beautifully amongst the mingled cirrostratus and cumulus clouds, with which the heavens became overcast.

In the afternoon, we passed the termination of the sand hills of the opposite shore. A fine male antelope was shot by Lieutenant Swift, and a skunk was also added to our stock of provisions. Distance twenty-five miles.

12th. Passed over a very wide bottom, of which the soil where not too sandy, produces a most luxuriant growth of grasses and other plants, but the river is still in a great measure destitute of trees, of which we passed but three, during the morning's ride, and not a bush over the height of about two and a half feet, being a few willows and barren plum bushes. We were again gratified with the appearance of the *prairie fowl*, running nimbly before us through the grass, the first we have seen since leaving the Platte. The bisons have now very much diminished in number; we passed unheeded, within a few yards of a young bull, whose glazed eye, and panting respiration, showed the operation of some malady, and it was curious to observe, that though he stood erect and firmly on his legs, the wolves which fled on our approach, were acquainted with his defenceless condition, and surrounded him in considerable numbers, awaiting his dissolution, and probably watching their opportunity to accelerate it.

The afternoon was calm, and the mercury at its greatest elevation, stood at 99 degrees. Soon after our departure from our resting place of noon, we observed a large herd of bisons on our left, running with their utmost rapidity towards us, from the distant bluffs. This was a sufficient warning to put us on our guard against another unwelcome war party. Looking attentively over the surface of the country in that direction, a mounted Indian was at length observed to occupy an elevated swell of the surface, at the distance of a mile or two from us. Our peace flag was as usual, immediately displayed, to let him know that we were white people, and to induce him to come to us, whilst we halted to wait for him. Assured by this pacific display, he approached a short distance but again halted, as if doubting our intentions. Julien was then sent forward towards him, bearing the flag, to assure him of our friendship. The Indian now advanced but with much caution, and obliquely from one side to the other, as if beating against the wind. Another Indian was now observed advancing rapidly, who joined his companion. After some communication, by means of signs with Julien, to ascertain who were, they approached with gunshot of us, and halting, desired to shake hands with our chief. After this ceremony they rode to an elevated ground, in order to give information to their party, which during this short interview, we had discovered at a long distance towards the bluffs, drawn up in a line, in a conspicuous situation. One of the horsemen halted, whilst his companion rode transversely twice between him and the party. This telegraphic signal was immediately understood by the party, that consequently came on towards us. But their movement was so tardy, that it required the exertion of the greater portion of our stock of patience to wait their coming, under the ardour of the heated rays of the sun to which we were exposed. They seemed peaceably disposed, and desired to accompany us to the river bank, in order to smoke with us, but such was the scarcity of timber, that we were unable to avail ourselves of the shade of a single tree.

We now ascertained that they were an Ietan or Camanch (a band of Snake Indians,) war party, thirty-five in number, of whom five were squaws. They had marched to attack the Osages, but were surprised in their camp of night before last, by a party of unknown Indians. In the skirmish that ensued, they lost three men, and had six wounded. They, however, escaped under cover of the darkness, with the further loss of fifty-six horses and all their clothing, which were captured by the enemy. They were indeed in a naked condition, being destitute of robes, leggings, and mockasins, with nothing to cover their bodies at night, or to protect them from the influence of the sun during the day. The squaws, however, had managed to retain their clothing, and one of the warriors had preserved an article of dress, resembling a coat, half red and half blue, ornamented with beads on the sleeves and shoulders. The usual decoration of beads about the neck, and in the hair, and ears, were preserved, and one warrior only was painted with vermillion. The hair of several was matted into flat braids with red clay, and one individual had seven or eight pieces of the pearl shell, so highly valued by these Indians, suspended from his ears. In every particular of form and feature, they were undistinguishable from the Kiawas, Kaskaias, and Arrapahoes. Much attention was devoted to the wounded, who were each accommodated with a horse, of which animals eight had been fortunately retained. These objects of sympathy, were assisted in alighting from their horses with great tenderness, particularly one of them, who was shot through the body. Another of them, who was one of the two mounted spies that first approached us, had lost his brother in the late battle, and to prove the sincerity of his grief for his loss, he had cut more than one hundred parallel transverse lines on his arms and thighs, of the length of from three to four inches, deep enough to draw blood, and so close to each other, that the width of the finger could not be interposed between any two of them.

They were armed with the bow and arrow, lance and shield, and thirteen guns, but by far the greatest number carried lances.

They begged stoutly for various articles, particularly clothing, and it was found necessary to separate from them a few feet, into a distinct body, in order to be prepared to act together in case of necessity. One of us, however, occupied with the appearance of these Indians, still remained amongst them, until one of the Indians attempted to seize his gun, when a slight scuffle ensued, which terminated by violently wresting the piece from the grasp of the Indian, and warily retreating from the midst of them.

All being seated, the pipe was passed round to a few principal persons, who sat directly in front of us. Some presents were likewise laid before the partizan, consisting of a blanket, a skin to make mockasins of, a dozen knives, and five twists of tobacco; and though some of them complained aloud, and with a violent shivering gesticulation, of the cold they suffered during the night, such was the state of our stores, both public and private, that it was not thought prudent further to enlarge our bounty.

One of our number, who was earnestly occupied in endeavouring to obtain a few words of their language, but who succeeded in recording but four, heard one of them whilst in conversation with the partizan, terminate a remark with a word or phrase, so exactly similar in sound to the words how is *it*, that he almost involuntarily repeated them aloud. The speaker seemed pleased with this, and believing from the exact similarity of the sounds, that he understood the language, immediately directed his discourse to him, but was answered only by signs, denoting ignorance of the languge.

Their words seem less harsh, more harmonious, and easier of acquisition, than those of their neighbours.

Whilst thus occupied, one of the soldiers who were behind us, called our attention to an Indian who had the effrontery to seize the Kaskaia horse by the halter, and as in a former instance, was making a noose to pass over his head. This procedure was pointed out to the partizan, who taking no notice of it, the fellow was ordered in a peremptory tone of voice and unequivocal manner, to desist, which he reluctantly complied with. Thus, this horse is immediately distinguished, and recognised by all the parties we have met with, since he has been with us.

We had remained about an hour with this party, when in consequence of this conduct, of their importunateness, and some incipient symptoms of disorder amongst them, we judged it prudent to leave them, without further delay, in order to avoid a quarrel.

We therefore mounted our horses, notwithstanding the earnest solicitations of these Indians, that we would pass the night with them, probably anticipating another night attack from some unseen enemy. But hardly had we proceeded an hundred yards, when Julien's voice called our attention to the precarious situation in which he was placed. He had been by an accident detained in the rear, and being separated a short distance from the party, he was now entirely surrounded by Indians, who appeared determined to strip him of every thing, and by pulling at his blanket, bridle, &c. they had nearly unhorsed him. Several of us, of course, at this critical juncture, turned our horses to assist him, and a soldier who was nearest, prepared his rifle to begin the onset. Observing our attitude, many of the Indians were in a moment prepared for battle, by placing their arrows across their bows, and a skirmish would, no doubt, have ensued, had not the partizan, observing our determination, and influenced perhaps by gratitude for the presents he had received, called off his men from Julien, and permitted us, without any further molestation, to proceed on our way.

In consequence of the desperate situation of this party, we could not entertain a doubt, that they would attempt to capture our horses during the night, and to appropriate to themselves our personal equipments. We therefore continued our movement until a later hour than usual, and after a day's journey of twenty-two miles, during which we saw but three trees, we encamped in a selected position, and made the best arrangements in our power, to repulse a night attack. The horses were staked as near to each other, and to ourselves as possible, the packs were arranged in a semi-circular line of defence, and each man reposed on his private baggage; the guard was doubled, and we remained wakeful during the night. No alarm however occured, and on the following morning we set out early. Our way led over an extensive bottom, from three to twelve miles in breadth, producing a luxuriant growth of grasses now glittering with drops of collected dew. Crossed a creek which is destitute of timber as far as the eye can trace its course. The depth of the water being to all appearance considerable, it became necessary to seek a fording place, which was found about a mile above its confluence. It was here knee-deep, flowing with a moderate current over a bed of sand and gravel, the surface of the water being depressed only about four feet below the general level. About an hundred yards beyond its confluence, we observed a canal of water backed up from the river, which from a little distance, gave a double appearance to the creek. We remained here until a large elk, which had been shot, was cut up and the meat packed upon the horses.

At our mid-day resting place were a few trees and some elevated sand hills, but as the situation was not an eligible one for the protection of the horses from

Indian depredation, we moved a few miles further, and encamped as usual on the bank of the river. The day had been very sultry, with an extreme temperature of 95 degrees, and the evening was accompanied by a display of lightning in the north-western horizon.

The bisons are yet numerous, and the white wolves also abundant; packs of the latter are still heard to howl about our camp in the night, responding to the harsh bellowing or grunting of the bulls. Our dogs, that formerly took part in this wild and savage concert, by barking fiercely in return, no longer rouse us from our sleep by noticing it.

14th. A slight dew had fallen. The wind was S.S.E. nearly calm, and our morning's journey was arduous, in consequence of the great heat of the atmosphere. Our dogs, these two or three days past, had evidently followed us with difficulty. Cæsar, a fine mastiff and the larger of the two, this morning trotted heavily forward and threw himself down directly before the first horse in the line: the rider turned his horse aside, to avoid doing injury to the dog, but had he noticed the urgency of this eloquent appeal of the animal for a halt, it would not have passed unregarded. The dog, finding this attempt to draw attention to his sufferings unavailing, threw himself successively between two or three other horses, but still failed to excite the attention he solicited, until a soldier in the rear observed that his respiration was excessively laborious, and his tongue to a great length depended from his widely extended mouth. He therefore took the dog upon his horse before him, intending to bathe him, in the river, which, however, being at the distance of a half mile, the poor exhausted animal expired in his arms, before he reached it. To travellers, in such a country, any domesticated animal, however abject, becomes an acceptable companion, and our dogs, besides their real usefulness as guards at night, drew our attention in various ways during the day, and became gradually so endeared to us, that the loss of Cæsar was felt as a real evil.

The afternoon continued sultry, the extreme heat being 97 degrees. Towards evening, a brisk northeast wind appeared to proceed from a nimbus which was pouring rain in that direction, and produced so instantaneous and great a change in the atmospheric temperature, that we were obliged to button up to the chin; but it revived and refreshed us all. As we were now approaching a well wooded creek, we hoped soon to assuage our impatient thirst; but great was the mortification, upon arriving at the naked bank, to see a dry bed of gravel of at least fifty yards in breadth. Crossing this inhospitable tract, which appears to be occasionally deluged with water, with the intention of passing down the opposite bank of the river, we were agreeably surprised to discover a fine limpid stream of cool water, meandering through a dense growth of trees and bushes, which had before concealed it from view. Here we remarked the Honey locust [Gleditsia *triacanthus*] and Button wood,] Platanus *occidentalis*,] though the principal growth is Cotton-wood, Elm, and Ash.

This stream of water, we believe, is known to a few hunters, who have had an opportunity to visit it, by the name of Little Arkansa.

The distance of the day's journey was twenty-three miles, during which but a single prairie-dog village was seen, and proved to be the last one that occurred on the expedition. Partridges and prairie fowls were numerous.

15th. Much lightning occurred during the night, pervading the eastern heavens, nearly from north to south. At the distance of a mile from last night's encampment we crossed a wooded ravine, and, further on, a small creek, when upon looking back on our right, we saw the appearance of an Indian village, situate near the confluence of the Little Arkansa with the river. Inspired with hope we turned towards the spot, but on arriving there, it proved to be a large hunting camp, which had probably been occupied during the preceding season. It exhibited a more permanent aspect than three others that occurred on our route of the three past days; much bark covered the boweries, and a few pumpkins, watermelons, and some maize, the seeds of which had fallen from unknown hands, were fortuitously growing as well within as without the rude but frail tenements. Of the maize we collected enough to furnish out a very slight but extremely grateful repast, and the watermelons were eaten in their unripe state.

Resuming our ride we crossed three branches of a creek, in one of which two of the horses entered in a part not fordable, and as the banks were steep and miry, it was with much exertion and delay that they were recovered. Oak and Walnut trees abound upon this creek, besides, Elm, Ash, and Locust. A kingfisher [Alcedo *alcyon*] was also seen.

The extreme heat was rather more intense than that of the preceding day, the mercurial column standing for a time at 97 1/2 degrees.

The bluffs hitherto more or less remote from the bed of the river, now approached it so closely, as to render it necessary to pursue our course over them. On ascending upon the elevated prairie, we observed that it had assumed a different appearance, in point of fertility, from that which we had been familiar with, nearer to the mountains. And although the soil is not entirely concealed from the view by its produce, yet the grass is from six inches to one foot in height.

But five bisons were seen today, a privation which communicates a solitary air to this region, when compared with the teeming plains over which we have passed, and of which these animals formed the chief feature.

Our distance this day on a straight line, may be estimated at fourteen and a quarter miles, though the actual travelled distance was much more considerable.

During the space of about one month, our only regular food, besides meat, has been coarsely ground parched maize meal, of which a ration of one gill per day, was shared to each individual. This quantity was thrown into common stock and boiled with the meat, into a kind of soup. This meal is nutricious, portable, not subject to spoil by keeping a reasonable length of time, and is probably to be preferred as a substitute for bread, to other succedanea by travellers in an uncivilized country. Our store of meal, however, was now exhausted, and we were obliged to resort to a small quantity of mouldy crumbs of biscuit, which had been treasured up for time of need.

At night almost incessant lightning coruscated in the north-western horizon.

16th. Several showers of rain with much thunder and vivid lightning fell during the night; and the early morning continued showery, but the clouds were evidently undergoing the change from nimbus to cirrostratus, in this instance, the harbingers of a fine day. Several ravines occurred on the morning's journey, containing, in the deeper parts of their bed, pools of standing water. The first was of considerable size, with steep banks, and thickly wooded as far up its course as the view extended. The trees were principally oak, some walnut, elm, ash, mulberry, button-wood, cotton-wood and willow.

A horse, presented by the Kiawa chief, could not be prevailed upon to traverse this occasional water course; he evaded the attempts of several men to urge him forward, and after being thus fruitlessly detained a considerable time, the animal was shot.

If he had been abandoned, he must have perished for want of water, having been accidentally deprived of sight, and more certainly, as that fluid, so indispensable for the support of animal life, was here of difficult access.

At the ravine, which served as a halting place during the mid-day heats, we first observed the plant familiarly known in the settlements, by the name of Poke, (Phytolacca *decandra.*) reclining over the bank with its fecundity in the midst of a crowded assemblage of bushes, and partially shading a limpid pool, that mantled a rocky bed below. A large species of mushroom, (Lycoperdon,) was not uncommon, nearly equal in size to a man's head.

We have now passed the boundary of the summer bison range, and the wolves, those invariable attendants on that animal, are now but rarely seen. The antelopes also have disappeared. The river banks, as well as those of creeks, and some ravines, from near the little Arkansa, are pretty well wooded, with but few interruptions. In many parts the growth is dense, but always, as yet, strictly limited to skirting the water courses.

During the afternoon, we crossed numerous ravines, some of which, judging from the infallible indications of dried grass, and floated wood lodged on high in the croches of the trees, pour down, at certain seasons, large volumes of water, from the prairies into the river.

Near our evening encampment, but on the opposite side of the river, appeared the entrance of a large creek, of the width of ninety or a hundred yards, and of considerable depth; it seems to be well wooded, and its course is nearly parallel to the river for a great distance, before it discharges into it. This stream is called Red Fork; its waters are turbid, opake, and red; great numbers of fresh water tortoises, closely allied to the Testudo ge*ographica* of Le Sueur, inhabited the basin formed by the entrance of this stream. Immediately below its junction, the bluffs on that side are washed by the stream of the river.

The bottom land on the left bank is still confined to a narrow strip.

The sun having been, during the chief part of the day, obscured by an interrupted sheet of cirrostratus, and a brisk northeast wind prevailing, rendered the day temperate and agreeable. Travelled distance nineteen and a half miles.

Having been entirely unsuccessful in hunting since the 13th instant, we remained in our position during the morning of the succeeding day, and sent out four hunters to procure fresh meat; but, towards noon, they all returned with but three turkeys, of which two were young; they saw no deer, but much elk sign.

At two o'clock, proceeded onward, upon a slightly undulated prairie, over which the eye roves to a great distance without impediment. Indeed, the surface of the country which extends along the upper portions of the Platte and Arkansa rivers, is generally less undulated than that on either side of the Missouri.

The ravines, which intersected our path were not so extensive or profound as those of yesterday, and, in one of them, we observed the common elder (Sambucus).

Should military possession ever be taken of this elevated country, eligible positions might readily be selected for military posts, at several different points below the Little Arkansa, where the bluffs almost impend over the river. Such a position was occupied by our evening encampment. This bluff is naked, of a gently rounded surface, presenting a high, rugged, and inaccessible front upon the river, which it commands to a considerable distance, in both directions. An adequate supply of wood, for fuel and architectural purposes, is afforded by a ravine which flanks its lower side, and by other points.

Two fawns were killed during this afternoon's journey of twelve miles, and a black bear was seen. The bitter-apple vine (Cucumis,) occurred now but rarely.

18th. The inequality of the surface increases as we proceed, the undulations being now much more abrupt and considerable, belted near their summits with a rocky stratum, and assuming much the same character with those spoken of in the account of our expedition to the Konza village. This stratum, which is gray and ferruginous sandstone, contains petrifactions of marine shells, so completely assimilated with the matrix, in which they repose, and decomposing so entirely simultaneously with it, when exposed to atmospheric action, that even their generic characters cannot be recognized. Amongst other appearances, however, we observed a bivalve, which seemed to differ from Terebratula and its congeners.

At the distance of eleven miles, we crossed a small river, flowing with a very gentle current over a gravelly bed, with a breadth of fifty or sixty yards, and an extreme depth of three feet. It has been named Stinking Fork. Its western bottom is of a very considerable width, well-wooded with the beforementioned description of trees, in addition to which the hackberry (Celtis) here first appears, together with a crowded undergrowth of pea vines, nettles, and rank weeds, which obstruct the passage of the traveller. The eastern bank, upon which our noonday encampment was established, was high, rocky and precipitous, requiring considerable exertion to surmount it.

Here the organic reliquiæ are somewhat more distinct, than those which we examined on the opposite side of this subsidiary river. They are referrible to those generally extinct genera, that inhabited the great depths of the primeval ocean. Amongst them we recognized a smooth species of Anomia, of the length of half an inch, a species of *Terebratula*, an *Encrinus*, and numerous insulated spines of a Linnæan E*chinus?*

At two o'clock, pursued our journey under an extreme heat of 92 degrees, which was hardly mitigated by the gentle fanning of a slight S.E. breeze. The appearance of the country had now undergone a somewhat abrupt change. Low scrubby oaks, the prevailing trees no longer exclusively restricted, as we have hitherto observed them, to the mere margin of a water course, now were seen extending, in little clusters or oases, in the low grounds. In the ravines, which are numerous, profound, abrupt, and rocky, we observed the hickory

(Caria of Nuttall.), which had not before occured since our departure from the forests of the Missouri.

The bluffs are steep and stony, rendering the journey much more laborious to our horses, that were almost exhausted by traversing a plain country, and their hoofs already very much worn by constant friction with the grass, will, we fear, be splintered and broken, by the numerous loose and angular stones which they cannot avoid. Near the summits of some of these bluffs, the stratum of rock assumes an appearance of such remarkable regularity as to resemble an artificial wall, constructed for the support of the superincumbent soil, and remind us of the extraordinary similar products of Chinese industry, mentioned by Barrow, intended for the acquisition of horizontal garden spaces on the sides of hills and mountains.

At the distance of eight miles from the small river before mentioned, we encamped for the night, on the east side of a creek which we call Little Verdigris.

It is about 40 yards in breadth, and not so deep as the Little Neosho; its bed is gravelly, but the foot of each bank is so miry, that we experienced some difficulty in crossing. There is but a slight skirting of forest, which denotes to the distant spectator, the locality of this creek.

One of the hunters returned with the information, of his having discovered a small field of maize, occupying a fertile spot at no great distance from the camp; it exhibited proofs of having been lately visited by the cultivators; a circumstance which leads us to believe that an ascending column of smoke seen at a distance this afternoon, proceeded from an encampment of Indians, whom, if not a war party, we should now rejoice to meet. We took the liberty, agreeably to the custom of the Indians, of procuring a mess of the corn, and some small but nearly ripe watermelons, that were also found growing there, intending to recompense the Osages for them, to whom we supposed them to belong.

During the night we were visited by a slight shower of rain from the southwest, accompanied by distant thunder.

CHAPTER XV

Indian hunting encampment—Brackish water—The party pressed by hunger—
Forked tailed flycatcher—An elevated, almost mountainous range of country—
Desertion of three men—Red water.

AUGUST 19th. Several small cornfields were seen this morning along the creek. At a short distance from our place of encampment, we passed an Indian camp, that had a more permanent aspect than any we had before seen near this river. The boweries were more completely covered, and a greater proportion of bark was used in the construction of them. They are between sixty and seventy in number.

Well worn traces or paths lead in various directions from this spot, and the vicinity of the cornfields induces the belief that it is occasionally occupied by a tribe of Indians, for the purposes of cultivation as well as of hunting.

The increasing quantity of forest, partially obscuring the course of the river, renders it now no easy to task to trace its inflexions.

After proceeding twelve miles, over a rugged country, at present destitute of water, we were rejoiced to find at our dining place, a puddle of stagnant rain water, which had been protected from the action of the sun, by the elevated and almost impending bank of the ravine, in which it was situate, and which, though "mantled o'er with green," was yet cool and grateful to our pressing thirst.

We left our cool and shady retreat, and again betook ourselves to the prairies, under a temperature of 96°. Our remaining dog, *Buck*, had been, since the regretted death of his companion, treated with all the kindness and attention due to an humble friend. He was very frequently accommodated with a ride on horseback before one of the men when he betrayed unusual exhaustion. But, notwithstanding all such attention, for which he seemed touched with feelings of gratitude, he experienced Cæsar's fate and was necessarily abandoned.

The evening camp was pitched upon a luxuriant grassy plain of the margin of the river. On tasting the water it was perceived to be slightly saline, though the proportion of that condiment was not so considerable as to render it unpleasant to the palate. This saline intermixture is, no doubt, due to the Red Fork, inasmuch as the river, above the entrance of that stream, appeared entirely destitute of saline contamination, and no stream enters on this side in which the slightest apparent degree of brackishness is to be detected by the taste.

The cotton tree is less numerous in this vicinity, than we have seen it higher up the river, and being intermixed with other trees, forms but an insignificant feature of the forest.

20th. Heavy rain, accompanied with much thunder and lightning, commenced early in the night, and continued until daylight this morning. Hunters, who had been sent out, detained us until nine o'clock, when they returned unsuccessful; in consequence of which, and of our having made a sparing meal last eavening, on a turkey that had been shot, we were obliged to depart fasting on our way.

The ravines were muddy, and their banks slippery in consequence of the rain; we had, however, the good fortune to fall upon an Indian trace, which complied with our proper direction, and which indicated the best points at which these gullies might be passed. In its course it conducted us to a creek which was pouring down a torrent of water. Here was an encampment that had obviously been occupied within a day or two, there being fresh rinds of water-mellons strewed about it.

One of the party, on attempting to cross this creek, was thrown into the water, in consequence of his horse having plunged suddenly beyond his depth; he, however, avoided being carried down with the rapid current by seizing the depending bough of a tree; the horse also was fortunately saved. By taking a different direction we all passed over without further casualty. But we were unable to trace any farther the party that we thus ascertained to have so recently preceded us, their footsteps being here entirely obliterated by the rain.

At the distance of sixteen miles, we encamped at an early hour on the bank of the river, and sent out hunters, who, however, after examining the vicinity, returned unsuccessful. Our three meals were, therefore, again, by stern necessity, reduced to a single frugal one, and our table, the soil, was set with a few mouldy biscuit crumbs boiled in a large quantity of water, with the nutricious addition of some grease.

Julien, who had been despatched for the peace flag, which was casually left at a ravine, to our great satisfaction returned with a skunk, or pole-cat, that he had fortunately killed. This we determined to preserve for a feast to-morrow.

21st. One of our horses strayed away last night, and could not now be found; we, therefore, set out without him, and as usual without breakfasting. The Indian trace was again discovered, and pursued abut nine miles to the dining place at noon. Here we were obliged to have recourse for food to a little treasured store of dried bison meat, which when all issued, amounted to the pittance of two ounces per man; this added to the *soup maigre* of the skunk, and a half pint of the crumbs of bread, afforded a tolerably good though far from abundant meal.

Proceeded on under an extreme atmospheric temperature of ninety degrees. Several deer were seen, but they proved to be so shy, that our hunters, perhaps through over eagerness, did not succeed in approaching them within gunshot. After accomplishing a distance of ten miles we pitched our camp on the river bank. Here the stream turns rather abruptly to the east, after having preserved a southerly and south of west direction for a considerable distance. A copious stream of water, called Neshetongo, or Grand Saline, flows into the river at this point, nearly opposite to our camp.

Supped on a few bread crumbs boiled in water. A black wolf, the first seen since our departure from the Missouri, made his appearance in the distance.

22nd. Three of the horses having strayed, detained us until eight o'clock, when a fall of rain commenced, which continued during the morning, and wet us thoroughly to the skin. A few hostile Indians, aware of our condition, might, perhaps, have disapppointed our hopes of a safe return to the settlements, inasmuch as the rain had rendered our arms and ammunition completely unfit for use, and left us defenceless.

A note, like that of the prairie dog, for a moment induced the belief that a village of the marmot was near; but we were soon undeceived by the appearance of the beautiful Tyrannus *forficatus* in full pursuit of a crow. Not at first view recognizing the bird, the fine, elongated tail plumes, occasionly diverging in a furcate manner and again closing together to give direction to the aerial evolutions of the bird, seemed like the extraneous processes of dried grass, or twigs of a tree, adventitiously attached to the tail, and influenced by currents of wind. The feathered warrior flew forward to a tree, from whence at our too near approach he descended to the earth at a little distance, continuing at intervals his chirping note. The bird seems to be rather rare in this region, and as the very powder within the barrels of our guns was wet, we were obliged to content ourselves with only a distant view of the bird.

The river margin, on which we held our course, has narrow and fertile, supporting a tolerably thick growth of mossy cup oaks, with walnut, cotton-wood, elm, and much underwood, through which it is sometimes rather difficult to force a passage. The river is now more serpentine in its course, than it was remarked to be nearer the mountains; but it is here wide, and still thickly studded with sand bars.

One of the hunters rescued the body of a small fawn from the wolves, that had killed and embowelled it. This afforded us all a good dinnner; and as we had, in the morning, drawn upon our almost exhausted store of sweet corn for a gill to each man, as a breakfast, we are to-day comparatively well fed.

Near our evening encampment were the remains of a large Indian hunting camp.

Our distance today nineteen miles.

On the following day we set out again fasting, and pursued our journey over a beautiful, open, level bottom. The bluffs on our left, of but moderate height, were partially clothed with oaks, and the river on the right skirted with the cotton tree. But a single ravine crossed our morning route. At eleven o'clock the mercury in the thermometer indicated 93 degrees.

At the distance of about two miles from our resting place of noon, we again halted, and pitched the tents in anticipation of a violent storm, as a nimbus of an unusually menacing aspect, was imposingly announced by wind and thunder, and seemed rapidly approaching from the south. In order to make amends for this delay, the hunters were sent out to endeavour to procure some food. But as the storm passed round, they were soon recalled, bringing with them the seasonable supply of four turkeys. On the subsequent part of the day we passed over a small stream, which we call Bitter-apple creek, with but a slow moving current, of the width of about ten yards, and three feet deep. Its bed was so muddy, that two of the pack-horses were mired, but were finally brought safely out. We then ascended into the prairie, where after labouring over an almost continual succession of ravines, we passed down to the river bank, and encamped for the night, having travelled about 20 miles. Numerous deer were seen today, but they were very shy.

The last Bitter-apple vine that occurred on the expedition was seen today. We were once again saluted by the notes of the Blue jay, and the Pine warbler, (Sylvia *pinus*) also occurred.

24th. As the high prairies offered almost continually a succession of steep and rugged ravines, which called for too much exertion from our horses to pass them, it was determined to endeavour to force our way through the undergrowth of the bottom. This we found to be now so intricate, that in many places it was really difficult to force a passage through the intertwined briars, and climbing plants. Our progress was however, at length altogether interrupted by a deep and miry slough of the river, over which no ford could be found. Fortunately, however, the sandy bed of the river itself offered a sufficiently firm footing to enable us to pass round the obstacle. Tired of the brambles, we again sought the prairie, and ascending an elevated hill, enjoyed a fine view of the river in its meanders, to a great distance, but the place of destination, Belle Point, which we now all anxiously looked out for, was not yet in sight.

A journey of 9 3-4 miles brought us to a large stream of clear water, but hardly perceptible current, passing over a bed of rock and mud; the banks were steep and high, and afforded us a very pleasant resting place during the presence of the mid-day heads. A flock of paroquets flew over our heads, uttering their loud note, with their usual loquacity. The kingfisher was flying from one withered support to another over the surface of the creek, and occasionally darting into the water in pursuit of some little scaly victim; and a large white crane, (Ardea *egretta*, Wilson,) stalked, with slow and measured strides, in the shallows of the creek. A Glass snake, (Ophisaurus *ventralis*) approached us, and was captured.

In the afternoon, small cumulous clouds arose in the horizon, and we again put forward, under a temperature of 95 degrees. Three miles farther, a large ravine occurred, containing much water in the deeper parts of its bed, but dry at intervals; it is wooded as far as we can trace it with the eye, and in the season of floods it must discharge a large volume of water at its confluence, which is distant about five miles from the creek crosssed this morning.

We passed by several singular, natural elevations, with conical summits, and halted early to hunt, for which purpose four men were sent out, who returned with two turkeys, which furnished a very light supper.

25th. Remained encamped, in order to give the hunters an opportunity to procure some game. We had nothing for breakfast or dinner, and as our meals a few days past, have been few and light, we have become impatient under the pressure of hunger; a few fresh water muscles, (Unio) and two or three small fishes, and a tortoise, which had been found in the mud of the ravine, were roasted and eaten, without that essential condiment, salt, of which we had been for some time destitute. The hunters so anxiously looked for, at length returned, bringing but three ducks, (Anas *sponsa*) one of them had shot down three deer, but they all escaped.

As we have no idea of our distance from Belle Point, and know not what extent of country we are doomed to traverse in the state of privation to which we have of late been subjected, we have selected from our miserable horses, an individual to be slaughtered for food, in case of extremity of abstinence, and upon which, although very poor, we cannot forebear to cast an occasional wishful glance.

Bijeau, before he parted from us, urged by his wishes for our safety, drew for our information, a sketch of the country over which we had to pass as far as he had travelled in that direction, on a former occasion, which sketch was terminated by two large streams, entering the river near to each other, and diverging in the opposite direction. As the remarkable relative course of these two streams as represented by Bijeau, corresponded to sufficient exactness with the representation of the Verdigris and Grand rivers, which terminated the sketch which Major Long drew to depict the country from Belle Point upwards; we believed that by joining the two sketches, we had a complete view of the country before us as far as the settlements. Bijeau's sketch proved to be a pretty faithful transcript of the country as far as the two water courses that we passed on the 18th inst., which as they terminated his map, we then supposed were of course, the Verdigris and Grand rivers. But not being able to recognise in Major Long's draft one single feature of the region we have since traversed, we finally concluded either that we had not yet arrived at the true Verdigris river, or, that we had passed by our place of destination without perceiving it. In this state of uncertainty it was determined to continue our course with as much speed as the exhausted situation of our horses would permit, with the hope of soon arriving at some settlement where we might obtain the proper direction.

The greatest heat of the day was 97 degrees. Two hunters were this evening sent forwards to encamp, and hunt early in the morning.

Another flock of paroquets were seen to-day.

26th. Penetrated through an intricate bottom of bushes interlaced by vines and briars, the timber chiefly oak. The hunters had procured nothing, but Lieut. Swift had the good fortune to kill a fine buck, and one of the hunters afterwards, a turkey. These were a happy alleviation to us, and at our noon halting place we enjoyed the rare luxury of a full meal. At this position was a large ravine containing much water, of the depth of 2 1-2 feet, and width of twenty or twenty-five yards, but without any visible current; its bed was muddy, and in some places rocky.

The journey of the afternoon was equally intricate with that of the morning; our way led along the fertile but narrow eastern margin of the ravine, or, as it would be called in the settlements of the Arkansa, *bayou*; and immediately on our left ascended the abrupt and rocky ridge of the bluff.

After a fatiguing journey of nineteen miles, we encamped on the river bank, in a fine clear bottom, surrounded semicircularly by the forest. The plum bushes, which abound in the country through which we have for several days been travelling, are generally killed, probably by conflagration, their black and defoliated branches strongly contrasting with the verdure around them; to-day, however, we met with some which had escaped uninjured,, and which afforded a few ripe plums.

27th. The river bottom becoming very narrow, obliged us to ascend upon the high grounds, which we found to be little less than mountainous, often rocky and steep, and as usual, intersected by profound ravines. Mr. Swift having succeeded in killing another deer, we halted, after a journey of twelve miles, in order to jerk the meat which we now possessed, and to rest the horses, whose feet were bruised and broken by fragments of rock.

The corporal did not join us until evening. The horse which he had rode became so exceedingly feeble as to be no longer able to support the weight of his rider, who therefore dismounted, and attempted to drive him on before him. In spite of his utmost endeavours the horse proceeded so slowly that the corporal was obliged to abandon him, in order to seek our trail that he had lost on the rocks over which we had passed. Not being able to regain the trail, and supposing we had directed our course towards the river, he wandered along its margin to a considerable distance, until almost exhausted with fatigue and vexation he at length ascended a high hill that commanded a view of the country around, and had the satisfaction to see a column of smoke rising above the forest at a distance. This sure indication he had pursued until, approaching with much caution, he was overjoyed to ascertain that his beacon was no other than the smoke from our meat drying process. Supposing that the horse would be able to travel after having rested during the night, the corporal was directed to accompany Julien to the spot where he had been left, and to bring him on, in the morning.

We availed ourselves of this leisure time to mend our horse gear, clothes, and mockasins.

In the evening a slight fall of rain took place, accompanied by thunder in the north east, which at night became heavy and loud.

28th. The horse that gave out yesterday was brought in, together with two others that had strayed, and for which we were hunting. We were now traversing an elevated and uneven ridge of country, which at many points may be safely estimated at five hundred feet above the surface of the river, and wooded to a great distance from that stream.

In the afternoon having descended to the river, we again laboured through the difficulties of dense underwood which such productive soils usually present, until towards evening, when we had the happiness to see a well worn Indian path, which had been interrupted by the river, and now took a direction towards our left. Wishing to pursue this route as well for the facility of travelling, as with the hope of soon arriving at some Indian town, we readily persuaded ourselves that it deviated from the course we were pursuing, only in compliance with the inequalities of the country. With little hesitation, therefore, we struck into the path, and night gathered around us before we threw ourselves, supperless, upon the ground to repose, after a fatiguing march of about twenty-one miiles, during which the greatest degree of heat was 92°.

Several small flocks of the common wild-pigeons flew by us both yesterday and to-day, in a southerly direction.

29th. After some detention in seeking a troublesome horse that had strayed, we again proceeded forward fasting. This abstinence, to which we had been several times subjected, affects one of our party in a singular and uniform manner: his voice becomes hollow-toned, and his hearing much impaired, a state that is popularly known, as he expresses it, by the phrase of *the almonds of the ears* being *down*.

We pursued the Indian path a considerable distance this morning, but as its course continued to diverge from the river, and we were fearful of deviating too far, we abandoned it, and by an oblique course endeavoured to regain the river. Here, however, the undergrowth being almost impervious, induced our return to the path, which we again attained near an Indian hunting camp of the past season, situate in a beautiful prairie, near a gently swelling hill. Here finding a little water in a ravine puddle, we halted, and served out a stinted ration of dried meat to each individual, instead of dinner, which so far from gratifying, tended to stimulate our desire for food.

Having been some days entirely destitute of tobacco in any shape, those of the party who are habituated to the use of it experience an additional and formidable privation. One of the men, who was erroneously supposed to have still a remnant of the precious stimulant in his possession, was heard to reply to an earnest and most humble petition for a small taste of it, or to be allowed to apply his tongue to it, "every man chaws his own tobacco, and them that has'nt any, chaws leaves."

During the prevalence of the greatest heat of the day, which was ninety-four degrees, we again set forward, and passed over a gently undulated surface supporting an open forest of young and scrub oak, intermixed with hickory. In the course of a few miles, we arrived at the edge of this forest, which here crowned a much elevated region. It was in fact higher, in proportion to the surface before us, than any other portion of the country we had seen on this side of the mountains. The eye, from this height, roved over a vast distance of prairie, and comparatively plain, country; and it was evident that we had now passed the hilly, and even mountainous, region which we have of late, been traversing. A few hills still interrupted the continuity of surface below, more particularly on the right of the landscape towards the river. Not a human being was yet to be perceived, nor a single trait indicative of their present existence. It seemed, for a moment, that our little cavalcade alone was endowed with the vital principle, and that the vegetable world held a solitary and silent dominion. Belle Point still evaded our sight; we might have passed it, or it might still have been very far before us, yet we could no longer struggle through the tangled underwood that inclosed the river, nor pick our passage amongst the loose stones of the bluffs, in order to preserve an uninterrupted view of the bank of the river, upon which that post is established. From this position the path winds rather abruptly downward, and at a little distance on the plain, conducted us through an abandoned Indian hunting camp.

The horse that gave out Sunday, having been since both packed and rode, this afternoon sunk under his rider, to the ground, and resisted our efforts to induce him to rise. As he appeared to be entirely exhausted we reluctantly abandoned him. He had been a sprightly, handsome, and servicable animal, and was chosen from a considerable number of horses, and presented to Mr. Say, by Major O'Fallon, when at the Pawnee villages.

After a day's journey of twenty-two miles, a favorable situation for an encampment offering timely, at a site which appeared to have been occupied by a tribe of Indians, during the late winter, induced us to pitch the tents, and prepare for the night. Lieutenant Swift, whose dexterity as a marksman had previously relieved us in times of need, now succeeded in killing a turkey for our evening meal.

30th. We pursued the path about ten miles further, with the hope of its soon terminating at some Indian village, but as it continued to diverge too widely from our apparent true course, we once again relinquished it, and turned towards the river, which we expected to regain in the course of a few miles, by tracing down the opposite bank of a large ravine, which now presented itself.

At our resting place of noon the banded rattlesnake, (C. *horridus*,) occurred; and five young turkeys were procured by the hunters.

Resuming our journey, it soon became obvious that the ravine we were tracing did not discharge into the Arkansa, but into some large tributary to that river, and which from an elevated ground we could distinctly see meandering to a great distance on the left. Another Indian path was now discovered, which, by its direction seemed to comply with our proper course. It led us to recross the ravine with its most luxuriant growth of trees, bushes, and weeds. On emerging from this intricate maze, we observed a large column of smoke arising in the southeast, as if from the conflagration of some entire prairie. This occurrence, combined with the effects of a large *burning* in the vicinity of our evening encampment, that seemed very recent, and the appearance of the well-worn pathways, inspired us with a renewed expectation of soon meeting with human beings, and of arriving at some permanent Indian village.

The highest temperature of the day was ninety-five degrees. Our distance this afternoon was ten miles.

31st. We arose early, and on looking at the horses that were staked around the camp, three of the best were missing. Supposing that they had strayed to a distance, inquiry was made of the corporal respecting them; who answered that three of the men were absent, probably in pursuit of them, and added, that one of those men who chanced to be last on guard, had neglected to awaken him to perform his duty on the morning watch. Forster, a faithful, industrious soldier, and who, in performing the culinary services for the party, had not lately been laboriously occupied, now exclaimed that his knapsack had been robbed; and upon examining our baggage, we were mortified to perceive that it had been overhauled and plundered during the night. But we were utterly astounded to find that our saddlebags, which contained our clothing, Indian presents, and manuscripts, had also been carried off.

This greatest of all privations that could have occurred within the range of possibility, suspended for a time every exertion, and seemed to fill the measure of our trials, difficulties, and dangers.

It was too obvious that the infamous absentees, Nowland, Myers, and Bernard, had deserted during the night, robbing us of our best horses, and of our most important treasures.

We endeavoured in vain to trace them, as a heavy dew had fallen since their departure, and rested upon every spear of grass alike, and we returned from the fruitless search to number over our losses, with a feeling of disconsolateness, verging on despair.

Our entire wardrobe, with the sole exception of the rude clothing on our persons, and our entire private stock of Indian presents, were included in the saddlebags. But their most important contents were all the manuscripts of Mr. Say and Lieutenant Swift completed during the extensive journey from Engineer Cantonment to this place. Those of the former consisted of five books, viz., one book of observations on the manners and habits of the mountain Indians, and their history, so far as it could be obtained from the interpreters; one book of notes on the manners and habits of animals, and descriptions of species; one book containing a journal; two books containing vocabularies of the languages of the mountain Indians; and those of the latter consisted of a topographical journal of the same portion of our expedition. All these being utterly useless to the wretches who now possessed them, were probably thrown away upon the ocean of prairie, and consequently the labour of months was consigned to oblivion, by these uneducated vandals.

Nowland, Myers, and Bernard, though selected, with others, by the officers of Camp Missouri, with the best intentions, for the purpose of accompanying our party, proved worthless, indolent, and pusillanimous from the beginning; and Nowland, we ascertained, was a notorious deserter in two former instances.

This desertion and robbery occurred at a most unfortunate period, inasmuch as we were all much debilitated, and their services consequently the less dispensable on that account, in the attentions necessarily due to the pack-horses, in driving these animals, loading and unloading them, &c.

We resumed our journey, upon our Indian pathway, in silence; and at the distance of sixteen miles we passed through the river forest, here three miles in width, and once again encamped upon the bank which overlooks the Arkansa. No trace of Belle Point, nor any appearance of civilization was yet in view. But we were all immediately struck with the change in the appearance of the water in the river. No longer of that pale clay colour to which we have been accustomed, it has now assumed a reddish hue, hardly unlike that of the blood of the human arteries, and is still perfectly opake from the quantity of an earthy substance of this tint, which it holds in suspension. Its banks and bars are formed from depositions of the same colour. This extraneous pigment has been contributed by some large stream flowing in from the opposite side, and which, in consequence of our late aberrance, we had not seen.

The hunters returned without game, but bringing us a few grapes, and some unripe persimmons, all of which were eaten.

The extreme heat of the day was ninety-five degrees, and in the evening thunder and lightning occurred in the western horizon.

CHAPTER XVI

The party meet with Osage Indians—Some account of this nation—
Manner of taking wild horses.

SEPTEMBER 1st. The hunters, who had been sent out at daylight, returned at 8 o'clock again unsuccessful, but after a journey of about three hours
we had an opportunity to appease the cravings of hunger, and halted to regale
ourselves on a small fawn that was shot. At three o'clock proceeded on, under
the extreme atmospheric temperature of the day of ninety-six degrees, and as
the current of air was scarcely perceptible, the day was, as usual, very sultry. We
were, at length, very agreeably surprised by hearing an Indian whoop, in our
rear, and, on looking back, a mounted Indian was observed upon a rising piece
of ground, contemplating our movements. The usual ceremony of displaying
our flag and deputing an individual to assure him of the pacific nature of our
mission, induced him readily to approach; and after some communication he
consented to encamp with us. He informed us that he was the son of Clermont,
principal chief of the Osages of the Oaks, or *Osage des Ghenes* of the French
traders, in whose territories we then were. Their village was at the distance of
about fifteen miles, but by far the greater portion of the inhabitants of it were

now on their way to the river, for the purpose of hunting. They had heard the reports of the guns of our hunters, and agreeably to their custom had sent out spies, of whom he was one, to ascertain from whom the sound proceeded; that he had fallen upon our trail, and consequently had no difficulty in finding us, and was moreover glad to see us. Indeed his conduct proved that he entertained towards us the most friendly and generous disposition. He was not tardy in ascertaining our wants, nor parsimonious in his attempts to relieve them. He passed his pipe around, a ceremony which signifies just as much, amongst these people, as the drinking to friendship and good fellowship does among the lower classes in civilized society; but to us, who had been so long deprived of the use of tobacco, it was an intrinsic gratification. He then laid before us some fine ripe blue plums; and remarking that the small portion of fawn meat, that constituted all our store, was very lean, he said that he would soon bring some more palatable food, and leaving his pipe and tobacco-pouch on the ground, with the request that we would partake freely of both, he disappeared in the forest.

It was dusk when he returned, with a fat buck hanging in pieces from his saddle; he was accompanied by five or six young warriors. These young men had visited the opposite side of the river, where they had discovered a herd of bisons, and as they were hastening back to Clermont with the intelligence, they observed our trail, which they mistook for that of a Pawnee war party, and were exerting their utmost speed homeward when they met with our friendly Indian, who smiled as he informed us of their mistake.

The remnant of our fawn had been cooked, and was partly eaten on their arrival, when they readily accepted our invitation to partake of it. In return for which, when their meat was prepared, the whole was set before us, and they respectfully waited until we were satisfied.

We now ascertained our position with respect to the settlements. We were within about four days' march of Belle Point, and the next large stream we would cross was the Verdigris.

Previously to retiring to rest the Osages performed their vespers, by chanting, in a wild and melancholy tone, a kind of hymn to the Master of Life.

Very remote lightning in the south-eastern horizon.

2nd. Our guests awakened early, and one of them retiring a short distance from his companions, began the well known ceremony common to this nation, of crying aloud with a voice of lamentation, intended probably as an invocation to the departed spirit of a relative or friend.

Messengers were despatched before sunrise to Clermont's camp, to inform that chief of the proximity of a party of white men on this side of the river, and of bisons on the other; and soon afterwards the remainder of our guests, with the exception of one that concluded to remain with us, departed to hunt.

Other Indians, attracted by curiosity, visited us in the course of the day, one of whom informed us that three men, whose appearance corresponded with the description of our deserters, were now at the village, and that the approaching hunting party, being already apprised of their character, Clermont, who was himself with the party, had forthwith despatched an order to the village to have them detained there, until the decision of our chief respecting them should be known.

The most welcome news induced Lieut. Swift and Julien, accompanied by Clermont's brother and two or three of the young warriors who were present, to set out immediately for the village, in order to seize the recreants, and conduct them to camp. Thus we were inspired with the most sanguine expectations not only of retrieving our losses, but also of subjecting the offenders to that punishment which was their due.

In the afternoon we had the company of numerous Indians from the hunting party, and an individual that left our camp early in the morning in pursuit of the bisons on the opposite side of the river, brought a horse-load of very lean meat. Their demeanour was pacific and kind, and they appeared disposed to serve us. They brought a considerable quantity of plums of a blue colour, and exceedingly agreeable taste, which were collected from trees growing in the adjacent forest. Our cook having intimated to one of them our want of salt, he instantly mounted his horse, and after a short absence, returned with a supply. One half of the hunting party was soon afterwards observed fording the river in a long line about a mile below our camp; the other portion we were told would cross the river at some point above the camp to-morrow morning, and would act in concert with the others, so as to surround the herd of bisons that they were now going in pursuit of.

In the evening Mr. Swift returned unsuccessful. When he left us in the morning he directed his course to Clermont's camp, which he found in the prairie, near a small puddle of impure water. He was very cordially and graciously received by the chief, who invited him to partake of some food. He assured Mr. Swift of his regret at being unable to induce any of his young men to pursue our fugitives, who, as he had but then been informed, departed from the village early in the morning. This unwillingness on the part of his young men, arose from their extreme anxiety to hunt the bisons, that were at this time unusually near, an enjoyment which they would on no account relinquish. He likewise regretted that he was at present so circumstanced as to be unable to comply with his wishes, by visiting our camp. "But" said Clermont, "if your chief will visit me at my camp, which will be established near yours in the evening, I will treat him well; I will present him with as much maize and dried meat as he wants; I will moreover furnish him with young men to serve as guides, and a horse or two if he wants them, to aid in the transportation of the baggage." Lieut. Swift assured him that we were much in want of such assistance as he had proffered, and that on our arrival at Belle Point his generosity should be requited; but the chief declared his indifference to any recompense for such services. Mr. Swift further learned that the deserters during their short stay at the village, had traded freely for provisions, with the trinkets they found in our saddle bags, and although dressed in our clothing, they appeared to imagine themselves suspected to be not what they seemed.

This idea was, in truth, well founded, for the Indians observing that they retained their guns constantly within their grasp, even when partaking of the hospitality of the different lodges, believed them to have committed some crime or outrage in consequence of which, they regarded themselves as unsafe in any asylum.

As the camp was about to move when Mr. Swift arrived there, he now took his leave to return, but inadvertently deviating from the proper course, he struck the river several miles above our camp. Clermont, meeting with his trail, perceived at once that he had gone astray, and immediately deputed one of his sons to pilot him to our camp.

In the acceptation of these Indians, white man and trader appear to be synonymous, and many of those who visited us, importuned us much to trade for leather, dried meat, pumpkins, both dried and fresh, &c.; in exchange for which, they desired our blankets, and even the clothing from our bodies.

The superiority of the hunting qualifications of the Indians over those of our hunters, was obvious, in an instance which occurred to-day. The corporal went to the forest for the purpose of killing a deer, and it was not long before an Indian who accompanied him pointed out one of those animals in a favorable situation. The corporal fired, but thought he had missed his object. The Osage, however, insisted that the animal was mortally wounded, and advanced forward a very considerable distance, where our hunter could see nothing of the usual sign of blood, or trodden grass, and found the victim dead upon the ground. One of the party, on an another occasion, saw an Osage shoot at a deer running, and wound him, another Indian, at a short distance further, fired at the same deer, and brought him down, both, of course, with single ball.

The extreme heat of the day was 95 degrees.

3rd. Our chief, who, upon the invitation of Clermont visited the Indian camp, accompanied by Julien and Clermont's son, returned this morning with two other sons of that chief, and a handsome young squaw, wife of one of them. His reception was not equal to his anticipations; Clermont, however, and one of his sons each presented a skin of maize, but that chief could not realize the almost splendid offers he had made us of guides and horses.

Word was brought to Clermont, that the information received yesterday of our deserters having departed from the village was incorrect, and that they still remained there. This induced at once, the offer of every thing they were in possession of, with the exception of the manuscripts alone, to any persons who should bring them to our camp. With this liberal offer, Clermont himself, accompanied by Julien, set out for the village to arrest them, but on their way, a messenger whom they met, assured them, that they had actually and finally departed this morning. Thus all our hopes of recovering our lost property vanished.

The stature of the Osages that fell under our observation was by no means superior to that of the Missouri Indians, and in very many instances, their form exhibited a beautiful symmetry. They do not seem to differ in point of features or colour from the Indians just mentioned. But the custom seems to be the more general in this nation of shaving the head, so as to leave only a scalp on the back part and above, which is, as usual, ornamented with silver plates, broaches, and feathers.

Their dresses and decorations are very similar to those of the Omawhaws, Otoes, and Konzas, but from their proximity to the settlements, they are furnished with a greater proportion of manufactured articles from the whites.

Their government, so far as we could ascertain, was of the same description with that of the other nations, and their manners, though perhaps less fierce and warlike, seem to be, with the exception of their vociferous matins, not very essentially distinct.

They have the usual armature of the bow and arrow, tomahawk, war-club, and scalping knife, but a large proportion of them have fusees, and we saw but very few who bore the lance and shield. They are freely branded by the Missouri Indians with the epithet of cowards. They are at present in amity with the Sauks and Foxes, and their friendship with the Konzas, with whom they freely intermarry, seems to have been uninterrupted since the expedition of Lieut. Pike.

The horses belonging to the Osages are by much the best we have seen amongst the Indian nations, and they are kept in the best order. The Indians generally of this country, appear to be excellent connoisseurs of horses, and to perceive any defects in them with a remarkable readiness. One of Clermont's sons possessed a very fine horse, for which the Kaskaia horse was offered, but the exchange was refused.

Horses are the object of a particular hunt to the Osages. For the purpose of obtaining these animals, which in their wild state preserve all their fleetness, they go in a large party to the country of the Red, or Canadian river, where these animals are to be found in considerable numbers. When they discover a gang of horses they distribute themselves into three parties, two of which station themselves at different and proper distances on the route, which, by previous experience, they know the horses will most probably take, when endeavouring to escape. This arrangement being completed, the first party commences the pursuit in the direction of their colleagues, at whose position they at length arrive. The second party then continues the chase with fresh horses, and pursues the fugitives to the third party, which generally succeeds in so far running them down as to noose and capture a considerable number.

The name of this nation, agreeably to their own pronunciation, is Waw-sash-e; but our border inhabitants speak of them under the names of *Huz-zaws* and *O-saw-ses*, as well as Osages. The word *Wawsashe* of three syllables has been corrupted by the French traders into *Osage*, and though the spelling of the latter has been retained by the Americans, we have still further swerved from the original, by pronouncing the word agreeably to the genius of our language.

The lodges or huts of their villages are yet covered with the bark of trees, but it is probable that they will adopt the more permanent and preferable architecture of dirt lodges, used by most of the Missouri nations.

As we proceeded to load our horses, at ten o'clock, in order to continue our journey, we perceived that several small articles, of no great value, had been pilfered from us, by our visitors. These are the only losses we have sustained from Indian theft during this protracted journey. . . .

CHAPTER XVII

*Verdigris river—Mr. Glen's trading house—New species of lizard—
Neosho, or Grand river—Salt works—Large spider—Illinois creek—
Ticks—Arrival at Belle Point.*

SEPTEMBER 4th. The face of the country exhibited the same appearance as that of yesterday's journey, until we arrived at a dense forest, which we supposed to margin the *Verdigris* river, or Was-su-ja of the Osages. There being no trace to direct us, we were obliged to penetrate the intricate undergrowth as we might, and after a tedious and laborious passage of something more than three miles, we attained, probably by a somewhat circuitous route, the river which we had so long vainly sought. At our crossing place the stream was probably eighty yards wide, and one foot in depth, running with a brisk stream over a rocky bed, though above and below, as far as we examined, the depth of water is much more considerable. This river is more rapid and pellucid than any tributary we have passed on this side of the mountain streams, and during the season of floods its volume is augmented by the tribute of those ravines over which we passed on the 29th and 30th ult. Late in the afternoon we struck the Osage trace leading from their village to the trading establishment, at the confluence of the Verdigris, whither we now directed our course. Our evening encampment was at a small ravine, in which were some plum bushes, bearing fruit yet unripe, of a fine red colour, and without the slightest exaggeration, as closely situate on many of the branches, as onions when tied on ropes of straw for exportation.

Distance 17 3-4 miles. Extreme heat 90 degrees.

5th. At ten o'clock we arrived at Mr. Glen's trading house near the Verdigris, about a mile above its confluence with the Arkansa. We were hospitably received by the interpreter, a Frenchman, who informed us that Mr. Glen was absent on a visit to Belle Point. In reply to our inquiries respecting the best and shortest route to the place of our destination, two Americans who were present, assured us that there was a path the whole distance, so obvious as not to be mistaken, and that they were so much occupied as to be unable to spare any one to pilot us. Unfortunately, however, for our informant, a military cap which was discovered suspended from a bean, betrayed him to be a soldier belonging to the garrison of Belle Point, temporarily employed at this place. When asked by what right he had entered into any other engagements whilst in the service of the United States, he replied, that he had the permission of his officers, but as he could not show a *permit* he was ordered to join our suite forthwith, as a guide, and to assist with the pack horses.

The interpreter informed us, that the distance to the town of the Osages of the Oaks is about fifty-five miles; from thence to the village of the second band of Osages, called the Little Osages, residing near the Neosho, or Grand river, more than sixty miles; thence to the village of the third band, called the Great Osages, resident near the head waters of the Osage river three miles. He assured us that Clermont had then four wives, and thirty-seven children! a number doubtless unprecedented amongst the North American Indians, and which may probably be attributed to this chief by mistake. We also learned that at the distance of twenty-five miles, was a copious salt spring, lately worked with the permission of the Indians, but at present it is abandoned, and the apparatus removed. Mr. Nuttall in his interesting journal of travels in the Arkansa territory has given an excellent account of this saline. It produces agreeably to his statement, under the management of the company, 1 bushel of salt, from 80 gallons of water, and 120 bushels were manufactured in a week.

A beautiful species of lizard, (agama) is occasionally met with in this territory. It runs with great swiftness. The forms of its scales, their arrangement and proportions, considerably resemble those of *Polychrus marmorata*, with the exception of the caudal ones, the series of which are equal, and the scales near the tip of the tail only are mucronate. A band over the shoulders somewhat resembles that of *Stelio querts-paleo*.

In addition to our usual fare served upon the earth, we enjoyed the luxury of wild honey, and Indian corn or maize bread, spread upon a table, and felt, perhaps, a little of that elation which the possession of a new garment gives to the beaux, when we found ourselves mounted on stools and benches around it.

The Sassafras, (Laurus *sassafras*) occurred this morning, and soon after our departure from the trading house we saw the Cane, (Miegia *macrosperma*) and were soon involved in a dense cane brake. Here we were hardly fanned by a breath of air, and during the prevalence of the extreme heat of the day, which was 96 degrees, the state of the atmosphere was extremely oppressive. A short ride brought us to the *Neosho*, or *Grand river*, better known to the hunters by the singular designation of the *Six Bulls*.

It enters the Arkansa very near to the confluence of the Verdigris, and at the ripple, which offers us a facility of crossing, is about 80 yards wide, the water clear, above and below, moving with a gentle current, and its bed and shores paved with large pebbles. At the entrance of the opposite forest, our guide, to whose tongue the direct and very obvious path was so familiar, now became bewildered, and after reconnoitring to his heart's content amongst the entangled briars, vines, and nettles, ushered us into a trace which conducted to an old Indian encampment, and terminated there. Further progress was in a great measure intercepted by the cane brake, which, not presenting any path, obliged us to break our passage with much labour. The dusk of the evening found us still pursuing a devious course through a world of vegetation, impenetrable to the eye, vainly seeking a spot upon which an encampment could be fixed; when to our unspeakable joy, and without previous intimation, the prairie of *Bayou Menard* appeared suddenly before us. The timber of these bottoms is large and various. The extreme heat of the day 96 degrees. Distance, eighteen miles.

Our pleasure at first seeing civilized white men was of no ordinary kind; it appeared as though we had already arrived at our own homes and families, in anticipation of Belle Point, which had hitherto seemed the utmost boundary, and terminus of our pilgrimage.

6th. A fine morning; and as on the days of the 1st inst. and 30th ultimo, no dew had fallen. Crossed the ravine at the head of Bayou Menard, and ascended the elevated hills, clothed with small oaks, and arrived at a branch of Green Leaf bayou, about nine o'clock, a distance of eight miles.

A slight shower of rain fell in the afternoon, and during our ride, we first observed the dog wood *(Cornus Florida;)* in the evening we arrived at Mr. Bean's salt works. These are situate on a small creek, which flows into the Illinois, about a mile below, and are at the distance of about seven miles from the Arkansa. Mr. Bean commenced his operations in the spring, and has already a neat farm house on the Illinois, with a considerable stock of cattle, hogs, and poultry, and several acres of Indian corn. Near the springs he has erected a neat log house, and a shed for the furnace, but his kettles, which were purchased of the proprietors of the Neosho establishment, were not yet fixed. He assured us that the water was so far saturated, as not to dissolve any perceptible quantity of a handful of salt that was thrown into it. On the side of a large well which he had sunk to collect the salt water, and perhaps two feet from the surface of the soil, he pointed out the remains of a stratum of charcoal of inconsiderable extent, through which they had penetrated, and which, to a by-stander was a certain proof that these springs had been formerly worked by the Indians. But as no other appearances justified this conclusion, a greater probability seems attached to the idea, that during some former conflagration of the prairies, the charred trunk or branches of a tree were here imbedded. Another agent, however, of sufficient efficacy to operate this carbonization of wood, resides in the sulphuric acid, liberated by the decomposing pyritous rocks, so abundant here.

Whilst waiting with a moderate share of patience, for our evening meal of boiled pumpkins, one of the children brought us a huge, hairy spider, which he carried upon a twig, that he had induced the animal to grasp with its feet. Its magnitude and formidable appearance surprised us. The boy informed us, that he had captured it near the entrance of its burrow, and that the species is by no means rare in this part of the country. Not having any box suitable to contain it, nor any pin sufficiently large to impale it, we substituted a wooden peg, by which it was attached to the inside of a hat. This species so closely resembles, both in form, colour, and magnitude, the gigantic bird-catching spider of South America, that from a minute survey of this specimen, which is a female, we cannot discover the slightest characteristic distinction. But as an examination of the male comparatively with that of the avicularia, may exhibit distinctive traits, we refrain from deciding positively upon the species.

Distance, twenty-four miles.

7th. The Illinois is called by the Osages, Eng-wah-con-dah, or Medicine-stone creek. At our fording place, near the saline, it was about sixty yards wide, with clear water, and pebbly shores, like those of the Neosho. We proceeded on through a country wooded with small oaks, interspersed with occasional small prairies, and crossed a deep ravine, called Bayou Viande. These bayous, as they are named in this country, unlike those of the lower portion of the Mississippi river, are large, and often very profound ravines or water courses, which, during the spring season, or after heavy rains, receive the water from the surface of the prairies, and convey it to the river; but in the summer and early autumn, the sources being exhausted, the water subsides in their channels, occupying only the deeper parts of their bed, in the form of stagnant pools, exhaling miasmata to the atmosphere, and rendering their vicinity prejudicial to health.

The extreme temperature of the day was 93 degrees, but it was rather abruptly reduced by a strong wind with thunder and lightning, from the S.E. which brought up a heavy rain, that continued to drench us until the evening, when, after a ride of fourteen miles, we encamped at Bayou Salaison, or meat salting Bayou. At our mid-day refectory, we were much annoyed by great numbers of small ticks, that were excessively abundant amongst the grass, and crawled by dozens up our leggins. Wherever they effected a lodgment upon the skin, their numerous punctures would cause an intolerable itching sensation that bid defiance to repose. In the evening, in addition to the needful process of drying our clothing and blankets, we had ample employment in scratching, and picking the pestiferous arachnides from our bodies. On entering the water for relief, the disagreeable sensation seemed to be mitigated for a time, only to be augmented on our return to the atmosphere. Mosquitoes, which were also abundant, were readily expelled from our tents by the smoke of burning wood; but the ticks, otherwise constituted, frustrated our endeavours to obtain the necessary rest and sleep during the night.

These ticks are of two different species, and in common with other species inhabiting different parts of the United States, are distinguished by the name of *seed ticks*, probably on account of their small size, when compared with others of the same genus.

The larger of the two kinds may be compared, in point of tranverse diameter, to the head of a small sized pin, but the other one is so much smaller, as to elude the sight, excepting on minute inspection.

The Cherokee Indians frequently visit this vicinity, on hunting excursions, and our guide informs us, that a hunting party of that nation is at present encamped at the mouth of this Bayou, at the distance of two and a half miles from our camp.

8th. The face of the country presents the same appearance with that we passed over yesterday, offering, in the arrangement of forest and fertile prairie, many advantageous sites for plantations, of which one is already established at the confluence of Big Skin Bayou.

During the afternoon's ride the country was observed to be more hilly.

Soon after the occurrence of the greatest heat of the day, which was 91 degrees, several showers of rain fell, accompanied by distant thunder.

On a naked part of the soil, gullied out by the action of torrents of water, we beheld a hymenopterous or wasp-like insect (Sphex) triumphantly, but laboriously, dragging the body of the gigantic spider, its prey, to furnish food to its future progeny. We cannot but admire the prowess of this comparatively pigmy victor, and the wonderful influence of a maternal emotion, which thus impels it to a hazardous encounter, for the sake of a posterity which it can never know.

Distance nineteen miles.

9th. Pursued our journey, with every hope of reaching the place of rendezvous appointed by Major Long, before noon. Since passing Bayou Viande we have observed the country, on either side of our path, to be distinguished by extremely numerous natural elevations of earth, of some considerable degree of regularity. They are of a more or less oval outline, and their general dimensions may be stated at one hundred feet long, by from two to five feet in greatest height. Their existence is doubtless due to the action of water. Should the rivers Platte and Arkansa be deprived of their waters, the sand islands of their beds would probably present a somewhat similar appearance.

An Indian who observed us passing, hallooed to us from a distance, and expecting some important communication, we waited some time, until he came up. He proved to be a Cherokee, dressed much in the manner of the whites, and not a little infected with the spirit of an interrogator, common, no doubt, to those with whom he has been accustomed to associate, and therefore probably regarded as a concomitant of civilization. We left him to his own surmises, respecting our object and destination, and soon arrived at the path which strikes off, for the river. After passing a distance of four miles through a cane brake, we arrived at a hut and small farm, belonging to a soldier of the garrison, and were shortly on the strand of the river, with the long-sought Belle Point before us. We were soon ferried over, and were kindly received on the landing by Captain Ballard and Mr. Glen. The former gentleman was at present invested with the command, in consequence of the temporary absence of Major Bradford on a visit to St. Louis. His politeness and attention soon rendered our situation comfortable, after a houseless exposure in the wilderness of ninety-three days.

The greatest heat of the day was 91 degrees, and distance travelled nine miles.

The Arkansa, below the great bend, becomes more serpentine than it is above, and very much obstructed by sand bars and islands, either naked or clothed with a recent vegetation; they are but little elevated above the surface of the water, and are covered, to some depth, during the prevalence of floods in the river. At Belle Point, and some distance above, these islands almost wholly disappear, but the sandy shores still continue, and are, as above, alternately situated on either side of the river, as the stream approaches or recedes from the opposite river bottoms. The colour of the water was now olive-green. All the red colouring matter, with which it is sometimes imbued, is contributed by streams entering on the southern side. The current of the Arkansa is much less rapid than that of the Platte, but the character of those two rivers in a considerable degree corresponds, in their widely spreading waters of but little depth, running over a bed of yielding sand. The rise of the waters at Belle Point takes place in the months of March and early April, with a less considerable freshet in July and August. But to this place navigation is seldom practicable for keel boats, from the month of August to February inclusive, though the autumnal freshet of October and November frequently admits their passage.

EPILOGUE

THE last two chapters of the Account *detail the experiences of the men at Fort Smith and their movements until the final dissolution of the party. At Fort Smith, which Long had helped establish in 1817 at Belle Point, the expedition members found welcome relief from the rigors of their journey:*

The gardens at Fort Smith afforded green corn, melons, sweet potatoes, and other esculent vegetables, which to us had, for a long time, been untasted luxuries. It is probable we did not exercise sufficient caution, in recommencing the use of these articles, as we soon found our health beginning to become impaired. We had been a long time confined to a meat diet, without bread or condiments of any kind, and were not surprised to find ourselves affected by so great and so sudden a change. It may be worth while to remark that we had been so long unaccustomed to the use of salt that the sweat of our faces had lost all perceptible saltiness, and the ordinary dishes which were brought to our mess table at the fort appeared unpalatable, on account of being too highly seasoned.

After this brief respite, Captain Bell, with two of the engagees, Dougherty and Oakley, left Fort Smith on September 19 bound for Cape Girardeau on the Mississippi. Two days later, a party consisting of Long, Say, Seymour, and Peale, along with four soldiers, set out for Cape Girardeau as well. A short time later, the parties were reunited and thereafter traveled together. Continuing through the Arkansas Territory, they made detailed observations of the country and the inhabitants:

The maize cultivated in the Arkansa territory, and in the southern and western states generally, is the variety called the gourd seed, having a long and compressed kernel, shrivelled at the end when fully ripe, and crops are not uncommon, yielding from sixty to ninety bushels per acre.

In all the uplands, the prevailing growth is oak. At the time of our journey the acorns were falling in such quantities, that the ground for an extent of many acres was often seen almost covered with them. Many recent settlers, indulging the disposition to indolence, which seized upon almost every man who fixes his residence in these remote forests, place as much dependence upon the crop of mast as on the products of their own industry. Vast numbers of swine are suffered to range at large in the forests, and in the fall of the year when they have become fat by feeding on the acorns, they are hunted and killed like wild animals, affording to the inhabitants a very important article of subsistence. It is remarked also, that the venison becomes fat somewhat in proportion as acorns are abundant. Turkies, which are still vastly numerous in the settlements of White river, feed upon them, but are said to grow poor in consequence.

Sweet potatoes grow in great perfection in many parts of the Arkansa territory, and are but too much cultivated and eaten, their constant use as an article of food, being little beneficial to health. The common, or Irish potatoe, as it is here universally called, succeeded but indiffferently, and few attempts are made to cultivate it.

A few of the roads which traverse the country from the Mississippi to the upper settlements of Red river and the Arkansa, have been sufficiently opened to admit the passage of waggons. Of these are seen many families migrating from Missouri to Red river, and from Red river to Missouri.

The first settlements in the wilderness are most commonly made by persons to whom hardihood and adventure have been confirmed, and almost indispensable habits, and who choose to depend upon the chase, and the spontaneous products of the unclaimed forest, rather than submit to the confinement and monotony of an agricultural life. They are therefore, of necessity, kept somewhat in advance of those settlers who intend a permanent residence in the situations they first occupy. Removing from place to place with their cattle, horses, and swine, they confine themselves to one spot no longer than *the range* continues to afford a sufficient supply of the articles most necessary to life. When the canes are fed down and destroyed, and the acorns become scarce, the small cornfield, and the rude cabin are abandoned, and the *squatter* goes in search of a place where all the original wealth of the forest is yet undiminished. Here he again builds his hut, removes the trees from a few acres of land, which supply their annual crop of corn, while the neighbouring woods, for an extent of several miles, are used both as pasture and hunting grounds. Though there is in this way of life an evident tendency to bring men back to a state of barbarism, we have often met among the rudest of the squatters with much hospitality and kindness. Near White river, we called at a house to purchase food for ourselves, and our horses, but having no silver money our request was refused, although we offered the notes of the Bank of Missouri, then in good credit. In a few miles we arrived at another cabin, where we found every member of the numerous family sick with ague and fever, except one young girl. But here they were willing to furnish every refreshment their house afforded. There were at this time very few houses, particularly in the settlements about White river, which did not exhibit scenes of suffering similar to those in the one, of which we were now the reluctant guests. We have seen some instances, where a family of eight or ten, not a single individual was capable of attending to the services of the household, or of administering to the wants of his suffering relatives. In these instances, we thought it better to pitch our tents at a little distance, and intrude ourselves no farther, than was necessary to procure corn, and other indispensable supplies.

Early the next month the party arrived at Jackson, Missouri:

On the 8th we arrived at Jackson, the seat of Justice for the county of Cape Girardeau, and after St. Louis and St. Charles, one of the largest towns in Missouri. It lies about eleven or twelve miles northwest of the old town of Cape Girardeau on the Mississippi, and is surrounded by a hilly and fertile tract of country, at this time rapidly increasing in wealth and population. Jackson is what is called a *thriving village*, and contains at present more than fifty houses, which though built of logs seem to aspire to a degree of importance unknown to the humble dwellings of the scattered and solitary settlers, assuming an appearance of consequence and superiority similar to that we immediately distinguished in the appearance and manners of the people. Our horses having never been accustomed to such displays of magnificence signified great reluctance to enter the village. Whips and heels were exercised with unusual animation, but in great measure without effect, until we dismounted, when by dint of coaxing, pushing, kicking, and whipping, we at length urged our clownish animals up to the door of the inn.

Meanwhile, James, Swift, and Capt. Stephen Watts Kearny, who had been visiting at the fort as inspector and paymaster, had left Fort Smith on September 20 bound for the "Hot Springs of the Washita." Arriving at the hot springs on September 28, the men provided a detailed picture of this feature of the landscape:

We have been informed, that these remarkable springs were unknown even to the American hunters, until the year 1779. At that time it is said, that there was but one spring discharging heated water. This is described as a circular orifice, about six inches in diameter, pouring out a stream of water of the same size, from the side of a perpendicular cliff, about eight feet from its base. At another place, near the top of the mountain, which rises abruptly towards the east, the heated water is said to have made its appearance near the surface of the ground, in a state of ebullition, and to have sunk and disappeared again upon the same spot. It is probable these representations are in a great measure fabulous. All we are to understand by them, is, that the gradual augmentation of the thermal rocks, which are constantly forming about the springs, has changed the position, and perhaps increased the number of the orifices.

These springs were visited by Hunter and Dunbar in 1804, and the information communicated by them, as well as much derived from other sources, together with an analysis of the waters, has been placed before the public by Dr. Mitchell. They have been subsequently examined by Major Long, in 1818, from whose notes we derive the greater part of the information we have to communicate respecting them. They are about seventy in number, and rise at the bottom, and along one side of a narrow ravine, separating two considerable hills of clay slate. A small creek enters the ravine from the north by two branches, one from the northwest, and the other from the northeast, flowing after their union, nearly due south, and blending with the water of the springs, increasing rapidly in size, and acquiring so high a temperature, that at the time of our visit the hand could not be borne immersed in it. After traversing from north to south, the narrow valley containing the springs, this creek meanders away to the southeast, and enters the Washita at the distance of eight or ten miles. All the springs are within six hundred yards below the junction of the two brooks, and all except one, on the east side of the creek.

After making these observations, the party proceeded on to Little Rock:

The village of Little Rock occupies the summit of a high bank of clay slate, on the southwest side of the Arkansa. Its site is elevated, and the country immediately adjoining in a great measure exempt from the operation of those causes which produce a state of the atmosphere unfavourable to health. It is near the commencement of the hilly country, and for a part of the year will be at the head of steam boat navigation on the Arkansa. The country in the rear of the projected town is high, and covered for the most part with open oak forests.

Leaving Little Rock on October 3, they continued through the "deep and gloomy forests of the Arkansas bottoms." Soon intercepting the route that Long and his group had traveled to Cape Girardeau, they retraced that path and reached the settlement on the Mississippi a few days later. In the following passages, editor James then traced the "progress of the exploring party to the place of their final separation . . .":

On the 12th October, the Exploring party were all assembled at Cape Girardeau. Lieutenant Graham with the steam boat Western Engineer, had arrived a day or two before from St. Louis, having delayed there, some time subsequent to his return from the Upper Mississippi. In the discharge of the duties on which he had been ordered, Lieutenant Graham and all his party, had suffered severely from bilious and intermitting fever.

A few days subsequent to our arrival at Cape Girardeau, the greater number of those who had been of the party by land, experienced severe attacks of intermitting fever, none escaped except Capt. Bell, Mr. Peale, and Lieut. Swift. Maj. Long and Capt. Kearny, who had continued their journey immediately towards St. Louis, were taken ill at St. Genevieve, and the latter was confined some weeks. The attack was almost simultaneous in the cases of those who remained at Cape Girardeau, and it is highly probable, we had all received the impression which produced the disease nearly at the same time. The interruption of accustomed habits, and the discontinuance of the excitement afforded by travelling, may have somewhat accelerated the attack. We have observed that we had felt somewhat less than the usual degree of health, since breathing the impure and offensive atmosphere of the Arkansa bottoms about Belle Point, and there, we have no doubt the disease fastened upon us. In every instance, we had the opportunity of observing, the attack assumed the form of a daily intermittent. The cold stage commenced with a sensation of languor and depression, attended with almost incessant yawning, and disinclination to motion, soon followed by shivering, and a distressing sensation of cold. These symptoms pass off gradually, and the hot stage succeeds. The degree of fever is usually somewhat proportioned to the violence of the cold fit, the respiration becomes full and frequent, the face is flushed, the skin moist, and the patient falls into a heavy slumber, on awaking after some time, extreme languor and exhaustion are felt, though few symptoms of fever remain. This routine of most uncomfortable feelings commencing at nine or ten in the morning, occupied for some time, the greater part of our days, late at evening, and during the night we suffered less.

Intermitting fevers are of such universal occurrence in every part of the newly settled country to the west, that every person is well acquainted with the symptoms, and has some favorite method of treatment. A very common practice, and one productive of much mischief, is that of administering large draughts of whiskey and red pepper, previous to the accession of the cold stage. Applications of this kind may sometimes shorten the cold fit, but the consequent fever is comparatively increased, and the disease rendered more obstinate. The Peruvian bark is much used, but often so injudiciously as to occasion great mischief.

Cape Girardeau, formerly the seat of justice, for a county of the same name, is one of the oldest settlements in Upper Louisiana, having been for a long time the residence of the Spanish intendant or governor. Occupying the first considerable elevation of the western bank of the Mississippi, above the mouth of the Ohio, and affording a convenient landing place for boats, it promises to become a place of some little importance, as it must be the *depot* of a considerable district of the country, extending from the commencement of the Great Swamp, on the southeast, to the upper branches of the St. Francis. The advantages of its situation must be considered greater, than those of the settlements of Tyawapatia and New Madrid, which are not sufficiently elevated. It is near the commencement of the hily country extending up the Mississippi to the confluence of the Missouri, northwest to the Gasconade and Osage rivers, and southwest of the province of Texas. Two or three miles below Cape Girardeau the cypress swamps commence, extending with little interruption far to the south.

The town comprises at this time about twenty log cabins, several of them in ruins, a log jail, no longer occupied, a large unfinished brick building, falling rapidly to decay, and a small one, finished and occupied. It stands on the slope and part of the summit of a broad hill, rising about one hundred and fifty feet above the Mississippi, and having a deep primary soil, resting on horizontal strata of compact and sparry limestone. Next the place where boats usually land, is a point of white rock, jutting into the Mississippi, and at a very low stage of water, producing a perceptible ripple. It is a white sparry limestone, abounding in remains of Encrini, and other marine animals. If traced some distances, it will be found to alternate with the common blue compact limestone, most frequently seen in secondary districts. Though the stratifications of this sparry limestone are horizontal, the rock is little divided by seams and fissures, and would undoubtedly afford a valuable marble, not unlike the *Darling* marble quarried on the Hudson.

The streets of Cape Girardeau are marked out, with formal regularity, intersecting each other at right angles, but they are now in some parts so gullied and torn by the rains as to be impassable, in others, overgrown with such a crop of gigantic vernonias and urticas, as to resemble small forests. The country back of the town is hilly, covered with heavy forests of oak, tulip tree, and nyssa, intermixed in the vallies with the sugar tree, and the fagus sylvatica, and on the hills with an undergrowth of the American hazle, and the shot bush or angelica tree. Settlements are considerably advanced, and many well cultivated farms occur in various directions.

Two or three weeks elapsed previous to Major Long's return from St. Louis, when, notwithstanding his ill health, he left Cape Girardeau immediately, as did Capt. Bell, both intending to prosecute without delay, their journey to the seat of government.

About the first of November, Messrs. Say, Graham, and Seymour, had so far recovered their health, as to venture on a voyage to New Orleans, on their way home. They left Cape Girardeau in a small boat, which they exchanged at the mouth of the Ohio for a steam boat, about to descend, Mr. Peale, who had escaped the prevailing sickness, accompanied them. . . .

Dr. James and Lieut. Swift only, were left with the steam boat Western Engineer at Cape Girardeau. Lieut. Swift had received instructions, as soon as the water should rise sufficiently, to proceed with the boat to the falls of the Ohio, where it was to remain during the winter. . . .

On the 22nd November, having been informed the Ohio had risen several inches, Lieutenant Swift determined to leave Cape Girardeau with the steam-boat on the following day. Dr. James had so far recovered as to be able to travel on horseback, and immediately set forward on the journey to the Falls of Ohio, intending to proceed, by the nearest route across the interior of Illinois.

The immediate valley of the Mississippi, opposite the little village of Bainbridge, ten miles above Cape Girardeau, is four miles wide, exclusive of the river, which washes the bluffs along the western side. Upwards it expands into the broad, fertile, and anciently populous valley, called the American bottom. On the east it is bounded by aburpt hills of a deep argillaceous loam, disclosing no rocks, and rather infertile, bearing forests of oak, sweet gum, tupelo, &c. The road crossing the hilly country between the Mississippi and the village of Golconda on the Ohio passes several precocious little towns, which appear, as is often the case in a recently settled country, to have outgrown their permanent resources. The lands, however, are not entirely worthless, and on some of the upper branches of the Cache, a river of the Ohio, we passed some fertile bottoms, though they were not entirely exempt from inundation at the periodical floods. The compact limestone about Golconda contains beautiful crystals of fluate of lime. Sulphuret of lead also occurs in that vicinity, as we have been informed, in veins accompanying the fluate of lime.

On arriving at Golconda, Dr. James had become so much indisposed, by a recurrence of fever and ague, as to be unable to proceed. This circumstance, with others, induced Lieutenant Swift to leave the steam-boat for the winter at the mouth of Cumberland river, twenty miles below. After a delay of a few days the latter continued his journey towards Philadelphia on horseback.

BIBLIOGRAPHY

Archival and Manuscript Sources

Much of the source material for the study of the Long expedition can be found within the various record groups of the National Archives and Records Administration, Washington, D.C. Of prime importance are Record Group 77, Records of the Office of the Chief of Engineers; Record Group 94, Records of the Adjutant General's Office; and Record Group 107, Records of the Office of Secretary of War (including Letters Received, Main Series, 1819-1823, and Letters Sent, Military Affairs, 1818-1820).

Edwin James's diary, "Notes of a part of the Expd. of Discovery Commanded by S. H. Long Maj. U.S. Eng. &c &c.," is in the Rare Book and Manuscript Library, Columbia University, New York, New York. Titian Peale's diary has been edited by A. O. Weese, "The Journal of Titian Ramsay Peale, Pioneer Naturalist," *Missouri Historical Review* 41 (January 1947):147-63. Captain John R. Bell's journal appears as volume 6 of the Far West and the Rockies Series, edited by Harlin M. Fuller and LeRoy R. Hafen, *The Journal of Captain John R. Bell, Official Journalist for the Stephen H. Long Expedition to the Rocky Mountains, 1820* (Glendale, Calif.: Arthur H. Clark Co., 1957).

The *Account of an Expedition from Pittsburgh to the Rocky Mountains,* edited by Edwin James, was published in Philadelphia by Carey and Lea (two volumes plus a book of maps and plates) and in London by Longman, Hurst, Rees, Orme, and Brown (three volumes) in 1823. In 1905 a four-volume edition prepared by Reuben Gold Thwaites was issued in the Early Western Travels Series (Cleveland: Arthur H. Clark Co., 1905); with extensive annotations, it remains the best scholarly text. A one-volume, limited edition, with an introduction by Howard R. Lamar, was published by the Imprint Society, Barre, Massachusetts, in 1972. For complete bibliographical information, see Henry R. Wagner and Charles L. Camp, *The Plains & the Rockies: A Critical Bibliography of Exploration, Adventure, and Travel in the American West, 1800-1865,* 4th ed. revised by Robert H. Becker (San Francisco: John Howell Books, 1982).

Exploration and Cartography

Allen, John L. "Geographical Knowledge and American Images of the Louisiana Territory." *Western Historical Quarterly* 2 (April 1971):151-70.

_____. "Patterns of Promise: Mapping the Plains and Prairies, 1800-1860." In *Mapping the North American Plains: Essays in the History of Cartography,* edited by Frederick C. Luebke, Frances W. Kaye, and Gary E. Moulton. Norman: University of Oklahoma Press, 1987.

Beers, Henry P. *The Western Military Frontier, 1815-1846.* Philadelphia: N.p., 1935.

[Everett, Edward]. "Long's Expedition." *North American Review* 16 (April 1823):242-69.

Friis, Herman R. "Stephen H. Long's Unpublished Map of the United States Compiled in 1820-1822 (?)." *The California Geographer* 8 (1967):75-87.

Gilbert, Bil. *The Trailblazers.* New York: Time-Life Books, 1973.

Goetzmann, William H. *Army Exploration in the American West, 1803-1863.* New Haven: Yale University Press, 1959.

_____. *Exploration and Empire: The Explorer and the Scientist in the Winning of the American West.* New York: Alfred A. Knopf, 1966.

_____. *New Lands, New Men: America and the Second Great Age of Discovery.* New York: Viking, 1986.

Goodwin, Cardinal. "A Larger View of the Yellowstone Expedition, 1819-1820." *Mississippi Valley Historical Review* 4 (December 1917):299-313.

Jackson, Donald L., ed. *The Journals of Zebulon Montgomery Pike, with Letters and Related Documents*. 2 vols. Norman: University of Oklahoma Press, 1966.

_____. *Thomas Jefferson & the Stony Mountains: Exploring the West from Monticello*. Urbana: University of Illinois Press, 1981.

Kane, Lucile M., June D. Holmquist, and Carolyn Gilman, eds. *The Northern Expeditions of Stephen H. Long: The Journals of 1817 and 1823 and Related Documents*. St. Paul: Minnesota Historical Society Press, 1978.

"Long's Expedition." *North American Review* 14 (April 1823):242-69.

Nichols, Roger. *General Henry Atkinson: A Western Military Career*. Norman: University of Oklahoma Press, 1965.

_____, ed. *The Missouri Expedition, 1818-1820: The Journal of Surgeon John Gale, with Related Documents*. Norman: University of Oklahoma Press, 1969.

_____. "Stephen H. Long." In *Soldiers West: Biographies from the Military Frontier,* edited by Paul Andrew Hutton. Lincoln: University of Nebraska Press, 1987.

_____. "Stephen Long and Scientific Exploration of the Plains." *Nebraska History* 52 (Spring 1971):50-64.

_____, and Patrick L. Halley. *Stephen Long and American Frontier Exploration*. Newark: University of Delaware Press, 1980.

[Schoolcraft, Henry Rowe]. Review of *La Decouverte des Sources du Mississippi, et de la Riviere Sanglante,* by J. C. Beltrami. *North American Review* 27 (July 1828):89-114.

Schubert, Frank N. *Vanguard of Expansion: Army Engineers in the Trans-Mississippi West, 1819-1879*. Washington, D.C.: Historical Division, Office of Administrative Services, Office of the Chief of Engineers, n.d.

[Silliman, Benjamin]. "Expedition of Major Long and Party, to the Rocky Mountains." *American Journal of Science and Arts* 6 (1823):374-75.

Tucker, John M. "Major Long's Route from the Arkansas to the Canadian River, 1820." *New Mexico Historical Review* 38 (July 1963):185-219.

Viola, Herman J. *Exploring the West*. Washington, D.C.: Smithsonian Books, 1987.

Wesley, Edgar B. "A Still Larger View of the So-Called Yellowstone Expedition." *North Dakota Historical Quarterly* 5 (July 1931):219-38.

Wheat, Carl I. *From Lewis and Clark to Fremont, 1804-1845*. Vol. 2 of *Mapping the Transmississippi West, 1540-1861*. San Francisco: The Institute of Historical Cartography, 1958.

Wood, Richard G. "Dr. Edwin James, A Disappointed Explorer." *Minnesota History* 34 (Autumn 1955):284-86.

_____. *Stephen Harriman Long, 1784-1864: Army Engineer, Explorer, Inventor.* Glendale, Calif.: Arthur H. Clark Co., 1966.

The Great American Desert

Alford, Terry L. "The West as a Desert in American Thought Prior to Long's 1819-1820 Expedition." *Journal of the West* 8 (October 1969):515-25.

Allen, John L. "The Garden-Desert Continuum: Competing Views of the Great Plains in the Nineteenth Century." *Great Plains Quarterly* 5 (Fall 1985):207-20.

Athearn, Robert G. "The Great Plains in Historical Perspective." *Montana, the Magazine of Western History* 8 (January 1958):21-26.

Blackmar, Frank W. "The Mastery of the Desert." *North American Review* 181 (May 1906):676-88.

Bowden, Martyn J. "The Great American Desert and the American Frontier, 1800-1882: Popular Images of the Plains." In *Anonymous Americans: Explorations in Nineteenth-Century Social History,* edited by Tamara K. Hareven. Englewood Cliffs, N.J.: Prentice-Hall, 1971.

Dick, Everett. *Conquering the Great American Desert.* Lincoln: Nebraska State Historical Society, 1975.

Dillon, Richard. "Stephen Long's Great American Desert." *Proceedings of the American Philosophical Society* 111 (April 14, 1967):93-108.

Hollon, W. Eugene. *The Great American Desert Then and Now.* New York: Oxford University Press, 1966.

Lewis, G. Malcolm. "Three Centuries of Desert Concepts in the Cis-Rocky Mountain West." *Journal of the West* 4 (July 1965):457-94.

Morris, Ralph C. "The Notion of a Great American Desert East of the Rockies." *Mississippi Valley Historical Review* 13 (September 1926):190-200.

Porter, Charlotte M. "The American West Described in Natural History Journals, 1819-1836." *Midwest Review* 2 (Spring 1980):18-37.

Prucha, Francis Paul. "Indian Removal and the Great American Desert." *Indiana Magazine of History* 59 (December 1963):299-322.

Smith, Henry Nash. *Virgin Land: The American West as Symbol and Myth.* Cambridge: Harvard University Press, 1950. Reprint. New York: Vintage Books, 1957.

Webb, Walter Prescott. "The American West, Perpetual Mirage." *Harper's* 194 (May 1957):25-31.

_____. *The Great Plains.* Boston: Ginn and Co., 1931.

————. "The West and the Desert." *Montana, the Magazine of Western History* 8 (January 1958):2-12.

Science

Beidleman, Richard G. "Edwin James, Pioneer Naturalist." *Horticulture* 44 (December 1966):32-34.

Benson, Maxine. "Edwin James: Scientist, Linguist, Humanitarian." Ph.D. diss., University of Colorado, Boulder, 1968.

Daniels, George H. *American Science in the Age of Jackson.* New York: Columbia University Press, 1968.

Ewan, Joseph. *Rocky Mountain Naturalists.* Denver: University of Denver Press, 1950.

————, and Nesta Dunn Ewan. *Biographical Dictionary of Rocky Mountain Naturalists: A Guide to the Writings and Collections of Botanists, Zoologists, Geologists, Artists, and Photographers, 1682-1932.* Utrecht/Antwerpen: Bohn, Scheltema, and Holkema, 1981.

McKelvey, Susan Delano. *Botanical Exploration of the Trans-Mississippi West, 1790-1850.* Jamaica Plain, Mass.: Published by the Arnold Arboretum of Harvard University, 1955.

Meisel, Max. *A Bibliography of American Natural History.* 3 vols. Brooklyn: Premier Publishing Co., 1924-29.

Merrill, George P. *The First One Hundred Years of American Geology.* New Haven: Yale University Press, 1924.

Nye, Russel Blaine. *The Cultural Life of the New Nation, 1776-1830.* New York: Harper and Brothers, 1960.

Oleson, Alexandra, and Sanborn C. Brown, eds. *The Pursuit of Knowledge in the Early American Republic: American Scientific and Learned Societies from Colonial Times to the Civil War.* Baltimore: Johns Hopkins University Press, 1976.

Osterhout, George E. "Rocky Mountain Botany and the Long Expedition of 1820." *Bulletin of the Torrey Botanical Club* 47 (December 1920):555-62.

Rodgers, Andrew Denney III. *John Torrey: A Story of North American Botany.* Princeton: Princeton University Press, 1942.

Sellers, Charles Coleman. *Mr. Peale's Museum: Charles Willson Peale and the First Popular Museum of Natural Science and Art.* New York: W. W. Norton and Co., 1980.

Smallwood, William M., in collaboration with Mabel S. C. Smallwood. *Natural History and the American Mind.* New York: Columbia University Press, 1941.

Weiss, Harry B., and Grace M. Ziegler. *Thomas Say, Early American Naturalist.* Springfield, Ill.: Charles C. Thomas, 1931.

Art and Literature

Bartlett, Richard A. "The Historian and Western Art: A Review Essay." *Colorado Heritage* 4 (1985):24-31.

Cooper, James Fenimore. *The Prairie.* 1827. Reprint New York: Viking Penguin, 1987.

Ewers, John C. "First Artists in the Great American Desert: Titian Ramsay Peale and Samuel Seymour." In *Artists of the Old West.* Garden City: Doubleday and Co., 1965; enlarged ed., 1973.

McDermott, John Francis. "Samuel Seymour, Pioneer Artist of the Plains and the Rockies." *Annual Report of the Board of Regents of the Smithsonian Institution, 1950.* Washington, D.C.: Government Printing Office, 1951.

Murphy, Robert Cushman. "The Sketches of Titian Ramsay Peale (1799-1885)." *Proceedings of the American Philosophical Society* 101 (December 1957):23-31.

Overland, Orm. *The Making and Meaning of an American Classic: James Fenimore Cooper's THE PRAIRIE.* New York: Humanities Press, 1973.

Poesch, Jessie. *Titian Ramsay Peale, 1799-1885, and His Journals of the Wilkes Expedition.* Philadelphia: American Philosophical Society, 1961.

Trenton, Patricia, and Peter H. Hassrick. *The Rocky Mountains: A Vision for Artists in the Nineteenth Century.* Norman: University of Oklahoma Press, in association with the Buffalo Bill Historical Center, Cody, Wyoming, 1983.

LIST OF ILLUSTRATIONS

Map, from the Philadelphia edition. Courtesy of the Denver Public Library, Western History Department.

Stephen Harriman Long, oil. Page ii. Courtesy of the Independence National Park Historical Collection.

Thomas Say, by Charles Willson Peale, oil. Page iv. Courtesy of the Academy of Natural Sciences.

Shell, T.R. Peale, May 13, 1819, watercolor. Page 20. Courtesy of the American Philosophical Society.

Western Engineer, T.R. Peale, 1819, ink and wash. Page 28. Courtesy of the American Philosophical Society.

Tern, T.R. Peale, May 28, 1819, watercolor. Page 29. Courtesy of the American Philosophical Society.

Turkey, T.R. Peale, June 3, 1819, watercolor. Page 37. Courtesy of the American Philosophical Society.

Sparrow, T.R. Peale, June 23, 1819, watercolor and pencil. Page 51. Courtesy of the American Philosophical Society.

Landscape, T.R. Peale, June 23, 1819, watercolor. Page 52. Courtesy of the American Philosophical Society.

INDEX

407